A PRIMER OF ITALIAN FASCISM

A PRIMER OF

ITALIAN FASCISM

Edited and with
an introduction by Jeffrey T. Schnapp
Translated by Jeffrey T. Schnapp,
Olivia E. Sears, and Maria G. Stampino

University of Nebraska Press
Lincoln and London

© 2000 by the University of Nebraska Press
Manufactured in the United States of America ⊗

Library of Congress Cataloging-in-Publication Data
A primer of Italian fascism / edited and with an introduction by Jeffrey T. Schnapp ; translated by Jeffrey
T. Schnapp, Olivia E. Sears, and Maria G. Stampino.
p. cm. — (European horizons) Includes bibliographi-
cal references and index. ISBN 0-8032-4279-4 (cloth :
alk. paper). ISBN 0-8032-9268-6 (paper: alk. paper).
1. Fascism — Italy History Sources.   2. Italy — Politics
and Government — 1922–1945 Sources.   I. Schnapp,
Jeffrey T. (Jeffrey Thompson), 1954– .   II. Sears, Olivia
E.   III. Stampino, Maria G.   IV. Series.
DG571.A2P75 2000 320.53'3'0945–DC21 99-32168 CIP

The following have generously given permission for
the use of copyrighted works: ANMA Libri for the
pieces in "Nine Selections from the Debate on Fascism and Culture: *Critica Fascista* (1926–1927)." Alda
Croce for the translation of Benedetto Croce, "La
protesta contro il *Manifesto degli intellettuali fascisti*,"
originally published in *La Critica* 23 (1925): 310–12.
The Carnegie Endowment for International Peace for
Alfredo Rocco, "The Political Doctrine of Fascism,"
originally published in *International Conciliation* 223
(October 1926): 393–415. Istituto dell'Enciclopedia
Italiana for translations from the entry "Fascismo"
in the *Enciclopedia italiana*, volume 14, general editor
Giovanni Gentile. Rome: Istituto dell'Enciclopedia
Italiana, 1929–   .

Contents

✳

Introduction
The Fascist Century
Jeffrey T. Schnapp

✳

In 1932 the fascist regime marked the tenth anniversary of its seizure of power with the sort of pomp and circumstance that were its trademark. Marches, parades, and public rituals were held in the streets of Rome involving veterans, members of the National Fascist Party, fascist youth groups, and ordinary citizens. The centerpiece of the commemorations was the Exhibition of the Fascist Revolution, held in Rome's Palace of Expositions and attended by nearly four million visitors. For the occasion, the palace's old neoclassical colonnade was replaced with a harsh new black, red, and silver geometrical façade built around a colonnade of four lictorian fasces covered with pop-riveted aluminum. The interior was no less transformed, containing an irregular sequence of halls within which spectators were treated to a graphically bold, kaleidoscopic representation of the history of fascism from its World War I origins to the Mussolini regime's present "conquests." As people paraded through the city streets and spectators traversed the exhibition halls, there were other shows as well, both aerial and architectural. Italo Balbo, perhaps fascism's most charismatic leader, embarked on his greatest mass transatlantic flight, or *crociera*, in early 1933, flying in a formation of twenty-four seaplanes from Orbetello to Chicago and back, becoming, in the process, an international celebrity. The medieval core of Rome was eviscerated in order to build the Via del' Impero (Boulevard of the Empire), a great avenue linking Mussolini's headquarters at Palazzo Venezia to the Coliseum. And there were expositions concerning farm tools, cereal production, and land reclamation, as well as cultural, juridical, and scientific congresses.

The year 1932 was far less joyous from the standpoint of the world economy. The 1929 Wall Street crash had sent the economies of the world into a collective tailspin, and Italy's was no exception. Production had declined by nearly one third, and unemployment was skyrocketing. But the spirit of the decennial festivities carried over into the domain of policy. The fascist regime was in the midst of effecting what it claimed would be a revolutionary transformation of the relationship between the economy and the state: its so-called corporative revolution. Laissez-faire capitalism, theorists like the integral corporativist Ugo Spirito (see chapter 11) argued, had envisaged society as made up of atomized individuals whose freedoms were best preserved by a weak liberal-democratic state, "agnostic" in social and cultural matters and with responsibilities in the economic domain reducible to ensuring fair practices and a level playing field. In response, socialism had envisaged society as made of conflicting social classes and devised an all-encompassing state that, as the advocate of the most downtrodden but universal of these social classes, the proletariat, seized the entire means of production, collectivized private property, and destroyed the individual. Fascism would offer a way out of this dialectic, a "third way" that would not only overcome the opposition between capitalism and socialism but also solve the greatest conflicts confronting the industrial world in the wake of the 1929 crash:

> Such is corporativism's essence. It is a hierarchical communism that denies both a leveling state and an anarchic individual, that opposes bureaucratic management but bureaucratizes the nation (turning every individual into an official), that resists private management and assigns a public value to the work performed by individuals. Wills unite to form a single will; multiple goals coalesce to form a single goal. All social life is rationalized. The economic world moves in the direction of unitary organization, which makes possible the realization of a dream: a planned economy that can overcome the chaos produced by liberal economics.[1]

Neither strictly capitalistic nor strictly socialistic, neither founded upon strict individualism nor strict collectivism, corporativism was purported to combine the best features of both prevailing systems while endowing economic reason with a higher, more spiritual logic: one attuned to values such as heroism, hierarchy, national identity, and imperial might; values that transcended purely material or pragmatic considerations. Corporativism relied upon the forced integration of representatives from labor and capital within self-governing but state-sponsored "guilds" or "corporations" (the Italian word *corporazione* signifies both), each responsible for a given sector of the national economy. Initially, there were seven corporations representing agriculture, commerce, banking, industry, transportation, navigation, and the professions, joined together at the level of a National Council of Corporations so as to coordinate their policies and bring them into line with national goals set by the state and its ministries. Later there would be twenty-three. But the experiment — never completed because the corporations were eventually stripped of meaningful powers vis-à-vis industry and of their autonomy vis-à-vis government—was at its peak as Mussolini penned the following lines in his 1932 contribution to the *Enciclopedia italiana* on the topic of fascism's "political and social doctrine":

> Granted that the nineteenth century was the century of socialism, liberalism, democracy, it does not follow that the twentieth century must also be the century of socialism, liberalism, democracy. Political doctrines pass; peoples remain. We are free to believe that this is the century of authority, a century tending to the "right," *a fascist century*. If the nineteenth century was the century of the individual (liberalism implies individualism) we are free to believe that this is the "collective" century and thus the century of the state.[2]

The claim that ours is a *fascist century* seems exaggerated if not quaintly absurd from an end-of-century vantage point. For us fascism necessarily stirs up black-and-white memories borrowed from the image bank of World War II documentaries: images in which Hitler plays the lead and Mussolini a supporting part; images that mark the beginning of the end of Italian fascism's dream of renewing the Roman empire and Roman salutes, the end of its empty posturing and cult of uniforms, the end of its rhetoric of might (soon to be unmasked by its actual military frailty and by the unprecedented devastation and human suffering that its German ally inflicted in the course of World War II). Instead of proving itself a revolutionary third way, Mussolinian fascism thus surfaces in the contemporary memory as a dead end; as a gap beyond which lies the Cold War, which is to say more "socialism, liberalism, democracy"; as an anachronism like Franco's Spain or the Ba'thist Iraq of Saddam Hussein.

There was a time when this was not so, a time when alarmist titles such as *The Coming American Fascism* found a prominent place on bookstore shelves and when radicals throughout the world were more than ready to pronounce capitalism dead and to announce that the choice now facing humankind was crystal clear: "fascism or communism; Rome or Moscow."[3] From the vantage point of 1932, Mussolini's claim seemed plausible enough to many within and outside Italy. Mass-based authoritarian political movements appeared on the rise across the globe while classical liberalism seemed on the verge of collapse. Witness Weimar Germany, where the year 1932 saw the once minuscule National Socialist Party knocking at the door of power. Even countries with long liberal-democratic traditions were experimenting with new forms of centralized planning and government intervention in the economic sphere, such as Roosevelt's New Deal in the United States. So the question of the day seemed to be which strong or strengthened state form was entitled to call the century its own: a reformist liberal-democratic one like the American New Deal; a totalitarian socialist one like that of Stalin's USSR with its much ballyhooed five-year plans; or an authoritarian fascist one? The purpose of this anthology is to provide the contemporary reader with the tools for understanding how the third option could have been taken seriously both by proponents and naysayers. By gathering together a representative sampling of key writings by the political leaders, political scientists, philosophers, historians, critics, and artists who were fascism's protagonists, it documents one of our century's characteristic cultural-political formations (and one that has left consistent traces on the present scene). In so doing, it also offers the reader firsthand experience of Italian fascism's historical evolution from outlaw movement to political party to prevailing force within a parliamentary regime to, finally, dictatorship.

And historical evolution there was, since, to a far greater degree than was the case with socialism or liberalism, fascism's doctrinal foundations were famously fluid. Far from a source of embarrassment, this fluidity was openly embraced by fascist thinkers, who regularly insisted upon subordinating thought to action and instinct and who celebrated their supreme leader as a supreme improviser. "Like all sound political conceptions," read the opening of the entry on fascism in the *Enciclopedia italiana* co-authored by Mussolini and the philosopher Giovanni Gentile, "fascism is action and it is thought: action in which doctrine is immanent, and doctrine arising from a given system of historical forces in which it inserts itself and works from within."[4] Should the "system of historical forces" shift, the doctrine embedded within actions necessarily shifts so as to better adapt itself to and shape reality.

The fascist espousal of fluidity bespeaks an essentially vitalistic concept of thought that stands in opposition to Enlightenment ideals. It repudiates all rationalistic models of human behavior and politics, be they liberal-democratic or socialist, as utopistic, abstract, universalistic, out of touch with anything but the practical and material realities of life. On the contrary, fascism sought to couple mind and body in the service not of utopias but of certain "life-enhancing" myths: secularized-sacred ideals such as self-sacrifice for the nation, the charismatic leader, or the race; service to the empire or the revolution or the state; the cult of danger, death, and fatigue in the pursuit of absolute heroism; a vision of history not as progress but as revelation or catastrophe. The individual was, for the fascist, neither the subject of liberal economics, reducible to a set of individual needs, appetites, and interests, nor the class subject of socialism, reducible to a set of collective needs, appetites, and interests. He or she was, rather, a "spiritual" being in whom instinct and thought were one: a being whose very flesh was inhabited by the intractable realities of history, nationality, race, climate, and the soil but summoned by these realities to an ethos transcending the narrow confines of individual self-interest.

A politics that celebrates improvisation and instinct is bound to be an inconsistent politics. Changes in the system of historical forces did precipitate some rather startling about-faces in the course of fascism's development: its shift from a fiercely anticlerical stance to the promotion of Roman Catholicism as "the distinctive, positive religion of the Italian people"[5]; its sudden adoption in 1938 of Nazi-type racial ideology, when Mussolini had hitherto mocked racism and anti-Semitism; its oscillating commitments to modernist and historicist cultural forms. These sorts of inconsistencies led critics like the communist leader Palmiro Togliatti to envisage fascist ideology as "nothing if not a chameleon. Analyze fascist ideology only in terms of the goal that fascism is aiming to achieve at a given moment with a given ideology."[6] Fascism's improvisatory ethos could of course harbor opportunistic motives, but Togliatti was well aware that there also existed an unchanging core of doctrinal features: ultranationalism; antiparliamentarianism; activism; elitism infused with populist rhetoric; the cult of youth; a totalitarian concept of the state reliant upon new voice and image technologies; the ideal of the fully mobilized and militarized nation; the celebration of authority, discipline, and hierarchical order; faith in the absolute primacy of the collective over the individual; a vision of history as driven not by class conflict but by the conflict between nations; war envisaged as the normative condition of humankind; romantic anticapitalism and the advocacy of a new yet old guild-based economy; aggressive promotion of industrialization and modernization (so long as it is reconcilable with the "intractable realities" of history, race, etc.); an ethos of heroism, intensification, acceleration, and sacrifice linking man to machine. Many if not most of the elements that make up this volatile mix were borrowed from sources such as anarcho-syndicalism, socialism, romantic nationalism, the writings of Mazzini, Nietzsche, Spengler, Gobineau, Sorel, and others. But their fusion cannot be dismissed simply as a smoke screen, an aberration, or a throwback. Rather, fascism put forward a distinctive (if asystematic) new vision of the individual, society, and the world, and however reliant upon nineteenth-century sources, that vision belongs to the twentieth century.

Ours was a fascist century, then, at least to the degree that fascism's advent represents a true novelty vis-à-vis liberal democracy (an eighteenth-century ideology that came to fruition in the nineteenth century) and socialism (a nineteenth-century ideology that came to fruition in the twentieth century alongside its fascist enemy twin). Ours was a fascist century also to the degree that fascism's rise, first in Italy and then in Germany, led to our century's hinge event and principal catastrophe: World War II. That fascism's crushing defeat in the latter context does not eliminate the potential for carryovers has been demonstrated by the resurgence of neofascist or fascistoid movements over the past few decades in the industrialized world, from the Nouvelle Droite in France to the Russian nationalists of Zhirinovsky to the American militias. But there are other more subtle or indirect ways in which fascism's limited though central place in the cultural and political history of the twentieth century may be felt, even as the modernity it crystallized is starting to ebb: its continuing hold on certain nihilistic youth subcultures; its certainty that Enlightenment ideals cannot overcome the enduring fact of ethnicity and nationalism; its conviction that modern political power consists in control over the production and management of images; its role as model for subsequent totalitarian mass-based regimes. On the policy front as well, interesting echoes and prefigurations may be found throughout the documents contained in this anthology, for example, in their accounts of the fascist version of the welfare state and proposals to abolish the state monopoly on postal and telegraphic communications, to form a European political and economic union, and, in the earliest phase of the movement, to promote worker self-management. It goes without saying that the documents in which they are found cannot always be taken at face value. More often than not they are declarations of intent and require careful decoding. (Even in the case of legal documents such as the Labor Charter and School Charter, full legal implementation and enforcement can never be taken for granted.)

This said, surface declarations matter enormously, and the ones included here are distinctive in a number of ways. First of all, they are limited to Italian sources. Whereas some of the excellent existing anthologies on the topic of fascism adopt a comparative perspective and survey fascist writings in a multiplicity of countries (principally, Italy, France, Germany, Belgium, Spain, and England), I have chosen a tightly focused, in-depth approach that emphasizes the historical development of fascist ideology in a single country. My presumption in this regard has been that the range of documents available in English on Italian fascism is still woefully limited, excluding as it does the entire second decade of fascist rule and a good many key legal, philosophical, and cultural texts, and that a single-country approach was uniquely appropriate in the case of Italian fascism to the degree that, historically speaking, it was the "original" fascism whose model was followed by subsequent movements, including Nazism. (That there were significant divergences between the original and its copies may be taken for granted.)

Second, to anthologize is necessarily to perform acts of inclusion and exclusion that advance a particular interpretation of the phenomenon under study. The present volume is no exception. Though its principal aim is historical inclusiveness and representativeness, it grants special emphasis to the role played by intellectuals and artists in defining the nature and scope of the fascist revolution. Another anthology, equally valid, might be built around the anti-intellectual oratory of squadron leaders like Roberto Farinacci and paint a picture whose foreground would be filled with violent, reactionary, and ultranationalist elements. I have chosen instead, even at the risk of some redundancy, to tilt the balance in favor of efforts to theorize fascism's socioeconomic and cultural program. This implies what some specialists may rightly view as an inordinate emphasis upon corporativist doctrine and the circle of fascist technocrats gathered around Giuseppe Bottai. Yet my aim has been to help readers grapple with the question of how and why fascism was able to elicit and maintain the support of a generation of distinguished artists, thinkers, and writers, most of whom embraced it as an authentic revolutionary alternative and third way. Corporativism, real or imagined, thus comes to play a central role in the Mussolini regime's mythology, no less important than the much celebrated "Battle for Grain," land reclamation programs, and public works projects.

Third, unlike its German counterpart, the Italian regime accommodated a wide range of definitions of fascist culture, and a good many of these are represented in the third part of this anthology. At one time or another, the regime identified itself with everything from Futurism and the Novecento (a kind of magic realism) to neo-Roman iconography to populist kitsch. But what it never renounced was an elitism that assigned to the makers of culture a primordial role while in turn aestheticizing the role of political leaders. In the words of Margherita Sarfatti, "Revolutions in every domain of religion, society, philosophy, and art are made by altering the watchword. They are made by launching a new watchword first within the governing elites [minoranze-guida] and then by extending it to the mob: a watchword that stops them, surprises them, makes them reflect, and places them under the spell of action."[7] Revolutions in politics were always already cultural revolutions (and, in Sarfatti's partisan account, both rely upon the modernist technique of defamiliarization). Ideologically fluid, fascism often sought answers to the question, What is a fascist revolution? in the domain of fantasies and images.

Lastly, it is worth noting that this anthology features a number of texts that are engaged in either open or covert critical struggles over fascism's nature, its history, or its revolutionary scope. The spectrum extends from the fiery rhetoric of a disaffected Futurist (chapter 19) to the ruminations of a battle-scarred conservative revolutionary (chapter 14) to an internal report in which the manifesto that provided the basis for the 1938 racial laws is subjected to sharp criticism (chapter 13) to an outright antifascist manifesto by the philosopher Benedetto Croce (chapter 22). While the range of positions begins to hint at the sorts of debates that characterized 1920s and 1930s Italy, this collection does not aspire to comprehensiveness. It aims, rather, to open up for the English reader a more complete, less monolithic vision of Italy's fascist decades.

The editorial criteria adopted in preparing and presenting the translated texts that make up this volume require some explanation. Each document is prefaced by an introduction that provides a brief biography of the author and a brief account of the circumstances of its composition. Where necessary, I have added annotations, principally in the case of political, cultural, and historical references that are unlikely to be familiar to the nonspecialist reader. Shaped as they were by Latinate models transmitted and enforced by rigorous classically grounded educations, 1920s and 1930s prose habits in Italian were florid and verbose and allow for a degree of redundancy that is ill-adapted to the English language. Frequent recourse to multiply nested subordinate clauses and to semicolons means that a single sentence can easily fill an entire paragraph. As a result, simplification and paring in the process of translation have often been necessary. My aim throughout has been to render the texts as accessible as possible, without any loss of accuracy. To this same end, the original Italian term has sometimes been inserted between brackets into passages where the English equivalent is unable to capture either a pun, an allusion, a specialized or technical valence, or a neologism.

Among the distinctive features of fascist-era Italian prose, none is more symptomatic of the cultural-political climate than the capitalization of terms of authority. Nouns such as nation, fatherland, state, empire, victory, fascism, government, monarchy, directorate, and black shirt, as well as all of Mussolini's titles—chief (*capo*), leader (*duce*), and so forth—were routinely capitalized in order to grant them the monumental status that was felt to be their due. Sometimes a single text will even make distinctions between capitalized and noncapitalized forms, for example, between the "weak and watered down" liberal-democratic state and the fascist totalitarian State, whose authority encompasses the private realm as well as the public one. Capitalization asserts the transcendent personhood of the collective (or, in the case of Mussolini, single) entities that fascism raises above the powers and rights of atomized individuals. This sort of political nominalism has an archaizing effect when carried over wholesale into English, where it recalls eighteenth-century orthographic practices. I have, therefore, been obliged to eliminate it from the translations except where absolutely essential to the meaning of a given passage. Even terms such as "fascism" have been decapitalized, as have the adjectives that are derived from them. The sole exception that I have made on a systematic basis is to preserve the title *Duce* ascribed to Mussolini. Derived from the Latin *dux*, which signifies "guide," "conductor," "commander," and "leader," it was regularly substituted for his proper name and represents so distinctive a usage that no English transla-tion could do it justice. Initially adopted by the Arditi (World War I assault troops), it was enshrined as the dictator's official title from 1926 onward and became one of the key features in the cult of Mussolini's personality.

Some other terminological clarifications are in order. As in the case of the title Duce, I have chosen not to translate only partially some other words and phrases with specialized meanings. A case in point are the terms *Fascio* and its plural *Fasci* (which I have left in the original) and *squadrismo* (translated as "squadrism"). The former refers in the first instance to the Roman lictorian fasces but became a standard turn-of-the-century label for political groupings or associations both on the left and on the right. In the context of the anthology it refers either to a specific fascist grouping, such as the pre–World War I Fasci di Azione Rivoluzionaria or Fasci di Combattimento within which the fascist movement first arose, or to the local fascist group or fascist headquarters (Casa del Fascio) which could be found in all Italian cities. The label "squadrism" is a neologism in English (much as *squadrismo* was in post–World War I Italian), but I have preferred it over various alternatives because it captures one of early fascism's distinc-tive features: its organization in military *squadre* (or "teams"), each with its own banners, slogans, and rituals. In the case of specialized vocabulary, such as the terminology revolving around the theory of corporativism, I have preferred literal translations over figurative ones. *Corporazione*, which, as indicated above, signifies both "company" (in the American sense) and "guild" (in the medieval sense), is translated literally as "corporation," and *corporativismo* is translated as "corporativism."

In closing, I should like to express my gratitude to several colleagues who were kind enough to offer their expert advice while I was in the process of assembling the present volume. Among them, I wish to single out Zygmunt Baranski, Cinzia Blum, Philip Cannistraro, Alexander De Grand, Robert Dombroski, and Claudio Fogu, whose suggestions have all contributed to the anthology's shape. Thanks are also due to my friend and collaborator Barbara Spackman for her work on chapter 16: an anthology of contributions to the *Critica Fascista* debate, which (in a modified version) appeared as "Nine Selections from the Debate on Fascism and Culture: *Critica Fascista* 1926–1927" in *Stanford Italian Review* 8.1–2: 239–72. To the late Renzo de Felice I am thankful for his encouragement regarding this project. The same goes for my colleague and friend Luigi Ballerini, whose persistence will have at last paid off. Last but not least, thanks are due to Olivia Erin Sears for her valuable help as a research assistant and translator, to Maria Galli Stampino for her contribution as a translator, and to Jobst Welge for his careful poring over the final manuscript. Any errors that have eluded their scrutiny are my own.

Notes

1. Ugo Spirito, "Corporatism as Absolute Liberalism and Socialism" (1932), cited from the translation contained in chapter 11 in the present volume.
2. Cited from Benito Mussolini, "Political and Social Doctrine," from the translation in chapter 5 in the present volume (my italics).
3. The first reference is to Lawrence Dennis's *The Coming American Fascism* (New York: Harper and Brothers, 1936), which indeed propounds that fascism will soon become inevitable in the United States. The closing quote is from p. 58 of a pamphlet entitled "Fascism" (New York: Vanguard Press, n.d.) by the American communist activist Scott Nearing.
4. Cited from Mussolini, "Fundamental Ideas," from the translation in chapter 5.
5. Mussolini, from chapter 5.
6. Palmiro Togliatti, *Lezioni sul fascismo* (1935) (Rome: Editori Riuniti, 1974), 15.
7. Cited from Margherita Sarfatti, "Art and Fascism," from the translation in chapter 17 in the present volume.

A Chronology of Fascism

✳

1883	Benito Mussolini born
1892	Foundation of the Italian Socialist Party (Partito Socialista Italiano)
1904	Giovanni Giolitti's nearly uninterrupted ten-year period as prime minister begins
1911–12	The Italo-Turkish war takes place along with Italy's conquest of Libya
June 1914	"Red week" actions (strikes, insurrections, etc.) take place
August 1914	World War I begins with Italy adopting a neutral stance; Mussolini argues for an "active" neutral stance against the more rigorous neutralists within the Socialist Party
October 1914	The Fascio Rivoluzionario d'Azione Internazionalista is founded; the interventionist movement is under way
November 1914	Mussolini is thrown out of the Socialist Party, founds *Il Popolo d'Italia*
December 1914	The Fascio d'Azione Rivoluzionaria is formed from out of the Fascio Rivoluzionario d'Azione Internazionalista
May 1915	Italy finally enters World War I on the side of the Triple Entente; the interventionist leaders enroll in the armed forces
Oct.–Nov. 1917	The Russian revolution brings the Bolsheviks to power; the Italian army suffers terrible losses in the Battle of Caporetto but triumphs over the Austrians at Vittorio Veneto
November 1918	The armistice ending World War I is signed
January 1919	The Italian Popular Party (Partito Popolare Italiano) is founded by Luigi Sturzo
March 1919	Mussolini founds the Fasci di Combattimento
June 1919	The Treaty of Versailles is signed and provokes a protest movement in Italy
September 1919	Gabriele D'Annunzio occupies the city of Fiume with a force made up principally of World War I veterans
November 1919	The socialists and the Italian Popular Party win the elections

August 1920	A wave of factory occupations begins in the north of Italy; the fascist squadrists respond with a wave of violent actions
December 1920	D'Annunzio and his followers are expelled from Fiume
January 1921	The Italian Communist Party (Partito Comunista Italiano) is formed
May 1921	Thirty-five fascists are elected to Parliament, among them Mussolini
August 1921	In the face of the wave of squadrist violence, a Pact of Pacification is signed between the fascists and socialists
November 1921	After years of insisting that fascism is an antiparty movement, Mussolini founds the National Fascist Party (Partito Nazionale Fascista) in order to rein in the unruly fascist groups
August 1922	The general strike called by the socialist labor unions fails and is disrupted by fascists
October 1922	The March on Rome takes place; Mussolini is appointed prime minister
January 1923	The Fascist Grand Council is created
March 1923	The Italian Nationalist Association merges with the National Fascist Party
May 1923	Giovanni Gentile's educational reform is put into place
April 1924	The new Acerbo electoral law permits the fascists to gain 374 seats in Parliament
June 1924	The socialist deputy Giacomo Matteotti is kidnapped and murdered by fascists after delivering a courageous speech before the Chamber of Deputies in which he denounced acts of violence and intimidation that had permitted the fascists to gain a two-thirds majority in the Chamber. Mussolini replies to demands for his resignation by instituting a series of inquiries into the murder and by keeping at arm's length all fascist officials tainted by the ensuing scandal
January 1925	Mussolini's dictatorship is declared
April 1925	The Congress of Fascist Intellectuals is held in Bologna under the aegis of Gentile, and the *Manifesto of Fascist Intellectuals* is published in its wake
May 1925	The *Reply to the Manifesto of Fascist Intellectuals* is published by Benedetto Croce
April 1926	The fascist youth organizations are reorganized under the umbrella of the Opera Nazionale Balilla

July 1926	The Ministry of Corporations is founded
November 1926	The communist leader Antonio Gramsci is arrested and tried by a special tribunal
April 1927	The Labor Charter is decreed
December 1928	The Bonifica Integrale land reclamation program begins
February 1929	The Lateran Pacts between Mussolini's government and the Holy See are signed, recognizing the Vatican's independence and relations between church and state and paying the Vatican reparations for its losses at the time of unification
October 1929	The Royal Academy of Italy is inaugurated
March 1930	The National Council of Corporations is created
October 1930	A press campaign leads to a crisis over the activities of Catholic Action
November 1931	Loyalty oaths are instituted as a requirement for university faculty
October 1932	The celebrations of the ten-year anniversary of the March on Rome take place along with the opening in Rome of the Exhibition of the Fascist Revolution
January 1933	The Nazis seize power in Germany; the Istituto per la Ricostruzione Industriale (IRI) is founded to strengthen the government's hand in the economic sphere
July 1933	The Four Power Pact between France, Germany, England, and Italy is signed; Italo Balbo leads the last and greatest aerial cruise: a mass flight of twenty-four seaplanes from Orbetello to Chicago and back
February 1934	The twenty-three corporations are formally established
July 1934	The first meeting between Mussolini and Adolph Hitler takes place in Venice
August 1934	Hitler is proclaimed Führer after the death of Hindenburg
October 1935	Italy invades Ethiopia; trade sanctions are imposed upon Italy by the League of Nations in retribution; the economic "autarchy" campaign is launched
May 1936	Mussolini announces the creation of the Italian Empire
October 1936	As Italy and Germany begin their joint intervention on the side of the antirepublican forces in the Spanish Civil War, the Rome-Berlin Axis is formalized
June 1937	Antifascist activists in exile Nello and Carlo Rosselli are assassinated outside of Paris by a group of French fascists

September 1937	Hitler and Mussolini meet in Vienna
March 1938	Germany invades and annexes Austria with Mussolini's approval
May 1938	Hitler and Mussolini meet in Italy
July 1938	The Italian racial laws are decreed
January 1939	The Chamber of Deputies is replaced with the Chamber of Fasci and Corporations
February 1939	The new fascist School Charter is approved by the Fascist Grand Council
April 1939	Italy invades Albania
May 1939	Foreign ministers Galeazzo Ciano and Joachim von Ribbentrop sign the Pact of Steel strengthening the alliance between fascist Italy and Nazi Germany
August 1939	The Nazi-Soviet Non-Aggression Pact is signed
September 1939	Germany invades Poland; France and Britain declare war on Germany
June 1940	Italy enters World War II on the side of Germany
September 1940	The Three Powers Pact between Italy, Germany, and Japan is signed
October 1940	Italy invades Greece; Hitler and Mussolini meet in Florence
June 1941	Germany declares war on Russia; the Italian army sends a corps of soldiers
January 1943	The Party of Action (Partito d'Azione) is founded in Paris by opposition leaders Ugo La Malfa and Fausto Parri
July 1943	The first Allied landings take place in Sicily; Hitler and Mussolini meet at Feltre; a coup is initiated against Mussolini's leadership by Dino Grandi; Mussolini is arrested; and the Fascist Grand Council names Marshal Pietro Badoglio as prime minister.
September 1943	Allied forces move from Sicily to the peninsula; the armed resistance swings into action under the leadership of the Committee of National Liberation; Badoglio negotiates an armistice with the Allies but is forced to flee Italy alongside King Victor Emanuel; Mussolini is rescued by the Germans and returned to Italy; the Italian Social Republic is instituted, with Alessandro Pavolini as secretary of the newly founded Fascist Republican Party (Partito Repubblicano Fascista)
January 1944	The coup participants, including Galeazzo Ciano, are executed

June 1944	Rome is liberated by Allied forces
July 1944	Mussolini and Hitler meet in Berlin; the resistance groups in northern Italy become increasingly effective; a plot against Hitler's life fails
April 1945	Milan is liberated; Mussolini is arrested by resistance forces and executed alongside Achille Starace; Hitler commits suicide in Berlin
May 1945	The Wehrmacht offers its unconditional surrender to Allied forces
December 1946	Former fascists from the Italian Social Republic found the Italian Social Movement (Movimento Sociale Italiano), which will become the principal bearer of the fascist torch in the postwar era
January 1948	After several years of coalition governments made up of the major partisan and resistance forces, the Italian Republic is formally proclaimed

A PRIMER OF ITALIAN FASCISM

PART 1

FOUNDATIONS

CHAPTER 1

Platform of the Fasci di Combattimento (1919)

The Fasci di Combattimento (Combat Leagues) first emerged in the spring of 1919 and brought together ex-socialists, revolutionary syndicalists, nationalists, Futurists, war veterans, and other militant but disaffected political forces within the fold of an antiparty movement. The original Fascio was organized by Mussolini in Milan for the 23 March 1919 rally at Piazza San Sepolcro (attended by one to two hundred supporters, subsequently known as Sansepolcristi). Although no formal program was adopted at the rally, the following document, which contains radical demands regarding income, property, and taxation, was developed over the ensuing months and published on 6 June 1919 in Mussolini's newspaper Il Popolo d'Italia.

Program of the Italian Fasci di Combattimento

On the political front WE DEMAND

a) The minimum age for voters lowered to eighteen years; the minimum age for members of the Chamber of Deputies lowered to twenty-five years; all government functionaries to be politically elected; a regional base for the multimember constituency.

b) The abolition of the Senate and the creation of a national technical council on intellectual and manual labor, industry, commerce, and agriculture.

c) A foreign policy aimed at expanding Italy's will and power in opposition to all foreign imperialisms; in other words, a dynamic policy that contrasts with one inclined to reinforce the hegemony of the current plutocratic powers.

On the social front WE DEMAND

a) The prompt enactment of a state law sanctioning a legal workday of eight *actual* hours of work for all workers.

b) A minimum wage.

c) The participation of workers' representatives in industry's technical affairs.

d) The management of industries and public services to be entrusted to proletarian organizations that are morally and technically up to the task.

e) The rapid and complete reorganization of the transportation industry and its personnel.

f) The modification of the bill on disability and old-age insurance, setting age limits according to the effort demanded by each type of work.

g) The forcing of property owners to cultivate their lands under the threat that uncultivated lands will be given to farmers cooperatives, with special regard for veterans returning from the front lines; and the obligation of the state to contribute to the construction of tenant farmhouses.

h) The development of hydroelectric power and the exploitation of the soil's riches, subject to the consolidation and correction of pertinent laws; the expansion of the Merchant Marines made possible by the operation of all naval shipyards thanks to the abolition of the import ban on steel plates and to financial arrangements (credits, consortia, etc.) likely to promote naval construction; the maximum expansion of inland navigation and of the fishing industry.

i) The obligation of the state to provide and maintain schools whose character decisively and soundly shapes a national conscience, impartial in character but rigidly secular; schools whose character disciplines minds and bodies in the defense of the fatherland so as to render short training programs [*forme brevi*] possible and free from danger, to raise the proletariat's moral and cultural condition; the obligation of the state to fully enforce the law concerning mandatory schooling, accompanied by the allocation of all necessary funds to the budget.

j) Reform of the state bureaucracy motivated by a sense of individual responsibility and leading to a significant reduction in bulk of the overseeing bodies; decentralization and simplification of services so as to free up productive energies, the treasury, and officials; purging of current personnel and the creation of economic conditions that would insure the influx of more suitable and effective workers into the administration.

On the military front WE DEMAND

a) The creation of an armed nation within which brief periods of instruction are designed with one precise aim in mind: to defend the nation's rights and interests alone, as determined by the soundly orchestrated foreign policy noted above, so as to attain its ends with utmost certainty.

On the financial front WE DEMAND

a) A large progressive tax on capital that would amount to a one-time *partial expropriation* of all riches.

b) The seizure of all goods belonging to religious congregations and the abolition of episcopal revenues, both of which represent an enormous liability for the nation and a privilege enjoyed by the very few.

c) The review of all contracts for war supplies and the sequestration of 85 percent of war profits.

∗

The Central Committee of the Italian Fasci di Combattimento

Italians!

This is the national platform of a soundly Italian movement.

Revolutionary because antidogmatic and antidemagogic; strongly innovative because antiprejudicial.

We value the revolutionary war above everything and everyone.

We will address other problems—of bureaucracy, administration, the law, the schools, the colonies, and so on—once we have created a new ruling class.

To this end, WE DEMAND

On the political front

a) Universal suffrage with regional list voting, proportional representation, and the vote and eligibility for women.

b) The minimum voting age lowered to eighteen years; the minimum age for representatives lowered to twenty-five years.

c) The abolition of the Senate.

d) The convocation of a national assembly for the duration of three years *whose primary task will be that of establishing the form of the national constitution.*

e) The *creation of national technical councils for labor,* industry, transportation, public health, communications, and so on, elected by professional or trade groups, with legislative powers and the right to elect a general commissioner with ministerial powers.

On the social front

WE DEMAND

a) The prompt enactment of a state law sanctioning a legal workday of eight hours *for all workers.*

b) A minimum wage.

c) The *participation of workers' representatives in industry's technical affairs.*

d) The management of industries and public services to be entrusted to proletarian organizations that are morally and technically up to the task.

e) The rapid and integral reorganization of railway workers and of all transportation industries.

f) *An urgent modification of the bill on disabilities* and old-age insurance, lowering the current sixty-five-year age limit to fifty-five years.

On the military front

WE DEMAND

a) The establishment of a national militia, with brief training periods and strictly defensive aims.

b) The nationalization of all arms and explosives industries.

c) A national foreign policy designed to promote the Italian nation abroad within the setting of the peaceful competition among civilizations.

On the financial front

WE DEMAND

a) A large progressive tax on capital that would amount to a one-time PARTIAL EXPROPRIATION of all riches.

b) *The seizure of all goods belonging to religious congregations* and the abolition of episcopal revenues, both of which represent an enormous liability for the nation and a privilege enjoyed by the very few.

c) The review of all contracts for war supplies and the sequestration of 85 percent of war profits.

translated by Olivia E. Sears

CHAPTER 2

Postulates of the Fascist Program (1920)

✶

The November 1919 elections saw the triumph of the Socialist Party and the Italian Popular Party and the defeat of the fascists. The movement seemed to be teetering on the brink of collapse, suffering from poor organization, inadequate funding, and low morale. The revised program, which accompanied the second congress of the Fasci di Combattimento, held in Milan on 24–25 May 1920, reflects the movement's rightward swing and growing alliance with industry. The sharpest divergences from the 1919 program are to be found in the treatment of industry and labor relations and in a general tendency to substitute concrete proposals for social legislation with less compromising theoretical statements. These "postulates" were largely authored by Cesare Rossi and were published a week before the opening of the May 1920 congress.

✶

Given current historical circumstances, the Fasci di Combattimento do not aspire to become a new party. Hence they feel bound to no specific doctrine or traditional dogma. Hence their refusal to schematize and reduce within the narrow, unnatural confines of an intangible program all the mutable multiform currents of thought, all the tendencies and experiences that time's passage and the reality of things suggest and dictate.

The nature of the enterprise that the Fasci di Combattimento propose to carry out right away can be resumed in the following three points: *Defense of the last national war— Consecration of our Victory— Resistance and opposition to the theoretical and practical degenerations of petty socialism.*

Against Political Parasitism

Inspired by their desire to affirm our nation's vitality and to glorify our victory, the Fasci di Combattimento express their disgust for the political bourgeoisie's men and organizations. Both have revealed their inadequacy in the face of domestic and foreign policy matters; both have proven resistant to profound renewal, hostile to spontaneous recognition of popular rights, and unwilling to reason except in terms of the concessions and renunciations that parliamentary manipulations dictate.

For a Working Bourgeoisie [*Una borghesia di lavoro*]

The Fasci recognize the tremendous merit of the "working bourgeoisie," whose contribution to progress and national supremacy in all fields of human endeavor (from industry to agriculture, from science to the professions) is precious and indispensable.

Against the Degeneration of Workers' Struggles

The Fasci di Combattimento aim to morally uplift the proletariat and to contribute to shaping independently minded union organizations. They therefore consider it their duty to rigorously oppose all labor battles in which purely economic issues are transmuted and distorted by vile, demagogic machinations.

The Problem of the Current Regime

For the Fasci di Combattimento, the question of whether the current regime ought to continue or not must be addressed as a function of the nation's present and future moral and material interests. The Fasci are thus not biased for or against current institutions.

Our Financial Postulates

a) Enactment of a large progressive tax on capital that would amount to a one-time partial expropriation of all riches, to be paid within a brief period of time.
b) The seizure of all goods belonging to religious congregations and the abolition of episcopal revenues, both of which represent an enormous liability for the nation and a privilege enjoyed by the very few.
c) The review of all contracts for war supplies and the sequestration of excess war profits left standing idle.

The Fasci and the Workers' Organizations

The Fasci wish to express their sympathy for and their intention to assist those minority groups within the proletariat who seek to harmonize the defense of their class interests with the interests of the nation. With regard to union tactics, they counsel the proletariat to adopt as its own forms of struggle and conquest that ensure the community's well-being as well as the well-being of individual producers, without narrow predilections and a priori exclusiveness.

For an Economy of Maximum Production

Faced with utopistic plans for reconstruction based on collectivizing economic solutions, the Fasci di Combattimento remain firmly planted in reality: a reality that does not allow for monolithic forms of autonomy and dictates an approach amenable to those forms—be they individualistic, collectivist, or of some other variety—that maximize productivity and well-being.

Our Demands in Defense of the Proletariat

a) The prompt enactment of a state law sanctioning a legal workday of eight hours for all workers.
b) The representation of workers in industry affairs, limited with respect to personnel matters.
c) The management of industry and public services entrusted to proletarian organizations that are morally and technically up to the task.
d) The formation of national technical councils for labor with legislative powers, consisting of representatives of industry, agriculture, transportation, intellectual work, public health, communications, and so on, and elected by each professional group.

On the Military Question

The Fasci di Combattimento demand the establishment of a national militia with brief training periods and defensive aims; the immediate acceptance of all demands made by veterans and disabled soldier associations, toward whom the fatherland's gratitude must be shown unambiguously and tangibly.

The Means of Struggle

As regards the tactics to be adopted in defense of the above platform, the Fasci di Combattimento will remain in contact with and work alongside (on a case-by-case basis) all groups and parties that assume the same antidemagogic, antibureaucratic, antiplutocratic oppositional stance and that seek to contribute to national reconstruction.

translated by Olivia E. Sears

CHAPTER 3

Program of the National Fascist Party (1921)

✴

In March 1921 Mussolini reaffirmed his long-standing position that fascism was not a party but a movement. But fascism's success in leading the armed reaction against the Socialist Party and the trade unions contributed to a rapid expansion into rural areas beyond the control of the Milanese leadership. This decentralization of authority prompted Mussolini to reverse himself and to consider the constitution of a party. The Program of the National Fascist Party represents an attempt to resolve the conflict between urban and agrarian fascism. It transforms the movement into a full-fledged political party with an official program and a formal hierarchy that was meant to check the power of local squadrist bosses. The program and statutes of the National Fascist Party were approved on 20 December and published on 27 December 1921.

✴

Fundamental Elements

Fascism constituted itself as a political party in order to strengthen its discipline and to individuate its beliefs.

A nation is not reducible to a sum total of living beings nor is it a tool that political parties may use for their own ends. Rather, it is an organism comprising an indefinite series of generations of which single individuals are but transient elements. The nation is the supreme synthesis of all material and nonmaterial values of a race.

A state is the juridical embodiment of a nation. Political institutions are effective as long as the nation's values are expressed and protected by them.

Autonomous values upheld by individuals, like the collective values upheld by multitudes and espoused by collective, organized bodies such as families, municipalities, corporations, and so on, ought to be promoted, developed, and defended. But this must always be done within the nation, an entity to which these values are subordinate.

The National Fascist Party maintains that the form of social organization predominant in today's world is the national society. It holds, moreover, that the destiny that awaits global life is not the unification of various societies into a single, immense society: "humanity" in the parlance of internationalists. Rather, destiny promises something better: fruitful and peaceful competition among all national societies.

The State

The state must be reduced to its essential functions: maintaining the political and judicial order.

The state bestows powers and responsibilities on associations. It also grants professional and economic corporations the right to vote in elections to the National Technical Councils.

It therefore follows that the powers and the duties currently assigned to the Parliament must be restricted. Under the Parliament's sway come all problems of the individual qua citizen of the state and of the state qua organ whose purpose consists in realizing and protecting the supreme national interest. Under the National Technical Councils' sway come all problems involving the activities undertaken by individuals qua producers.

The state is sovereign. Such sovereignty cannot and ought not be damaged or diminished by the Church, to which ample freedom must be granted so that it may carry out its spiritual ministry.

The National Fascist Party's attitude regarding the forms assumed by individual political institutions depends upon the moral and material interests of the nation, understood both in its reality and in its historical becoming.

Corporations

The rise of corporations is a historical fact that fascism cannot oppose. It aims at coordinating corporative development in the pursuit of national objectives.

Corporations must be promoted with two fundamental goals in mind: as an expression of national solidarity and as a means for the development of production.

Corporations must not strive to submerge the individual in the collectivity by arbitrarily leveling his or her abilities and strength. Rather, they must aim at making good use of and developing them.

The National Fascist Party will advocate the following positions in support of blue- and white-collar workers:

1. The enactment of a state law establishing an official standard workday of eight hours for all employees, with possible exceptions being granted due to special agricultural or industrial needs;

2. The enactment of welfare legislation adapted to current needs—particularly in the domains of accident, disability, and old-age protections provided agricultural, industrial, or office workers—so long as it does not hamper production;
3. Obligatory representation of workers in the management of factories, limited with respect to personnel issues;
4. The management of industry and public services entrusted to union organizations that are morally and technically up to the task;
5. Promotion of the diffusion of small landholdings in those regions where it makes sense for certain types of agricultural production.

Cornerstones of Domestic Policy

The National Fascist Party aims to bring a new dignity to our political habits, so that the life of the nation is not characterized by antithetical forms of public and private morality.

It aspires to the supreme honor of governing the nation and aims to restore the ethical principle that governments ought to administer the commonwealth as a function of the nation's supreme interest and not as a function of the interests of political parties and cliques.

The prestige of the nation-state must be restored. The state in question does not look with indifference upon the outbreak of arrogant forces attempting or threatening to materially and spiritually weaken its structure. It is a jealous keeper, defender, and propagator of national tradition, sentiment, and will.

The freedom of individual citizens is subject to a twofold limit: the freedom of other juridical persons and the sovereign right of the nation to live and develop.

The state must favor the nation's growth by promoting (but not monopolizing) all efforts that foster the ethical, intellectual, religious, artistic, judicial, social, economic, and physiological development of the national collectivity.

Cornerstones of Foreign Policy

Italy must reaffirm its right to complete historical and geographical unity, even in cases where unity has not yet been fully achieved. It must fulfill its duty as bulwark of Latin civilization in the Mediterranean basin. It must firmly and serenely assert the sway of its laws over the peoples of different nationalities annexed to Italy. It must provide real protections to Italians abroad, Italians who are deserving of the right to political representation.

Fascism finds the founding principles of the so-called League of Nations wanting, because irrespective of whether they are members or nonmembers, nations do not enjoy an equal footing within the League.

Fascism does not believe in the vigor or effectiveness of the color-coded internationals, whether red, white, or other. The latter are artificial, formal constructions gathering small minorities of individuals with varying degrees of conviction. They are to be contrasted with the great masses of the population whose lives, whether on an upward or a downward trajectory, provoke shifts in power and, in turn, the collapse of all internationalist constructions. (Recent history has proven as much.)

The diffusion of Italianness [*italianità*] throughout the world must be the aim of Italy's commercial growth and of the international treatises through which it asserts its influence. International treatises must be reviewed and altered, particularly where they contain clauses that are clearly inapplicable; they must fulfill the needs of the national and worldwide economy.

The state must make the most of Italian colonies in the Mediterranean and overseas by means of economic and cultural institutions, as well as by developing rapid informational and transportation links.

The National Fascist Party openly supports a policy of friendly contacts with the peoples of the Near and Far East.

The defense and growth of Italy abroad must be placed in the hands of an army and navy that are equal to Italy's policy needs and on a par with the armies and navies of other nations. It must also be placed in the hands of a diplomatic corps that, aware of its role, is endowed with culture, courage, and the requisite skills necessary to express Italy's greatness at once materially and symbolically.

**Cornerstones of Fiscal Policy and Policies
for National Economic Reconstruction**

The National Fascist Party will insist upon the following:

1. That concrete sanctions be imposed on individuals and corporations when labor contracts that were freely entered into are not respected;
2. That, in cases of acts of negligence, public employees and their supervisors be subject to civil sanctions to the benefit of the injured party;
3. That taxable income and assessments of inherited estates be made public, in order to facilitate the monitoring of each citizen's financial obligations to the state;
4. That all future state initiatives that aim to protect certain branches of

agriculture and manufacturing from dangerous foreign competition be designed as a stimulus to our nation's productive forces and not for the benefit of parasitic, plutocratic groups whose intention it is to exploit our national economy.

The following will be the short-term objectives of the National Fascist Party:

1. Balancing state and local budgets (when necessary) by means of rigorous cutbacks to all parasitic or redundant entities and via reductions in expenditures neither crucial to the well-being of the beneficiaries nor justified by more general objectives;

2. Decentralization of the public administration so as to simplify the delivery of services and to streamline our bureaucracy, without falling into the trap of political regionalism (which we firmly oppose);

3. Shielding the taxpayers' money from misuse by means of the abolition of all state or local government concessions and subventions to consortia, cooperatives, factories, special clienteles, and other entities similarly incapable of surviving on their own and not indispensable to the nation;

4. Simplifying the tax code and distributing tax burdens according to proportional criteria (that do not amount to "proportional plundering") such that no category of citizens is unduly favored or handicapped;

5. Opposition to financial and fiscal demagoguery that hampers the spirit of enterprise and saps our nation's savings and production;

6. Cessation of policies favoring public works projects that are botched, undertaken for electoral reasons, or supposedly to insure law and order, projects that are unprofitable because of the irregular and fragmentary way in which they are distributed;

7. Crafting of an organic public works plan in harmony with the nation's new economic, technical, and military needs. The plan proposes:

    a. Completion and reorganization of the Italian railway system, so as to insure better links between newly liberated regions and the peninsula and to improve transportation links within the peninsula itself, especially north-south links across the Apennines;

    b. Maximum acceleration of the electrification of railways and, more generally, the exploitation of hydroelectric power in our mountainous river basins so as to promote the growth of industry and agriculture;

    c. Repair and expansion of the roadway system, especially in the South, where this is a necessary precondition for resolving countless economic and social problems;

    d. Creation and reinforcement of maritime links between the Italian peninsula and the islands, the eastern Adriatic shore and our Mediterranean colonies, as well as between the North and South, so as to shore up the railroads and/or to encourage Italians to take to the sea;

    e. Concentrating expenses and efforts in a few key harbors on the three seas surrounding the peninsula, outfitting them with the most up-to-date equipment;

    f. Struggle and resistance against all forms of localism inasmuch as, in the field of public works, they lead to uncoordinated efforts and thwart projects of national interest.

8. Return to the private sector of industries that the state has managed poorly, in particular, the telephone system and the railroads. Regarding the latter, competition needs to be enhanced between the major lines, which need, in turn, to be managed differentially with respect to regional and local lines;

9. Abolition of the state monopoly on postal and telegraphic communications so that private enterprise may supplement and eventually replace the state-run service.

Cornerstones of Social Policy

Fascism recognizes the social function of private property. At once a right and a duty, private property is the form of management that society has traditionally granted individuals so that they may increase the overall patrimony.

    In its opposition to socialist projects for reconstruction that rely upon a dogmatically collectivist model of economics, the National Fascist Party has its feet firmly planted in the soil of our historical and national reality. This reality does not allow for a single type of agricultural or industrial economy. The party, accordingly, supports any and every solution, be it individualistic or of any other kind, that will guarantee the maximum level of production and well-being.

    The National Fascist Party advocates a regime that would strive to increase our national wealth by unleashing individual enterprises and energies— the most powerful and industrious factor in economic production— and by abolishing, once and for all, the rusty, costly, and unproductive machinery of state-, society-, and municipality-based control. The party thus supports all efforts to enhance Italy's productivity and to eliminate forms of individual and group parasitism.

    The National Fascist Party will argue for the following:

1. That disorderly clashes between divergent class and socioeconomic interests be disciplined, to which end it is essential that organizations representing

workers and employers be granted legal recognition (so that they may, in turn, be made legally responsible);

2. That a law be promulgated and strictly enforced prohibiting strikes on the part of public servants. Moreover, arbitration boards must be set up that are made up of representatives from the executive, from among the blue- or white-collar workers on strike, and from the taxpayers.

School Policy

The schools' overall objectives ought to be the shaping of individuals who can contribute to the nation's economic and historical progress, the raising of the masses' moral and cultural level, and a continual renewal of the ruling elite via the training of the best elements within every social class.

To these ends, the following measures are urgently needed:

1. Reinforcement of the battle against illiteracy through the building of schools and of access roads and by means of all state measures that may be deemed appropriate;

2. Mandating that compulsory schooling extend through the sixth grade in municipalities where schools are available and can accommodate all students who do not continue on to middle school after the sixth-year exam. In all other municipalities, mandatory schooling at least through the fourth grade;

3. The institution of rigorously national elementary schools whose task it is to physically and morally shape Italy's future soldiers. In order to carry out this mandate, intensive state monitoring of programs, teacher selection, and teacher performance are necessary (especially in municipalities in the hands of antinationalist forces);

4. Free middle schools and universities, though state monitoring of academic programs and of the spirit of what is being taught is required, as is the state's direct involvement in premilitary instruction, aimed at facilitating the training of officers;

5. Teacher-training colleges governed by the same principles that govern the schools where teachers will be employed. Therefore, schools training elementary school teachers must retain a rigorously national character;

6. Development of a master plan for the establishment of professional, industrial, and agrarian schools that would make use of funding and a wealth of experience provided by manufacturers and farmers. These schools would have as their purpose an increase in the nation's productivity and the training of an intermediate class of technicians, between workers and managers.

To this end, the state will have to supplement and coordinate existing private sector efforts, while displacing these where they are found wanting;

7. Endowing middle and high schools with an overall "classical" character. All types of middle schools should be unified, so that Latin is studied by all students. French must no longer be the only language studied alongside Italian. The second modern language ought to be chosen as a function of regional need, especially in those areas that border on other nations;

8. Centralization of all educational benefits, grants, and so on, under the aegis of a single institute managed by the state. Such an institute would single out the most intelligent and hardest-working pupils in the earliest grades and insure that they go on into higher education. It would counteract (when necessary) parental selfishness and provide needy students with substantial financial aid;

9. Improvement of the salary and status of teachers, professors, and army officers (who are, after all, the nation's military educators). This should provide them with the increased respect and with the means to expand their cultural horizons. It will also inspire in them and in the general public a higher awareness of the national importance of their mission.

Justice

Preventative and therapeutic anticrime methods must be promoted such as reform schools, schools for the deranged, criminal asylums, and the like. Penal sentences are a means of self-defense on the part of a national society whose laws have been injured. They are usually meant to have both intimidatory and corrective value. From the standpoint of the second, it is essential that the hygiene of jails be improved and that, via the introduction of prison work, their social function be perfected.

Special tribunals should be abolished. The National Fascist Party is in favor of a reform of the military criminal code.

Trial proceedings ought to be swift.

National Defense

Every citizen is obliged to serve in the military. Our army must start to see itself integrated within a single armed nation, a nation within which all individual, collective, economic, industrial, and agricultural forces converge for the supreme purpose of defending our national interests.

To this end the National Fascist Party advocates the immediate creation of a complete and perfect army, an army that watches over newly conquered borders like a vigilant sentry and that, on the domestic front, makes sure that the nation's infinite reserve of spirits, men, and military means is always trained, organized, and regimented so that it is always ready for times of danger and glory.

With this same goal in mind, the army, along with schools and sports clubs, must infuse citizens' bodies and spirits with the aptitude and knowledge required for battle and sacrifice in the name of the fatherland (premilitary instruction).

Organization

Fascism in action is an organism with goals that are:
   a. political
   b. economic
   c. combative.

In the political field, fascism opposes sectarianism. It welcomes any person sincerely espousing its principles and obeying its discipline. It stimulates and values those endowed with genius, gathering them together in expert groups according to their specialty. It participates intensely and regularly in all aspects of political life, putting into contingent practice that which does not lie outside its doctrine's pragmatic framework, while at the same time reaffirming the doctrine as an overarching whole.

In the economic field, fascism supports the creation of professional corporations that, depending upon historical or geographical circumstance, may be either genuinely fascist or independent in character. Only one thing is crucial: that they be deeply informed by the tenet that the nation stands above all social classes.

As concerns its bellicose character, the National Fascist Party is one and the same as its squadrons. The squadrons are voluntary militias fighting in the service of the nation-state. They are a living source of strength in which and through which the fascist idea embodies itself and defends itself.

translated by Maria G. Stampino and Jeffrey T. Schnapp

CHAPTER 4

Excerpt from "History of the Fascist Movement" (1932)

Gioacchino Volpe

✳

Volpe (1876–1971) was the most eminent historian to join the fascist ranks. A specialist in medieval history and a war veteran, he served as a fascist deputy in Parliament between 1924 and 1929. Thanks to his "History of the Fascist Movement," published in 1932 as the historical appendix to Mussolini's and Gentile's "Foundations and Doctrine of Fascism" in the Enciclopedia italiana, *Volpe emerged as the official historian of the regime. Despite the status that this conferred upon him, Volpe's loyalties during the early years of World War II turned toward the monarchy and against the Italian Social Republic. The following extract from his "History of the Fascist Movement" covers the foundation of the Fascist Party up through the March on Rome (chapters 4 and 5), both recounted in harmony with the Fascist National Party's own mythology.*[1]

✳

By 1922 the Fascist Party had become the principal organized force within the country, even though its adversaries continued to claim that the fascist program was so vague that it was no program at all. Subtle reasoners and clever ideologues, they confused philosophy with life, forgetting that feelings and passions are or can be inchoate thoughts and, at the very least, have the capacity to shape events. They viewed fascism as "extraneous to political culture" and condemned it as such.

But the Fascist Party continued to grow, as did fascism itself, even beyond the confines of the party. There were greater unity and discipline. There was greater confidence felt by the mass of members, that confidence in oneself and in one's work that verges on a sense of faith. By this time fascism had come to believe that it possessed not only [practical] ends but also a [historical] mission. The word "mission" thus surfaced anew in Italian history for the first time since the Risorgimento, the era of Gioberti and Mazzini, thanks in part to the direct influence of those who had felt a new sense of youthfulness during the wartime and postwar years.[2] Fascism began to develop its own myths. To have belonged to the tiny band of forerunners that made up the first Fascio of Milan, the Fascio Mussolini so often invoked as a paragon of perfect discipline and equilibrium, was now becoming a mark of glory. March 1919 was surrounded by a bright halo, because the year in question signaled the start of a new era in Italy's history. "Nineteenism" [*diciannovismo*] became synonymous with enthusiasm and faith. How much was accomplished in so little time! How many comrades had fallen in daily battles! The dead had founded and solidified a tradition. For the most part they were youths. Some were mere adolescents. They belonged to every social class and began their [adult] lives in the fascist movement. Some were interventionists at the age of seventeen and eighteen, volunteers in the Great War, legionnaires at Fiume and then fascists. . . . These truly representative figures of their generation, these near exemplary men, succumbed under the blows of communists or deserters. Such was the fate that befell the soul and leader of the Prato fascists, Federico Florio, in January 1922.[3]

Towering ever higher above the mass that was growing in unity, discipline, and dedication was their leader — *the leader* — Mussolini. Mussolini did not hold any special position within the party hierarchy. Yet from this time on he was designated il Duce.[4] Not only was Mussolini the founder of the Fasci, but for three years he had taken part in the daily struggle to promote their growth, urging them on and restraining them, laboring to train and hone himself as well as others. Mussolini had always risen above the contingent, above the individual, above particulars and petty passions [*il particolare e passionale*]. Now he came to embody the very movement whose essential elements he himself brought into being. More than to any other person, it was thanks to him that, even as fascism defined and differentiated itself, it was able to grow spiritually, to become consonant with what most (and the best) Italians were saying, to ever increasingly identify itself with the "public interest" and with Italy. No one was more agile than Mussolini in preventing deviations and disruptions, in resisting the pull exercised by far right or far left currents, in fighting both "agrarian" (i.e., not properly "rural") fascists who wished to entirely demolish the socialist economic organizations with the pretext of wanting to crush socialism, and fascists who wished to lead peasants and workers converted to fascism down the same road followed by communists and Bolsheviks. Day after day he hammered away in his newspaper. And on important occasions, his weapons were his living presence and his living word (the latter despite a growing disdain for empty chatter).

Unlike their hollow counterparts, Mussolini's words translated into works. They penetrated deep into the soul of his listeners. He knew well how to stir up emotions so close to action's edge as to be nearly synonymous with action. He repudiated the "verbose, prolix, inconclusive" eloquence of his democratic opponents and crafted an "essentially fascist" eloquence, an eloquence "that is essential [*schelettrica*], biting, sincere, and firm." He never lost himself in details or in everyday occurrences. Rather, he sketched out visions, charted the course to be followed, pointed to goals. Whether writing or speaking, he kept his followers in a constant state of anticipation. He always insisted not on things done but on things yet to be done. He was always looking toward the future. He imbued fascists with a soldier's mindset: a soldier who is always prepared because he knows that the hour of battle may come in ten years or in ten days. His entire vocabulary was that of a soldier or a general. For him, fascism was a militia [*milizia*]. Problems were enemies to be confronted and conquered. The Italian people were an army on the march in closed ranks. Officers, corps, foot soldiers, recruits, discipline; the party card as military dogtag; don't argue, believe!; fight and obey. He radiated an air of intolerance, verging on contempt, for men who were too wise or "too clever," for "intellectuals" who, in their presumption and in their overestimation of culture and science, often proved little more than sterile sophists "capable of splitting a hair into four" but incapable of acting upon the world of things. He endorsed Adriano Tilgher's definition of fascism as "absolute activism transplanted into the field of politics."[5] To this he added that if relativism is the logical consequence of scientific reason [*scientificismo*] and if relativism acknowledges the absolute supremacy of life and action over intelligence, then the fascist movement, thanks to its refusal to give a definitive or programmatic form to its complex and powerful currents of feeling [*stati d'animo*] and its reliance upon fragmentary intuitions, may be designated a form of "superrelativism." If relativism is linked to Nietzsche and to his *Willen zur Macht* [will to power], fascism is the most formidable creation of an individual and national will to power (cited from "Relativism and Fascism" in *Il Popolo d'Italia* [22 November 1921]).

Mussolini's critical attitude toward the intellect lent itself to misinterpretation among his followers, often degenerating into a general contempt. And crude expressions of irony and contempt for culture and cultural figures there were, provoking, in turn, cold and hostile attitudes toward fascism on the part of many intellectuals. To a degree, this irony and contempt may have reflected the intellectual horizons of a generation shaped by four years in the trenches or that had distractedly completed its studies or that was simply predisposed to fisticuffs rather than to patient paging through books. But it also bespoke unsatisfied desires, the sorts of desires that always arise in times when men are beginning to undertake new things and to experience life in a brand new way but find little help, guidance, or support because the prevailing wisdom, schools, and professors are out of touch with the times. In point of fact, this moment marked the beginnings of a cultural renewal. Fascism now possessed its own ideal of culture, a fascist culture alive, mobile, capable of penetrating, animating, and unifying all things—not detached but one with life. It aspired to a "fascist culture," a "fascist art," a "fascist style," a "fascist way of life."

During the second half of 1921 and, even more strikingly, in 1922, overall conditions—or at least some conditions—within the country had improved, and there were a few comforting economic signs. People returned to work. The infatuation with Russia and Bolshevism was on the wane, partly owing to the return of socialists who had seen Russia firsthand. From his retreat in Gardone, [Gabriele] D'Annunzio reinforced their despair.[6] He declared that Russia, through her act of self-immolation, had freed the world from a puerile illusion and a sterile myth. Her terrible experiment had proven that a government based upon the dictatorship of a single social class was unable to create tolerable living conditions. Italians became reconciled to the war, which is to say, to one another. The war was purified of its dirt and dross. The pain and suffering that it inflicted were no longer the stuff of insults and reprimands hurled by Italians against fellow Italians. At the end of 1921, the minister [of war, Ivanoe] Bonomi, carried out the translation of the remains of the Unknown Soldier to the Altar of the Fatherland [Altare della Patria], stirring up deep emotions and renewed feelings of brotherhood from one end of the peninsula to the other.[7] Fascism claimed the lion's share of credit for this change of heart. And rightfully so, although the shift itself transcended fascism or any other individual agent or ideological current, much to the credit of the Italian nation, its intrinsic health, and its inexhaustible vitality. The army had quickly recovered from the debacle of October 1917 (a debacle largely due to military causes but aggravated by an impending moral collapse). In similar fashion, the body politic now overcame the collapse of 1919–20, expelling its evil humors and the mighty viruses associated with four years of wartime suffering.

All this needs to be recognized. The justification of [Italy's] intervention [in the Great War], the exaltation of her victory, the damming up of the Bolshevik flood: all these contingent and negative responsibilities shouldered by fascism began to diminish in importance around this time. From the very start, fascism had, of course, harbored other possibilities: convictions and thoughts, for instance, shared with nationalist, liberal, and socialist groups but transformed into actions and accomplishments by fascism alone. If three years of struggle had weakened the enemy, their impact upon fascism was the opposite. Fascism found itself enhanced as a political doctrine. It now was eyeing grander horizons and more ambitious aims. The appearance of Fasci abroad during 1921–22 in places such as Alexandria, Cairo, Reims, Rhodes, Lugano, Paris, Smyrna, New York, Tripoli, and so on, places where there was no need to check the growth of Bolshevism, is ample proof. Even among its sympathizers, there were many who expected that fascism would soon begin to demobilize and disarm, placing Italy back in the hands of the men and parties who had always divided up power among themselves. Instead, fascism continued to mobilize. Its chief target now became the government or, rather, the parliamentary regime that, under Bonomi (who fell in 1922) and, worse still, under his successor, [Luigi] Facta, reached new heights of incompetence and chaos.[8] Parliament was always on the verge of a new crisis brought on by organized and officially recognized groups who fought among themselves for supremacy and who viewed the government as little more than the administrator of their personal interests. The government, likewise founded upon the principle of proportional representation of parliamentary groups and, hence, always bickering, was accustomed to living from day to day and to viewing itself as the momentary exponent of momentary situations. Was all this disorder attributable to the reform that had instituted proportional representation? Many thought so and found in it a further reason to heap abuse upon [Francesco Saverio] Nitti, the author of the 1919 electoral reforms.[9] But one had to dig deeper to find the causes: in the egotism of parties that felt and acted neither as a whole nor even as part of a larger whole but instead as partisan entities; in the absolute preponderance of legislative power (especially in the lower chamber) over executive power; in the stripping away of the Crown's authority and its reduction to a nearly passive spectatorial role in the setting up of the Cabinet. Hence the desire that the king should make himself more forcefully present. Hence also the demand for a military dictatorship. Mussolini himself advocated the latter one day in Parliament, adding that it was a very risky step, to be considered only in extreme circumstances because either it succeeded or the result was sure to be utter chaos.

But cries of "Down with Parliament!" and "Long live the dictatorship!" began to sound everywhere, whether in fascist or nonfascist demonstrations before the prefectures and army headquarters. Incidents of this kind occurred in Bologna and Florence. Commenting on this outcry, Mussolini observed that "the best part of the nation is moving toward the right, not toward the left, in the pursuit of order, discipline, and hierarchy. For three years it has demanded a government but none has been provided. The government does not exist. The current crisis proves that the chamber is incapable of providing the nation with a government. Today's cry from Bologna may tomorrow become the roaring chorus of the whole nation" (*Il Popolo d'Italia*, 12 February 1922). . . .

A series of fascist mass rallies occurred during the spring. The Milanese one, held on 26 March to mark the third anniversary of fascism's foundation, was attended by workers, peasants, and members of the lower middle class. "No profiteers [*pescecani*]! Ours is a movement inspired by idealistic impulses," commented Mussolini in *Il Popolo d'Italia*. On 21 April there was the first fascist commemoration of the Birthday of Rome and Labor Day, celebrated by means of gatherings, processions, and so on, designed to displace those traditionally held on May Day.[10] An article in *Gerarchia* called attention to Rome's central place in the history of the Italian people.[11] In his newspaper, Mussolini added, "In Rome we see the promise of the future. Rome is our myth. We dream of a Roman Italy, which is to say, of an Italy wise and strong, disciplined and imperial. Much of the immortal spirit of Rome has risen again in fascism. Roman is our lictorian fasces, Roman the organization of our fighting forces, Roman our pride and our courage. Great builders were the Romans. . . . With these thoughts the fascists commemorate the first furrow traced on the Palatine to erect the four-square city."[12] In the middle of May, fifty thousand fascist workers from the labor organizations flocked to Ferrara. They came from every direction, on foot, on bicycles, in trucks and river boats, cloaks and blankets tossed across their shoulders in military fashion. Italo Balbo acted as their leader.[13] Theirs was a great "fascist strike": a strike for work and not for subsidies. They demanded the immediate initiation of long-ago-approved work projects, protested against the government's slowness, affirmed the principle that "those who fought the war have a right to a decent life." On 24 May, date of the anniversary of Italy's entry into the war, a fascist funeral procession was fired upon, a procession transporting the mortal remains of Erico Toti back to his native Rome. (Toti was a popular hero and storm trooper [*bersagliere*] who, having lost his leg in the Great War while fighting in a cyclist battalion, continued to fight and, mortally wounded in a later battle, hurled his wooden peg leg at the enemy.) Many were wounded or killed. Mussolini, writing in *Il Popolo d'Italia*, declared: "To all

Italian fascists: consider yourselves materially and morally mobilized from this moment on. Repair to the places that you are told with the speed of lightning. Everything will crumble under the impact of your blow." A few days later, further acts of violence against fascists in Bologna and its province took place. Suspecting the existence of a government plan to destroy the fascist labor and political organizations in cooperation with the other parties, all the powers and duties of the leaders of provincial Fasci were transferred to [central] action committees [*comitati d'azione*]. The Fasci of Bologna mobilized. Michele Bianchi, the party secretary, transferred his command to Bologna.[14] Squadrons from Ferrara, Modena, and Venice also converged upon the city. A total of ten thousand men bivouacked under Bologna's porticos with nightly rounds, reveilles at dawn, c-rations . . . which is to say, with discipline worthy of an army. A veritable occupation of the city! They called for the head of [Cesare] Mori, the city prefect.[15] And when they succeeded in having the police placed under the authority of army general [Sebastiano] Sani, they departed. The occasion put on display for the first time the power of fascism's new politico-military organization: its alertness, discipline, and agility. Nonfascist newspapers took note, even abroad, where a mix of genuine interest and curiosity was developing around this movement whose sights were set not only on domestic matters but also on Italy's foreign policies (in terms more benevolent toward ex-enemies than toward ex-allies).

Along with Bologna came Florence. On 28 May, the Tuscan Fasci, from Grosseto and Carrara to Arezzo and Livorno, assembled. Thousands strong, they gathered in Padua, Legnano, and Sestri Ponente. Then there was the first national assembly of once socialist, now fascist labor groups whose passage was carried out to cries of "Long live Italy, long live fascism!" By this time, the battle with socialism for the heart of the masses was being won all the way down the line, particularly in the countryside. Speaking in the Po valley, Mussolini drew attention to the ruralization of fascism. To this he added that "patriotism is no longer a sentiment monopolized (or exploited) by the cities, for it now belongs to the countryside as well. Once practically unknown, the tricolor now billows over even the smallest villages." One of fascism's great achievements was to have managed to integrate the vast masses of rural folk into the living body of Italian history (*Gerarchia*, 22 May 1922). [Edmondo] Rossoni echoed this, declaring that workers were now full-fledged participants in the nation's history.[16] For the first time, a true *national* syndicalism had come about. Workers were no longer asking only for material benefits, as had been the case when they were under the sway of socialists. "New affirmations of the Italian nation will now surge forth directly from the people and especially from the rural masses."

The spectacle of armylike masses, mobilized and demobilized in the blink of an eye, masses that, though seemingly aligned with the state, were in reality acting outside the state, astonished and disquieted many in Italy and abroad. Did fascism intend to restore or to destroy the public order and the state, they wondered. Is it possible to restore and to destroy at one and the same time? Mussolini replied: there exists an absolute antithesis between the state as understood and advocated by fascism and the current "liberal" state that pretends to rise above the party and class fray and refuses to make any distinction between forces that are pronation and prostate, and antination and antistate ones. This antithesis must cease. Fascism itself, that is, must incarnate in the state.

But how to put Mussolini's words into practice? Ought one to do so without violating the law? Perhaps. Two paths, two solutions emerged from within the ranks of the Fasci. One entailed a legal approach: fascism's gradual spread to every region and municipality (especially the largest) with the goal of gaining the support of an overwhelming majority, reforming electoral laws, holding new elections, achieving a majority in the chamber, and, finally, taking over the government. The other was military and insurrectionary in character and favored acting outside the law. Legality or illegality? Fascism's dilemma was openly posed in the Chamber of Deputies. Mussolini seemed to favor the first (or, at the very least, was willing to give it a shot). He could readily foresee the difficulties posed by an insurrection, among which the possibility that an uprising might grant primacy to military actors and activities rather than to political ones. This said, Mussolini was hardly averse to the second course of action. One can easily imagine him secretly fascinated by visions of an army on the march and of a victory achieved by assault (and not by means of negotiation and a steady transition). Then there is the matter of his deep-rooted conviction that no solution should ever be ruled out, that all avenues need to be left open, all the more so given that legality and illegality were not readily distinguishable or extricable from one another. July saw a series of "battles for purges on the local level," as Mussolini dubbed them: sackings or, rather, resignations of mayors and socialist communal councils. By midmonth fascism had triumphed in Rimini. Rimini and Bologna became the two arms of a pair of pincers squeezing the Romagna region as a whole. Rimini opened the door to the Marches, where, heretofore, there had been only a few fascist Avanguardie.[17] Next came a series of victories: first in Andria, in the center of Puglia; then in Cremona, the battlefield of Roberto Farinacci; and, finally, at Novara and Viterbo.[18]

At this juncture the antifascist camp seemed ready to spring into action in an effort to fill the ever widening breech. First there was the late July railway strike that began in Novara (where the Chamber of Labor [Camera del lavoro] was assaulted) and subsequently spread to the surrounding regions, inspired and encouraged by the communists through their Turin newspaper, *Ordine Nuovo*.[19] The fascists responded by threatening to occupy Milan with thirty thousand men if the strike did not end by 21 July. And end it did on 21 July, either due to the fascist threat or due to the strike's only partial success. A few days afterward came the socialist attempt to reconquer Ravenna, marked by a battle between workers affiliated with the Red Leagues and those who had switched over to fascist labor unions. Quick on the skirmish's heels came the occupation of Ravenna by fascists from the surrounding areas and Ferrara in particular, all gathered around Balbo, an event that came to be referred to as "the taking of Ravenna." New and bigger strikes were proclaimed on 31 July with the Facta government in crisis. One day earlier, the leader of the socialist Right, Filippo Turati, had been received by the king and consulted on the ministerial crisis.[20] It was the first time that a member of the Socialist Party with a strong base of support in Parliament and in the General Confederation of Workers had been welcomed to the Quirinale.[21] A partnership, the daily dream of many democratic groups since the start of 1919, suddenly seemed within reach. But the fascists were opposed, not because Mussolini didn't think that, sooner or later, it might be possible to build a coalition between the three great mass parties that now ruled Italy: socialism, fascism, and the Italian Popular Party—a coalition within which fascism must figure as *primus inter pares*.[22] (He had said as much one year earlier in the chamber and now repeated himself in his newspaper on 30 July 1922.) Rather, Mussolini could not simply stand by and watch as the socialists rose to power alongside members of the Popolari, whose antifascism was growing ever more intransigent. A Socialist–Popular Party coalition government was intolerable to him because it could only be interpreted as an act of war against fascism and, therefore, as the declaration of a civil war.

The general strike destroyed any hopes for collaboration with the government, irrespective of the attitude of the party and of the General Confederation of Workers (CGL) toward a strike that was revolutionary in both intent and inspiration. In this situation, as before, the fascists issued a public injunction and an ultimatum to the strikers and to the government:

either an end is called to the strike within forty-eight hours or we will act in the place of the public authorities and end it ourselves. Forty-eight hours later the strike was still ongoing. The fascist squadrons sprung into action, occupying train stations, taking over railway lines, operating and escorting trains, protecting railwaymen who had refused to strike. In a few days the strike was broken. At the same time, on 3 August, the fascist squadrons expelled the socialists from the Commune of Milan, attacking and destroying [the headquarters of their newspaper] *Avanti* but not without bloodshed.[23] The tricolor was hoisted anew over Palazzo Marino, and D'Annunzio returned to Milan for the first time since the night of Ronchi to address the people from its balcony.[24] If tensions had existed between Mussolini and D'Annunzio, they now evaporated. Then came battles in Savona, Parma, and Livorno, the latter led by Commander Costanzo Ciano, a gold medal recipient.[25] The Commune of Livorno was also occupied at this time, and, as if to consecrate this victory, twenty thousand citizens fell to their knees and prayed for those who had lost their lives. On 5 August the Genovese Action Committee decided to occupy the port, long a stronghold of socialists, whose cooperatives monopolized all work. The rallying cry was freedom for the port, revocation of all existing contracts between the Port Authority and the socialist cooperatives, recognition of multiple cooperatives in all industrial sectors. This too was a victory. The Palace of San Giorgio, the glorious palace of the old Republic located in the heart of maritime Genoa and now the seat of the presidency of the Genovese Port Authority, was occupied. The socialist newspaper was destroyed.

All these events were highly significant and rich in consequences. They showed what a few thousand men could accomplish when determined to fight, animated by clear ideals and powerful passions, and buoyed by the applause or consent of the great majority of citizens. They showed that socialism succeeded neither in inculcating into the proletariat a sense of national law and order nor in arousing revolutionary sentiments and capacities. Mussolini's sarcasm was right on target. The socialists, he said, had failed at both collaboration and revolution. So what came of all this? Fascism achieved an almost definitive consecration. It now managed to attract many who had been sitting on the fence. The list of new Fasci, unions, Avanguardie, new squadrons grew ever longer. The socialist and red communes crumbled as if in an earthquake. Chambers of Labor were occupied; cooperatives, like those in Verona and Venice, were taken over. The Socialist Party was losing ground as additional segments of the working class, in particular urban workers, now turned toward fascism. The way was led, however, by the middle- and low-tier segments of the bourgeoisie, hitherto disorganized and inclined to endorse various models of socialist collaboration with the government. But hadn't socialism now disqualified itself as an upholder of national values? Certainly its contribution to the public disturbances, to disarray, to financial demagogy in the administration of the communes was a bad omen as regarded its future governance of the state.

In short, a multitude of new converts from the bourgeoisie as well as from the people swelled fascism's ranks and raised concerns. Adversaries hoped that what befell socialism in 1919–20 would now befall fascism, namely, that, now fully fattened up, it would collapse under its own weight. "No way," answered Mussolini. "We are unlike the socialists. We have not made false promises. We speak of Italy and of Italy's future. We will not renounce some of our imperialistic claims. Too many members [*accoliti*] may harm a party that is split, but not a party of soldiers such as ours. For us political discipline is also military discipline. Our young recruits want to fight, not to argue. We have never promised unrealistic benefits [*felicità*] to labor unionists. We will fight to defend workers' gains but, if necessary, we will also demand sacrifices" ("La Fiumana," from *Il Popolo d'Italia*, 26 August). This was all a bitter, near fatal blow to socialism, both to its size and to its prestige [*credito*]. Already weakened by its failure to put a new order in place, by its waiting in vain for the advent of a messiah, and by its lethargy toward the communists, socialism was wounded yet again, wounded by the failure of the general strike and by the contradiction between its own conciliatory invocations of law and order, including appeals that the state do battle with fascist violence, and its recourse to even greater violence. The socialists themselves admitted their defeat as a consequence of the strike, with which they had hoped to smash fascism. "The August strike," they said, "has been our Caporetto."[26] It was our last card. We have played it and lost. Our opponents have taken Milan and Genoa away from us, two at once seemingly impregnable bastions. They have torched our two principal newspapers, *Avanti* in Milan and *Il Lavoro* in Genoa. Wherever present, the fascist gales have blown us away. The various solutions we adopted to solve the problems with which our existence confronted us have all come too late. Too late our embrace of collaborationism, which should have been tried after the elections of May 1921. Too late our embrace of revolutionism, attempted in the form of a general protest strike only when many of our fortresses had already fallen. The fault lies with internal disagreements over method and with deviations from the original course charted by socialism.

We must return to our beginnings, go back to the constitutional charter of Italian socialism of 1892 (*La Giustizia*, Reggio Emilia, [22 August 1922]).

In all likelihood, the August victory reinforced the strength of revolutionary, rather than the legalistic or gradualist currents, within the Fascist Party. Or, at least, it hastened the pace of change. Ever more serious were the problems confronting fascism as a result of its growth: problems that were now national in scope. And ever greater was the gap between the passivity of the legitimate government and the hyperefficient activity of the de facto fascist government. It became increasingly urgent to attend to southern Italy, whose reaction to northern developments was, as always, slow and cautious. The South had resisted the influence of Mazzini's movement [*mazzinianesimo*] in the middle of the nineteenth century. Variable were its reactions to "Piedmontism" (the encounter with which represents the South's first contact with the Italian unity movement). During 1919–20, the socialists worried that the South might become Italy's Vendée.[27] Now the South worried the fascists as well. . . . How to conquer and hold Rome without the South? How to avoid the dangers of schism and disunity? On 11 August Mussolini called for a Black Shirt rally in Naples on 24 October as a show of force that would also launch a more rapid penetration of the region. Fascism, he stated, will make the southern question into the nation's most pressing question. It will tap the political and economic energies capable of reinvigorating the South. The South will heal the South, but the state will promote the self-healing effort. When it looks south, fascism sees a great reserve of men, workers, and soldiers. It sees a great feeling of togetherness and a great resistance to subversive plagues. . . .

Already the phrase "The March on Rome" was in the air. To those who questioned him about it, Mussolini answered that, in the highest possible historical sense, the march had already begun. Fascism's progress toward fully incarnating the state was under way. Also under way was the formation of a new class of political leaders to whom would be entrusted the task of governing the Italian nation, governing in the true sense (for Facta's was not a government but merely a cabinet). There was talk of a march of some one to three hundred thousand Black Shirts in military formation, all converging from three directions: the Adriatic, the Tyrrhenian Sea, and the valley of the river Tiber. A possibility, but neither strictly necessary nor inevitable. . . . In short, there was uncertainty. Michele Bianchi, the party secretary, admitted as much when on 13 August, addressing a meeting of the party's central committee in Milan, he told the regional delegates that "we have now reached the reconstructive phase. The great mass of workers has come to us and is looking to us. So it's *aut, aut*; it's *either, or*. Either we become the state's vital fluid or we take the state's place. Either new political elections are called so that our political representation is proportional to our actual power or there will be further fascist actions. The decision must be made quickly. (Let's hope that Italy's elites are listening carefully. . . .)" The head of the squadrons, Balbo, requested the creation of a technical and strategic office within the party directorate so as to unify the command structure of the fascist military organizations and to render them more efficient. Balbo was always to the left. He was always the advocate of a fully mobilized, unfettered fascism. He opposed the Pact of Pacification and the transformation of the fascist movement into a political party.

On 20 September in Udine, the Fasci of Venezia Giulia held a great rally on the anniversary of the breach of Porta Pia.[28] An important speech was given by Mussolini, whose thoughts turned to Rome: the city of the spirit, the city that, for Mazzini and Garibaldi, had been an exalted symbol and goal and that would play a key role in the life of the new Italy, becoming "the palpitating heart of the dreamed-of Italian empire." But Rome had to be earned: earned through internal and external discipline, earned by means of a politics denouncing cowardice and compromise at any cost. From Rome, fascism would transmute the regime. How so? A month before the Rome rally, Mussolini felt obliged to shed some anticipatory light on his attitude toward the monarchy: "I believe that it is possible to renew the regime while leaving the monarchy intact." There were other, greater targets at which to take aim! And an antimonarchical stance would turn a large number of Italians against fascism. It would foster regional separatism. "We must have the courage to be monarchists," said il Duce. The monarchy means continuity. Great are the responsibilities that it shoulders! Besides, the fascist revolution doesn't aspire to wipe the slate clean or to give people the impression that everything is collapsing around them, thereby provoking waves of panic. It suffices to demolish the socialist-democratic [*socialistoide democratica*] superstructure. At present, the Italian state has no moral substance. It is always at the mercy of the strong (however momentary their strength). It approaches every problem individually and as if strictly a political matter. It possesses no deep sense of duty or of a mission. It therefore builds without using mortar. Overloaded with activities, it must be lightened. You fear that the state will diminish as a result? On the contrary. More than ever, its domain will remain the great domain of the spirit. . . .

Mussolini's Udine speech echoed powerfully throughout the nearby recovered territories [*regioni redente*] and even as far as the distant South (to which it was especially addressed).[29] Immediately thereafter came several weeks of rallies and shows of strength: in Vicenza, Novara, Alessandria, and Cremona. At the last of these, on 24 September, Mussolini declared: "The Piave was not an end but a beginning. From there our banners set out on their march, a march that can only end in Rome. Nothing can stand in our way." On 29 September a meeting of members of the party directorate was held in Rome at the headquarters of the confederation of cooperatives: Mussolini, Bianchi, Balbo, Ciano, Terruzzi, de Vecchi, Dudan, Bastianini, and others.[30] Plans for the March on Rome, the actual March on Rome, seemed decided upon. A clash with the army was to be avoided; the monarchy was to be respected; the government was to be snatched away from the Parliament. Internal disagreements arose here and there among the Fasci. Certain [local] leaders had to be admonished: fascism's march cannot be interrupted and must advance along a single road—that which leads to Rome!

A number of important events came to fruition in the Alto Adige between September and October. At the beginning of September, the party secretary, Bianchi, presented a memorandum to the head of the government, asking that he cut right to the quick of the autonomy question by wiping out the traces of the past regime and by bringing the Alto Adige region within the nation's laws and powers. Negotiations with local municipal authorities took place and bore fruit, as in Merano, for instance, where the Italian flag would now be flown on holidays and both Italian and German would now be employed as official languages. . . . Negotiations in Bolzano, however, proved fruitless. Here Italian children were bereft of schools, the police exercised political functions, and Mayor Perathoner retained absolute control over the city. No less fruitless were negotiations with the region's German-born deputies. The government continued to vacillate. The fascists had to step in yet again. Come September, Francesco Giunta, who had led attacks in Trieste and Fiume, received permission from Mussolini to intervene and, if necessary, to take extreme measures. Late on the night of 30 September, squadrons from Vicenza, Mantua, Trento, Cremona, and Brescia . . . speedily converged upon Bolzano and, after a brief initial clash, occupied the Empress Elizabeth School and changed its name to the Queen Elena School. They then took over city hall, where they hoisted the tricolor flag and hung a portrait of the king. Next they occupied the government offices of the province of Trento, headed by Commissioner Credaro, and issued peremptory demands to the government, namely, the abolition of the commissariat and dismissal of the commissioner himself, the subjection of lands reclaimed [in World War I] to Italian law, and the creation of a single Trento-Bolzano province. The attack was not truly directed at the region's two hundred thousand Germans, whose presence could hardly be ignored and toward whom no one wished to pursue a policy of violence. No, its principal target was against the Italian government that had allowed these Germans—a minuscule minority within a nation more ethnically homogeneous than most in Europe—to completely ignore Italy and to treat Italians as if they were foreigners.

Outside the fascist and antifascist folds, the country reacted to these events with varying emotions: satisfaction, disquiet, bewilderment. "At last we have a [real] government!" said some. "How many governments are there? It's intolerable for there to be more than one!" said others. By this they implied both that the fascists should swiftly take the government's place and that the government should swiftly return to truly governing. The contradiction had to be resolved and resolved anon. For the fascists the solution was, of course, already at hand, and they made no mystery of the course that they would follow. Addressing the Antonio Sciesa action squadrons in Milan on 4 October, Mussolini spoke in no uncertain terms about "the air of expectation that has taken hold of the souls of all Italians, presaging an event which is sure to come." He also recalled the August attack on *Avanti* through barbed-wire entanglements and a hail of bullets. "Here was the true violence of Milanese fascism at work," he declared. "Not the petty violence of individuals, occasional and often fruitless, but the grand, the beautiful, the inexorable violence of decisive moments [*ore decisive*]." Again the aim was to shift the fascists' focus away from a myriad of minor actions and to concentrate it squarely on "decisive moments." It is no secret that Mussolini prepared the proclamation he later made to the Italian nation at this time. But Mussolini, as already indicated, was not one to leave any stone unturned. In this case, his strategy was two-pronged. Persuaded that it was impossible to achieve an acceptable outcome by legal means, the outcome now anticipated by all fascists, he never excluded a legal solution so that he could better justify his eventual recourse to violent methods to the undecided majority. Before the young men of the Sciesa squadron Mussolini insisted that "Italy's need for a [true] government is ever more pressing." . . . He said that the government should call the Chamber of Deputies into session at the beginning of November, pass a new voting law, and hold immediate elections. The Facta crisis was not enough, he continued.[31] Given the composition of the current Parliament, thirty new crises would simply give rise to another thirty Factas. If the government doesn't choose this line of action, the other line of action will be ours. Our cards are now fully laid out on the table, even if few are capable of reading them because parliamentary politics have so dulled their minds. But a new Italy filled with impetus and life has risen up from out of the trenches. And, like a man who feels his hands about to grasp the helm of the ship of state, he indicated the course he intended to take with a sweeping gesture: "Ours will be a politics of rigor [*severità*] and reaction, the latter because we are also reactionaries. We react against democratic habits of mind, according to which everything must be rendered gray, mediocre, equal; and according to which the authority of the state—from the all-too-democratic king to the lowliest employee—must also be rendered ephemeral and drab. Democracy has stripped Italians of any sense of 'style,' that is, of an overall line of conduct [*linea di condotta*], of color, power, the picturesque, the unexpected, the mystic—all that which has a real impact upon the soul of the multitudes. We will bring all of this back. We will cover the entire gamut, from violence to religion, from art to politics. We are politicians and warriors. . . ."

A man who could speak like this to young followers already filled with great expectations, a man capable of envisioning such a profound transformation [*rivoluzione*] of the nation's life, could hardly have attached much importance to the negotiations that were going on with the leader of the government. Yet, all the same, the negotiations went forward, irrespective of the fascists' deeper aims. They had commenced right after the Bolzano incidents, which is to say in a context within which even blind men could see just how paralyzed were the government and the Italian state and just how efficient were the new fascist paragovernment and parastate. And they stumbled forward.

As during the war, Rome, official Rome, was the last to see and to understand the new Italy. What filtered through from the peninsula was a fictitious version of the real. An illusory life was lived in official Rome, a life made up of traditional habits and thoughts. Parliament, party squabbles, talk about crises all assumed a disproportionate importance with respect to the actual conditions these phenomena bespoke of or reflected within the nation. Suddenly, the government staked out its entire response upon the respect for law and order. It declared its inability to weigh the relative merits of the political ideas that were fighting for Italy's heart and soul and its unwillingness to abandon a neutral stance. The fascists demanded a large share of power. They wanted the most important ministries: foreign affairs, war, the marine, public works, aviation. The government instead offered them posts as undersecretaries and as ministers without portfolio, which makes it all the less surprising that the Fascist Party hastened its military preparations. On 18 October, a meeting was held under the aegis of the Milanese Fasci, involving Mussolini, Bianchi, de Vecchi, Balbo, General de Bono (commander of the fascist squadrons), and Generals Fara and Ceccherini.[32] A quadrumvirate [*quadrumvirato*] made up of Bianchi, Balbo, de Vecchi, and de Bono was named for purposes of leading the impending revolutionary action.[33] Mussolini suggested 21 October as a date. The earlier the better, he probably thought. Some felt hesitant as to whether fascism's military organization had yet achieved a sufficient degree of efficiency. Others wondered whether the South's support or, at the very least, its benevolent neutrality was guaranteed. So it was decided that the 24 October Naples rally should go forward as planned. In the meantime, however, Balbo, de Bono, and de Vecchi would develop a plan for mobilization and fix the massing points for the various columns that would advance on Rome.

Such were the circumstances under which the Naples rally unfolded. The day before, Bianchi and the three squadron leaders had already finalized their plans, issued orders, and fixed the date for the March on Rome. Speaking at the San Carlo Theater, Mussolini announced: "We have reached that point when either the arrow must leave the bow or the string will break due to excessive tension." And what he meant was that the moment of truth had arrived. The truth in question was left obscure. But Mussolini did rebuke Facta's lack of understanding, his petty legalism, his laughable offers, and he did insist that fascism wouldn't "enter the government by the back door" because its aim was "to infuse the liberal state with all the vitality [*forza*] of the new generation that had emerged victorious from the war." The future of the monarchy, he added, was not in doubt. The point was driven home by some further friendly words concerning the throne, words well attuned to the feelings of a region whose political traditions (to the degree that political traditions exist at all) remained monarchical. "The monarchy represents the basis of [national] unity," he said, "and fascism has no interest in demolishing it. By the same token, the monarchy has no interest in opposing fascism. Did it oppose the charter of 1848? Did it oppose the war in 1915?"[34] Next came a paean to Naples and its citizens. Last came his reply to those who continued to argue that this vast region had never faced a Bolshevik threat and, therefore, had no need for fascism. "But there are so many other ills to cure and problems to solve!" he argued. "We must disinfect the local atmosphere [*disinfettare gli ambienti locali*], coordinate all forces, make of Naples, along with Palermo and Bari, one of the engines of growth [*forze d'impulso*] that propels the South out across the three seas and continents that surround the peninsula. . . ."

Afterward there occurred a great parade, with Mussolini standing in review. The fascists massed in the city's outskirts and, after a three-hour march, converged upon Piazza San Ferdinando in the heart of Naples. There were forty thousand squadrists, twenty thousand members of the workers unions, mounted squadrons from the Campania and Puglia regions, special squadrons of cyclists and of veterans decorated with gold medals. At their head marched legions representing the recovered lands [terre redente], with the loudest cheers reserved for the representatives of Fiume and Dalmatia. (The passion for both had fueled fascism ever since 1919.) Shouts of "On to Rome! On to Rome!" also resounded. And Mussolini endorsed them in a brief address. This demonstration, he said, is but a demonstration and cannot metamorphose into a battle proper, "but I must tell you with all the solemnity that the occasion imposes that either the government [governo] is handed over to us or we will seize power by advancing on Rome." By now it was a matter of days, maybe even of hours. He exhorted everyone to quickly return to their home bases with the aim of "simultaneously seizing by the throat Italy's dreadful ruling class throughout the entire nation." The National Council of the Fasci met over the next two days. In attendance was the entire political, military, and union hierarchy of fascism: the party directors, the central committee, the inspector general of the squadrons, the provincial secretaries, even representatives of the confederation of cooperatives. All the most urgent problems were discussed: the party, trade unions, specialized task forces [gruppi di competenza], elections, foreign policy, schools. But a wave of impatience swept over everyone. Even the party secretary, Bianchi, had to concede that "the events of the past days have outstripped a good number of points on our agenda." Until a few days ago hesitations were still being expressed, "but now all the turmoil is giving way to a rock-solid sense of determination that will and must prove victorious." He summed up the situation as follows: "The Chamber of Deputies no longer represents the country. So, every minister the chamber votes in is exercising his powers illegitimately. Our duty is to restore legitimacy to Italy's political institutions [ridare la legalità agli istituti rappresentativi in Italia]." In other words, to reestablish a true correspondence between the juridical Italy [Italia legale] and the real Italy [Italia di fatto] by circumventing the chamber's powers.

The situation preceding the March on Rome was not unlike that in May 1915, when the interventionists appealed directly to the king for the appointment of a prowar minister, an appointment to which the chamber was opposed. In the case of the Naples rally, however, the oratory and discussion ran the risk of dragging on. Hence Michele Bianchi's quip: "But fellow fascists, it's pouring [ci piove] in Naples, and you're just standing around?"

On 26 October secret orders were issued to the *principi* and *triarî* for an immediate nationwide mobilization.[35] By midnight the plan was fully carried out. All political, military, and administrative authority was placed in the hands of a secret quadrumvirate granted dictatorial powers. Mussolini drafted a proclamation, signed by the quadrumvirate. It recalled the fact that it was the fourth anniversary of the day on which the army had launched its victorious offensive on the Piave: "Today, the Black Shirt army commemorates the mutilated victory [*vittoria mutilata*] and, bearing down intensely upon Rome, brings victory back to the glorious capital."[36] He warned the army and the police not to intervene. The battle was not against them but "against a ruling political class made up of fools and idiots who haven't managed to provide the nation with anything like a real government during four years of rule." He went on to reassure the industrious middle and upper classes [*la borghesia produttrice*]: "fascism wishes to impose discipline on the nation as a whole and to aid all those who contribute to its well-being and economic growth." Workers too had nothing to fear. Their rightful interests would be safeguarded: "I call on God almighty and on the spirits of the [fascist] dead to bear witness to the fact that a single impulse, a single desire, a single passion drives us: that of contributing to the salvation and greatness of the fatherland."

Meanwhile, in the larger cities, local leaders formed action committees and took charge of the movement. Public buildings, city halls, postal and telegraphic offices, police stations, and prefectures were occupied nearly everywhere. Wherever possible, caches of arms were seized by means of lightning strikes [*colpi di mano*]. Necessities were commandeered. There were clashes with soldiers and police. Much blood was shed at Casal Monferrato, Cremona, in the Bologna region, and elsewhere. Bloodshed was averted in most cases either because astute, daring, and surprising actions left the forces of order unable to react or because their momentary acquiescence was obtained. This attitude of wait and see, once confronted by the event itself and by fascism's success in Rome and Italy as a whole, soon turned into acceptance and solidarity. The soldiers did their duty. They continued to man their posts and withstood as best they could the fascist onslaught: the onslaught of a mass rather than of an army. (Few fascists were armed right from the outset.) The soldiers' was hardly an easy position. Faced with strict orders that they employ any and all methods required to crush the uprising, the majority obeyed, though some came over to the other side (or, at least, some conversions were reported by officers in the course of 1922). A widespread sympathy for fascism existed within the lower army ranks. It was reinforced by the fact that, though it often called for the arming of ordinary citizens [*nazione armata*], fascism gave daily evidence of its warm feelings toward the army and of its view that the army was integral to Italy and to fascism itself, so uncompromising orders were rare. A sense of tragedy was in the air. Everyone knew that the unfolding events were, to a degree, a matter of fate; everyone knew that they were legitimate in large part. The fascists were neither a faction nor a band of armed rebels nor were they subversives or antimilitarists given to vilifying the army. No: they were the nation itself, its best and brightest, those best able to embody the traditions established during the war. This was in contrast to a morally isolated government whose claim to represent Italy was little more than a legal fiction. Would it really have been conceivable for them to do battle with a mass of mostly unarmed or poorly armed young men, young men singing the praises of Italy, the army, and the king as they marched? The squadron commanders were themselves veterans decorated with medals for valor and for injuries sustained [on the World War I battlefront]. Many declared that they would never have opened fire on their comrades in gray-green uniforms. If ordered to shoot, they would have stood at attention and simply let themselves be fired upon. Of course, such orders never came. The army's defection was never at issue. At issue was the army's swift adaptation to new circumstances that very quickly assumed a legal form.

The *triari* stayed behind to guard the cities while the *principi* marched on Rome. . . . General command headquarters were located in Perugia, which had fallen into fascist hands on the night of 28 October after the city prefect surrendered so as to avoid bloodshed. The work of bringing together and coordinating troops was in the hands of experienced generals and upper-echelon officers who had retired from active duty after the war. Some had served as leaders of the Fiume legionnaires. And if their efforts weren't always perfect, they were effective enough.

Back in Rome, the Council of Ministers seemed blind to the fact that they were facing an entirely new kind of crisis as well as ignorant regarding the fascists' plans. They met on the evening of 26 October and decided to resign, leaving the president free to form a new cabinet. The king was better informed and rushed back to the capital the next night. Cheered by fascists and nationalists as he arrived at the Rome train station, he accepted the resignation of the Facta cabinet. Facta himself carried on as prime minister so as to maintain order in the streets. Urged on by some of his ex-ministers, he immediately announced a series of harsh measures: the arrest of fascism's quadrumvirate and its regional leaders, an armed defense of Rome's bridges and gates, a national state of siege to begin on 28 October. So certain was

Facta that the king would sign his declaration that news of the state of siege was broadcast over the wires of the Agenzia Stefani.[37] Yet the king refused. By midday, the state of siege had been officially suspended. Hours of deep emotion and anxious expectation followed. Luigi Federzoni (head of the Roman nationalist forces), Dino Grandi (Bologna's representative in the Chamber of Deputies), Costanzo Ciano, Cesare de Vecchi, and others shuttled back and forth between the government and the courts, the courts and Mussolini, and Mussolini and the government in an attempt to negotiate a solution.[38] A wave of support for the king swept through Rome once his decision became known. Fascist and nationalist squadrons began to circulate freely. Finally, after efforts to establish a joint Salandra-Mussolini government failed (due to Salandra's refusal), Mussolini himself was instructed to form a government on 29 October 29.[39] He arrived in Rome, introduced himself to the king, and immediately formed a cabinet that included General Armando Diaz, duke of Italy's Victory, and Admiral Paolo Thaon di Revel, duke of the Seas, commanders in chief, respectively, of the army and the navy during the final victorious phase of the war.[40] In the meantime, the fascist columns had begun their March on Rome. (Some, due to impatience on the part of both commanders and followers, had done so on their own initiative and in defiance of orders.) A march that saw little bloodshed: an occasional ambush carried out by communists or Arditi del Popolo, sniper fire from rooftops in Rome's working-class San Lorenzo neighborhood aimed at columns from the Abruzzo region, and so on.[41] So a drama that could have ended in tragedy came to a happy close. On 31 October the order for demobilization was issued, but not before one hundred thousand Black Shirts gathered at Villa Borghese and paraded past Mussolini. They continued on in formation, first to pay homage to the Altar of the Fatherland and then at the Quirinale, to salute the king, who, with Diaz and Thaon di Revel standing at his side, passed the river of youth in review during five long hours. There were cheers, songs, and hymns of praise; resounding *alalàs*[42]; banners and flags flapping in the wind; Garibaldian red shirts interspersed among the Black Shirts; overflowing enthusiasm. Immediately afterward, the fascist squadrons left Rome and returned home.

translated by Jeffrey T. Schnapp

Notes

1. It is worth noting that there exists a prior translation into English of Volpe's *History of the Fascist Movement* by an anonymous period translator. The volume

was published in Rome in 1936 by the Edizioni di Novissima (a propaganda house). Often incomprehensible and filled with mistranslations, this volume can be consulted only at the reader's own risk.

2. Risorgimento (Resurgence) is the term commonly used to describe the period of Italy's struggle for national unification between 1815 and 1870. Vincenzo Gioberti (1801–52), a priest and philosopher, was one of the Risorgimento's moderate leaders. Premier of Sardinia between 1848 and 1849, he initially favored a federation of Italian states under papal supervision but later embraced the ideal of a unified constitutional monarchy. Giuseppe Mazzini (1805–72), one of the key figures in Italian unification, represented the revolutionary, anticlerical wing of the Risorgimento. Exiled from Italy during much of his adult life, he advocated a united Italian republic to be created by means of a popular uprising.

3. "Blood Bonds," in *Diuturna* (Milan: Alpes, 1930), 256. The allusion is to Guglielmo Federico Florio, commander of the *squadre d'azione* (action squadrons) of Prato, killed by a deserter in January 1922. Florio was commemorated as a martyr in room O of the 1932 Exhibition of the Fascist Revolution by means of a display of photographs, medals, letters from Mussolini to Florio's mother and sister, and articles from *Il Popolo d'Italia*.

4. As indicated by Volpe, the title Duce (derived from the Latin *dux* or "leader") took root early in the history of the fascist movement. After the fascist dictatorship was declared in 1925, the title became one of Mussolini's official titles and was ritually repeated in a wide array of public ceremonies. In the public eye, Mussolini became more than prime minister, president of the Council of Ministers, foreign minister, or minister of corporations: he was first and foremost the *Duce del fascismo*, fascism's leader and guide.

5. One of the signatories of Croce's *A Reply to the Manifesto of Fascist Intellectuals*, Adriano Tilgher (1887–1941) was a prominent antifascist philosopher and literary critic, noted for his writings on contemporary poetry and theater.

6. Gabriele D'Annunzio (1863–1938) was Italy's leading literary figure during the period extending from World War I through the mid-1930s. Elected to the Chamber of Deputies in 1897, D'Annunzio briefly flirted with both the extreme Right and Left before identifying himself with the nationalist current. During the campaign to provoke Italy's entry into the war, he emerged as the interventionists' most charismatic leader and orator, a role he further developed by means of a series of daring gestures carried out during the war that established him as the symbol of Italy's victory. In the wake of the war, surrounded by veterans and radical nationalist supporters, he led the seizure of the city of Fiume (now Rijeka, Croatia), where he became commander of the so-called Regency of Carnaro between September 1919 and December 1920. A supporter of fascism in the early 1920s, he received the title of prince of Monte Nevoso in 1924 from King Victor Emanuel in recognition of his heroism and literary accomplishments, a title to

which corresponded ownership of the villa on Lake Garda in the town of Gardone known as the Vittoriale. D'Annunzio's aestheticizing and elitist vision of politics, inspired in part by his readings of Nietzsche, led him to denounce socialism as an expression of the "slave morality."

7. Ivanoe Bonomi (1873–1951) was a reformist socialist with nationalist leanings who, as prime minister between June 1921 and February 1922, played a key role in the transition from democracy to fascism. The allusion is to the period when Bonomi was minister of war under the government of Giovanni Giolitti (1920–21).

8. Luigi Facta (1861–1930) was prime minister during the final fateful months that led up to the March on Rome. His inability to respond the surging wave of violent actions carried out by the fascist squadrons contributed to the impasse that permitted Mussolini's rise to power.

9. Francesco Saverio Nitti (1868–1953) was one of the leaders of the Radical Party and, having occupied various ministerial positions between 1911 and 1919, served as prime minister during the period of D'Annunzio's occupation of Fiume (1919–20), during which time he carried out the electoral reform alluded to by Volpe.

10. 21 April was the legendary date of the founding of the city of Rome, and, inspired by D'Annunzio's classicizing rhetoric and ceremonials at Fiume, the fascists adopted this date as a fascist holiday to be commemorated by an austere Roman-style march.

11. *Gerarchia* was the title of a monthly journal founded by Mussolini in 1921 and published by the regime's principal organ, *Il Popolo d'Italia.* Its director during the 1920s was Margherita Sarfatti (see chapter 17).

12. The allusion is to Rome's mythical foundation by Romulus and Remus. According to Roman historians such as Livy, Romulus plowed a squared-off furrow to mark the sacred boundaries of the city walls.

13. Italo Balbo (1896–1940) was the leader of fascism in Ferrara and one of the most powerful and charismatic members of the fascist hierarchy. Balbo's political career included various ministerial positions, but his emergence as a celebrity and symbol of the regime (and even rival to Mussolini) is connected to the mass aviation stunts that he led between 1928 and 1933. Volpe's underscoring of Balbo's role omits any mention of the fact that until early 1921, Balbo had belonged to the republican ranks.

14. Bianchi (1883–1930) was the first general secretary of the National Fascist Party, appointed in November 1921. A leading figure in Ferrarese revolutionary syndicalist circles and in the interventionist movement, Bianchi participated in the founding of the Combat Fasci [*fasci di combattimento*] and was one of Mussolini's closest allies during fascism's first half-decade. So close was he during the period here evoked by Volpe that, alongside Italo Balbo, Emilio de Bono, and Cesare Maria de Vecchi, Bianchi became one of the so-called Four Men, or Quadrumviri, selected by Mussolini to coordinate the March on Rome.

15. Cesare Mori (1872–1942) was noted for the firm hand with which he fought both the fascists and organized crime in Bologna. Though driven from his position due to fascist pressures, his career continued under fascist rule as prefect of various Sicilian cities, where he distinguished himself for his anti-Mafia campaigns.

16. Rossoni (1884–1965) was a revolutionary syndicalist labor union leader who went on to become the first head of the fascist labor unions and a major theorist of fascist corporatism. Despite his vigorous efforts to implement what Rossoni had labeled "integral syndicalism," his efforts failed, and the fascist unions never attained the importance or autonomy that Rossoni had intended. Rossoni himself went on to occupy a series of largely symbolic, high profile positions in Mussolini's regime.

17. The Avanguardie (Avant-Gardes) first arose in the early 1920s as a national youth organization closely tied to the fascist movement. From the original Milanese Avanguardia Studentesca dei Fasci di Combattimento (Student Avant-Garde of the Combat Fasci), founded in January 1920, the movement spread rapidly, and by mid-1920 there were over thirty such groups working side by side with the local Fasci.

18. As Cremona's undisputed fascist boss and an intransigent defender of fascist purity, Roberto Farinacci (1892–1945) was one of the leading advocates within the National Fascist Party of authoritarian rule. His virtual rulership over the city of Cremona and tendency to act independently of party directives led to recurring tensions with Mussolini and to Farinacci's retreat from politics between 1926 and 1933. After 1933 the two reconciled, and Farinacci reemerged as a key hierarch and an enthusiastic supporter of the racial laws and alliance with Hitler.

19. *Ordine Nuovo*, the title of Antonio Gramsci's socialist journal and newspaper, served as a key incubator within which was hatched the splinter movement within Italian socialism that, after the 1921 Livorno congress, gave rise to the Italian Communist Party.

20. Filippo Turati (1857–1932) was the main founder of the Socialist Party and led its mainstream, reformist wing—the so-called minimalists—during the prefascist era. Confronted by the rising tide of fascist violence in 1921 and 1922, Turati set out to build a coalition with the parties in power, in return for which he was expelled from his own party.

21. Volpe is referring to the Confederazione Generale del Lavoro (General Confederation of Workers), the leading socialist-affiliated trade union of the prefascist era. In February 1922 the union joined an antifascist alliance known as the Alleanza del Lavoro (Alliance of Labor), made up of republican, socialist, anarchist, and communist forces, and spearheaded the (only partly successful) August general strike. The Quirinal Palace currently serves as the official residence of the Italian president but, at the time, was the king's residence.

22. Founded by Luigi Sturzo in 1919, the Partito Popolare Italiano (Italian Popular Party) was a mass-based Catholic party that sought to counter the rise of socialism

with a platform advocating proportional representation, Italian cooperation with international entities like the League of Nations, small-scale rural farming, decentralization, Catholic unionism, and the protection of families. Its initial success led to participation in the first Giolitti government (1920–21), though it was in the opposition by the time of Facta (1922). Antifascist in both theory and practice, the Italian Popular Party inadvertently facilitated fascism's triumph through its own intransigence. It was a frequent target of squadrist attacks and was dismantled in November 1926 under the Exceptional Decrees that justified the creation of the fascist dictatorship.

23. *Avanti* was the official newspaper of the Italian Socialist Party. From 1912 through 1914 Mussolini was editor in chief of the paper, but, expelled from the party because of a sudden shift in favor of Italy's intervention in World War I, he left his position to found *Il Popolo d'Italia* in November 1914. During the post–World War I years, the headquarters of *Avanti* became a favorite target of the fascist squadrons.

24. The "night of Ronchi" refers to the evening of 11 September 1919, on which D'Annunzio's troops gathered at the foot of the Carso and set off to occupy the city of Fiume.

25. Costanzo Ciano (1876–1939), not to be confused with his son and Mussolini's son-in-law, Galeazzo Ciano, was a navy admiral and World War I hero celebrated for the so-called *beffe* (pranks) of Cortellazo and Buccari. A fascist "of the first hour" and participant in the March on Rome, he served as minister of postage and communications between 1924 and 1934 and as president of the Chamber of Fasces and Corporations between 1934 and 1939.

26. The Battle of Caporetto took place in October and November 1917 and marked the worst military defeat that Italy suffered during World War I. It became the symbol of Italy's humiliation, just as, one year later, Vittorio Veneto (the battle in which Italy triumphed over Austria) became the symbol of Italy's victory.

27. The reference is to the Vendée region in western France, where an alliance between fiercely devout Catholic peasants and the local nobility led in 1793 to a revolt against the revolutionary government.

28. The so-called breach (*breccia*) of Porta Pia, one of the gateways to the city of Rome, occurred on 20 September 1870 in the midst of the events associated with the completion of Italian unification and with the downfall of the Papacy's temporal power. In the mythology of the fascist regime, the event was viewed as a foreshadowing of the fascist March on Rome.

29. As indicated elsewhere in the essay, the "reclaimed" or "redeemed" lands referred to here are those that Italy had laid claim to in the context of World War I, in particular the German-speaking border areas and the Adriatic city of Fiume (Rijeka).

30. The World War I hero Cesare Maria de Vecchi (1884–1959), also mentioned later in the essay as one of the Quadrumviri, was a leading exponent of the conservative-

monarchist current within fascism from 1919 onward. During the course of a tumultuous career that saw him repeatedly pass in and out of Mussolini's favor, de Vecchi served as governor of Somalia, representative to the Holy See, minister of national education, member of the Fascist Grand Council, and governor of the Dodecanese.

31. The allusion is to the first Facta crisis, namely, that occasioned in early October 1922 by ever increasing violent actions on the part of fascist squadrons and open talk of a march on Rome. A lieutenant of Giovanni Giolitti within the Liberal Party, Luigi Facta served as prime minister between February and late October 1922, resigning when King Victor Emanuel III refused his request for a state of siege decree to combat the fascists' March on Rome.

32. Generals Gustavo Fara (1859–1936) and Sante Ceccherini (1863–1932) were, as Volpe indicates, involved in directing the March on Rome. Both argued for its postponement, and, after the fascist seizure of power, both were offered positions within the fascist militia.

33. The Latin label "quadrumvirate" was adopted to designate the four-man team personally selected by Mussolini to lead the March on Rome. The leadership role actually played by Bianchi, Balbo, de Vecchi, and de Bono would, however, prove mostly symbolic.

34. The reference is to the charter, signed on 4 March 1848 by the king, that served as the basis for the constitution of a newly unified Italy. The charter specified a two-tiered Parliament (divided between a nominated Senate and an elected Chamber of Deputies), abolished censorship of the press, and granted the king veto powers vis-à-vis laws enacted by the Parliament. The answer to these questions regarding the monarchy's support of Italian unification and participation in World War I is, of course, yes.

35. As indicated elsewhere in Volpe's text, fascism frequently imagined its own forms of military organization in ancient Roman terms. The words *principi* and *triari* refer, respectively, to the second- and third-line soldiers in the Roman army. The lead line was formed by the *hastati*, the second by *principes*, and the third by *triarii*.

36. The phrase "mutilated victory," coined by Gabriele D'Annunzio, registers the widespread dissatisfaction felt throughout Italy with the settlement reached at Versailles in the wake of World War I. Italy had claimed a number of border regions to its north and east and, despite figuring among the war's victors, achieved few territorial gains. Hence the talk of a *mutilated* victory, the word "mutilated" hinting, in the original Italian, at a hobbled or crippled success.

37. Italy's national wire service.

38. A major figure in the nationalist movement and (at first) reluctant supporter of the 1923 Pact of Union between the nationalists and fascists, Luigi Federzoni (1878–1967) was appointed minister of the interior in the immediate wake of the Matteotti assassination so as to restore order within the ranks of the National Fascist Party.

This he did by means of a series of decrees that tightened up central government control over local authorities and expanded the powers of prefects, particularly in the domain of the press, where they were now free to impede or halt the printing of publications hostile to the central government. One of fascism's leading figures, Dino Grandi (1895–1988) is remembered principally for the key roles that he played in the domain of foreign relations and in the events surrounding the formation of the Badoglio government (July–September 1943). Grandi served as minister of foreign affairs between 1929 and 1932, after which he spent seven years as Italy's English ambassador. Opposed to intervention along with the Germans in World War II, he was the author of the so-called Grandi Motion, approved at the 24–25 July 1943 Fascist Grand Council meeting, that unseated Mussolini and restored the king's powers as commander in chief over the army. Though Grandi's rapport with Mussolini was conflictual from the start, he was named as one of the four Quadrumviri who were to lead the March on Rome.

39. Prime minister during the initial years of World War I, Antonio Salandra (1853–1931) was one of the leaders of Italian liberalism and strove, mostly in vain, to keep the fascists within the constitutional/legal orbit. His efforts to create a transitional liberal-nationalist government with fascist participation in the wake of the Facta crisis failed in late October 1922 and led to Mussolini's first mandate.

40. Armando Diaz (1861–1928) was chief of staff of the Italian army from 1917 to 1919 and, though not a fascist, was instrumental in ensuring the army's neutral stance during the March on Rome. A member of Mussolini's first cabinet (where he served as minister of war), he was the recipient of the title "duke of Italy's Victory" in 1924. Paolo Thaon di Revel (1859–1948) served with distinction as commander in chief of Italy's naval forces during and after World War I, as a result of which he was promoted to the rank of admiral. Though, like his army counterpart Armando Diaz, he was not a fascist, Revel accepted the position of minister of the navy in Mussolini's first cabinet.

41. The Arditi del Popolo (Assault Troops of the People) were antifascist veterans groups, mostly of republican inspiration, who engaged in direct combat against the fascists during the years 1921 and 1922. Harshly treated both by their fascist opponents and by the police, their ranks included many anarchists, socialists, and communists.

42. The war cry "Eia! Eia! Eia! Alalà!" was first devised by D'Annunzio within the framework of the civic liturgy that he developed during the occupation of Fiume. Borrowed from the Homeric epics, it was adopted also by the fascists.

CHAPTER 5

Foundations and Doctrine of Fascism (1932)

Benito Mussolini (in collaboration with Giovanni Gentile)

The entry that appeared under the heading of "Fascism" in Gentile's monumental Enciclopedia italiana *consisted of Gioacchino Volpe's historical overview (see preceding text) and the following text, signed by Mussolini. Widely published, cited, and translated, the latter document was enshrined as Mussolini's official definition of fascism, even though it was largely based on Gentile's philosophical writings and coauthored by the philosopher. The first, more theoretical section was in fact drafted by Gentile, while the second part, concerned with fascism's conception of the state and nation, seems to have been directly penned by Mussolini, as were the annotations (keyed to letters in parentheses here), which contain excerpts from his speeches. See also the introduction to chapters 18 and 21.*

I. Fascism's Fundamental Ideas

Like all sound political conceptions, fascism is action and it is thought: action in which doctrine is immanent, and doctrine arising from a given system of historical forces in which it inserts itself and works from within (A). It is, therefore, informed by contingencies of time and space, but it retains an ideal content that makes it an expression of truth in the higher region of the history of thought (B). There is no way to have a spiritual impact on the world as a single human will dominating the will of others, unless one has a conception of the transient and specific reality on which that action is to be exercised and of the permanent and universal reality in which the transient dwells and has its being. To know men one must know man. To know man one must be acquainted with reality and its laws. There can be no conception of the state that is not, at base, a conception of life. Whether it consists in a philosophy or in an intuition, a system of ideas developed within the framework of logic or shaped by a vision or a faith, such a conception of the state is always, at least potentially, an organic conception of the world.

Thus many of the concrete expressions of fascism—such as its party organization, system of education, discipline—can only be understood when considered in relation to its general attitude toward life, a spiritual attitude [*modo spiritualistico*] (C). In the eyes of fascism, the world is not a superficial material entity that casts man in the role of a self-sufficient and self-centered individual, subject to natural laws that instinctively predispose him to embrace a life of selfish momentary pleasures. Fascist man is not only an individual but also a nation and a country. He embodies the ideal of individuals and generations bound together by a moral law, sharing traditions and a common mission. This moral law supplants the instinctual lure of a life enclosed within the circle of evanescent pleasures with a higher life founded upon duty; a life free from limitations of time and space; a life in which the individual, by means of self-sacrifice, the renunciation of self-interest, through death itself, can achieve that purely spiritual existence in which his value as a man consists.

Accordingly, fascism's conception of life is a spiritual one, in keeping with our century's general revolt against the flaccid materialistic positivism of the nineteenth century. Antipositivist but positive; neither skeptical nor agnostic; neither pessimistic nor passively optimistic as, generally speaking, are all those doctrines (entirely negative in character) that locate the center of life outside of man. A fatal error, for man can and must create a world for himself through the exercise of his free will.

Fascism wants man to be active and engaged in action with all his energies. It wants him to be manfully aware of the difficulties facing him and ready to confront them head on. It conceives of life as a struggle in which man is called upon to conquer for himself a truly worthy place, first of all by fashioning himself (physically, morally, intellectually) into the instrument required for achieving victory. And what applies to the individual applies to the nation and to mankind as a whole (D). Hence the high value of culture in all its forms (artistic, religious, scientific) (E) and the tremendous importance of education. Hence also the essential value of work, by means of which man subjugates nature and creates the human world (the world of economic, political, ethical, intellectual forces).

This positive conception of life is, obviously, an ethical one. It encompasses the whole field of reality as well as the field of human activities that master reality. No action is exempt from moral judgment; no activity can be despoiled of the value that a moral purpose confers on all things. Therefore, life, as envisaged by the fascist, is serious, austere, religious. Its manifestations are poised in a world built upon moral forces and spiritual responsibilities. The fascist disdains the life of ease [*la vita comoda*] (F).

The fascist conception of life is a religious one (G), according to which man must be viewed in his immanent relation to a higher law, an objective Will that transcends the individual and raises him to conscious membership in a spiritual community. Those who choose to view the fascist regime's religious policies in purely opportunistic terms fail to realize that fascism is not only a system of government but also (and above all) a system of thought.

In the fascist conception of history, man is man only by virtue of the spiritual process to which he contributes as a member of a family, a social group, a nation, and a function of history to which all nations contribute. Hence the great value of tradition as transmitted through records, language, customs, the rules of social life (H). Outside history man ceases to exist. This is the reason why fascism is opposed to any and all individualistic abstractions based on eighteenth-century materialism and to Jacobinistic utopias and innovations. It denies the possibility of "happiness" on earth as imagined in the eighteenth-century economistic literature. It rejects the teleological notion that sometime in the future the human family will definitively resolve all of its difficulties, because there is no escaping history and life, both of which are founded upon continual flux and change.

In politics, fascism aims at realism. It wishes to deal only with those problems that are the spontaneous product of actual historical conditions, problems that find or suggest their own solutions (I). Only by entering into the process of reality and taking hold of the forces at work within it can man act upon man and upon nature (J).

Anti-individualistic, the fascist conception of life stresses the importance of the state. It affirms the value of the individual only insofar as his interests coincide with those of the state, which stands for the conscience and the universal will of man in history (K). It opposes classical liberalism, which arose as a revolt against absolutism and exhausted its historical function when the state became the expression of the conscience and will of the people. Liberalism denied the state in the name of the individual; fascism reasserts the state as the true reality of the individual (L). And if liberty is to be the attribute of living men and not of the sort of abstract dummies invented by individualistic liberalism, then fascism stands for liberty. Fascism stands for the only liberty worth possessing: the liberty of the state and of the individual within the state (M). The fascist conception of the state is all-embracing. Outside of it no human or spiritual values can exist, much less have value. Thus understood, fascism is totalitarian, and the fascist state—in which all values are synthesized and united—interprets, develops, and heightens the life of the people (N).

No individuals outside the state; no groups (political parties, associations, trade unions, social classes) outside the state (O). This is why fascism is opposed to socialism, which sees in history nothing but class struggle and neglects the possibility of achieving unity within the state (which effects the fusion of classes into a single economic and moral reality). This is also why fascism is opposed to trade unionism as a class weapon. But when brought within the orbit of the state, fascism recognizes the real needs that gave rise to socialism and trade unionism, giving them due weight in the corporative system in which divergent interests are harmonized within the unity that is the state (P).

Grouped according to their interests, individuals make up classes. They make up trade unions when organized according to their economic activities. But, first and foremost, they make up the state, which is no mere matter of numbers or simply the sum of the individuals forming the majority. Accordingly, fascism is opposed to that form of democracy that equates a nation with the majority, reducing it to the lowest common denominator (Q). But fascism represents the purest form of democracy if the nation is considered—as it should be—from the standpoint of quality rather than quantity. This means considering the nation as an idea, the mightiest because the most ethical, the most coherent, the truest; an idea actualizing itself in a people as the conscience and will of the few, if not of One; an idea tending to actualize itself in the conscience and the will of the mass, of the collective ethnically molded by natural and historical conditions into a single nation that moves with a single conscience and will along a uniform line of development and spiritual formation. Not a race or a geographically delimited region but a people, perpetuating itself in history, a multitude unified by an idea and imbued with the will to live, with the will to power, with a self-consciousness and a personality (R).

To the degree that it is embodied in a state, this higher personality becomes a nation. It is not the nation that generates the state (an antiquated naturalistic concept that afforded the basis for nineteenth-century propaganda in favor of national governments); rather, it is the state that creates the nation, granting volition and therefore real existence to a people that has become aware of its moral unity.

The right to national independence is not based upon any merely literary and idealistic form of self-consciousness. Still less can it be derived from a more or less passive and unconscious de facto situation. Rather, such a right depends upon an active, self-conscious political will expressing itself in action and ready to enforce its rights. It depends, in short, upon the existence, at least in fieri, of a state. Indeed, it is the state itself, by virtue of being the expression of a universal ethical will, that creates the right to national independence (S).

A nation, as expressed in the state, is a living, ethical entity to the degree that it is capable of evolving. Inactivity on its part would signal death. It follows that the state is more than just an authority that governs and imposes legal form and spiritual value upon individual wills. "More" because the state is also a power that makes its will felt and respected beyond its own borders, thus affording practical proof of the universal character of the decisions necessary to guarantee its growth. This implies organization and expansion, potential if not actual. In this way the state becomes attuned to the will of man, which grows by overcoming obstacles and actualizes itself by demonstrating its own infinity (T).[1]

A higher, more powerful expression of personality, the fascist state embodies a spiritual force encompassing all manifestations of the moral and intellectual life of man. Its functions cannot be limited to those of maintaining order and keeping the peace, as liberal doctrine would have it. The fascist state is no mere mechanical device for delimiting the sphere within which individuals may exercise their supposed rights. It represents an inwardly accepted standard and rule of conduct. A discipline of the whole person, it permeates the will no less than the intellect. It is the very principle, the soul of souls [*anima dell'anima*], that inspires every man who is a member of a civilized society, penetrating deep into his personality and dwelling within the heart of the man of action and the thinker, the artist, and the man of science (U).

Fascism, in short, is not only a law giver and a founder of institutions but also an educator and a promoter of spiritual life. It aims to refashion not only the forms of life but also their content: man, his character, his faith. To this end it champions discipline and authority; authority that infuses the soul and rules with undisputed sway. Accordingly, its chosen emblem is the lictor's fasces: symbol of unity, strength, and justice.[2]

II. Fascism's Political and Social Doctrine

When in the now distant March of 1919, through the columns of the *Popolo d'Italia*, I summoned to Milan the surviving interventionists who had followed me ever since the foundation of the Fasci of Revolutionary Action in January 1915, I had no specific program in mind.[3] The only doctrine of which I had practical experience was socialism: a decade-long experience both as a follower and a leader extending from 1903–4 through the winter of 1914. But mine was not a doctrinal experience, for, even during that decade, I was committed to the doctrine of action. A uniform, universally accepted socialist credo had not existed since 1905, when the revisionist movement, headed by Bernstein, arose in Germany and, in the midst of various ideological tides, found itself countered by a leftist revolutionary movement that in Italy never went beyond the domain of slogans, though it set the stage for Bolshevism in the case of Russian socialism.

Reformism, revolutionism, centrism: this terminology has faded away without leaving a trace, while into the great river of fascism flowed currents traceable to Sorel, Péguy, Lagardelle of *Le Mouvement Socialiste*, and the cohort of Italian syndicalists associated with Olivetti's *Pagine Libere*, Orano's *La Lupa*, and Enrico Leone's *Divenire Sociale*, who, between 1904 and 1914, set Italian socialism, emasculated and chloroformed due to its fornications with Giolitti's party, on a vigorous new course.[4]

When the war ended in 1919, socialism was already dead as a doctrine. It continued to exist only as a grudge, especially in Italy, where its only chance lay in inciting reprisals against the men who had willed the war and who were to be made to pay for it.

Il Popolo d'Italia described itself in its subtitle as "the daily organ of fighters and producers." The word "producers" was already the expression of an intellectual trend [*indirizzo mentale*]. Fascism was not the nursling of a doctrine previously drafted at a desk. It was born of the need of action and was action. It was not a party but, in the first two years, an antiparty and a movement. The name I gave the organization fixed its character.

Yet if anyone were to take the time to reread the now yellowing papers that document the meeting at which the Italian Fasci di Combattimento were founded, he would encounter not a doctrine but a series of pointers, forecasts, and hints. When freed from the inevitable matrix of contingencies, these very elements developed in a few years' time into a series of doctrinal positions entitling fascism to rank as a political doctrine differing from all others, past or present.

"If the bourgeoisie believe that we are their lightning rods," I wrote back then, "they are mistaken. We must reach out toward the world of work. . . .[5] We wish to accustom the working classes to the responsibilities of management so that they realize that it is no easy matter to run a business. . . . We will fight both technical and spiritual rear-guardism. . . .

Now that the present regime is nearing its end we must not be faint-hearted. We must rush forward. If the regime is to be superceded, it is we who must take its place. The right of succession is ours, because we urged the country to enter the war and we led it to victory! . . . Existing forms of political representation cannot satisfy us. We demand direct representation of competing interests. . . . It may be objected that this program implies a return to guilds [*corporazioni*]. No matter! . . . I therefore hope this assembly will accept the economic claims put forward by national syndicalism. . . ."

Is it not remarkable that from the very first day, at Piazza San Sepolcro, the word "guild" [*corporazione*] was pronounced: a word that, as the revolution unfolded, would come to express one of the basic legislative and social creations of the new regime?

The years preceding the March on Rome mark a period during which the need for action forbade research or systematic doctrinal elaborations. Fighting was taking place in the towns and villages. Discussions there were, but something more sacred and more important was occurring: death. Fascists knew how to die. A full-blown doctrine, divided up into chapters and paragraphs with learned annotations, may have been lacking. But its place was taken by something far more decisive: faith. This said, should someone who knows how to seek and select care to reconstruct those days on the basis of books, articles, resolutions passed at congresses, major and minor speeches, he will find that fascism's doctrinal foundations were laid while the battle was still raging. It was during those very years that fascist thought armed itself, refined itself, and proceeded with its organization. The problem of the individual and the state, the problem of authority and liberty, political, social, and especially national problems were discussed. The struggle against liberal, democratic, socialistic, Masonic doctrines and with the Popular Party (Partito Popolare) was pursued at the same time as punitive expeditions were carried out.[6] Fascism's then lack of a formal system was used by disingenuous adversaries as an argument for proclaiming its inability to elaborate a doctrine at the very time when the doctrine in question was being formulated. As is the case with all new ideas, the process of elaboration (however tumultuous) began in the guise of violent dogmatic negations that soon assumed the positive guise of constructive theories, subsequently incorporated, in 1926, 1927, and 1928, into the laws and institutions of the regime.

Fascism is now clearly defined not only as a regime but as a doctrine. This means that fascism, exercising its critical faculties on itself and on others, has studied from its own special standpoint and judged by its own standards all the problems affecting the material and intellectual interests now causing such grave anxiety to the nations of the world, and it is ready to deal with these problems by means of its own distinctive policies.

First of all, as regards the future development of humankind (and quite apart from all present political considerations), fascism, generally speaking, believes neither in the possibility nor in the utility of perpetual peace. It therefore discards pacifism as a cloak beneath which are concealed renunciation of struggle and cowardice in the face of self-sacrifice. War alone keys up all human energies to their maximum tension and impresses the seal of nobility upon those peoples who have the courage to face up to it. All other tests are pale substitutes that never place a man face to face with himself in the moment of decision between life or death. Accordingly, all doctrines postulating peace at all costs are incompatible with fascism. Equally foreign to the spirit of fascism, even if in special political circumstances they occasionally prove useful, are all internationalistic and league superstructures [*corruzioni internazionalistiche e societarie*]. Time and again history has demonstrated that these corrupting agents tend to crumble to the ground whenever the heart of nations is deeply stirred by sentimental, idealistic, or practical considerations. Fascism applies this antipacifistic attitude to the life of the individual. "I don't give a damn" [*me ne frego*], the proud motto of the fighting squadrons scrawled by the wounded on their bandages, not only refers to a gesture of philosophic stoicism but also sums up a doctrine that is not merely political. It describes a fighting spirit that accepts all risks. It signifies a new style of Italian life. The fascist accepts and loves life. He rejects and despises suicide as cowardly. To him life means duty, elevation, conquest. Life must be lofty and full. He lives for himself, but, most of all, he lives his life for others, be they close or distant, of the present or of the future.

The regime's population policy is based upon these premises. The fascist too loves his neighbor, but for him the word "neighbor" is not a vague and ungraspable abstraction. Love of one's neighbor does not rule out the need for educational severity. Still less does it exclude notions of differentiation and rank. Fascism will have nothing to do with universal embraces. As a member of the community of civilized nations, it looks other peoples straight in the eyes. It is vigilant and diffident. It tracks others' mood shifts as well as changes in their interests. And it does not allow itself to be deceived by mutable and fallacious appearances.

Such a conception of life makes fascism the resolute negation of the doctrine underlying so-called scientific and Marxian socialism: the doctrine of historical materialism, according to which the history of mankind is reducible to class struggle and changes in the processes and instruments of production. No one denies that the vicissitudes of economic life—discoveries of raw materials, new technical processes, scientific inventions—have their importance. But it is absurd to argue that they suffice to explain human history to the exclusion of other factors. Fascism believes and will always believe in sanctity and heroism, which is to say, in acts in which no economic motive, be it remote or immediate, is at work. Having denied historic materialism, which sees in men mere puppets on the surface of history, appearing and disappearing on the crest of the waves while in the depths the real directing forces move and work, fascism also denies the immutable and irreparable character of the class struggle as the natural outcome of this economic conception of history. Above all else, it denies that the class struggle is the predominant agent of social change. This twofold blow struck against the pillars of socialist doctrine leaves intact only socialism's sentimental dream, as old as humanity itself, of creating social relations in which the sufferings and sorrows of the humbler folk will be alleviated. But here again fascism differs, for it rejects the economic view of happiness as something to be secured socialistically, almost automatically, at a given stage of economic development when all will be assured a maximum of material comfort. Fascism refutes the possibility of a materialistic conception of happiness and abandons it to the economists of the mid–eighteenth century. It denies the equation well-being equals happiness, which sees in men mere animals, content when they can feed and fatten, thus reducing them to a pure and simple vegetative existence.

After socialism, fascism trains its guns on the whole complex of democratic ideologies and rejects both their premises and their practical applications and policies. Fascism denies that numbers, as such, can be the determining factor in human society. It denies the right of numbers to govern by means of periodic consultations. It asserts the irremediable, fertile, and beneficial inequality of men who cannot be leveled by any device as mechanical and extrinsic as universal suffrage. Democratic regimes may be described as those under which the people, from time to time, are deluded into thinking that they exercise sovereignty, while real sovereignty resides in and is exercised by other, sometimes irresponsible and secret forces. Democracy is a kingless regime with many kings who are sometimes more exclusive, tyrannical, and destructive than a single king, even if he is a tyrant. This explains why fascism, which, for contingent reasons, was tendentially republican prior to 1922, abandoned that stance before the March on Rome, convinced that the form a government assumes is no longer of preeminent importance. The study of past and present monarchies and past and present republics demonstrates, rather, that neither monarchies nor republics can be judged sub specie aeternitatis. Each is in reality little more than the expression of the political development, the history, the traditions, and the psychology of a given country.

Fascism has outgrown the dilemma of monarchy versus republic, a dilemma over which democratic regimes have for too long dallied, ascribing every failure to the former and celebrating the latter's perfection. Experience teaches, on the contrary, that some republics are profoundly reactionary and absolutist while some monarchies embrace the most daring political and social experiments.

In one of his philosophical meditations, Renan, who had prefascist intuitions, remarks:

free spirit, eh?

Reason and science are the products of mankind, but it is chimerical to seek reason directly for the people and through the people. It is not essential to the existence of reason that all should be familiar with it. Even if all had to be initiated, this could not be achieved through base democracy, which seems fated to promote the extinction of all arduous forms of culture and of all the highest forms of learning. The maxim that society exists only for the well-being and freedom of the individuals who make it up does not seem to be in conformity with nature's plans, solely concerned with the species and ever ready to sacrifice the individual. It is much to be feared that democracy so understood—and let me hasten to add that democracy could well be understood otherwise—will breed a form of society in which a degenerate mass would have no other thought than that of enjoying the ignoble pleasures of the vulgar.[7]

So argues Renan. By rejecting democracy, fascism rejects the absurd conventional lie of political egalitarianism, the habit of collective irresponsibility, the myth of material happiness and indefinite progress. But if democracy is instead understood as referring to a regime in which the masses are not driven to the margin of the state, then the writer of these pages has already defined fascism as "an organized, centralized, authoritarian democracy."

Fascism is definitely and absolutely opposed to the doctrines of liberalism, both in the political and the economic sphere. The importance of liberalism in the nineteenth century should not be exaggerated for present-day polemical purposes, nor should we transform only one of the many doctrines that flourished during that century into the object of a cult for the present and future of humankind. Liberalism flourished for only fifteen years. It arose in 1830 as a reaction to the Holy Alliance's efforts to turn Europe's clocks back to before 1789. Its high point came in 1848, when even Pius IX was a liberal, and its decline began immediately thereafter. If 1848 was a year of light and poetry, 1849 was a year of darkness and tragedy. The Roman Republic was killed off by its sister republic, that of France. In that same year, Marx proclaimed the gospel of socialism in his famous *Communist Manifesto.* In 1851 Napoleon III carried out his illiberal coup d'état, ruling France until 1870, when he was overturned by a popular uprising following one of history's worst military defeats. His vanquisher was Bismarck, who knew nothing about liberalism and its prophets. It is symptomatic that throughout the nineteenth century the religion of liberalism was completely unknown to so highly civilized a people as the Germans (except for the brief parenthesis known as the "ridiculous parliament of Frankfurt"). Germany attained national unity outside the framework of liberalism and in opposition to liberalism, a doctrine foreign to the German temperament, which is essentially monarchical, whereas liberalism is the historic and logical stepping stone to anarchy. The wars of 1864, 1866, and 1870 represent the three key stages in the development of German unity, and all three were led by "liberals" such as Moltke and Bismarck. And in the unification of Italy liberalism played a very minor part when compared to the contributions made by Mazzini and Garibaldi, neither of whom was a liberal. Were it not for the intervention of the illiberal Napoleon III, we would not have had Lombardy; without that of the illiberal Bismarck at Sadowa and at Sedan, very probably we would not have had Venetia in 1866. Which is to say that without illiberalism we might not have entered Rome in 1870. The years extending between 1870 and 1915 mark the twilight of the religion of liberalism (even in the opinion of liberalism's high priests), which found itself under attack from decadentism in literature and from activism in the realm of political practice. Activism, which is to say nationalism, futurism, fascism.

The liberal century, after tying innumerable Gordian knots, tried to cut them with the hecatombs of the world war. Never has any religion claimed so cruel a sacrifice. Were the gods of liberalism thirsting for blood? Now liberalism is preparing to close the doors to its temples. It has been deserted by peoples who feel that its agnosticism in the economic sphere and indifference [*indifferentismo*] in the political and moral sphere will have future consequences just as ruinous as its legacy in the past. This explains why all of today's political experiments are antiliberal. And it is supremely ridiculous to endeavor, on this account, to place them outside the pale of history, as if history were a preserve set aside for liberalism and its advocates, as if liberalism were the last word in civilization beyond which one cannot go.

The fascist negation of socialism, democracy, and liberalism does not imply a desire to drive the world backward in time to before 1789, the year commonly referred to as that which inaugurated the liberal-democratic century. History does not travel backward. Fascist doctrine has not embraced de Maistre as its prophet.[8] Monarchical absolutism is of the past, and so is ecclesiolatry. Dead and gone are feudal privileges and the division of society into closed, uncommunicating castes. Nor does the fascist conception of authority have anything in common with that of a police state.

A party governing a nation in totalitarian fashion marks a new departure in history. There are no points of reference nor of comparison. From beneath the ruins of liberal, socialist, and democratic doctrines, fascism extracts whatever vital elements remain. It preserves what may be described as "the acquired facts" of history. Everything else it rejects. Which is to say that it rejects the idea that any doctrine is suited to all times and to all people. Granted that the nineteenth century was the century of socialism, liberalism, democracy, it does not follow that the twentieth century must also be the century of socialism, liberalism, democracy. Political doctrines pass, peoples remain. We are free to believe that this is the century of authority, a century tending to the "right," a fascist century. If the nineteenth century was the century of the individual (liberalism implies individualism), we are free to believe that this is the "collective" century and thus the century of the state. It is eminently reasonable for a new doctrine to make use of still-vital elements from other doctrines. No doctrine was ever born brand spanking new. No doctrine can boast absolute originality. Every doctrine is linked, at the very least historically, both to the doctrines that preceded it and to those that will follow. The scientific socialism of Marx connects up with the utopian socialism of the Fouriers, Owens, and Saint-Simons. Nineteenth-century liberalism traces its origins back to the Enlightenment. Democratic doctrine harks back to the Encyclopedists. All doctrines aim at directing the activities of men toward a given goal. But these activities, in turn, interact with the doctrine itself, modifying and adjusting it to new needs or outstripping it. A doctrine, therefore, must be a vital act [un atto di vita] and not a rhetorical exercise [un'esercitazione di parole]. Hence the pragmatic strain in fascism, its will to power, its will to life, its attitude toward the fact of violence, and hence its value.

The cornerstone of fascist doctrine is its conception of the state: of the state's essence, its functions, and its ends. For fascism the state is absolute, while individuals and groups are relative. Individuals and groups are thinkable to the degree that they operate within the state. Instead of directing the game and guiding the material and moral progress of the community, the liberal state limits its activities to recording results. The fascist state is wide awake and has a will of its own. For this reason it may be described as an "ethical" state. At the first quinquennial assembly of the regime, in 1929, I declared:

> The fascist state is not a night watchman, solicitous only of the personal safety of its citizens; nor is its sole purpose that of guaranteeing material prosperity and relatively peaceful conditions of life (a board of directors could do as much). Neither is it a purely political entity, divorced from practical realities and aloof from the multifarious activities of citizens and peoples. The state, as conceived and actualized by fascism, is a spiritual and moral entity whose purpose is that of securing the political, juridical, and economic organization of the nation, an organization that is an outgrowth of the spirit. The state guarantees the internal and external security of the country, but it also safeguards and transmits the spirit of the people, elaborated through the ages within its language, its customs, its faith. The state represents not only the present but also the past and, most especially, the future. Transcending the individual's brief existence, the state stands for the immanent conscience of the nation. The forms in which it finds expression change, but the need for it remains. The state educates citizens about civic duty [*virtù civile*], makes them aware of their common mission, urges them to unite. Its justice harmonizes their divergent interests. It transmits to future generations achievements in the fields of science, art, law, human solidarity. It raises men up from primitive tribal life to that highest manifestation of human power, imperial rule. The state hands down to future generations the memory of those who laid down their lives to insure its safety or to obey its laws. It commemorates as examples for future generations the names of the captains who enlarged its territory and of the men of genius who won it glory. Whenever respect for the state declines, whenever the disintegrating and centrifugal tendencies of individuals and groups prevail, nations are sure to decay.

Since 1929, economic and political developments have further confirmed these truths. The importance of the state is growing by leaps and bounds [*giganteggia*] in all parts of the world. Only the state can resolve capitalism's dramatic contradictions. The so-called crisis can only be settled by state action and within the orbit of the state. Where are the shades of the Jules Simons, who, in the early days of liberalism, proclaimed that the "state should endeavor to render itself useless and prepare to hand in its resignation"?[9] Or of the MacCullochs, who, in the second half of last century, urged that the state should desist from governing too much?[10] And what of the English Bentham, who thought that the only thing that industry needed from government was to be left alone?[11] And what of the German Humboldt, who expressed the opinion that the best government was a "lazy" one?[12] What would they say now about the constant, inevitable, and urgent requests on the part of business for government intervention? It is true that the second generation of economists was less uncompromising in this domain than the first, and that even [Adam] Smith left the door ajar, albeit cautiously, for government intervention in business.

If liberalism spells individualism, fascism spells government. The fascist state, however, is a unique and original creation. It is not reactionary but revolutionary, for it provides solutions to a number of universal problems that have arisen elsewhere. In the political domain it combats the fractiousness of parties, the usurpation of power by parliaments, and the irresponsibility of assemblies. In the economic domain it takes on the increasingly numerous and important functions performed by labor unions and trade associations, whose disputes and agreements affect both capital and labor. In the moral domain it promotes order, discipline, obedience to the moral dictates of the fatherland.

Fascism wants a strong, organic state that enjoys a broad popular base of support. The fascist state claims the right to rule over the economic domain no less than over other domains. It makes its presence felt throughout the length and breadth of the country by means of its corporative, social, and educational institutions. All the political, economic, and spiritual forces of the nation, each organized into its respective associations, circulate within the state.

A state founded upon the support of millions of individuals who recognize its authority, feel it in action, and are ready to serve its ends is not the tyrannical state of a medieval lord. It has nothing in common with the despotic states that existed prior or subsequent to 1789. Far from crushing the individual, the fascist state multiplies his energies, just as in a regiment a soldier is not diminished but multiplied by the presence of fellow soldiers. The fascist state organizes the nation but leaves the individual adequate elbow room. It has curtailed useless or harmful liberties while preserving those that are essential. In such matters, only the state—not the individual—can be the judge.

The fascist state is not indifferent to religious phenomena nor does it cultivate an indifferent attitude toward the distinctive, positive religion of the Italian people, Roman Catholicism. The state has no theology, but it has a moral code [*una morale*]. The fascist state views religion as one of mankind's deepest spiritual manifestations, and, for this reason, it not only respects religion but defends and protects it. The fascist state does not attempt, as did Robespierre at the height of the revolutionary delirium of the Convention, to set up a god of its own, nor does it seek in vain, as does Bolshevism, to efface god from the soul of man. Fascism respects the god of ascetics, saints, and heroes, and it also respects the god cultivated in the people's ingenuous and primitive heart, the god to whom their prayers are addressed.

The fascist state expresses the will to exercise power and to command. Here the Roman tradition is embodied in a conception of strength. Imperial power, as understood by fascist doctrine, is not only territorial, military, and commercial. It is also spiritual and moral. An imperial nation, in other words, a nation that directly or indirectly leads other nations, can exist without conquering a single square mile of territory. This said, fascism considers the imperialistic spirit—that is, the tendency for nations to expand—an expression of their vitality. It considers the opposite tendency—that is, the tendency to limit a nation's purview to its domestic affairs—a symptom of decadence. Peoples who rise or rise again are imperialistic; renunciation is characteristic of dying peoples. Fascist doctrine is best suited to the impulses and feelings of a people, like the Italian, that after lying fallow during centuries of foreign servitude is now reasserting itself in the world.

But imperialism demands discipline, the coordination of efforts, a deep sense of duty, and a spirit of self-sacrifice. This explains many aspects of the regime's actual practice as well as the course taken by many of the forces within the state. It also argues for a firm hand in responding to those who would oppose the spontaneous and inevitable transformation of twentieth-century Italy by championing outgrown nineteenth-century ideologies, ideologies rejected wherever daring experiments in political and social change are under way.

Never before have peoples thirsted so much for authority, direction, and order as they do now. If each age has its own doctrine, then there are countless indications that fascism is the doctrine of our age. Fascism's vitality is proven by the fact that it has aroused a faith. That this faith has conquered souls is proven by fascism's fallen heroes and martyrs. Throughout the world, fascism has now acquired the universality befitting of all doctrines that, by achieving self-expression [*realizzandosi*], crystallize a moment in the history of human thought.

III. Appendix: Notes Extracted from Mussolini's Speeches

(A) If fascism does not wish to die or, worse still, to commit suicide, it must now arm itself with a doctrine. Yet the doctrine in question will not and cannot be a robe of Nessus clinging to us for all eternity, for tomorrow is mysterious and unpredictable. This doctrine will serve as a norm to guide our daily political and individual actions. I who myself dictated this doctrine am the first to realize that the modest tables of our laws and programs—the theoretical and practical guidelines of fascism—must be revised, corrected, enlarged, and developed, because some portions have already suffered injury at the hands of time. I believe that the doctrinal essence and fundamentals are still to be found in the postulates that, during the past two years, have acted as a call to arms for the recruits of Italian fascism. Those fundamental postulates, however, must now serve as the basis for extending our program out into a vaster field.

All Italian fascists must cooperate in this task, a task of vital importance to fascism, especially in those regions where (with and without formal agreements) peaceful coexistence has been achieved between antagonistic movements.

The word I am about to employ is a grandiose word, but it expresses my sincere wish that during the two months that are still to elapse before our National Assembly, a *philosophy* of fascism might be elaborated. Milan is already making its contribution in the form of the first fascist school of propaganda.

It is not merely a question of putting together a program that can then be used as the constitution of the party that will inevitably arise from the fascist movement. It is also a question of refuting the silly myth that fascism consists only of violent men. In point of fact, there are many fascists who belong to the restless but meditative class.

The new course taken by fascist activity will in no way diminish the fighting spirit typical of fascism. To equip the mind with doctrines and creeds does not mean to disarm. Rather, it signifies a strengthening of our power to act and of our consciousness. Soldiers who fight in full awareness of their cause make the best warriors. Fascism has made its own the twofold motto of Mazzini: *Thought and Action.*[13]

Fascists must remain in contact with one another, their activity must be informed by doctrine, it must be an activity of spirit and of thought. . . .

Had our adversaries been present at our meeting, they would have been convinced that fascism is not only action, but also thought.[14]

(B) Today I hold that fascism is universal: universal as an idea, a doctrine, an accomplishment. It is Italian in its particular institutions but universal in spirit (and cannot be otherwise). The spirit is universal by its very nature. It is, therefore, easy to foresee a fascist Europe that draws its inspiration from the doctrine and practice of [Italian] fascism; a Europe, in other words, that adopts fascist solutions to the problems that beset the modern state, a state profoundly different from those existing before 1789 or formed immediately thereafter. Today fascism fulfills universal needs. It solves the threefold problem of relations between the state and the individual, between the state and associations, between associations and [other] organized associations.[15]

(C) This political process is accompanied by philosophical developments. If it is true that matter was placed on an altar for one century, today it is spirit that has taken its place. All the distinctive expressions of the democratic spirit are discredited as a result: a carefree ethos, improvisation, lack of a personal sense of responsibility, the exaltation of numbers and of that mysterious divinity called *The People.* All creations of the spirit — religious ones first among them — are coming to the fore, and anticlericalism, which for several decades was the policy embraced by democrats in the Western world, is on the wane. By saying that God is returning, we mean that spiritual values are returning.[16]

There is a field reserved for meditations concerning the supreme goals of life that transcends research into these goals themselves. Consequently, science finds its point of departure in experience, but it is fated to branch out into the field of philosophy. In my opinion, philosophy alone can enlighten science and lead to the universal idea.[17]

In order to understand the fascist movement one must first appreciate the underlying spiritual phenomenon in all its vastness and depth. The movement's [outward] manifestations have been of a powerful and decisive nature, but one must dig deeper. In point of fact, Italian fascism marked much more than a political revolt against weak and incapable governments that allowed state authority to decay and that were threatening to arrest the nation's progress. It also signaled a spiritual revolt against old ideas that had corrupted the sacred principles of religion, of faith, of country. Fascism has thus been a revolt of the people.[18]

(D) Struggle is at the origin of all things, for life is full of conflicts. There is love and hatred, white and black, day and night, good and evil, and until these conflicts achieve resolution, struggle is fated to remain at the root of human nature. This said, it is good for life to be so. Today we indulge in wars, economic battles, and clashes of ideas, but if a day were to arrive when struggle ceased to exist, that day would be tinged with melancholy. It would be a day of ruin, the final day. But because history unveils ever new horizons, this day will never come. By attempting to restore calm, peace, and tranquility, one is fighting the dynamism of the present period. One must be prepared for other struggles and for other surprises. Peace will only come when people surrender to a Christian dream of universal brotherhood, when they link hands across the oceans and over the mountains. Personally, I do not believe in such forms of idealism, but I do not rule them out, for I rule out nothing.[19]

(E) For me the honor of nations consists in the varying contributions that they have made to human civilization.[20]

(F) I dubbed our organization the Fasci Italiani di Combattimento. This hard metallic name encapsulated the entire program of fascism, as I dreamed it up, willed it, and carried it out!

Comrades, this remains our program: to fight.

Life for the fascist is a continuous, ceaseless battle that we eagerly embrace with great courage and with the requisite sense of intrepidness.[21]

You touch the core of fascist philosophy. When a Finnish philosopher recently asked me to explain to him in a single sentence the significance of fascism, I wrote in German: "We are against the *easy* life."[22]

(G) If fascism were not a creed, how could it infuse its followers with courage and stoicism! Only a creed that has soared to the heights of religion can inspire such words as crossed the lips, now lifeless, alas, of Federico Florio.[23]

(H) Tradition is certainly one of the greatest spiritual strengths possessed by a people to the degree that it represents the sustained and constant creation of their soul.[24]

(I) Our temperament leads us to address concrete aspects of problems, rather than their ideological or mystical sublimation. We therefore easily regain our balance.[25]

Our battle is a thankless one, yet it is a beautiful battle since it compels us to rely exclusively upon our own forces. We have torn to shreds revealed truths, spat upon dogmas, rejected all theories of paradise. We have baffled the charlatans: the white, red, and black charlatans who placed panaceas on the market that promised humankind eternal "happiness." We do not believe in programs, in plans, in saints, or in apostles. Most of all we do not believe in happiness, in salvation, or in the promised land.[26]

We do not believe in a single solution, be it economic, political, or moral. There is no linear solution to life's problems because—O illustrious choristers from all the sacristies!—life is not linear and can never be reduced to primordial needs.[27]

(J) We are not and do not wish to be immobile mummies whose faces are forever turned toward the same horizon. Nor do we wish to lock ourselves within the narrow confines of subversive bigotry, where formulas, like the prayers of a professed religion, are muttered in mechanical fashion. We are men, living men who wish to make a contribution, however modest, to the creation of history.[28]

We uphold moral and traditional values neglected or despised by socialism. But, above all, fascism is horrified by anything that implies an arbitrary mortgage on the mysterious future.[29]

Despite the various theories of conservation and renovation, of tradition and progress, expounded by the Right and the Left, we do not cling desperately to the past as if it were the sole remaining life boat. Yet neither do we dash headlong into the seductive mists of the future.[30]

Negation and eternal immobility mean damnation. I am all for motion. I am one who marches on.[31]

(K) We were the first to state, in the face of liberal-democratic individualism, that the individual exists only insofar as he is within the state and subject to the requirements of the state and that, as civilization becomes more and more complex, individual freedom becomes more and more restricted.[32]

A feeling for the state is growing within the consciousness of today's Italians. They increasingly sense that the state is the irreplaceable defender of their unity and independence, that the state alone represents the future prolongation of their stock and their history.[33]

If Italy has made such astounding progress in the course of the past eight years, it seems eminently reasonable to suppose and to foresee that the next fifty or eighty years will ensure that this Italy whose overwhelming power and vitality we already feel will be greater still. All the more so if harmony reigns among its citizens, if the state continues as the sole mediator of political and social conflicts, if all remains within the state and nothing outside the state (because it is impossible for an individual to exist outside the state unless he is a savage who makes his home in the solitude of the desert sands).[34]

Fascism has restored to the state its sovereign functions by claiming for it an absolute ethical meaning that opposes the egotism of classes and categories. It has restored dignity to state rulership, which elected assemblies had reduced to the status of a mere political tool, insisting instead that it represents the state's personality and its imperial power. It has freed state administration from the burdens of factions and party interests.[35]

(L) Let no one attempt to deny fascism's moral character, for I would be ashamed to speak from this podium if I did not know that I represent the state's moral and spiritual powers. What would the state be if it did not possess its own spirit and morality, for these are what lend power to the laws in virtue of which the state is obeyed by its citizens?

. . . The fascist state affirms its ethical character. It is Catholic, but, first and foremost, it is fascist. It is, in fact, exclusively and essentially fascist. Catholicism completes fascism, and this we openly declare. But let no one believe that they can turn the tables on us under the veil of metaphysics or philosophy.[36]

. . . a state fully aware of its mission and that represents a people on the march; a state that necessarily transforms the people even in their physical aspect. In order to be more than a mere administrator, the state must utter great words, expound great ideas, and place great problems before the people.[37]

(M) The concept of freedom is not absolute because nothing in life is ever absolute. Freedom is not a right, it is a duty. It is not a gift, it is a conquest. It is not equality, it is a privilege. The concept of freedom changes with the passing of time. Freedom in times of peace is not the same as freedom in times of war. Freedom in prosperous times is not the same as the freedom allowed in times of poverty.[38]

Within our state the individual is not deprived of freedom. In fact, he possesses greater liberty than an isolated individual because the state protects him, and he is part of the state. The isolated individual is defenseless.[39]

(N) Today we proclaim to the world the creation of a strong and united Italian state, extending from the Alps to Sicily. This state assumes the form of a well-organized, centralized, unified democracy wherein people circulate with ease. Indeed, gentlemen, either you admit the people into the citadel of the state, and they will defend it, or you shut them out, and they will assault it.[40]

Under fascism, class unity—the political, social, and moral unity of the Italian people—is realized within the state and only within the state.[41]

(O) We have created a unified Italy. Remember that Italy had not been a unified state since the Empire! I wish to solemnly reaffirm our doctrine of the state. I wish to reaffirm with equal vigor the formula that I expounded at La Scala in Milan: "everything within the state, nothing against the state, nothing outside the state."[42]

(P) In other words, ours is a state that controls all the forces acting in nature. We control the political, moral, and economic forces. Ours is thus a full-blown corporative state . . . It represents an entirely new principle: a categorical, definitive antithesis to the world of democracy, plutocracy, and Freemasonry and to the world that still abides by the fundamental principles laid down in 1789.[43]

The Ministry of Corporations is not a bureaucratic organ. Nor does it wish to take over the work performed by labor unions, whose independence is essential if they are to fulfill their mission of organizing, selecting, and improving union members. The Ministry of Corporations is the institution through which, both at the nation's center and the periphery, integral corporativism becomes a reality, and economic interests and forces are kept in balance. Only within the state can such a balance be maintained, for the state alone can transcend conflicting group and individual interests and can mediate such conflicts in the pursuit of higher goals. The rapid realization of such goals is facilitated by the fact that fascism brings within its orbit economic organizations at all levels, each recognized, protected, and supported by the corporative state. In other words, these organizations accept fascism's ideals both in theory and in practice.[44]

We have constituted a corporative fascist state, a state that corresponds to a national society, a state that focuses, controls, harmonizes, and tempers the interests of all social classes in such a way as to protect them in equal measure. During the years of liberal democratic rule, labor looked with diffidence upon the state, for it was outside the state and against the state. It considered the state its perpetual enemy. Today there is not a single working Italian who does not seek his or her place in a corporation or federation, who does not wish to become a living atom within that great, immense, living organism that is the fascist national corporate state.[45]

(Q) The war was revolutionary. Its rivers of blood washed away the century of democracy, the century of numbers, majorities, and quantities.[46]

(R) Race: a feeling and not a reality; 95 percent a feeling.[47]

(S) A nation exists inasmuch as it represents a people. A people is on the rise so long as it is numerous, hard-working, and well regulated. Power is a function of this threefold principle.[48]

Fascism does not deny the state. Fascism maintains that a civic society, be it national or imperial, can assume no other form than that of a state.[49]

For us the nation is mainly spirit (and not just territory). There are states that possessed vast territories yet left not a trace in the history of humankind. Neither is number the only yardstick, for small, microscopic states have sometimes left behind immortal, imperishable documents in the fields of art and philosophy.

A nation's greatness is the sum of all these virtues and conditions. A nation is great when its spiritual might is translated into reality.[50]

We wish to unify the nation within a sovereign state, sovereign because, above everyone, it can afford to be against everyone, representing the moral continuity of the nation in history. Without the state there can be no nation, only temporary human aggregations vulnerable to history's forces of disintegration.[51]

(T) I believe that . . . if a people wishes to live it must develop a will to power. Otherwise it will vegetate, live miserably, and fall prey to stronger peoples, in whom this will to power is developed to a higher degree.[52]

(U) Fascism has remade Italians' character. It has removed spiritual impurities, made us able to confront all kinds of sacrifices, restored the strength and beauty of the Italian mien.[53]

It is fitting here to point to the profound significance of the fascist levy [leva fascista].[54] Far more than a ceremony, it represents a crucial phase in the education and integral preparation of Italian men that the fascist revolution considers one of the fundamental duties of the state. So fundamental that, if the state does not fulfill this duty or allows doubts to be cast on this subject, the state simply forfeits its right to exist.[55]

anonymous translation revised by Jeffrey T. Schnapp

Notes

1. The word "infinity" is employed here in its etymological sense and reflects the impact upon Mussolini of the French philosopher Henri Bergson (1859–1941). It refers to the human will's lack of finitude, to its insatiable appetite for ever enhanced powers and ever new stimuli.

2. Symbol of the Roman state's power over life and limb, the lictor's fasces was adopted early on as the symbol of Mussolini's movement. In ancient Rome the fasces typically consisted of a bundle of birch or elm rods belted together by a red strap, out of which jutted an ax head. The symbol had also been adopted as an emblem of popular sovereignty during the French Revolution and hence evoked both democratic and imperial ideals.

3. The Fasci di Azione Rivoluzionaria (Fasci of Revolutionary Action) emerged out of the slightly earlier Fascio Rivoluzionario d'Azione Internazionalista (Revolutionary Fascio of Internationalist Action) in late January 1915. The purpose of both was to promote Italian intervention in World War I, and both were led by revolutionary syndicalist elements. Mussolini was, in reality, only one member of a leadership cadre that included Alceste de Ambris and Angelo Olivetti, among others.

4. Georges Sorel (1847–1922) was the author of *Reflections on Violence* and numerous other works associated with the syndicalist critique of reformist socialism. As France's most eminent theorist of revolutionary syndicalism, he exercised considerable influence on the Italian scene and was referred to by the early Mussolini as "our master."

   The French essayist and poet Charles Péguy (1873–1914) left behind his socialist beginnings to embrace a distinctive brand of mystical, socially committed, and heterodox Catholicism. He is remembered as the author of ferocious polemics against Jean Jaurès, the French socialist leader, and of incantatory works such as *Le Mystère de la charité de Jean d'Arc* (1910) and *Le Mystère des saints innocents* (1912).

   Hubert Lagardelle (1875–1958) was the founder and editor of *Le Mouvement Socialiste*, the revolutionary syndicalist journal to which Sorel was a regular contributor between 1906 and 1909, alongside other key Italian syndicalists (Labriola, Orano, Olivetti, and Panunzio).

   Later to emerge as one of fascism's principal advocates of corporatism, Angelo Olivetti (1874–1931) was the founder and publisher of the review *Pagine Libere* between 1906 and 1911, 1914 and 1915, and 1920 and 1921, a review that, along with *La Lupa*, set the stage for a convergence between nationalist and revolutionary syndicalist themes.

One of the regime's most influential journalists and propagandists, Paolo Orano (1875–1945) began in October 1910 to publish the review *La Lupa,* within which the syndicalist-nationalist confluence began to crystallize for the first time.

Between 1905 and 1910, Enrico Leone's *Divenire Sociale* was perhaps Italy's leading journal advocating a "scientific" socialism with strong revolutionary syndicalist components. Featuring authors such as Arturo Labriola, it typically argued that only by completing its bourgeois revolution (via the dismantling of protectionist trade barriers and the monarchy) could Italy's proletarian revolution succeed.

Giovanni Giolitti (1842–1928) was leader of the left wing of the Liberal Party, which, through a series of complex and ever-shifting coalitions with republicans, radicals, and socialists, managed to control the nation's political fate during the decades preceding the fascist seizure of power.

5. The precise phrase employed here is *andare incontro al lavoro,* which underscores fascism's syndicalist, antibourgeois roots. The phrase would undergo a slight shift in the later slogan *andare verso il popolo* [to reach out toward the people], which was meant to call attention to the mass character of the fascist regime and to its efforts to forge a politics founded upon immediate contact between people and state.

6. The Italian Popular Party was founded in 1919 by Luigi Sturzo as a Catholic alternative to socialism. With a platform that emphasized civic protections and freedoms, social reforms, and democratic values, it achieved immediate success in the elections of November 1919 and became a major political player in the ensuing years. Initially antifascist, thanks to Sturzo's views, the party attempted to collaborate in 1923–24 with the new fascist regime, only to fall victim, first, to acts of squadrist violence and, finally, to the 1926 decrees that officialized Mussolini's dictatorship.

7. Ernest Renan (1823–92) was the prolific author of classic studies of biblical history such as *La Vie de Jésus* (1863), *Histoire des origines du christianisme* (1863–83), and *Histoire du peuple d'Israël* (1887–93). His production included numerous moral and philosophical works that figured among the young Mussolini's readings.

8. A ferocious critic of Enlightenment ideals, Joseph de Maistre (1754–1821) had advocated in works such as *Du pape* (1817) the unification of the entire world under the power of a single spiritual monarch, the pope.

9. Jules Simon (1814–96), the French politician and philosopher.

10. Presumably John Ramsay MacCulloch (1789–1864), the British economist and statistician who belonged to the circle of John Stuart Mill.

11. Jeremy Bentham (1748–1832), the noted exponent of utilitarianism.

12. Alexander von Humboldt (1769–1859), the German naturalist, philosopher, and explorer.

13. Mussolini, "Letter to Michele Bianchi," written on 27 August 1921 for the opening of the School of Fascist Culture and Propaganda in Milan; reprinted in *Messaggi e proclami* (Milan: Libreria d'Italia, 1929), 39.

14. Mussolini, "Speech before the National Council of the Fascist Party," 8 August 1924; reprinted in *La nuova politica dell'Italia*, vol. 3 (Milan: Alpes, 1928), 267.

15. Mussolini, "Message for Year IX," 27 October 1930; reprinted in *Discorsi del 1930* (Milan: Alpes, 1931), 211.

16. "Where the World Is Headed," in *Tempi della rivoluzione fascista* (Milan: Alpes, 1930), 34.

17. "To the Congress of Science at Bologna," 31 October 1926, in *Discorsi del 1926* (Milan: Alpes, 1927), 268.

18. "Message to the British People," 5 January 1924, in *Messaggi e proclami*, 107.

19. "At the Politeama Rossetti, Trieste," 20 September 1920, in *Discorsi politici* (Milan: Stab. Tipografico del *Popolo d'Italia*, 1921), 107.

20. Cited from Emil Ludwig, *Talks with Mussolini* (London: Allen and Unwin, 1932), 199.

21. "On the Seventh Anniversary of the Foundation of the Fasci," 28 March 1926, in *Discorsi del 1926*, 98.

22. Cited from Ludwig, *Talks with Mussolini*, 190.

23. "Bonds of Blood," in *Diuturna* (Milan: Alpes, 1930), 256.

24. "A Brief Prelude," in *Tempi della rivoluzione fascista* (Milan: Alpes, 1930), 13.

25. "Aspects of the Drama," in *Diuturna*, 86.

26. "Time to Set Sail," in *Diuturna*, 223.

27. "Time to Set Sail," 233.

28. "Audacity," in *Diuturna*, 11.

29. "After Two Years," in *Diuturna*, 242.

30. "A Brief Prelude," 14.

31. Cited from Ludwig, *Talks with Mussolini*, 203.

32. "To the General Staff Conference of Fascism," in *Discorsi del 1929* (Milan: Alpes, 1930), 280.

33. "Message on the Seventh Anniversary," 25 October 1929, in *Discorsi del 1929*, 300.

34. "Speech before the Senate," 12 May 1928, in *Discorsi del 1928* (Milan: Alpes, 1929), 109.

35. "To the Council of State," 22 December 1928, in *Discorsi del 1928*, 358.

36. "To the Chamber of Deputies," 13 May 1929, in *Discorsi del 1929*, 182.

37. "To the Chamber of Deputies," 183.

38. "Fifth Anniversary of the Foundation of the Fasci di Combattimento," 24 March 1924, in *La nuova politica dell'Italia*, 3: 30.

39. Cited from Ludwig, *Talks with Mussolini*, 129.

40. "Speech before the Chamber of Deputies," 16 May 1927, in *Discorsi del 1927* (Milan: Alpes, 1928), 159.

41. "Speech before the Chamber of Deputies," 9 December 1928, in *Discorsi del 1928*, 333.
42. "Speech before the Chamber of Deputies," 16 May 1927, in *Discorsi del 1927*, 157.
43. "Speech before the New National Directorate of the Party," 7 April 1926, in *Discorsi del 1926*, 120.
44. "Speech at the Opening of the Ministry of Corporations," 31 July 1926, in *Discorsi del 1926*, 250.
45. "On the Fourth Anniversary of the March on Rome," 18 October 1926, in *Discorsi del 1926*, 340.
46. "Where the World Is Headed," 37.
47. Cited from Ludwig, *Talks with Mussolini*, 75.
48. "To the General Assembly of the Party," 10 March 1929, in *Discorsi del 1929*, 24.
49. "The State, the Antistate, Fascism," in *Tempi della rivoluzione fascista*, 94.
50. "Speech in Naples," 24 October 1922, in *Discorsi della rivoluzione* (Milan: Alpes, 1928), 103.
51. "Speech before the National Council of the Fascist Party," 8 August 1924, in *La nuova politica dell'Italia*, 3: 269.
52. "Speech to the Senate," 18 May 1926, in *Discorsi del 1926*, 109.
53. "Speech Delivered at Pisa," 25 May 1926, in *Discorsi del 1926*, 193.
54. The *leva fascista* was a ceremony held on 21 April, the anniversary of the legendary founding of Rome, that celebrated the interconnections between the various fascist youth groups. Patterned after Roman ceremonials for the passage into manhood, it involved the ritualized transfer of symbols — the musket, blue neckerchief, white ribbon — from one generational group to another.
55. "Speech before the Chamber of Deputies," 28 May 1928, in *Discorsi del 1928*, 68.

PART 2

CORE AND PERIPHERY

CHAPTER 6

Fascism as Intellectual Revolution (1924)

Giuseppe Bottai

finding meaning in what someone established

✳

Bottai (1895–1959) was one of the fascist regime's foremost intellectuals, though his intellectual influence often exceeded his political success. He delivered this speech on 27 March 1924. A journalist for much of his career, he fought in World War I with the Arditi, assault troops who later formed the core of Gabriele D'Annunzio's Fiume occupation force. Bottai joined in the Fiume adventure, formed ties to early Futurism, and in 1921 served in Parliament as a fascist deputy. From this time through 1943 he held numerous important positions, among them, minister of corporations, governor of Rome, minister of national education. Advocating of an elitist vision of the National Fascist Party, Bottai vigorously defended the need for internal debate and criticism within the party and resisted its violent authoritarian wing. (See also the introductions to chapters 14, 16, and 24.)

✳

Tonight I will speak to you in the language of a National Fascist Party member, one who is proud to carry the card of the National Fascist Party.

Do not view this preliminary statement as superfluous. Today, nothing predisposes our party to internal fractures. The inner moral and spiritual unity of our organization in its fivefold structure — political, military, trade union, cooperative, and technical — is wholly admirable, especially when one considers the pressures exerted by adversaries who remain unconvinced that the new era demands a revision of their doctrines and methods. The party retains its compact and urgent strength in the face of some recent polemics and silly splits. This is the reason why I open my speech, a speech of the highest composure whose polemics are driven more by inner passion than by artful virulence, with the explicit statement that I very concretely belong to the official organization of the National Fascist Party.

Buoyed with strength in the wake of our victory, I chose to shoulder the most challenging of tasks: to remind the victors of their responsibilities and not of the advantages victory has procured. As a result, accusatory fingers have been pointed at me with increased frequency. The fingers of severe judges filled with scorn for my serenely critical language. The fingers of the timorous, eager to shore up their irrational, catastrophic pessimism through my objective analysis.

But I am a man for whom passions [*infatuazioni*] of this sort are entirely alien, whether due to factors of temperament or of education. A mad passion for discipline leads to blindness. A mad passion for the critical spirit leads to intellectual anarchy.

I served fascism from its origins in March 1919, embracing it as an intellectual and spiritual reaction and advancing its cause with my intelligence and spirit. Standing firm against adversaries who asserted the rights of culture in order to oppose us, I felt emboldened by knowing that I possessed a more valid and ready force than muscular strength alone. In my recourse to the latter, I let necessity and measure be my guides, aided by my experience of the battlefields as an Ardito (that remarkable expression of young Italians' intelligence in the form of audacity).

I have always recognized the genesis of fascism as nontheoretical and nonlogical in the sense that it was the product neither of a systematic, preordained set of ideas nor of a stone-cold calculation. Indeed, I view this antitheory and antilogic bias as one of the merits of the fascist movement and as one of the reasons that it unfolded so rapidly and impetuously, progressing almost instinctively, as if according to a natural chain reaction. But I never believed that intelligence, in the purest sense of this beautiful Latin and Italian term, was absent at fascism's origin.

I feel it imperative to reestablish a simple truth in the light of various cudgel-driven deformations [*deformazioni manganellistiche*] of fascism that critics have disingenuously seized upon to chalk up all the merits of the national movement to the rough bravado of a few individuals engaged in a crazed pursuit of posthumous heroism. That truth in question is that, as consecrated in the chronicles of March 1919, fascism's earliest constitutive nucleus was made up of intellectuals. These intellectuals belonged to different (even opposing) schools, disciplines, and tendencies. But, renewed due to the shared sacrifices in the trenches, they found themselves united, thanks to the sudden emergence of a new understanding [*intelligenza*] of life in general and of Italian political life in particular.

Fascism's origins were decidedly intellectual.

When, in a recent speech in Naples, Deputy Giovanni Amendola scornfully denounces us for our *half culture*, he misses the point.[1] Our scorn is for his brand of culture, of which we refuse even that half that he so generously ascribes to us.[2]

Placed on jeweler's scales and measured numerically, it is entirely possible that our culture will weigh but a fourth of Deputy Amendola's, a fact we readily admit. But, just as Deputy Arturo Labriola is a living example of the discrepancy between cultural refinement and an upright moral character, Amendola illustrates the enormous difference between being cultured and having a lively, up-to-date intelligence, an intelligence able to understand the deeper meaning of changes in the course of life.[3]

We reject Giovanni Amendola's culture.

Fascism did not wait until 1921 to become revolutionary, as Ivanoe Bonomi's theory would have it.[4] On the contrary, it arose as a revolutionary gesture of refusal: of the culture that preceded it, of the practices and governing methods employed by the old ruling classes.

Refusing the culture of the nineteenth century does not mean endorsing ignorance. Nor does it imply a wholesale rejection of the historical period or turning the clock back to a prior century's tradition.

Simply put, it means enabling one's intelligence to grasp things with immediacy, that is, to understand them anew and to reevaluate them.

Deputy Amendola claimed in Naples that he "set out to show through his own example that public life imposes discipline on those who understand public life as a noble calling. Such a discipline obliges one not to relinquish one's positions, to stick to them even when all avenues appear closed, to resist for resistance' sake." Evidently, the speaker is overcome with nostalgia for his culture, which is all fine and well. Nostalgias are solitary, undeniable pleasures. One gets the nostalgia that one deserves.

What we fascists ask of Amendola and his generation is that they permit us to leave behind their nostalgia for well-worn paths to instead anxiously embrace new positions in the world of culture. They must allow a new generation of intellectuals to embark on both a destructive and a constructive revision of modern civilization (irrespective of whether we someday come to accept many of the works that we now denounce as outdated).

Fascism is a revolution of intellectuals. To be even more explicit, it is an intellectual revolution.   *new nostalgia – establ th.*

Fascism's central problem remains the creation of a new ruling class, whether externally, at the national level, or internally, within the party apparatus. To declare this openly is not to suggest that the core group gathered around Benito Mussolini in March 1919 failed to live up to its pretense of contesting the old culture and creating a new one. What it does suggest, on the contrary, is that fascism's weighty mission has not changed during the five years since the movement's foundation. *truly for its people*

The hard necessities of the anti-Bolshevik fight—a secondary (not primary) feature of fascism, in my view—kept us from immediately turning to the task. There was no time for philosophizing with the enemy so near at *no point in rationalizing with others.*

hand. But the situation has altered now that this obstacle has been removed and power is ours, so the problem of our origins faces us once again in its entirety.

The problem of fascism's intellectual revolution.

This is how we reply to our opponents, who have been busy disseminating the lie that our revolution was the result only of muscular effort and denying our right to create a new Italian politics. This is also how we reply to those fascists who play into the hands of our enemies when they try to raise to the status of theory some obsolete or transitory aspects of our political action.

Sources and Targets of Antifascist Misunderstanding

Misapprehensions regarding fascism arise when aspects of the National Fascist Party's actions or temporary positions assumed by the fascist government are deliberately distorted by men accomplished in the art of manipulating sentiments and resentments.

The result is a contradiction. The same adversaries who, when in power, grope after the realities of our national life among the clouds and address concrete problems abstractly adopt the opposite method when approaching the fascist party and government; namely, they automatically endow events of a concrete and transitory nature with universal meanings.

When the men in the current national government came to power, they were not faced with the theoretical problem of human freedom but rather with the practical problem of establishing law and order [*autorità*].

Who was responsible for confronting Italy with such a terrible dilemma? Who was it that permitted this problem to fester? The answer is clear: the very social class from which we seized power and to which today's antifascists belong. It was democracy that permitted an assault so violent on the state's sovereignty that only an exceptional measure could reestablish authority: dictatorship.

The dictatorship currently in place is not a fundamental or essential defining feature of our methods or policies (as confirmed by countless indications, noted by men of good faith, that it is already tending toward self-overcoming). Nor was dictatorship unavoidable. It was the postwar ruling class's aversion to making use of physical force (alongside its lack of genuine efforts to garner popular support) that created the need to employ force in a more rigorous and sustained manner.

The problem is not strictly an Italian one. It is European, not to mention global, in scope. But no country experienced a crisis of authority as serious or as enduring as did Italy: so serious and enduring that it profoundly shaped our movement's practical orientation and mode of action. Among the contributing factors to the ongoing crisis it is plausible to consider a residual tendency toward rebellion among some within our ranks, but it must be noted that the habit of exerting authority locally when confronted with absent or ineffectual governments can be expected to disappear only gradually, thanks to endless and heartfelt efforts. Fascism has not yet come into its own from the standpoint of political policy making. It is still expiating the past. It is still battling a crisis created by others. It is still remedying mistakes that were not its own. It is still treating illnesses that it inherited on the level of nation and its party organization.   *people 7 govt*

A long list of examples is unnecessary to prove the accuracy of my thesis. To justify some of the errors or abuses of today by citing the errors or abuses of yesterday is hardly productive if one wishes to rise above everyday polemics. This said, it would be improper to overlook the principal historical reasons for the present need to impose the authority principle with greater force than under ordinary circumstances. Suffice it to recall that in 1920 there were train workers who impeded the passage of trains carrying the Italian armed forces and that the government then in place not only accepted these sorts of disruptions but also sanctioned the principle that its own employees could disobey it. In the same year, train and cable car workers refused to obey the decree establishing daylight savings time; a prefect of the kingdom legally sanctioned the violent seizure of some factories belonging to the Mazzonis Company in Piedmont; the porters' trade union imposed fines upon the judicial authorities; and the Bologna Chamber of Labor freely encroached upon the state's sovereignty by requisitioning grapes, fixing their price, and placing a cap on the price of fuel, textiles, clothes, and so on. Suffice it to recall these and similar events in order to show just how systematic was the ruling class's abdication of its responsibilities and how citizens thereby developed the habit of not observing the law.

Today it is necessary to dispel the effects of those years when the Italian people ignored the state's authority. When Mussolini asserts that freedom is a duty, his is not a generic utterance but rather a truth that reflects the deep convictions of the Italian people. Deputy Amendola has no right to assert that he "defend[s] the people's ability to carry out the highest duties of civic life" when it was precisely the men in his political party who were responsible for the citizenry's loss of any sense of civic duty.

One cannot repair a lacerated moral fabric in a single year. The lawless perversions of yesteryear are still firmly imprinted on the souls and consciences of an infinite number of Italians of all political stripes, which is to say that if one were simply to enact the abstract principle of unlimited freedom, anarchy's powers, dormant but not yet defeated, would be unleashed anew. The democratic decay of the four years between 1919 and 1922 is an undeniable fact. For the damage to be reversed, one would have to reestablish a feeling for the interdependence between the concepts of freedom and of authority and to strengthen the latter's hold on the people, so that once it counterbalances the concept of freedom, a superior harmony can arise. The constitution embodies this very harmony. Tracing at the same time the state's ideal form and its practical structure, it stands as the first and foremost guarantee that the balance between freedom and authority will be achieved in terms of spirit, conscience, and the will of the people.

The current efforts of the fascist government aim at redressing this balance. Arduous efforts, undertaken at the unrelenting rhythms that befit an urgently needed reconstruction.

On 21 February [1924] Deputy Claudio Treves had the shameless courage to sign a manifesto drafted by his party's leadership that contained the phrase "Victory, that freed the farthest boundaries of the fatherland."[5] This from the same individual who in March 1920 told the Chamber of Deputies that the postwar social unrest was "the necessary and inevitable consequence of what took place; nobody can undo what had been done. Behold the inevitable corollary of the crime!" A crime: this is clearly Treves's image of the great war! Is it not then fair to turn the tables and to yell back at those who are now groaning under our pressure that the restoration of authority is the inevitable corollary of their crime against the fatherland and against freedom?

Dictatorship is the inevitable corollary, the unavoidable consequence of what was carried out not by us but by our opponents. Let the Italian people ask them for explanations!

The antifascists play their strongest card at this point: they try to show the Italian people that, by virtue of its nature and its goals, fascism is inexorably committed to dictatorship.

We reply that the fundamental character of the fascist movement is otherwise! After all, it was fascism and only fascism that stood up and defended not the freedom of a single class but *the freedom of all Italians* in their fatherland. This at the precise historical moment when beastlike hordes of Italians were foaming at the mouth with Lenin's slogan "freedom is a bourgeois prejudice"; when Deputies Turati and Treves voted for a platform stating that "when the proletariat reaches a position of political power it must proceed to a regime of class dictatorship" at their party's October 1919 convention; when the socialist newspaper *Avanti* justified the October 1920 death sentence pronounced by a workers tribunal against the guards Santagata and Crimi with the following words: "In these young men, in these women, in this sentence, one no longer must see a group of individuals, outlaws, or inhuman beings; one must instead envisage a social class that defends itself like a cohesive body, perhaps not fully conscious of itself, but driven by a blind instinct for self-preservation." . . .

It is still easy for our enemies to try to hinder us by summoning up the sullen ghost of reaction! But recall that our martyrs died with the phrase "fascism is the savior of our freedom" on their lips. They did not sit around waiting for the various champions [*gigini*] of a free Italy to do their bidding in the wake of the war. Their spirit lives on among the liveliest of our comrades. Immune to the lure of murky nostalgias and determined to contribute to fascism's apotheosis, they declare that the dictatorship serves as guarantor of the pure idea of freedom; that it is in harmony with the best and healthiest of Italian political traditions and entirely compatible with ideas of order and nationhood; and that the antifascists' spurious claim that fascism is reactionary must be classed as one of the filthy carryovers from the old Italy now in demise.

The Fascist Revolution and Modern Civilization

In one of his occasional moments of lucidity, an adversary wrote the following in the July 1923 issue of a political magazine (and fascists who want to understand and not be misunderstood ought to think hard about these words):

> Antifascists have two goals in mind when they define fascism as a pure and simple form of conservatism. First, they aim to limit the term's meaning and thereby hope to stir up and mobilize all those oppositional conservative forces that rally around liberal, democratic, populist, and so on, ideas. Second, they aim to deflate the event's importance by proclaiming that fascism's past (and hence future) strength falls short of what would be required to effect substantial change and precipitate a revolution.

One could hardly have pinpointed the antifascist misunderstanding any better. Here words such as liberalism, democracy, and populism are attributed social objectives that are not their own so that fascism may, in turn, be judged absolutely antiliberal, antidemocratic, and opposed to the people's interests.

The time has come to confute our opponents and to reestablish the truth by precisely situating fascism's intellectual revolution within that characteristic complex of political and economic forms, philosophical doctrines and ideologies that make up modern post-Reformation civilization. The time has come to elucidate just how the fascist revolution as a form of political action and fascism as a governing method are antidemocratic and antiliberal.

Born of the struggle between the Reformation and the Catholic Church, tied to the emergence of a capitalist bourgeoisie and to contemporaneous philosophical elaborations, the principle of individual rights attained its highest political expression in the French Revolution and in the proclamation of the rights of man and of the citizen.

The French Revolution and the Napoleonic occupation brought to light two different, even opposing interpretations and political practices, both derived from the same principle. According to the first, man constitutes the only reality of social life, and the state, deprived of any autonomous value, must place itself at the mercy of individuals, gradually annihilating itself, following the inexorable degenerative course that leads to anarchy. According to the second, the state constitutes the only reality of social life in the face of the discordant and incoherent multiplicity of individuals, and, as the only source of law, the state is entitled to treat its citizens as an instrument of its will.

This oscillation between anarchy and despotism, democratic principles and social reality proved fateful. And against it there arose, first in France and Germany and later in Italy, a vast critical movement starting in the Romantic period but extending well into the twentieth century that called into question the mind set and principles of the French Revolution.

Fascism's intellectual revolution is part of this movement, though in an original, distinctive, Italian way.

Fascism and Democracy

Those who respond to fascist critiques of democracy by arguing that fascism too will eventually give way to a democratic regime are deliberately confusing ideology and historical fact.

If by democracy one understands the possibility granted all citizens of actively participating in the life of the state, then nobody will deny democracy's immortality. The French Revolution rendered this possibility historically and ethically concrete, so much so that an ineradicable right was born that exercises a tenacious hold on individual consciousness, independent of abstract invocations of immortal principles or developments in modern philosophy. Within our own ranks it is true that some have philosophized against this fundamental truth of the democratic principle. Far more than the attacks of adversaries, they damage our cause with their feverish and eccentric thoughts.

Democracy, in the term's everyday meaning, is above all a concept and a political practice that is best defined as *atomistic.* There are as many kinds of democracies as there are democratic regimes. Two extreme examples come to mind: French democracy (now on the verge of anarchic dissolution) and American democracy (a system within which the federal courts limit and control the interpretation of democratic dogmas—dogmas that thrive in North America, according to European legend).

In Italy we experienced the worse kind of democracy: an ochlocracy defined by the transfer of sovereign power from the law to the mob. We experienced democratic tyranny, the multiple and monstrous dictatorship of the people as sovereign.

For this reason we deny the creators of this variety of democracy any right of appeal (which doesn't mean that we are either able or willing to call into question the component of democracy that history has consecrated).

Fascism and Liberalism

The opposition's sleight of hand also extends to the word liberalism.

Liberalism qua political doctrine is the affirmation of a unitary historical process to which all parties and all individuals contribute. It is politics understood as fight and conquest. Marking history in its recent development, liberalism is an eminently realistic doctrine that contains elements from our best native traditions.

Liberalism is also a distinctive political ideology that arose alongside democracy. It holds that states are the mechanical result of the interplay of competing political forces and, therefore, that their duties consist in little more than administration and policing.

This conception is typical of eras of transition and change. Silvio Spaventa, a political thinker whose work Senator Albertini and Deputy Amendola have made frequent use of for their own ends,[6] has written: "The liberal principle has proven able and even necessary when it comes to changing the status quo. But it has proven unable and ineffective when it comes to reforming what must be preserved. No European government, past or present, liberal or nonliberal in its origins, has been able or will be able to survive thanks to liberalism."

For better or for worse, Italy provides irrefutable proof of this verity. Liberalism played the determining role in our national revolution. But it also created an ineffective government. Fascism takes over from liberalism as expression of historical progress the same spirit of freedom (which determines its very nature and organization and the spirit that informs its actions), but freedom understood not as individual will but as a higher will, opposed to individual whims, that emerges from the synthesis of freedom and authority. It is from this higher universal freedom that fascism draws its deepest inspiration.

Fascist Revolution and Antidemocratic Tradition

Now that the field has been cleared of the most damaging antifascist detritus, I wish to dismantle the trite commonplace that fascism lacks any spiritual and doctrinal significance by briefly elucidating its close connections to recent historical developments. As already stated, fascism's intellectual revolution builds upon the critique of the French Revolution. Contrary to what Amendola, with his usual casuistry, has suggested, this in no way implies agreement with thinkers like Bonald, de Maistre, Burke, or Taine, who are all committed to chipping away at the very idea of the nation-state (which lies at the heart of the fascist revolution).[7] Numerous key intellectual precursors bridge the gap between their critiques and fascist thought. In the first place, there is the idealist philosophy of Kant and Hegel, which placed the principles of 1789 in a new critical light. Second, one must mention Georges Sorel's revolutionary contribution. Aiming to exalt spiritual and moral values, Sorel established a continuity between the Enlightenment and the positivist culture of the mid–nineteenth century (with all its corruption, lies, and mediocrity), debunking the cult of egalitarian utopias and positivist claims that socialism would soon become a science in a manner different from de Maistre and Bonald. Third, there is Alfredo Oriani's distinctively Italian contribution.[8] Renewer of the cult of heroes and high ideals, Oriani preached the religion of an immortal fatherland against the leveling effects of democracy and against socialist materialism. Last but not least comes Enrico Corradini, who had the pleasure of presiding over the fusion between nationalist and fascist forces, a fusion that launched the first phase of fascism's intellectual revolution, providing a link to a powerful political tradition that can be criticized but never denied. "Never denied" because nationalism's firm and fruitful traditions provide us with unbreachable defenses against two anarchic manifestations: the opposition's criticism and the ignorance that infiltrates our organizations in order to corrupt their spirit.

The Fascist State's Modernity

The view that fascism is immune to moral, spiritual, intellectual, cultural, or doctrinal reason has now been dispelled, as have definitions of fascism as mindless and unlimited brute force or blind reaction. Connections with tradition have also been demonstrated, as has the need to go beyond certain stances in the pursuit of fascism's intellectual revolution, at which point the opposition immediately cries out, "What about the state?"

What is this fascist state of yours? In his inimitable way, Benito Mussolini answered this question last Sunday in words that he has been repeating at least since 1 January 1923: "A state is the embodiment of a moral idea that finds expression in a system of individual hierarchies, each with its own responsibilities: hierarchies whose members—from the highest to the humblest—feel a sense of pride and privilege in carrying out their duty." Over a year ago, Mussolini laid the foundations for an ethical state: a state that is more than an association entered into on the basis of the free will of individuals or a social contract; a state opposed to liberal-democratic models inasmuch as it proposes a productive solution to the democratic antithesis between state and individual.

This modern concept of the ethical state was first formulated by Machiavelli. It matured in the philosophical writings of Vico, Spaventa, and de Meis.[9] It was propounded by Nationalism and elucidated in Croce's and Gentile's philosophy. It provides a basis for fascism as it marches toward victory, not because of fascism's material might but rather because, far from marking an unnatural return, its advent coincides with the rebirth of Italian thought.

At last we reach the final bulwark of antifascist error: the claim that fascists are at the mercy of the overbearing will of a man whose natural temperament finds expression in a dictatorship.

Our opponents (I limit myself to those who are worthy of consideration) ignore our suffering, the suffering of the young generations in the wake of the war.

They do not understand the war experience of men who enlisted at nineteen, their souls fresh and open.

They do not understand the turmoil experienced by young men who, in the immediate postwar era, were caught between the people and the fatherland.

They did not share our eagerness to obey.

They did not share the despair we felt at the absence of worthy rulers.

They do not know how long we waited for a chief [*Capo*].

This is why they fail to understand how much we love this chief of ours, this great national leader who molded our soul, sensibility, and intelligence, this man on whose behalf we gladly left behind our lives of leisure and faced death, time and again.

This is why our opponents are blind to the fact that we are faithfully waiting for him to perform the most painful and noble of efforts. This creator of order, beauty, and intelligence must now relentlessly, even cruelly infuse the souls of all his faithful with faith in the newborn nation-state!

translated by Maria G. Stampino and Jeffrey T. Schnapp

Notes

1. Giovanni Amendola (1882–1926) was one of fascism's leading opponents between 1919 and 1926. A conservative liberal for most of his distinguished career as a politician and journalist, he served as minister of the colonies in Luigi Facta's 1922 government. Amendola began publishing the overtly antifascist *Il Mondo* after the March on Rome (where Croce's antifascist manifesto appeared) and was one of the leaders of the post–Matteotti assassination revolt against Mussolini. His courageous defense of Italian democracy made him a favorite target of squadrist beatings.

2. As the essay makes clear, Bottai is employing the word "culture" in the broadest possible sense. The term encompasses at once the prior era's aesthetic production and its entire cultural, political, and social atmosphere.

3. Arturo Labriola (1873–1959) was one of the historic leaders of the revolutionary syndicalist movement in Italy. Despite his antireformist stance, he remained committed to mainstream antiprotectionist and antimonarchical views and even served as minister of labor in the 1921–22 Giolitti cabinet. His opposition to fascism was based on the conviction that it represented a force of reaction that would keep Italy from completing its bourgeois revolution (which he viewed as a necessary precondition for proletarian revolution).

4. Bonomi had put forward this view during the period (1921–22) when, as prime minister, he was directly confronted with the task of responding to squadrist violence.

5. Claudio Treves (1869–1933) was a prominent reformist socialist, deeply committed to the defense of liberal democratic institutions. Affiliated with the "minimalist" (i.e., gradualist) wing of the Italian Socialist Party, he was forced to flee Italy in 1926 for Paris, where he became one of the leaders of the antifascist opposition.

6. Silvio Spaventa (1822–93) was Benedetto Croce's teacher and a distinguished parliamentarian and political philosopher. Among his other writings are *Lo stato e le ferrovie* (1876), *La politica della destra* (1910), and *Lettere politiche* (1926). Luigi

Albertini (1871–1941) had been a member of the Senate since 1915. As director of *Corriere della Sera*, Albertini was a vocal liberal opponent of Mussolini's regime.

7. The Catholic monarchist Louis de Bonald (1754–1840) was a fierce opponent of empiricist materialism and democratic ideals. The British statesman Edmund Burke (1729–97) is remembered here as the author of *Reflections on the Revolution in France* (1790). Hippolyte Adolphe Taine (1828–93), the prominent French philosopher, critic, and historian, is alluded to here with reference to his six-volume study *Les Origines de la France contemporaine* (1874–94).

8. Alfredo Oriani (1852–1909) was a prolific essayist and novelist with strongly nationalistic, antidemocratic leanings. Thanks to Nietzschean works such as *La rivolta ideale*, Oriani was celebrated as a fascist precursor, and his collected works, published in thirty volumes between 1923 and 1933, were edited by Mussolini himself.

9. The allusions are to Giambattista Vico (1668–1744), noted author of the *Scienza nuova* (1725–44); the Italian Hegelian and teacher of Gentile, Bertrando Spaventa (1817–83); and Angelo Camillo de Meis (1817–91), the political philosopher and author of *Il sovrano* (1868).

CHAPTER 7

The Two Faces of Fascism (1924)

Sergio Panunzio

✳

Panunzio (1886–1944), a major fascist theorist and political scientist, directed the first fascist institution of higher learning: the Fascist Faculty of Political Science at the University of Perugia. He joined the fascist movement in 1921, out of the ranks of revolutionary syndicalism and the interventionist movement. He ultimately advocated a brand of corporativism that focused on politicizing the population and substituting centralized bureaucracy with self-governing corporative bodies. He is perhaps best remembered for his contribution to spreading fascism's myths and revolutionary image, as in this piece from his Che cosa è il Fascismo.

✳

I

Defining fascism is no easy task, and it is precisely this difficulty that many people use to justify their spiteful and negative—but always superficial—criticisms. Nevertheless, after the exuberant triumphs and orgies of pragmatist philosophy, it shouldn't prove difficult for intellectuals, critics, and hypercritics to admit that a great historic movement of national and international importance can arise without a previously elaborated doctrine, defined and expressed in a platform. Fascism as an idea is undefinable. It is a fact that is still unfolding. As I see it, to fix its meaning today would be a contradiction in terms. Some foolishly conclude that, because of the impossibility of a definition and the logical advantage of avoiding one, fascism does not exist or, better still, that it is neither real nor serious. On the contrary, seeing that in the beginning actions preceded words, it is better to conclude with Goethe that it is preferable to stick to facts and to shunt aside all "utopic" intellectual traditions (to echo Sorel): traditions that imagine that it is necessary to start from doctrine in order to arrive at facts and institutions, that view facts and institutions as nonexistent if they cannot claim a point of departure that is logical, doctrinal, and programmatic.[1]

II

That is not all. Fascism is not susceptible to definition because it is a highly complex movement that presents two fundamental aspects, sharply opposed and simultaneous. Thus it follows that some people define it in one way while others define it in another, diametrically opposite way. Some apply the label "left" to it, while others apply the label "right." Oversimplification (as noted by Spencer and Pareto)[2] is the most serious and fatal error that one can commit in life and in thought, especially in the social sciences. And no greater obstacle to the comprehension of fascism exists than oversimplification.

III

This said, there does exist a social philosophy—a glorious achievement of the Italian mind alone—that, from the point of view of method, provides some help in understanding fascism and determining its historical value. The philosophy in question is contained in Vilfredo Pareto's *Sociology*. Fascism could be considered largely the experimental proof of this philosopher's doctrines, which are essentially based on nonlogical actions and on the supremacy of the irrational in history.

What can safely be said about fascism thus far is that it is a purely Italian movement and, by consequence, neither exportable nor comparable to other movements occurring in other places and at other times.

Fascism is a movement unto itself, original, atypical; there are no copies or imitations, nor can there be. Hence its essentially historical nature. It is the product of two crises:

1) the general crisis of socialism throughout Europe, rendered more acute in Italy because of its peculiar economic and social conditions and by Italians' moral sensibility and keen political intelligence (it is no exaggeration to assert that the most important product of European Marxist revisionism was Italian syndicalism, in which Georges Sorel recognized a great part of himself);

2) the crisis of the war and of the postwar in Italy; victorious in war, Italy was defeated in peace until the day the Black Shirts entered Rome.

These two crises define the historical foundations of fascism. If they are ignored, it is impossible to understand anything about the fascist phenomenon. As we have said, fascism has two opposing faces. This contradiction must be fully explained.

IV

Fascism, in its dual character, is revolutionary and conservative. How and why? This contradictory nature makes for definitional difficulties. It stupefies pure conservatives and makes them wary of accepting it as conservative.

It gives pause to revolutionaries, who don't know whether to embrace it as a revolutionary phenomenon. It gives rise to global astonishment and to local confusion when public opinion—especially foreign public opinion—is confronted with the indisputable majesty of fascism's advent. Finally, it resists critics' efforts to judge it in its naked form or, rather, their tendency to judge it with every sort of prejudice and preconception (which amounts to the same thing). So, is fascism revolution or restoration? This is the nub of the question, a question that seems to haunt opinion abroad, especially in countries with a long history and ancient culture, though it is insignificant (or nearly so) in Italy. (I leave to one side the despicable slander of fascism committed by foreign journalists and reporters and by our transplanted or voluntarily exiled compatriots. Criticism should be leveled by critics and not by slanderers.) Generally speaking, it stands to reason that men and social classes are divided into conservatives and revolutionaries. The first, taking into consideration only one face of fascism, will spread the news that fascism is conservative. The second, considering only the other face, which is just as visible as the first, will proclaim that fascism is revolutionary.

It would appear that the scholastic doctrine of the *double truth* finds confirmation in this comparison: a single object is both this and that, both white and black![3] But this is not at all the case. Fascism is neither exclusively conservative nor exclusively revolutionary. It combines (from two separate perspectives, naturally) one thing *and* the other. To invoke a phrase that is not a meaningless cliché but a dialectical concept, I would say that fascism is a great "conservative revolution." I wrote as much in November 1919 in *Il Popolo d'Italia*, the newspaper that Benito Mussolini founded in 1914, a newspaper intimately tied to the new Italy's history. I wrote that it was necessary to *preserve* everything from prior economic, familial, and political institutions that cannot be destroyed without prompting the body politic's dissolution, not just in this or that given form of society but in every society qua society. I wrote that it was necessary to *destroy* everything that cannot be preserved by grafting new branches onto the age-old trunk, by organically melding new and old.

We renew by preserving, we preserve by innovating. These are the two faces of fascism, apparently contradictory but fundamentally united in a single reality of thought, life, and history. What constitutes the magnificent originality of the "Italian revolution," what makes it greatly superior to the French and Russian Revolutions, is that it has remembered and profited from the teachings of Vico, Burke, Cuoco, and all the critical historiography on the revolution of 1789.[4] As such it has preserved the past, acted in the present, and directed all its energies toward the future: all this, within the limits imposed by the present historical context. In certain respects, fascism is ultraconservative, for example, in its insistence upon familial, religious, authoritarian, and legal values. These are values that have been attacked and destroyed by the encyclopedic cultural ideals of the Enlightenment, an era whose legacy has been carried over to the proletariat's ideology, democratic socialism, which is principally responsible for today's corruption. In other respects, fascism is innovative to such a degree that it terrifies conservatives, as does, for example, its advocacy of a "labor state" [*stato sindacale*] and its demolition of the "parliamentary state."

We are contemporaries, so our judgments are necessarily partial. Conservatives find fascism too revolutionary. Revolutionaries accuse it of being too conservative. But let history be the judge. History has no preconceptions. What is visible today and will further develop in time is the *analysis* of the two tendencies that today are already referred to as the *two spirits* of fascism: the conservative spirit and the revolutionary spirit. The synthesis will come later on, and time will tell.

V

The nature of things is their birth, said our great G. B. Vico.[5] This principle explains in practical terms the "how" and the "why" of fascism, as well as its contingent features.

It should never be forgotten that fascism is the unexpected progeny of two crises: that of socialism and that of wartime Italy.

During the fateful month of August 1914, the Italian Socialist Party was at a crossroads. If it was to be revolutionary in deed and not just in word, it would have had to commit itself to being both strongly *national* and decisively *in favor of the war*. But it was neither because its constitution disallowed it. Mussolini immediately intuited this. He abandoned the Socialist Party and, in the company of other subversives, founded and infused with life the *revolutionary interventionist* movement. Many people with disparate ideas joined the movement for reasons of interventionist opportunism. Among them were numerous democrats whose mentality (as later became clear) was diametrically opposed to that of the subversives and revolutionaries who would make up the future leadership of fascism. If the war had been embraced and led by a national socialist party, Italy's diplomatic and *military* conduct would doubtless have been different, particularly in its interactions with the Triple Entente [l'Intesa].[6] Perhaps the European war might have ended sooner and better without American intervention. The interventionist movement had to content itself with resisting socialist neutralism and defeatism and with struggling desperately against weak liberal governments. It fought to keep the war from becoming the disaster that neutralists and socialists desired. If, in May 1915, Salandra had brought Mussolini to power with him, if he had instituted a revolutionary government free from liberals, the outcome would have been much improved.[7] The history of interventionist efforts (nationwide but especially in Milan) to avoid Caporetto is still little known. All the same, the war ended in victory. The democrats immediately raised the Adriatic question and split the interventionists. It became sadly necessary to boo Bissolati at La Scala in Milan.[8]

The democrats took advantage of the veterans. Mussolini would have done the contrary. Even before the Paris Conference he should have taken power with the support of front-line veterans, and, if it hadn't been for the democrats' defection and for Nitti's pseudo-Machiavellian maneuvers, he might well have done so.[9]

VI

It is pointless to rehearse here the sad history of the Adriatic question. Rome we were unable to conquer, but Fiume we did, with D'Annunzio. God knows how we were able to face the gloomy elections of 1919. Well, it was thanks to Mussolini. Mussolini who, already before Vittorio Veneto, had announced that it was necessary to march not *against* but *toward* labor; who, immediately after Vittorio Veneto, championed the formula of the eight-hour workday. It was that same Mussolini who, *for the 1919 elections*, provided the newborn Fasci di Combattimento with a party platform that, far from being reactionary, was boldly and wisely innovative and revolutionary.

So if the Adriatic question hadn't helped the socialist party, the dregs of society that fornicated with it, and Italy's other dead and moribund forces to recover their strength, *we might well have seen the fulfillment, from 1919 on, of fascism's revolutionary spirit.* This proved impossible because of circumstances. Faced with an obscene socialist revolution, supported not only by the plutocratic anti-Italian governments of the Triple Entente but also tolerated, promoted, and protected by the Italian government, fascism was forced to adopt a reactive, repressive, even *punitive* stance. This explains fascism's reactionary semblance during the period from the elections of November 1919 to the March on Rome.

VII

Now, it would be inaccurate to claim that fascism's restorative phase is entirely over. We are still far from the end of the road, and our path is still obstructed.

If a Bolshevik revolution had taken place, the task of reacting would have proven easier and simpler.

Socialism was negative. What it did not destroy, it corrupted, spoiled, and ruined. Hence the need to restore the values of the past. We have had a socialist revolution, it is true, but a revolution that failed and was unable to triumph. Hence the enormous ills of a *failed* revolution: a revolution that yielded none of the benefits of a subversive revolution. The immediate task of fascism remains unfinished. It consists in the energetic restoration of the public order, something fascism has done magnificently, eliciting the amazement and admiration of everyone in the world who thinks, feels, and understands. The energetic restoration, that is, of the prestige of authorities, the state treasury, and those traditional social units that are sacred and inviolable (and cannot, therefore, be tampered with)—first and foremost among them, religion and the family. But the spirit of renewal exists and is imminent within fascism. I believe that I have demonstrated this by means of these historical notes. It will permeate the history of Italy and of Europe.

translated by Olivia E. Sears

Notes

1. In his prefatory letter to Daniel Halevy, Sorel had written, "a utopia is . . . an intellectual product; it is the work of theorists who, after observing and discussing the known facts, seek to establish a model to which they can compare existing society in order to estimate the amount of good and evil it contains." Cited from *Reflections on Violence*, trans. T. E. Hulme (New York: Peter Smith, 1941), 32–33.

2. The allusion is to Herbert Spencer (1820–1903), the British philosopher who in works such as *The Principles of Biology* (1864–67) and *The Principles of Sociology* (1876–96) sought to apply the doctrine of evolution to all knowable phenomena. One of the fathers of modern sociology, Vilfredo Pareto (1848–1923) was an economist and sociologist who, through the application of mathematical analysis to economic theory, attempted to differentiate between rational and irrational motives in social action and to examine the rise and fall of ruling elites. A critic of liberal democratic theories of politics, Pareto was much admired by Mussolini and, at the time of his death, was associated with the new-born review *Gerarchia*.

3. Believed by certain radical Aristotelians of the high Middle Ages, this doctrine held that when the truths of revealed theology conflict with those provided by logic and philosophy, the conflict is to be resolved by recognizing that there exist two autonomous categories of truth.

4. Vincenzo Cuoco (1770–1823), the political philosopher and advocate of Italian unification under a republican government.

5. Book 1.148 of Vico's *New Science* reads: "The inseparable properties of institutions

must be due to the modification or guise with which they are born. By these properties we may therefore verify that the nature or birth was thus and not otherwise." Cited from *The New Science of Giambattista Vico*, trans. Thomas G. Bergin and Max H. Fisch (Ithaca: Cornell University Press, 1984), 64.

6. The Triple Entente was the informal alliance binding England, France, and Russia together at the outbreak of World War I.

7. Antonio Salandra (1853–1931) rose to the position of prime minister in March 1914 right before the outbreak of World War I. He initially staked out a neutralist position but by the end of the year reversed himself (having failed to win concessions from Austria in return for Italy's continuing neutrality) and began negotiating the Pact of London with the powers of the Triple Entente, committing Italy to intervene in the war. Signed in April 1915, the pact set off a ferocious battle between pro- and anti-interventionist forces, with the former triumphing by the subsequent month, when Italy formally entered the war. Despite the clamor for a pro-interventionist reshuffling of his government, Salandra made only minor concessions and had been driven out of power by June 1916.

8. One of the founders of the Socialist Party, Leonida Bissolati (1857–1920) was a moderate socialist who favored the Libyan war of 1911–12 as well as Italian intervention in World War I. During the immediate postwar years, Bissolati served as minister of military assistance and war pensions and split with Sidney Sonnino and others who favored intransigence toward Yugoslavia at the Treaty of Versailles negotiations. In December 1918 he was forced to resign his position.

9. The Paris Conference was called in early 1919 to negotiate the treaties (principally the Treaty of Versailles) needed to bring World War I to a formal close.

CHAPTER 8

Fascism's Problems and Realities (1924)

Camillo Pellizzi

✳

Pellizzi (1896–), a noted journalist and literary critic, was a prominent member of the "new technocratic" group close to Giuseppe Bottai. He completed a law degree at Pisa before fighting in World War I. A professor at the University of Pisa, he also regularly taught literature and language at the University of London between 1920 and 1939, developing close ties to writers such as Ezra Pound. This selection is from his book Problemi e realtà del Fascismo. *From 1940 to 1943 Pellizzi was president of the National Institute of Fascist Culture, capping a career of deep involvement in the definition of fascist cultural policies and politics.*

✳

Fascism's Unity and Form

Within the postwar setting, fascism was the sole movement that not only had recourse to violence but also systematically integrated violence into a highly distinctive "national rhetoric." Fascism's "national rhetoric" challenged some aspects of the prior bourgeois and conservative concept of nationality and supplemented the latter with inspirational elements and mythological principles that were vaster in their scope and more substantial. Fascism potentially included all orders of society within its myth of the nation. It approached society not on the basis of social classes or individual monads but in terms of values and concrete functions that contribute to the ultimate common myth. In other words, fascism repudiated the abstract, amorphous nation with no internal differentiation; a nation in which every individual has the same privileges and rights; a nation in which a single class (spiritually unformed yet economically close-knit) can rule over all others. On the contrary, fascism was uncompromising and intolerant in its demand that each and every individual fully subject himself to the existing hierarchy and to common goals. It demanded, in short, the shaping [*formazione*], differentiation, and hierarchical arrangement of social groups. If fascism has often stood in opposition to the rich (and will continue to do so), this opposition is not based on hostility toward the notion of a ruling class. It is rooted, rather, in the conviction that the current ruling class was and remains historically ill formed. Insufficiently solid, it holds itself only indirectly and partially responsible. It is not yet animated by the myth that fascism is bringing to gradual if confused fruition in the hearts of the Italian people.

The early shaping of fascism's personality and character took place, as already noted, at the beginning of the European war [World War I]. In the course of the war, these features developed further, underwent diffusion, and asserted themselves more forcefully. After the war they coalesced slowly and actualized themselves as a full-blown political force. Fascism's personality and character are of a concrete type. They do not belong to an abstract category but rather express the concrete qualities of individuals. The idea advanced by some at the end of the war of bestowing a direct political function on veterans qua veterans was devoid of truth and has nothing to do with fascism's formation or with its central intuitions. Most veterans would in fact have objected that "there's too much politics in Italy to begin with; those of us who fought during the war don't want to become politicians" (or something to that effect). The truth of the matter is that there was too much rhetorical posturing in our political life. Violence, strength, an exacting creative will were all sorely absent. To go beyond the rampant rhetoricity of public life, to build up an alternative force, these veterans had to *choose sides*. They had to enter the fray, even to fight among themselves over the concrete problems that were surfacing. Sometimes internecine strife constitutes a healing fate. Besides, when the time for formulating and preaching new programs expires and it becomes necessary to confront the enemy in the trenches face to face, all confusion and exaggeration cease. True friends reveal themselves as such. The enemy is unmistakably identified and defeated on the field.

Some posed the question, "Why select the name Fasci di Combattimento [Combat Leagues]? Are you a political party or a gang of armed outlaws?" The small founding group from *Il Popolo d'Italia* did not want to avoid the adjective *political* as much as the noun *party*. In its view, to make use of the word *party* would have meant validating the entire constitutional framework and the then-current methods of electoral and parliamentary struggle. At which point, like heralds, Italy's stalest political camouflage artists raised an outcry over the fact that some true patriots wanted to continue the war within, after it was over at the borders. Yet the first fascists had always found their main antagonists less in Austria and Hungary than within Italy! Had the crisis been less intense; had the internationalist, class-based rhetoric not pushed the entire country so close to the brink of disaster; had the collapse of the old order of dissimulation not been so complete; then maybe the fascist aristocracy could have bided its time, toned down its demands, shown tolerance, compromised with the impulses of its own soul. Fortunately for Italy, the storm proved serious. All the old guidance systems showed just how little they could be trusted. Hence, the name Fasci di Combattimento.

A program—the much sought-after fascist *program*—is embedded within these three words. Some asked, "But what is the goal of this fight [*combattimento*] of yours?" The answer consisted in a single but great word, a sovereign and overpowering rhetorical formula: Italy. The reply was predictable: "Yes, but whose Italy? There are at least as many Italies as there are individual consciousnesses and wills."

The question might have been answered as follows: "*Our* Italy. You will see. For the time being we recognize our enemies, and, by fighting them, we are building up our strength. You, the rulers of the old regime, have proven unable to wage war or to make peace. You have created *no Italy* at all. We will start by stripping away as many of your powers as possible."

Hence, from its beginning, fascism was squadrism: a disciplined and militant volunteerism characterized by regular recourse to *direct action*. And so fascism will remain until squadrism's historical function is exhausted. It can by no means be taken for granted that squadrist force, discipline, and vigor must be forever channeled into the sort of political police functions that squadrism has performed thus far. Unless it were to find itself stupidly persecuted and humbled, the squadrist mind-set is fated to blossom and develop in other guises. It is fated to give rise to new social forces in unforeseeable new domains (a matter better taken up elsewhere).

Here I wish to stress a point regarding squadrism that antifascist polemics always touch upon. Early squadrism was muddled and chaotic. It was made up of curious and varied individuals: former Arditi; legionnaires from Fiume; former terrorists, back from the front; unemployed workers of various stripes; idealistic young intellectual drifters; the worst of scoundrels. . . . Yes, even scoundrels: scoundrels of the sort to which the future will build monuments; bandits like those who laid Rome's first stone; pirates like those who gave birth to the Venetian Republic or to the British Empire; adventurers like the paladins of chivalric epics or the noblemen of the Crusades. Sublime scoundrels these who redeemed themselves in the embrace of a passionate ethical principle, in the fire of a collective spirit, in the inner discipline of obedience and sacrifice. Take, for instance, the story of Sarza Madidini from Cremona. A deserter and subversive, rejected from the Fasci as unworthy, he volunteered for all the riskiest sorties. Wounded, he submitted an application for membership, but, once again, the request was turned down. Nevertheless, he continued to endure all the risks of the fascist battle until, wounded anew and close to death, he requested and was finally granted membership, which he considered the consecration of his human dignity and of his nobility as an Italian. Admittedly, there were excesses committed by the squadrists. Various leaders—Mussolini first and foremost—rose to condemn them, but they were often unavoidable. Yet the spiritual strain that permeates Sarza Madidini's story recurs with great regularity: the desire for a new form of human and civic nobility to be conquered by means of warlike violence and exposure to constant danger.

This concrete (but, in those days, hard-to-define) movement did not attract individuals with closed or rigid mind-sets or vested interests. For a long time, many viewed fascism as deeply antihistorical. Suspecting concealed interests, they sought to find out who was lending the movement trucks or who was providing it with headquarters space and money. As a result, many episodes surfaced that seemed incomprehensible and even shameful to true believers in the cause. But what remained unacknowledged was the fact of fascism's deep spiritual force: an autonomous, coherent force, fully consistent with its embryonic *personality* despite thousands of incidental variations and local facets. Far from an antihistorical paradox, fascism marked, instead, the beginning of a new historical formation.

It is indeed true that fascism's exterior surface seemed multifaceted. No more multifaceted, though, than the contingent reality of the problems it had to solve: problems which change from place to place and from class to class. This is true because Italy was and is a country characterized by a divine multiformity and spiritual plurality. In Italy no two countenances, no two heads, no two hearts look exactly the same. For this reason alone it is hardly surprising that early fascism abounded in contradictions, misunderstandings, even acts of undiscipline (mostly carried out in good faith in the service of its ideals) or that it was sometimes obstructed by complicated, harsh, crude, and thoughtless egotism. To overemphasize such differences and divergences within fascism, however, is to deny oneself any deep intuition of the phenomenon in its living, deeper unity, a unity that Mussolini was wont to liken to an organ with a thousand pipes on which "if you hit certain keys, it produces the sound of a military fanfare." Fascism is the first *singular* methexic force that Italian history has ever engendered.[1] Indifferent to region and class, it is singular because it enlists people from all regions and from all classes. It has Italy as its necessary premise but aims at the world.

Chiefs, Followers, and Hangers-On

With an eye toward resolving the internal crisis provoked by the famous "pacification pact" made with the socialists, the Fasci reconstituted themselves as the National Fascist Party.[2] Critics immediately predicted that fascism would die because it "would lose any originality once it ceased being an outlaw movement." They were wrong. Even functioning as a party, fascism retained its extralegal status and originality. And it certainly did not disappear. A party program was printed up, and it took part in the 1921 elections. Thanks to its so-called program, it was now able to choose among those who presented themselves as new followers. The elections brought fascism into Parliament so that it could limit the damage done as it awaited the moment to fully accomplish its revolution.

The fascist movement was now under way and was coming into its own, day by day, outside the confines of Parliament and its program. It no longer consisted only in faith, devotion, and force. Some of its chiefs had begun to manifest the ethical virtues possessed by only the most fruitful aristocracies: a historical sense of responsibility; a feeling of independent, free selfhood; a sense of duty not to others but to oneself. In short, a *consciousness* [*coscienza*]. Linked to this emerging consciousness, another symptomatic feature was in the process of surfacing: the cult of *authority*. On the streets and in the fields, fascism fought for authority and admitted to it openly.

Authority, but not derived from written law, a monarch, a constitutional system, or any fixed dogma. On the contrary, authority born from and as a function of a creative action. The authority of a dynamic, ethical state. Fascists experienced this state not as something pre-existing that was in need of resuscitation but rather as something entirely new, something that must arise entirely out of *their* work, *their* discipline, *their* heroism. Who might have guessed that all this would take place in the old Italy of the pandects and decretals; the Italy of endless legal quibbling, with its Spanish-inspired legal formalism, Jesuit casuistry, byzantinism, and academies; an Italy where political *self-camouflage* [*mimetismo*] was once held up as one of the nation's distinctive characters!

Mussolini was consistent in his affirmation of the absolute primacy of spiritual values and of the need for hierarchy. He condemned the idolatry of the masses and contested all "economistic" accounts of society's key problems.

Thus, the methexic current that had been held in check and that, under the aegis of superficial, second-hand theories, had propelled Italy toward unity and independence this time revealed itself with greater amplitude, with greater ambition, and with its own distinctive perspective. A perspective that, though still in embryonic form, strove heroically to rid itself of all the dross of the past and of all foreign contamination. So fascism was not just a physical force, aiming at an external renewal. It was also a mystical force of liberation and of inner exaltation. Throughout fascism's mythical and heroic phase, spiritual powers germinated within its violence, as if arising directly out of the violence itself. This spirituality brought about miracles that physical violence alone could never have carried out. And with the return of miracles came the return of rites that were distinctly religious and at the same time indicative of our past grandeur. The squadrons became centuries, cohorts, legions and resurrected the Roman army's forms of discipline. Survivors cried out that killed companions were "present!" in the course of roll calls. These archaic, mystical, beautiful forms are not "rhetorical," as some have claimed, for in them an operative force has taken on a spontaneous shape. They are genuine expressions of an emerging personality, not external or artificial manifestations.

Soon this germinal force started to push certain leaders to the forefront. They were all original and curious types. Take Lanfranconi, a bizarre mix of ascetic, bohemian, and tenant farmer who rose against the entire red tide of Lomellina and, with only a few faithful companions, conquered the region in a matter of months.[3] Take Farinacci, the former railroad employee who galvanized a few scattered youngsters against the Cremonese reds and blacks and became the province's popular dictator. (He made it a point of honor to carry no weapon except for a simple riding whip.) Take Scorza from Lucca, who led a few faithful followers to clean up Garfagnana, a region that had caused even Rome's legions to tremble.[4] Take Ricci, who, in Carrara, managed to enthrall hardened, dour masses of quarrymen, imposing fascist discipline upon a region once wracked by acute upheavals.[5] It is impossible to recall them all. Perrone-Compagni in Florence; Bottai in Latium; de Vecchi in Turin; Terruzzi and Forni in Milan; Balbo in Parma; Baroncini in Bologna; Rossi in Ancona; Lantini and Mastromattei in Liguria; Santini in Pisa; Sansanelli in Naples; Bolzon in Sicily; later, Gandolfo in Sardinia; and many, many more.[6] It was a blossoming of strong-willed, eager men, men of the people chosen from among our very best youth in the name of national necessity.

I am well aware that Lanfranconi will not be chosen as minister of education, nor will Farinacci, for example, become minister of foreign affairs. History casts even the most exalted aristocrat in but one key role. Nowadays, fascism requires men to carry out more delicate tasks. The need is dire because the movement is largely made up of boys or of young men who have lost many years of study and of technical and cultural training as a consequence of the European and the civil wars. Fascism mobilized certain character types and formed or will form others. As these new Italians improve their managerial, administrative, and technical skills, the laws of motion will drive them to take on weightier tasks. The result will be an Italy governed (as it is beginning to be governed today) by much stronger, more creative, and more responsible hierarchies. The very presence, be it actual or potential, of these powerful cadres within the state will imperil the careers of cowards, meddlers, and swindlers. Let me add that some of the choicest spirits from the preceding generation have joined the fascist ranks so as to find and define themselves more fully, the most famous case being that of Giovanni Gentile.

The methexic spirit, in short, abounds (to the point of overflowing in fascism's chiefs). Though the mass of followers is still mostly chameleon-like, it shows flashes of commitment that bode well for a gradual broadening and deepening of the fascist hierarchy. For the time being, what is necessary is a gradual, cautious development of the movement's vital principles, as well as careful and appropriate use of many indispensable (and celebrated) instruments of fascist rhetoric. It is also necessary to make use of certain men. As regards the occasional unfortunate sign of political regression, it will be considered below in the context of an analysis of the elements that make up what one might call *fascist (dis)simulation* [*mimetica fascista*].

I note in closing that even the structuring of the fascist party as a single militia, complete with military oaths and regulations (which sharply differentiate it from what one ordinarily refers to as a "party"), has not prevented our nation's worst leeches from hanging on to the winners' chariot. I am referring to the spineless, the timorous, and the disoriented, to the meddlers and half-virgins of the old Italian political scene. In some places they have even managed to prevail "in the name of the fasces" [*in nomine Lictorum*]. But they mostly adapt themselves so as to continue their usual barratry. Accustomed to bending their backs, they ignore the bitter scorn of pure-souled fascists.

If I had to define these hangers-on by way of an historical example, I would compare them to the mobs of jesters, peddlers, and prostitutes who followed the Crusaders' armies into the Holy Land.

In addition, traces of the old mentalities still exercise a tenacious hold. Their ability to latch onto the national organism represents the gravest and most dangerous of threats. For example, the breakup of the Masons offers no guarantees that the old Masonic-democratic mind-set will not pollute our ranks and cadres, giving rise to frictions and resurgences at the expense of healthy and vital elements. Because in the south the fight was against individual and local gangs, some thought that the Masons (who are simply a larger, more impersonal gang) would be fascism's natural ally, if not an outright blood-sister. But time will explode such tumors and misunderstandings.

Fascism must be understood as a spiritual and historic reality, a reality that exists above and beyond individual episodes, above and beyond contingent formations and specific individuals. The deeper needs of the entire movement and the energies of many superior men stand firm between the many flaws inherited from the past and the possibilities opened up by the future.

translated by Maria G. Stampino and Jeffrey T. Schnapp

Notes

1. The adjective "methexic," repeatedly employed by Pellizzi in the second half of the essay, refers to the notion borrowed from the nineteenth-century philosopher Vincenzo Gioberti (but based upon Plato) of absolute participation of the real in the ideal within the framework of the cyclical return of existence to full Being.

2. The allusion is to the Pacification Pact signed in August 1921 between the socialists and fascists, which aimed to curb squadrist violence and the reprisals that it provoked. Signatories included not just the two political parties but also the General Confederation of Labor. Difficulties in enforcing its terms led to Mussolini's decision to transform the Fasci into a political party and to the pact's dissolution in November of the same year.

3. Lanfranconi was apparently the local leader of the Lomellina Fascio. The Lomellina is located in the vicinity of the cities of Pavia and Mortaro.

4. Carlo Scorza (1897–1988) was the founder and leader of the Lucca Fascio and a leading figure in the fascist hierarchy during the regime's two decades. Renowned for his brutality, he occupied numerous positions of responsibility, including that of secretary of the National Fascist Party during its final year (1943).

5. Renato Ricci (1896–1956) was the founder and leader of the Carrara Fascio. In the wake of the March on Rome, he was elected to Parliament, served as vice-secretary of the party, and assumed leadership of the Opera Nazionale Balilla between 1927 and 1937.

6. Pellizzi's list surveys most of the founders of the early local Fasci.

CHAPTER 9

The Political Doctrine of Fascism (1925)

Alfredo Rocco

Right-wing fascist theorist Rocco (1875–1935) began his political career as a nationalist, joining the fascist movement only in 1923, when it merged with the Nationalist Association. Nonetheless, he rapidly rose to a prominent role within the regime. As minister of justice between 1925 and 1932, he was responsible for a wide range of legislation that included many of the key laws governing labor relations and insuring the domination of the executive branch of government over the legislative and judicial branches. With the regime's reorganization in 1932, Rocco left office to become a senator in 1934 and rector of the University of Rome.

✴

Fascism as Action, as Feeling, and as Thought

Much has been said and is now being said for or against this complex political and social phenomenon that in the brief period of six years has taken complete hold of Italian life and, spreading beyond the borders of the kingdom, has made itself felt in varying degrees of intensity throughout the world. But people have been much more eager to extol or to deplore than to understand—which is natural enough in a period of tumultuous fervor and of political passion. The time has not yet arrived for a dispassionate judgment. For even I, who noticed the very first manifestations of this great development, saw its significance from the start and participated directly in its first doings, carefully watching all its early uncertain and changing developments, even I do not feel competent to pass definite judgment. Fascism is so large a part of myself that it would be both arbitrary and absurd for me to try to dissociate my personality from it, to submit it to impartial scrutiny in order to evaluate it coldly and accurately. What can be done, however, and it seldom is attempted, is to make an inquiry into the phenomenon that shall not merely consider its fragmentary and adventitious aspects but strive to get at its inner essence. The undertaking may not be easy, but it is necessary, and no occasion for attempting it is more suitable than the present one afforded me by my friends of Perugia.

Suitable it is in time because, at the inauguration of a course of lectures and lessons principally intended to illustrate that old and glorious trend of the life and history of Italy that takes its name from the humble saint of Assisi, it seemed natural to connect it with the greatest achievement of modern Italy, different in so many ways from the Franciscan movement but united with it by the mighty common current of Italian history. It is suitable as well in place because at Perugia, which witnessed the growth of our religious ideas, of our political doctrines, and of our legal science in the course of the most glorious centuries of our cultural history, the mind is properly disposed and almost oriented toward an investigation of this nature.

First of all let us ask ourselves if there is a political doctrine of fascism, if there is any ideal content in the fascist state. For in order to link fascism, both as concept and system, with the history of Italian thought and find therein a place for it, we must first show that it is thought, that it is a doctrine. Many persons are not quite convinced that it is either the one or the other, and I am not referring solely to those men, cultured or uncultured, as the case may be and very numerous everywhere, who can discern in this political innovation nothing except its local and personal aspects and who know fascism only as the particular manner of behavior of this or that well-known fascist, of this or that group of a certain town, who therefore like or dislike the movement on the basis of their likes and dislikes for the individuals who represent it. Nor do I refer to those intelligent and cultivated persons, very intelligent indeed and very cultivated, who because of their direct or indirect allegiance to the parties that have been dispossessed by the advent of fascism have a natural cause of resentment against it and are therefore unable to see, in the blindness of hatred, anything good in it. I am referring rather to those—and there are many in our ranks too—who know fascism as *action* and *feeling* but not yet as *thought*, who therefore have an intuition but no *comprehension* of it.

It is true that fascism is, above all, *action* and *sentiment* and that such it must continue to be. Were it otherwise, it could not keep up that immense driving force, that renovating power that it now possesses and would merely be the solitary meditation of a chosen few. Only because it is feeling and sentiment, only because it is the unconscious reawakening of our profound racial instinct, has it the force to stir the soul of the people and to set free an irresistible current of national will. Only because it is action, and as such actualizes itself in a vast organization and in a huge movement, has it the conditions for determining the historical course of contemporary Italy.

But fascism is thought as well, and it has a theory that is an essential part of this historical phenomenon and that is responsible in a great measure for the successes that have been achieved. To the existence of this ideal content of fascism, to the truth of this fascist logic we ascribe the fact that though we commit many errors of detail, we very seldom go astray on fundamentals, whereas all the parties of the opposition, deprived as they are of an informing, animating principle, of a unique directing concept, do very often wage their war faultlessly in minor tactics, better trained as they are in parliamentary and journalistic maneuvers, but they constantly break down on the important issues. Fascism, moreover, considered as action, is a typically Italian phenomenon and acquires a universal validity because of the existence of this coherent and organic doctrine. The originality of fascism is due in great part to the autonomy of its theoretical principles. For even when, in its external behavior and in its conclusions, it seems identical with other political creeds, in reality it possesses an inner originality due to the new *spirit* that animates it and to an entirely different theoretical approach.

Common Origins and Common Background of Modern Political Doctrines: From Liberalism to Socialism

Modern political thought remained, until recently, both in Italy and outside of Italy, under the absolute control of those doctrines that, proceeding from the Protestant Reformation and developed by the adepts of natural law in the seventeenth and eighteenth centuries, were firmly grounded in the institutions and customs of the English, of the American, and of the French revolutions. Under different and sometimes clashing forms, these doctrines have left a determining imprint upon all theories and actions, both social and political, of the nineteenth and twentieth centuries, down to the rise of fascism. The common basis of all these doctrines, which stretch from Languet, from Buchanan, and from Althusius down to Karl Marx, to Wilson and to Lenin, is a social and state concept that I shall call *mechanical* or *atomistic*.[1]

Society according to this concept is merely a sum total of individuals, a plurality that breaks up into its single components. Therefore, the ends of a society, so considered, are nothing more than the ends of the individuals that compose it and for whose sake it exists. An atomistic view of this kind is also necessarily *antihistorical*, inasmuch as it considers society in its spatial attributes and not in its *temporal* ones, and because it reduces social life to the existence of a single generation. Society becomes thus *a sum of determined individuals,* namely, the generation living at a given moment. This doctrine, which I call atomistic and which appears to be antihistorical, reveals from under a concealing cloak a strongly materialistic nature. For in its endeavors to isolate the present from the past and the future, it rejects the spiritual inheritance of ideas and sentiments that each generation receives from those preceding and hands down to the following generation, thus destroying the unity and the spiritual life itself of human society.

This common basis shows the close logical connection existing between all political doctrines; the substantial solidarity that unites all the political movements, from liberalism to socialism, that until recently have dominated Europe. For these political schools differ from one another in their *methods,* but all agree as to the *ends* to be achieved. All of them consider the welfare and happiness of individuals to be the goal of society, itself considered as composed of individuals of the present generation. All of them see in society and in its juridical organization, the state, the mere instrument and means whereby individuals can attain their ends. They differ only in that the methods pursued for the attainment of these ends vary considerably one from the other.

Thus the liberals insist that the best manner to secure the welfare of the citizens as individuals is to interfere as little as possible with the free development of their activities and that therefore the essential task of the state is merely to coordinate these several liberties in such a way as to guarantee their co-existence. Kant, who was without doubt the most powerful and thorough philosopher of liberalism, said, "Man, who is the end, cannot be assumed to have the value of an instrument." And again, "justice, of which the state is the specific organ, is the condition whereby the freedom of each is conditioned upon the freedom of others, according to the general law of liberty."

Having thus defined the task of the state, liberalism confines itself to the demand of certain guarantees that are to keep the state from overstepping its functions as general coordinator of liberties and from sacrificing the freedom of individuals more than is absolutely necessary for the accomplishment of its purpose. All the efforts are therefore directed to see to it that the ruler, mandatory of all and entrusted with the realization, through and by liberty, of the harmonious happiness of everybody, should never be clothed with undue power. Hence the creation of a system of checks and limitations designed to keep the rulers within bounds; and among these, first and foremost, the principle of the *division of powers,* contrived as a means for weakening the state in its relation to the individual by making it impossible for the state ever to appear, in its dealings with citizens, in the full plenitude of sovereign powers; also the principle of the *participation of citizens in the lawmaking power,* as a means for securing, on behalf of the individual, a direct check on this, the strongest branch, and an indirect check on the entire government of the state. This system of checks and limitations, which goes by the name of *constitutional government* resulted in a moderate and measured liberalism. The checking power was exercised only by those citizens who were deemed worthy and capable, with the result that a small elite was made to represent legally the entire body politic for whose benefit this regime was instituted.

It was evident, however, that this moderate system, being fundamentally illogical and in contradiction with the very principles from which it proceeded, would soon become the object of serious criticism. For if the object of society and of the state is the welfare of individuals, severally considered, how is it possible to admit that this welfare can be secured by the individuals themselves only through the possibilities of such a liberal regime? The inequalities brought about both by nature and by social organizations are so numerous and so serious that, for the greater part, individuals abandoned to themselves not only would fail to attain happiness but would also contribute to the perpetuation of their condition of misery and dejection. The state therefore cannot limit itself to the merely negative function of the defense of liberty. It must become active, on behalf of everybody, for the welfare of *the people*. It must intervene, when necessary, in order to improve the material, intellectual, and moral conditions of the masses; it must find work for the unemployed, instruct and educate the people, and care for health and hygiene. For if the purpose of society and of the state is the welfare of individuals, and if it is just that these individuals themselves control the attainment of their ends, it becomes difficult to understand why liberalism should not go the whole distance, why it should see fit to distinguish certain individuals from the rest of the mass, and why the functions of the people should be restricted to the exercise of a mere check. Therefore the state, if it exists for *all*, must be governed by all and not by a small minority; if the state is for the people, sovereignty must reside in the people; if all individuals have the right to govern the state, liberty is no longer sufficient, *equality* must be added; and if sovereignty is vested in the people, the people must wield *all* sovereignty and not merely a part of it. The power to check and *curb the government* is not sufficient. The people must be the government. Thus, logically developed, liberalism leads to democracy, for democracy contains the promises of liberalism but oversteps its limitations in that it makes the action of the state positive, proclaims the equality of all citizens through the dogma of *popular sovereignty*. Democracy therefore necessarily implies a *republican* form of government even though at times, for reasons of expediency, it temporarily adjusts itself to a monarchical regime.

Once started on this downward grade of logical deductions it was inevitable that this atomistic theory of state and society should pass on to a more advanced position. Great industrial developments and the existence of a huge mass of working men, as yet badly treated and in a condition of semiservitude, possibly endurable in a regime of domestic industry, became intolerable after the Industrial Revolution. Hence a state of affairs that toward the middle of the last century appeared to be both cruel and threatening. It was therefore natural that the following question be raised: "If the state is created for the welfare of its citizens, severally considered, how can it tolerate an economic system that divides the population into a small minority of exploiters, the capitalists, on one side, and an immense multitude of exploited, the working people, on the other?" No! The state must again intervene and give rise to a different and less iniquitous economic organization by abolishing private property, by assuming direct control of all production, and by organizing it in such a way that the products of labor be distributed solely among those who create them, namely, the working classes. Hence we find socialism, with its new economic organization of society, abolishing private ownership of capital and of the instruments and means of production, socializing the product, suppressing the extra profit of capital, and turning over to the working class the entire output of the productive processes. It is evident that socialism contains and surpasses democracy in the same way that democracy comprises and surpasses liberalism, being a more advanced development of the same fundamental concept. Socialism in its turn generates the still more extreme doctrine of Bolshevism, which demands the violent suppression of the holders of capital, the dictatorship of the proletariat, as means for a fairer economic organization of society and for the rescue of the laboring classes from capitalistic exploitation.

Thus liberalism, democracy, and socialism appear to be, as they are in reality, not only the offspring of one and the same theory of government but also logical derivations one of the other. Logically developed liberalism leads to democracy; the logical development of democracy issues into socialism. It is true that for many years, and with some justification, socialism was looked upon as antithetical to liberalism. But the antithesis is purely relative and breaks down as we approach the common origin and foundation of the two doctrines, for we find that the opposition is one of *method,* not of *purpose.* The end is the same for both, namely, the welfare of the individual members of society. The difference lies in the fact that liberalism would be guided to its goal by *liberty,* whereas socialism strives to attain it by the *collective organization* of production. There is therefore no antithesis or even a divergence as to the nature and scope of the state and the relation of indivduals to society. There is only a difference of evaluation of the means for bringing about these ends and establishing these relations, which difference depends entirely on the different economic conditions that prevailed at the time when the various doctrines were formulated. Liberalism arose and began to thrive in the period of small industry; socialism grew with the rise of industrialism and of worldwide capitalism. The dissension therefore between these two points of view, or the antithesis, if we wish so to call it, is limited to the economic field. Socialism is at odds with liberalism only on the question of the organization of production and of the division of wealth. In religious, intellectual, and moral matters it is liberal, as it is liberal and democratic in its politics. Even the antiliberalism and antidemocracy of bolshevism are in themselves purely contingent. For bolshevism is opposed to liberalism only insofar as the former is revolutionary, not in its socialistic aspect. For if the opposition of the bolsheviks to liberal and democratic doctrines were to continue, as now seems more and more probable, the result might be a complete break between bolshevism and socialism, notwithstanding the fact that the ultimate aims of both are identical.

Fascism as an Integral Doctrine of Sociality Antithetical to the Atomism of Liberal, Democratic, and Socialistic Theories

The true antithesis, not to this or that manifestation of the liberal-democratic-socialistic conception of the state but to the concept itself, is to be found in the doctrine of fascism. For while the disagreement between liberalism and democracy and between liberalism and socialism lies in a difference of method, as we have said, the rift between socialism, democracy, and liberalism on one side and fascism on the other is caused by a difference in concept. As a matter of fact, fascism never raises the question of *methods,* using in its political praxis now liberal ways, now democratic means, and at times even socialistic devices. This indifference to method often exposes fascism to the charge of incoherence on the part of superficial observers who do not see that what counts with us is the *end* and that therefore even when we employ the same means we act with a radically different *spiritial attitude* and strive for entirely different results. The fascist concept, then, of the nation, of the scope of the state, and of the relations obtaining between society and its individual components rejects entirely the doctrine that I said proceeded from the theories of natural law developed in the course of the sixteenth, seventeenth, and eighteenth centuries and that form the basis of the liberal, democratic, and socialistic ideology.

I shall not try here to expound this doctrine but shall limit myself to a brief summary of its fundamental concepts.

Man—the political animal—according to the definition of Aristotle, lives and must live in society. A human being outside the pale of society is an inconceivable thing—a nonman. Humankind in its entirety lives in social groups that are still today very numerous and diverse, varying in importance and organization from the tribes of Central Africa to the great Western empires. These various societies are fractions of the human species, each one of them endowed with a unified organization. And as there is no unique organization of the human species, there is not "one" but there are "several" human societies. Humanity therefore exists solely as a biological concept, not as a social one.

Each society, on the other hand, exists in the unity of both its biological and its social contents. Socially considered it is a *fraction of the human species endowed with unity of organization for the attainment of the peculiar ends of the species.*

This definition brings out all the elements of the social phenomenon and not merely those relating to the preservation and perpetuation of the species. For man is not solely matter; and the ends of the human species, far from being the materialistic ones we have in common with other animals, are, rather, and predominantly, the spiritual finalities that are peculiar to man and that every form of society strives to attain as well as its stage of social development allows. Thus the organization of every social group is more or less pervaded by the spiritual influxes of unity of language, of culture, of religion, of tradition, of customs, and in general of feeling and of volition, which are as essential as the material elements: unity of economic interests, of living conditions, and of territory. The definition given above demonstrates another truth that has been ignored by the political doctrines that for the last four centuries have been the foundations of political systems, namely, that the social concept has a biological aspect, because social groups are fractions of the human species, each one possessing a peculiar organization, a particular rank in the development of civilization with certain needs and appropriate ends, in short, a life that is really its own. If social groups are then fractions of the human species, they must possess the same fundamental traits of the human species, which means that they must be considered as a succession of generations and not as a collection of individuals.

It is evident, therefore, that as the human species is not the total of the living human beings of the world, so the various social groups that compose it are not the sum of the several individuals that at a given moment belong to it but, rather, the infinite series of the past, present, and future generations constituting it. And as the ends of the human species are not those of the several individuals living at a certain moment, being occasionally in direct opposition to them, so the ends of the various social groups are not necessarily those of the individuals that belong to the groups but may even possibly be in conflict with such ends, as one sees clearly whenever the preservation and the development of the species demand the sacrifice of the individual, to wit, in times of war.

Fascism replaces, therefore, the old atomistic and mechanical state theory that was at the basis of the liberal and democratic doctrines with an organic and historic concept. When I say organic I do not wish to convey the impression that I consider society as an organism after the manner of the so-called organic theories of the state but rather to indicate that the social groups as fractions of the species receive thereby a life and scope that transcend the scope and life of the individuals identifying themselves with the history and finalities of the uninterrupted series of generations. It is irrelevant in this connection to determine whether social groups, considered as fractions of the species, constitute organisms. The important thing is to ascertain that this organic concept of the state gives to society a continuous life over and beyond the existence of the several individuals.

The relations, therefore, between state and citizens are completely reversed by the fascist doctrine. Instead of the liberal-democratic formula, "society for the individual," we have "individuals for society" with this difference, however: that while the liberal doctrines eliminated society, fascism does not submerge the individual in the social group. It subordinates him but does not eliminate him, the individual as a part of his generation ever remaining an element of society however transient and insignificant he may be. Moreover, the development of individuals in each generation, when coordinated and harmonized, conditions the development and prosperity of the entire social unit.

At this juncture the antithesis between the two theories must appear complete and absolute. Liberalism, democracy, and socialism look upon social groups as aggregates of living individuals; for fascism they are the recapitulating unity of the indefinite series of generations. For liberalism, society has no purposes other than those of the members living at a given moment. For fascism, society has historical and immanent ends of preservation, expansion, improvement, quite distinct from those of the individuals that at a given moment compose it, so distinct in fact that they may even be in opposition. Hence the necessity, for which the older doctrines make little allowance, of sacrifice, even up to the total immolation of individuals, on behalf of society; hence the true explanation of war, eternal law of mankind, interpreted by the liberal-democratic doctrines as a degenerate absurdity or as a maddened monstrosity.

For liberalism, society has no life distinct from the life of the individuals, or, as the phrase goes, *solvitur in singularitates.* For fascism, the life of society overlaps the existence of individuals and projects itself into the succeeding generations through centuries and millennia. Individuals come into being, grow, and die, followed by others, unceasingly; social unity remains always identical to itself. For liberalism, the individual is the end and society the means; nor is it conceivable that the individual, considered in the dignity of an ultimate finality, be lowered to mere instrumentality. For fascism, society is the end, individuals the means, and its whole life consists in using the individuals as instruments for its social ends. The state, therefore, guards and protects the welfare and development of individuals not for their exclusive interest but because of the identity of the needs of individuals with those of society as a whole. We can thus accept and explain institutions and practices that, like the death penalty, are condemned by liberalism in the name of the preeminence of individualism.

The fundamental problem of society in the old doctrines is the question of the rights of individuals. It may be the right to freedom as the liberals would have it, or the right to the government of the commonwealth as the democrats claim it, or the right to economic justice as the socialists contend, but in every case it is the right of individuals or groups of individuals (classes). Fascism, on the other hand, faces squarely the problem of the right of the state and of the duty of individuals. Individual rights are only recognized insofar as they are implied in the rights of the state. In this preeminence of duty we find the highest ethical value of fascism.

The Problems of Liberty, of Government, and of Social Justice in the Political Doctrine of Fascism

This, however, does not mean that the problems raised by the other ideologies are ignored by fascism. It means simply that it faces them and solves them differently, as, for example, the problem of liberty.

There is a liberal theory of freedom, and there is a fascist concept of liberty. For we, too, maintain the necessity of safeguarding the conditions that make for the free development of the individual; we, too, believe that the oppression or annihilation [*un annullamento o una mortificazione*] of individual personality can find no place in the modern state. We do not, however, accept a bill of rights that tends to make the individual superior to the state and to empower him to act in opposition to society. Our concept of liberty is that the individual must be allowed to develop his personality on behalf of the state, for these ephemeral and infinitesimal elements of the complex and permanent life of society determine by their normal growth the development of the state. But this individual growth must be normal. A huge and disproportionate development of the individual or of classes would prove as fatal to society as abnormal growths are to living organisms. Freedom, therefore, is due to the citizen and to classes on the condition that they exercise it in the interest of society as a whole and within the limits set by social exigencies, liberty being, like any other individual right, a concession of the state.

What I say concerning civil liberties applies to economic freedom as well. Fascism does not look upon the doctrine of economic liberty as an absolute dogma. It does not refer economic problems to individual needs, to individual interest, to individual solutions. On the contrary, it considers economic development, and especially the production of wealth, as an eminently social concern, wealth being for society an essential element of power and prosperity. But fascism maintains that in the ordinary run of events economic liberty serves the social purposes best; that it is profitable to entrust to individual initiative the task of economic development both as to production and as to distribution; that in the economic world individual ambition is the most effective means for obtaining the best social results with the least effort. Therefore, on the question also of economic liberty the fascists differ fundamentally from the liberals; the latter see in liberty a principle, the fascists accept it as a method. By the liberals, freedom is recognized in the interest of the citizens; the fascists grant it in the interest of society. In other terms, fascists make of the individual an economic instrument for the advancement of society, an instrument that they use so long as it functions and that they subordinate when no longer serviceable. In this guise fascism solves the eternal problem of economic freedom and of state interference, considering both as mere methods that may or may not be employed in accordance with the social needs of the moment.

What I have said concerning political and economic liberalism applies also to democracy. The latter envisages fundamentally the problem of sovereignty; fascism does also, but in an entirely different manner. Democracy vests sovereignty in the people, that it to say, in the mass of human beings. Fascism discovers sovereignty to be inherent in society when it is juridically organized as a state. Democracy, therefore, turns over the government of the state to the multitude of living men that they may use it to further their own interests; fascism insists that the government be entrusted to men capable of rising above their own private interests and of realizing the aspirations of the social collectivity, considered in its unity and in its relation to the past and future. Fascism, therefore, not only rejects the dogma of popular sovereignty and substitutes for it that of state sovereignty, but it also proclaims that the great mass of citizens is not a suitable advocate of social interests for the reason that the capacity to ignore individual private interests in favor of the higher demands of society and of history is a very rare gift and the privilege of the chosen few. Natural intelligence and cultural preparation are of great service in such tasks. Still more valuable perhaps is the intuitiveness of rare great minds, their traditionalism [*la tradizione*] and their inherited qualities. This must not, however, be construed to mean that the masses are not to be allowed to exercise any influence on the life of the state. On the contrary, among peoples with a great history and with noble traditions, even the lowest elements of society possess an instinctive discernment of what is necessary for the welfare of the race that in moments of great historical crises reveals itself to be almost infallible. It is therefore as wise to afford to this instinct the means of declaring itself as it is judicious to entrust the normal control of the commonwealth to a selected elite.

As for socialism, the fascist doctrine frankly recognizes that the problem raised by it as to the relations between capital and labor is a very serious one, perhaps the central one of modern life. What fascism does not countenance is the collectivistic solution proposed by the socialists. The chief defect of the socialistic method has been clearly demonstrated by the experience of the last few years. It does not take into account human nature, it is therefore outside of reality, in that it will not recognize that the most powerful spring of human activities lies in individual self-interest and that therefore the elimination from the economic field of this interest results in complete paralysis. The suppression of private ownership of capital carries with it the suppression of capital itself, for capital is formed by savings, and no one will want to save but will rather consume all he makes if he knows he cannot keep and hand down to his heirs the results of his labors. The dispersion of capital means the end of production since capital, no matter who owns it, is always an indispensable tool of production. Collective organization of production is followed therefore by the paralysis of production since, by eliminating from the productive mechanism the incentive of individual interest, the product becomes rarer and more costly. Socialism, then, as experience has shown, leads to increase in consumption, to the dispersions of capital, and therefore to poverty. Of what avail is it, then, to build a social machine that will more justly distribute wealth if this very wealth is destroyed by the construction of this machine? Socialism committed an irreparable error when it made of private property a matter of justice while in truth it is a problem of social utility. The recognition of individual property rights, then, is a part of the fascist doctrine not because of its individual bearing but because of its social utility.

We must reject, therefore, the socialistic solution, but we cannot allow the problem raised by the socialists to go unsolved, not only because justice demands a solution but also because the persistence of this problem in liberal and democratic regimes has been a menace to public order and to the authority of the state. Unlimited and unrestrained class self-defense, evinced by strikes and lockouts, by boycotts and sabotage, leads inevitably to anarchy. The fascist doctrine, enacting justice among the classes in compliance with a fundamental necessity of modern life, does away with class self-defense, which, like individual self-defense in the days of barbarism, is a source of disorder and of civil war.

Having reduced the problem to these terms, only one solution is possible, the realization of justice among the classes by and through the state. Centuries ago the state, as the specific organ of justice, abolished personal self-defense in individual controversies and substituted for it state justice. The time has now come when class self-defense also must be replaced by state justice. To facilitate the change fascism has created its own syndicalism. The suppression of class self-defense does not mean the suppression of class defense, which is an inalienable necessity of modern economic life. Class organization is a fact that cannot be ignored, but it must be controlled, disciplined, and subordinated by the state. The labor union, instead of being, as formerly, an organ of extralegal defense, must be turned into an organ of legal defense that will become judicial defense as soon as labor conflicts become a matter of judicial settlement. Fascism, therefore, has transformed the labor union, that old revolutionary instrument of syndicalistic socialists, into an instrument of legal defense of the classes both within and without the law courts. This solution may encounter obstacles in its development (the obstacles of malevolence, of suspicion of the untried, of erroneous calculation, etc.), but it is destined to triumph even though it must advance through progressive stages.

Historical Value of the Doctrine of Fascism

I might carry this analysis further, but what I have already said is sufficient to show that the rise of a fascist ideology already gives evidence of an upheaval in the intellectual field as powerful as the change that was brought about in the seventeenth and eighteenth centuries by the rise and diffusion of those doctrines of *ius naturale* that go under the name of "philosophy of the French Revolution." The philosophy of the French Revolution formulated certain principles, the authority of which, unquestioned for a century and a half, seemed so final that they were given the attribute of immortality. The influence of these principles was so great that they determined the formation of a new culture, of a new civilization. Likewise, the fervor of the ideas that go to make up the fascist doctrine, now in its inception but destined to spread rapidly, will determine the course of a new culture and of a new conception of civil life. The deliverance of the individual from the state carried out in the eighteenth century will be followed in the twentieth century by the rescue of the state from the individual. The period of authority, of social obligations, of "hierarchical" subordination will succeed the period of individualism, of state feebleness, of insubordination.

This innovating trend is not and cannot mark a return to the Middle Ages. It is a common but erroneous belief that the movement, started by the Reformation and heightened by the French Revolution, was directed against medieval ideas and institutions. Rather than as a negation, this movement should be looked upon as the development and fulfillment of the doctrines and practices of the Middle Ages. Socially and politically considered, the Middle Ages wrought disintegration and anarchy; they were characterized by the gradual weakening and ultimate extinction of the state, embodied in the Roman Empire, driven first to the East, then back to France, thence to Germany, a shadow of its former self; they were marked by the steady advance of the focus of usurpation, destructive of the state and reciprocally obnoxious; they bore the imprint of a triumphant particularism. Therefore, the individualistic and antisocial movement of the seventeenth and eighteenth centuries was not directed against the Middle Ages but rather against the restoration of the state by great national monarchies. If this movement destroyed medieval institutions that had survived the Middle Ages and had been grafted upon the new states, it was as a consequence of the struggle primarily waged against the state. The spirit of the movement was decidedly medieval. The novelty consisted in the social surroundings in which it operated and in its relation to new economic developments. The individualism of the feudal lords, the particularism of the cities and of the guilds had been replaced by the individualism and the particularism of the bourgeoisie and of the popular classes.

The fascist ideology cannot therefore look back to the Middle Ages, of which it is a complete negation. The Middle Ages spell disintegration; fascism is nothing if not sociality. It is if anything the beginning of the end of the Middle Ages prolonged four centuries beyond the end ordinarily set for them and revived by the social democratic anarchy of the past thirty years. If fascism can be said to look back at all it is rather in the direction of ancient Rome, whose social and political traditions at the distance of fifteen centuries are being revived by fascist Italy.

I am fully aware that the value of fascism, as an intellectual movement, baffles the minds of many of its followers and supporters and is denied outright by its enemies. There is no malice in this denial, as I see it, but rather an incapacity to comprehend. The liberal-democratic-socialistic ideology has so completely and for so long a time dominated Italian culture that in the minds of the majority of people trained by it, it has assumed the value of an absolute truth, almost the authority of a natural law. Every faculty of self-criticism is suppressed in the minds, and this suppression entails an incapacity for understanding that time alone can change. It will be advisable, therefore, to rely mainly upon the new generations and in general upon persons whose culture is not already fixed. This difficulty to comprehend on the part of those who have been thoroughly grounded by a different preparation in the political and social sciences explains in part why fascism has not been wholly successful with the intellectual classes and with mature minds, and why, on the other hand, it has been very successful with young people, with women, in rural districts, and among men of action unencumbered by a fixed and set social and political education. Fascism, moreover, as a cultural movement is just now taking its first steps. As in the case with all great movements, action regularly outstrips thought. It was thus at the time of the Protestant Reformation and of the individualistic reaction of the seventeenth and eighteenth centuries. The English revolution occurred when the doctrines of natural law were coming into being, and the theoretical development of the liberal and democratic theories followed the French Revolution.

At this point it will not be very difficult to assign a fitting place in history to this great trend of thought that is called fascism and that, in spite of the initial difficulties, already gives clear indication of the magnitude of its developments.

The liberal-democratic speculation both in its origin and in the manner of its development appears to be essentially a non-Italian (that is, a German, French, and English) formation. Its connection with the Middle Ages already shows it to be foreign to the Latin mind, the medieval disintegration being the result of the triumph of Germanic individualism over the political mentality of the Romans. The barbarians, boring from within and hacking from without, pulled down the great political structure raised by Latin genius and put nothing in its place. Anarchy lasted eight centuries, during which time only one institution survived and that a Roman one—the Catholic Church. But as soon as the laborious process of reconstruction was started with the constitution of the great national states backed by the Roman Church, the Protestant Reformation set in, followed by the individualistic currents of the seventeenth and eighteenth centuries, and the process of disintegration was started anew. This antistate tendency was the expression of the Germanic spirit, and it therefore became predominant among the Germanic peoples and wherever Germanism had left a deep imprint even if afterward superficially covered by a veneer of Latin culture. It is true that Marsilius of Padua is an Italian writing for Ludwig the Bavarian, but the other writers who in the fourteenth century appear as forerunners of the liberal doctrines are not Italians: Ockham and Wycliff are English; Oresme is French.[2] Among the advocates of individualism in the sixteenth century who prepared the way for the triumph of the doctrines of natural law in the subsequent centuries, Hotman and Languet are French, Buchanan is Scotch.[3] Of the great authorities of natural law, Grotius and Spinoza are Dutch; Locke is English; l'Abbé de St. Pierre, Montesquieu, d'Argenson, Voltaire, Rousseau, Diderot, and the encyclopedists are French; Althusius, Pufendorf, Kant, Fichte are German.[4]

Italy took no part in the rise and development of the doctrines of natural law. Only in the nineteenth century did she evince a tardy interest in these doctrines, just as she tardily contributed to them at the close of the eighteenth century through the works of Beccaria and Filangeri.[5]

While therefore in other countries such as France, England, Germany, and Holland the general tradition in the social and political sciences worked on behalf of antistate individualism and therefore of liberal and democratic doctrines, Italy, on the other hand, clung to the powerful legacy of its past in virtue of which she proclaims the rights of the state, the preeminence of its authority, and the superiority of its ends. The very fact that Italian political doctrine in the Middle Ages linked itself with the great political writers of antiquity, Plato and Aristotle, who in a different manner but with equal firmness advocated a strong state and the subordination of individuals to it, is a sufficient index of the orientation of political philosophy in Italy. We all know how thorough and crushing the authority of Aristotle was in the Middle Ages. But for Aristotle the spiritual cement of the state is "virtue," not absolute virtue but political virtue, which is social devotion. His state is made up solely of its citizens, the citizens being either those who defend it with their arms or who govern it as magistrates. All others who provide it with the materials and services it needs are not citizens. They become such only in the corrupt forms of certain democracies. Society is therefore divided into two classes, the free men or citizens, who give their time to noble and virtuous occupations and who profess their subjection to the state, and the laborers and slaves, who work for the maintenance of the former. No man in this scheme is his own master. The slaves belong to the freemen, and the freemen belong to the state.

It was therefore natural that St. Thomas Aquinas, the greatest political writer of the Middle Ages, should emphasize the necessity of unity in the political field, the harm of plurality of rulers, the dangers and damaging effects of demagogy. The good of the state, says St. Thomas Aquinas, is unity. And who can procure unity more fittingly than he who is himself one? Moreover, the government must follow, as far as possible, the course of nature, and in nature power is always one. In the physical body only one organ is dominant — the heart; in the spirit only one faculty has sway — reason. Bees have one sole ruler; and the entire universe one sole sovereign — God. Experience shows that countries that are ruled by many perish because of discord while those that are ruled over by one enjoy peace, justice, and plenty. The states that are not ruled by one are troubled by dissensions and toil unceasingly. On the contrary, states that are ruled over by one king enjoy peace, thrive in justice, and are gladdened by affluence. The rule of the multitudes cannot be sanctioned, for where the crowd rules it oppresses the rich as would a tyrant.

Italy in the Middle Ages presented a curious phenomenon: while in practice the authority of the state was being dissolved into a multiplicity of competing sovereignties, the theory of state unity and authority was kept alive in the minds of thinkers by the memories of the Roman imperial tradition. It was this memory that supported for centuries the fiction of the universal Roman Empire when in reality it existed no longer. Dante's *De Monarchia* deduced the theory of this empire conceived as the unity of a strong state. "It is best, whenever possible, for something to be carried out by one single means rather than by several," he says in the fourteenth chapter of the first book, and further on, considering the citizen as an instrument for the attainment of the ends of the state, he concludes that the individual must sacrifice himself for his country: "If the part should sacrifice itself for the sake of the whole, and man is a member of his community . . . then a man should be ready to sacrifice himself for his fatherland."[6]

The Roman tradition, which was one of practice but not of theories—for Rome constructed the most solid state known to history with extraordinary statesmanship but with hardly any political writings—influenced considerably the founder of modern political science, Nicolo Machiavelli, who was himself in truth not a creator of doctrines but a keen observer of human nature who derived from the study of history practical maxims of political import. He freed the science of politics from the formalism of the scholastics and brought it close to concrete reality. His writings, an inexhaustible mine of practical remarks and precious observations, reveal dominant in him the state idea, no longer abstract but in the full historical concreteness of the national unity of Italy. Machiavelli, therefore, is not only the greatest of modern political writers, he is also the greatest of our countrymen in full possession of a national Italian consciousness. To liberate Italy, which was in his day "enslaved, torn and pillaged," and to make her more powerful, he would use any means, for to his mind the holiness of the end justified them completely. In this he was sharply rebuked by foreigners, who were not as hostile to his means as they were fearful of the end that he propounded. He advocated, therefore, the constitution of a strong Italian state, supported by the sacrifices and by the blood of the citizens, not defended by mercenary troops, well-ordered internally, aggressive, and bent on expansion. "Weak republics," he said, "have no determination and can never reach a decision."[7] "Weak states were ever dubious in choosing their course, and slow deliberations are always harmful."[8] And again: "Who so undertakes to govern a multitude either in a regime of liberty or in a monarchy without previously making sure of those who are hostile to the new order of things builds a short-lived state."[9] And further on, "the dictatorial authority helped and did not harm the Roman republic," and "kings and republics lacking in national troops both for offense and defense should be ashamed of their existence,"[10] And again: "Money not only does not protect you but rather it exposes you to plundering assaults. Nor can there be a more false opinion than that which says that money is the sinews of war. Not money but good soliders win battles."[11] "The country must be defended with ignominy or with glory and in either way it is nobly defended."[12] "And with dash and boldness people often capture what they never would have obtained by ordinary means."[13] Machiavelli was not only a great political authority, he taught the mastery of energy and will. Fascism learns from him not only its doctrines but its action as well.

Different from Machiavelli's, in mental attitude, in cultural preparation, and in manner of presentation, G. B. Vico must yet be connected with the great Florentine from whom in a certain way he seems to proceed. In the heyday of "natural law" Vico is decidedly opposed to *ius naturale,* and in his attacks against its advocates, Grotius, Seldenus, and Pufendorf he systematically assails the abstract, rationalistic, and utilitarian principles of the eighteenth century.[14] As a recent scholar correctly states:

> While the "natural jurists," basing justice and state on utility and interest and grounding human certitude on reason, were striving to draft permanent codes and construct the perfect state, Vico strongly asserted the social nature of man, the ethical character of the juridical consciousness, and its growth through the history of humanity rather than in sacred history. Vico therefore maintains that doctrines must begin with those subjects that take up and explain the entire course of civilization. Experience and not ratiocination, history and not reason must help human wisdom to understand the civil and political regimes that were the result not of reason or philosophy but rather of common sense, or if you will of the social consciousness of man,

and farther on,

> to Vico we owe the conception of history in its fullest sense as teacher of life, the search after the humanity of history, the principle that makes the truth progress with time, the discovery of the political "course" of nations. It is Vico who uttered the eulogy of the patrician "heroic hearts" of the first founders of states, magnanimous defenders of the commonwealth and wise counsellors of politics. To Vico we owe the criticism of democracies, the affirmation of their brief existence, of their rapid disintegration at the hands of factions and demagogues, of their lapse first into anarchy, then into monarchy, when their degradation does not make them a prey of foreign oppressors. Vico conceived of civil liberty as subjection to law, as just subordination, of the private to the public interests, to the sway of the state. It was Vico who sketched modern society as a world of nations, each one guarding its own empire, fighting just and not inhuman wars. In Vico, therefore, we find the condemnation of pacifism, the assertion that right is actualized by bodily force, that without force, right is of no

avail, and that therefore "he who cannot defend himself against injury is enslaved."[15]

It is not difficult to discern the analogies between these affirmations and the fundamental views and the spirit of fascism. Nor should we marvel at this similarity. Fascism, a strictly Italian phenomenon, has its roots in the Risorgimento, and the Risorgimento was influenced undoubtedly by Vico.

It would be inexact to affirm that the philosophy of Vico dominated the Risorgimento. Too many elements of German, French, and English civilizations had been added to our culture during the first half of the nineteenth century to make this possible, so much so that perhaps Vico might have remained unknown to the makers of Italian unity if another powerful mind from southern Italy, Vincenzo Cuoco, had not taken it upon himself to expound the philosophy of Vico in those very days in which the intellectual preparation of the Risorgimento was being carried on.

An adequate account of Cuoco's doctrines would carry me too far afield. The author of the article quoted above gives them considerable attention. He quotes among other things Cuoco's arraignment of democracy: "Italy has fared badly at the hand of democracy, which has withered to their roots the three sacred plants of liberty, unity, and independence. If we wish to see these trees flourish again, let us protect them in the future from democracy."

The influence of Cuoco, an exile at Milan, exerted through his writings, his newspaper articles, and Vichian propaganda, on the Italian patriots is universally recognized. Among the regular readers of his *Giornale Italiano* we find Monti and Foscolo.[16] Clippings of his articles were treasured by Mazzini, and Manzoni, who often acted as his secretary, called him his "master in politics."

The influence of the Italian tradition summed up and handed down by Cuoco was felt by Mazzini, whose interpretation of the function of the citizen as duty and *mission* is to be connected with Vico's doctrine rather than with the philosophic and political doctrines of the French Revolution.

"Training for social duty," said Mazzini, "is essentially and logically unitarian. Life for it is but a *duty*, a *mission*. The norm and definition of such mission can only be found in a collective term superior to all the individuals of the country—in the people, in the nation. If there is a collective mission, a communion of duty . . . it can only be represented in the national unity." And farther on: "The declaration of rights, which all constitutions insist on copying slavishly from the French, express only those of the period . . . that considered the individual as the *end* and pointed out only one half of the problem," and again, "assume the existence of one of those crises that threaten the life of the nation and demand the active sacrifice of all its sons . . . will you ask the citizens to face martyrdom in virtue of their rights? You have taught men that society was solely constituted to guarantee *their* rights, and now you ask them to sacrifice one and all, to suffer and *die* for the safety of the 'nation'?"

In Mazzini's conception of the citizen as instrument for the attainment of the nation's ends and therefore submissive to a higher mission, to the duty of supreme sacrifice, we see the anticipation of one of the fundamental points of the fascist doctrine.

Unfortunately, the autonomy of the political thought of Italy, vigorously established in the works of Vico, nobly reclaimed by Vincenzo Cuoco, kept up during the struggles of the Risorgimento in spite of the many foreign influences of that period, seemed to exhaust itself immediately after the unification. Italian political thought, which had been original in times of servitude, became enslaved in the days of freedom.

A powerful innovating movement, issuing from the war and of which fascism is the purest expression, was to restore Italian thought in the sphere of political doctrine to its own traditions, which are the traditions of Rome.

This task of intellectual liberation, now slowly being accomplished, is no less important than the political deliverance brought about by the fascist revolution. It is a great task that continues and completes the Risorgimento; it is now bringing to an end, after the cessation of our political servitude, the intellectual servitude of Italy.

Thanks to it, Italy again speaks to the world, and the world listens to Italy. It is a great task and a great deed, and it demands great efforts. To carry it through, we must, each one of us, free ourselves of the dross of ideas and mental habits that two centuries of foreign intellectualistic tradition have heaped upon us; we must not only take on a new culture but create for ourselves a new soul. We must methodically and patiently contribute something toward the organic and complete elaboration of our doctrine, at the same time supporting it both at home and abroad with untiring devotion. We ask this effort of renovation and collaboration of all fascists, as well as of all who feel themselves to be Italians. After the hour of sacrifice comes the hour of unyielding efforts. To work, then, fellow countrymen, for the glory of Italy!

Translated by Dino Bigongiari in 1926, revised by Jeffrey T. Schnapp

Notes

1. Rocco's list includes Hubert Languet (1518–81), French diplomat and author of *Vindiciae contra tyrannos*; the Scottish humanist and dramaturge George Buchanan (1506–82); the German jurist and advocate of natural law Johannes Althusius (1556–1637); Karl Marx; Woodrow Wilson; and Vladimir Ilyich Lenin.

2. Marsilius of Padua (1270–1342) was the author of the *Defensor pacis* (1324), one of the key political and religious works of the fourteenth century. The work was dedicated to King Louis of Bavaria and set out to prove the supremacy of the Roman emperor's claims over those of the Holy See. The list of writers includes William of Ockham (died 1349), the Franciscan scholastic and critic of the papacy; John Wycliffe (1328–84), the educational reformer and critic of the Church; and Nicholas Oresme (1320–82), the philosopher and translator.

3. The allusion is to François Hotman (1524–90), the French jurist and early critic of absolute monarchy.

4. Rocco's list extends from Hugo Grotius (1583–1645), author of the first codes of international law, to Samuel Pufendorf (1623–94), historian, jurist, and author of *Du droit de la nature et des gens* (1672), which makes the social contract the rational foundation of the state.

5. The jurist Cesare Beccaria (1738–94) was the author of *Dei delitti e delle pene* (1764), a treatise in which he denounced contemporary injustices as well as the recourse to torture and the death penalty. Gaetano Filangeri (1752–88), also a distinguished jurist, was the author of *La scienza della legislazione* (1780), a classic early study of the rules that ought to govern legislation.

6. *De monarchia* 1.14.1, 2.7.2.

7. *Discorsi sopra la prima deca di Tito Livio* 1.38.1.

8. *Discorsi sopra la prima deca di Tito Livio* 2.15.1.

9. *Discorsi sopra la prima deca di Tito Livio* 1.16.12.

10. *Discorsi sopra la prima deca di Tito Livio* 1.34.1, 1.21.2.

11. *Discorsi sopra la prima deca di Tito Livio* 2.10.7–8.

12. *Discorsi sopra la prima deca di Tito Livio* 3.41.1.

13. *Discorsi sopra la prima deca di Tito Livio* 3.44.1.

14. The reference is to John Selden (1584–1654), whom Vico regularly criticizes in his *Scienza nuova*.

15. Rocco attributes the quotation and several subsequent ones to an essay by the contemporary jurist Montemayor published in *Rivista Internazionale di Filosofia del Diritto* 5 (1926): 351, 262, 370.

16. *Giornale Italiano* was perhaps the leading organ of Italian resistance to French occupation during the early years of the nineteenth century. It was indeed read by many leading writers and intellectuals, including the poets Vincenzo Monti (1754–1828) and Ugo Foscolo (1778–1827), and the novelist Alessandro Manzoni (1785–1873).

CHAPTER 10

Fascism, Nationalism, and Reactions (1931) and Fascism, Revolution, and European Nonreaction (1931)

Delio Cantimori

✳

Cantimori (1904–66) was a prominent historian of the first fascist generation and went on to become a very influential postwar historian and a teacher at the Scuola Normale of Pisa. He was the author of numerous studies ranging over such topics as Renaissance humanism and religion, the history of heresy and the Church, international relations, and nineteenth-century socialism. One of the principal Italian interpreters of the writings of the conservative Catholic (and, later, Nazi) political philosopher Carl Schmitt during the 1930s, Cantimori shifted his allegiance to the Communist Party after the war. The following piece, written at the age of twenty-seven for the review Vita Nova, *is indicative of his early view that fascism represents not only a genuinely revolutionary force but also the dialectical synthesis between the political forces of reaction and revolution.*

✳

Fascism, Nationalism, and Reactions

In its astute commentary on Mussolini's speech at Palazzo Venezia, the magazine *Critica Fascista* made the following acute observation:

> If in the past people (as we did not) overstated the importance of nationalism to fascism's character, nowadays one must be cautious in invoking its universality. Nobody, we believe, should delude themselves into thinking that a fascist-style revolutionary movement will sprout up in every country threatened by the same kind of crisis that we overcame between 1919 and 1922. A given context cannot be reproduced, and history does not repeat itself on a daily basis. (1 November 1930)

I seriously doubt that there are politicians or politically engaged individuals among us so unsophisticated that they would be prone to fall into the precise trap described by *Critica Fascista*. This said, the delusion in question is a dangerous one not so much in the realm of actual political events as in the realm of ideas and ideologies. In point of fact, genuine reactionaries or chauvinistic nationalists from various countries often appeal to fascism and call themselves fascists solely on the basis of the equation fascism equals reaction advanced by antifascist propagandists. My task is not to analyze our government's foreign policy, but I must question the confusion of political pacts with a convergence of ideas, of diplomatic support provided by our government for political reasons with sympathies or ideological affinities felt by the entire population. Not only are such confusions unnecessary, but they are also detrimental (because unfascist, which is to say, frivolous), equivocal, and demagogic. One would fall into this trap if one were to accept at face value the protestations of enthusiasm of little known or irresponsible movements and groups whose sole aim is find support for their retrograde nostalgias. Authority, order, and justice are not equivalent to reaction and restoration. The corporative state is not an absolutist or capitalist medieval state, and it openly embraces the freedom of private enterprise. Such enterprise undertaken by a single individual—channeled, naturally, by the state and the nation—cannot be called "enterprise" if it is not free, for, logically speaking, without freedom there is no enterprise. The corporative state is not a state of bureaucrats and white-collar workers, unless one is willing to endow the term "bureaucrat" with such an ample meaning that it coincides with the term "citizen." The fascist order is not the order of Warsaw. For someone accustomed to disorder or temperamentally prone to rebelliousness, it might feel restrictive. But for those who, for reasons of age, are only now starting to become seriously involved in politics, there is no feeling of restriction as they pursue debates and deepen their explorations. Whatever course this new generation wishes to follow is acceptable, because what felt restrictive to its predecessors, it considers a given: the foundation stone upon which one must necessarily build. Authority is recognized in and of itself, that is, as fully aware of itself and of its responsibilities for embodying the very morality that it aims to impose on others. This is why the best of our journalists—foremost among them, those from *Critica Fascista*—are right in insisting that our party leaders carry out the duties that they must impose on others with modesty and seriousness. Because fascism conceives of the party as an aristocracy that must distinguish itself by means of great sacrifice and hard work, as well as via the rigorous fulfillment of all duties, its concept of authority is new. For fascism, freedom is not an abstract right but something to be conquered moment by moment; it provides the means to better an always vigilant selfhood [*miglioramento di sè continuamente vigile*]. It would be useless to hope for or to fear the turning back of the clock (this being impossible, as even children realize). Fascism's vitality shows that it is no throwback to the past, nor is it a defender of outdated ideas and attitudes, derived from a past so distant that it can be romantically idolized by reactionary philo-Catholics, hungry for new forms of nobility and the renewal of absolutism. Negative in their very essence, committed to the renewal of dead institutions, these sorts of groups declare themselves "antimodern" inasmuch as the "modern" designates anything that to them appears corrupt.

An even more pernicious source of confusion is to be found in these groups' claims that they are "revolutionary," claims that must be fought at all costs so as not to create stumbling blocks to our government's own action. This self-definition on the part of various European philo-Catholic and chauvinistic groups relies upon a spurious, fencing-based [*schermistica*] interpretation of history's dialectic and is informed by terminology borrowed from prior party politics and class struggles.[1] They reason in the following manner:

> Parties in power must preserve the power they have achieved with all their might, because it is in their interest to do so. (A purely class-based concept of political struggle and a purely materialistic vision of politics, to say the least!) If these parties wish to preserve their power, they must become conservative irrespective of whether their ideology is liberal. But conservatism entails the adoption of a defensive stance: a loser's stance whether in a fencing match or a parliamentary battle! Since victory is essential, better to call ourselves revolutionary and our enemies conservative. Our victory then becomes certain because we are in the opposition, which is to say, on the attack. Moreover, our enemies are obliged to grant us the freedom to oppose them (even if we would never reciprocate), because, if they do not, they will violate their own principles. In the end, we will bring the opposition-conservation cycle to a close and usher in a new age.

Tactically speaking, their logic is unimpeachable. But it is devoid of any ideal or ideological content. It is reducible to the old maxim that "opponents take advantage of those who are discontented." It also helps us to understand why the old parties' and ruling elite's adoption of the principle of "blessed be all owners" [*beati possidentes*] ends up proving the reactionary circles right.

It is obvious, then, that these reactionary circles don the mask of revolutionism for reasons of pure demagoguery (or, if you will, for didactic or propagandistic purposes). They do so while remaining fully aware of their true character and goals. Close observation suggests that their objectives range from the pure and simple repression of what true revolutionaries have laboriously obtained, to the restoration either of the absolute monarchy or of the Germanic nation of the Holy Roman Empire or of the Catholic Europe of bygone days (dreamed of by Novalis), and so on and so forth. Which is to say, they advocate Bourbonism and Austrianism. They dub themselves "realists" because they are skeptical aesthetes. They dub themselves "aristocrats" because they think that they are in tune with the latest trends in the nobility's thought.

It is perfectly clear that all this has nothing to do with fascism. Fascism is not communism, and, despite its fundamental unity, one finds a wide range of attitudes among its followers, including some that are reactionary. Calling fascism reactionary on the basis of the presence of reactionaries within its fold is about as useful as calling it Einsteinian on the grounds that there are fascists who are followers of Einstein. It is useless to dwell on this point: every fascist who remains faithful to his oath of allegiance and who is ready to obey his leaders' orders is free to develop and assert his own views, as well as to debate those of others. However superfluous it may seem to restate the obvious, we must beware of the (at the very least) erroneous tendency to automatically identify one's convictions with those of the government and of the government's chief. Certain reactionary groups, especially the most chauvinistic ones, seem to consider fascism not as the wholly human and historical movement/party that it was. Rather, they choose to view fascism as an agent of divine providence, sent from on high by superhuman or supernatural powers to liberate them from those irritating modern individuals who still harbor the perverse idea that they are men, not serfs: men capable of thinking and not simply of repeating dogmas; men endowed with dignity as workers and as citizens that is not dependent upon paternalistic concessions made by those who are sublimely privileged whether due to birthright, self-delusion, wealth, or acquired status. Were circumstances to change, the chauvinists are always ready to abjure fascism, to mock it, even to fight it. (For a case in point, consider the stance adopted by French nationalists toward Italy.)

The nationalism espoused by foreign pseudofascist reactionary groups is another element that contributes to misunderstandings, since the creation of a national consciousness [coscienza] is one of the main goals of fascist action. There is no point in rehearsing the obvious differences between the political ideals of nationalism and those of fascism. The fascist struggle to forge a national consciousness has as little to do with the cult of Camelot

[*Camelot du roi*] as its conception of the state has to do with communist collectivism. The words of *Critica Fascista* are apposite, since the aim of this essay is not to delineate a tendency so much as to clarify some basic facts:

> Fascist Italy must not be confused with warmongering Germany of Wilhelm II, because neither will we ever view war as an end in itself *nor will we ever be able to restrict our spirit within the nation's narrow boundaries. For us, the nation is a necessary premise and starting point for expansion. And expansion means not so much territorial conquest as spiritual and political conquest.*

This stance leads to the conviction that "the necessity of a European union has never been felt as much as today, and yet it has never been more difficult to bring it about" ("Toward Europe," *Critica Fascista*, 15 August 1930). Even clearer are the words of Camillo Pellizzi, who likes to express important truths in the form of extravagant paradoxes . . . : "if we stop to consider a map (on which Italy is printed in green) and get lost in calculations regarding the future greening of this or that piece of turf, then we are no better than the polite, Protestant merchants of Northern Europe, who invented and implemented nationalism out of whole cloth (while the Latins theorized it)" (*L'Italiano*, 15 August 1930). It might appear that Pellizzi's poking fun at others is meant to soften his condemnation of nationalism or to chastise their bad habits with laughter. But a few years back he expressed his views more openly:

> At stake is determining if and how the nation as concept should constitute one of the inspiring and propelling principles of fascism. *I believe that it should not.* My thesis is that the national principle is based on an empirical myth or pseudoconcept, endowed with a contingent value . . . In the fascist era it is no longer the nation that should move us, but rather the nation itself that must move toward the fascist idea of state and of empire. (*Vita Nova*, 1927)

This is to say that there is no inherent connection between chauvinist nationalism and fascism. The former, as revealed by demagogic actions outside of Italy, is racist in origin and reactionary from an ideological standpoint. Fascism, on the contrary, pursues serious revolutionary ends, advocates the corporative state, and works toward the elimination of all residues of the past, from Bourbonism to the clerical/anticlerical antinomy. Fascism is not self-enclosed. It is European and puts itself forward as European. And it does so wholeheartedly: not in order to champion some new Holy

Alliance and Restoration but rather in the name of a new revolution that will triumph over the modern materialist plutocracy.

The challenge is not just to differentiate nationalism from fascism (because everyone is aware that fascism absorbed many nationalist forces and that the process of absorption proved that one was not reducible to the other). The deeper challenge lies in coming to grips with other movements: movements that *define themselves* as fascist and that, though fascist *in part*, are *first and foremost* nationalist; movements entirely lacking in universal ambitions. . . . In such cases, political and tactical advantages can sometimes be gained by uniting against common enemies. But this means keeping one's distance when it comes to common ideals. Nobody is so naive as to believe other people's pleasantries, even when fighting side by side. Uniting against a common adversary, however, can foster delusions, delusions that, in turn, give rise to disappointments. It is not *their* vision of the state that will form the core of the new Young Europe [*Giovine Europa*], it is *ours*.[2]

For this reason, caution must be exercised in granting our friendship and allowing others to defend our flag, even with allies.

At this juncture, one might ask, What then should one make of fascism's claims to universality? The question presupposes that the person asking it is a reactionary or a democrat (which is pretty much the same thing) because the equation fascism equals reaction is a purely antifascist one that has gained credibility only thanks to profascist sympathies expressed by genuine reactionaries like Wilhelm II and various political parties. Such expressions of support have given rise to accusations of philo-Prussianism, philo-Austrianism, and the like: accusations so meaningless and abstract as to persuade only latter-day Romantics. . . . For our belated Romantics, the antithesis between fascism and communism does not involve two *new* movements fighting to conquer an *old* world; rather, it opposes a newness defined as communism to an oldness defined as fascism. The former they view as the latest product of the Reformation and the Renaissance, the Enlightenment and the Romantic movement (much as Mazzini or Hegel viewed the French Revolution as a consequence of Christianity); they identify it with revolution, disorder, freedom (in the bad sense), corruption, dynamism. The latter they instead identify with everything old-fashioned, civilized, and orderly; with *Kultur* as opposed to *Civilization*; with what is static and perfect because motionless, and motionless because immutable like some supernatural creation. According to this scheme, fascism amounts to little more than the antithesis to the communist thesis. Instead of providing a synthesis of all the modern world's most vital elements, it allows for the preservation of abstract dogmas or, at best, for the adaptation or dressing up of tradition as a superhuman, untouchable given. (No thought is given to the possibility that fascism might represent the living legacy of our Risorgimento and the affirmation of a truly new form of life.) Fascism is reduced to conservation and defense. No longer a vehicle for Latinity and a sober fascist rationality, no longer a force of assault and conquest, the fascist spirit is reduced to—the phrases are theirs—a Romantic aestheticism that idolizes fragments from the past.

Clearly, one could choose to be "universal" in this way, but, in so doing, one would cast fascism in a secondary role. Fascism would become a mere reflection of the universality of the "progressive" action carried out by communism. It is self-evident, however, that fascism is action, not reaction. Its universality has nothing to do with Primo de Rivera.[3] . . . It cannot be reduced to our government's successes (attributable to the genius of its leader) or to the defeats suffered by democrats (attributable to their weakness). The latter circumstances do, however, bring into focus fascism's true universality; they foreshadow it by showing our opponents' weakness as well as our strength. No more, no less.

As already stated, fascism's true claim to universality is founded upon the corporative state and upon the general concept of economic life that undergirds it. Let me close as I began, anchoring my words in the more authoritative ones of *Critica Fascista*:

> Our corporative experience provides clear and detailed rules to govern interactions within the web of interference made up by the state, groups, and individuals. A strong state; the integration of all citizens into the corporative order; a reconstituted family unity; and, above all, a new heroic, virile morality, characterized by volunteerism and solidarity: these are some of the measures that will help to solve Europe's crisis.

All this has European, which is to say, universal, applicability, an applicability that contrasts sharply with the plans of those who still worship "the states that existed before 1789 and were founded afterward." The fascist state, in Mussolini's own words, is "quite another thing."

This is the goal toward which we need to work with clarity and a cool head.

✳

Fascism, Revolution, and European Nonreaction

The party's semi-official propaganda has for some time now been stressing fascism's revolutionary character. That highly placed officials and organizations above suspicion should endorse this view is much for the better because a hateful concept of fascism as reaction was gaining ground: a vision of fascism as restorer of a past that will never return (despite the elegance of its ladies, the splendor of its courts, and the solemnity of its priesthood).

I will now offer a clear and detached explanation of these words so as to avoid contributing to the proliferation of misunderstandings that impede fascism's progress in the modern world and play into the hands of political and ideological propagandists. Valid critiques and concepts elaborated in the domain of theory have been transferred to the domain of practice and employed as tools to analyze the actions of our government and regime with deleterious results. Public opinion has become no less disoriented than have foreign readers who wish to understand Italian life from the standpoint of its international implications, particularly in the European context.

The biggest misunderstanding hinges on the much abused term "revolution." For some Romantic spirits, "revolution" is a sort of scarecrow that evokes the massacres and guillotines of 1789. For other Romantic spirits, the term "revolution" provokes excitement and thrills for the very same reason: the promise of violent change, . . . of violent release of one's overflowing forces, of a Jacobin-like destruction of the past that would negate all traditional values in the name of a pure and simple ideal (however vague and abstract).

The recent polemic concerning Catholic Action and the pope's encyclical on fascism offered a sobering spectacle.[4] Writers who until then had been among the fiercest defenders of the altar and had professed an authoritarian, Counter-Reformationist and de Maistre–like brand of Catholicism were suddenly heard proclaiming fascism a revolution. This they did with the sole aim of recycling the usual Jansenist ideas: that the Church must be spiritual, poor, Franciscan, and so on. What these good men forgot is that any revolution whose essence consists in such things is a lousy revolution.

There are still a few people left who conceive of a "revolution" as a total, violent upheaval along French and Russian lines. Their biggest mistake results from an abstract, aestheticized understanding of the term "revolution." They say that a revolution overturns ideals and conditions that are firmly established and commonly accepted (or, rather, they leave this implicit so as not to have to think about what will follow the old order's destruction). In its Marxist/communist version this view prophesies the fatal, necessary, mechanical victory of the proletariat over capitalism on the basis of dialectical reasoning. None of this has anything to do with fascism, nor do its reactionary analogues. Just as chauvinistic nationalists once exploited socialist collectivism in forging their myths, so reactionaries of all stripes now take advantage of the Romantic-aesthetic concept of revolution to dress up their aging, rotting ideologies in revolutionary garb. For many of them, the "revolutionary" character of fascism amounts to little more than an assault—an absurd and disgraceful assault!—on the ideals of the Risorgimento.

Their psychological stance is clear. They recognize that the deference felt for the ideals of the Risorgimento represents a moral and cultural patrimony shared by all patriotic and civilized Italians. Respect and admiration, a civic and moral sense of duty: these are conservative elements, according to their abstract and superficial mind-set. So, if they are to be "revolutionary," it is necessary for them to deny this past, to destroy the idols that stand in their way! At this point they unleash the full brunt of their iconoclastic fury against the Risorgimento, its ideals, and its men. Italy, they maintain (with an astonishing lack of historical and critical insight), is the homeland of the Counter-Reformation, and what came after represents its downfall. Mazzini was either a Protestant or something worse. Cavour's relatives were Calvinists, his mind-set was pro-English, and so on.[5] So, how could the Italian nation possibly succeed given that it was the creation of heretics and excommunicates? . . . Better to borrow one's exemplars of national pride from the Bourbons, whose aim was to secure Sicilian sulfur all for themselves!

Nobody in their right mind would argue against the pursuit of a fair-minded critical understanding of the Bourbon dynasty or of the various Risorgimento-era separatist and particularist movements, any more than anyone would advocate an acritical, wholesale embrace of Risorgimental ideas and ideology. The attempt to pass off fascism as a negation of the Risorgimento or its overcoming—unless "overcoming" means the preservation and vital transformation of its fundamental elements, or unless one counts among these "fundamental elements" peripheral features such as Mazzini's mysticism of the Third Italy and Gioberti's recently defeated neo-Guelphism—and as a proponent of the restoration of the ancien régime is an extremely dangerous mistake.[6] Although the circumstances may vary, the harsh anti-Italianism of the old Austria's clerical or socialist journalists is still targeting the irredentism both of Mazzini followers and of their opponents. Other journalists, with the courtly unctuousness of faithful yet always useless servants, worry about the fate of the Hapsburgs and the good name of the Bourbons, may God bless their souls!

Fascism goes beyond, not against, the Risorgimento. It pursues the same path and embraces the same fundamental ideals. Let the following

be admitted: that in 1930 Italy may not need to resurrect Garibaldi or
Mazzini or Cavour. But even less does it need to resurrect Count Solaro
della Margherita, from whom so many erroneous and pseudocontem-
porary teachings are derived![7] Count Solaro has been cited in the recent
debates over Catholic Action and correctly so when it comes to answering
clerical polemics that view the altar as always threatened and preach that
any curtailment of ecclesiastical authority also curtails the state. But this
citation is, at core, mistaken. It omits mention of the fact that, in its
absolute totalitarianism, the modern state contains nothing that is specifically Catholic. Furthermore, it harks back to a jurisdictional position that
was explicitly and definitively refuted by fascism's own Duce. To make
things worse, a misleading example was appended to the citation of Count
Solaro: that of the Bourbons and their ecclesiastical policy. The example
is meaningless. Which Bourbons are we talking about here? Those of the
eighteenth century? If so, they were deeply embroiled in a jurisdictionally
based, enlightened, and free-thinking Jansenistic fight. Are we talking about
the Bourbons of the Italian restoration? If so, what then of the disastrous
agreement of 1818?[8] Better to leave the dead in peace, especially when they
turn out to be so dangerous! Let us not displace the cult and celebration
of the great men to whom we owe our Risorgimento with a snobbery that
is at once aestheticizing, iconoclastic, and pseudorevolutionary. The less
pleasant features of this cult—Mazzinian sectarianism, liberal moralism of
purportedly Cavourian derivation—vanished long ago. Why then resurrect their reactionary, ridiculous, purely abstract counterparts, given their
irrelevance in the modern world?

The French Revolution was not a true revolution simply because it replaced the tolerance, the critical mind-set, and the individualistic freedoms
that still prevailed in Voltaire's France with fanaticism, intolerance, and
oppression. Nor was the Russian Revolution a great revolution simply
because it resurrected pan-Slavic ideas, replaced the czar's police with
the GPU, or doubted the progressivism of the intelligentsia.[9] Nor is the
fascist revolution a great or true revolution simply because the Bourbons
are exalted, Solaro della Margherita's writings are reprinted, or Papini's
followers invoke de Maistre.[10] Many are inclined to identify the strength
and intransigence of our revolution with reactionary principles: a purely
exterior identification and one that gravely compromises the effectiveness
of our propaganda and of fascist national education.

To create such an artificial genealogy for fascism's intransigence and
rightful rigor would mean dressing it up in moldy old rags, depriving it of

its youthful revolutionary élan. For legalists and loyalists, for authoritarians like Solaro della Margherita who believe in subjects not citizens, for advocates of the state as a pure abstraction, Oberdan was a traitor, Nazario Sauro and Cesare Battisti were deserters, as were the legionnaires of Fiume, and Mazzini was a rebel who had been sentenced to death, while Garibaldi was an irregular soldier to be kept always at arm's length.[11] Fascism has gone beyond all of this; it refuses to drag along with it such distorted and aberrant mental baggage.

Fascism is not revolutionary in the Jacobin sense, nor is it revolutionary simply because it rejects the guiding principles of the last one hundred years of European history. Yet fascism is not a proponent of backward motion. To advocate a return to abstract authoritarianism, to absurdly argue for intolerance, to justify one's actions in terms of the actions of medieval or seventeenth-century tyrants reveals a lack of courage and faith in oneself. It reveals a desire to replace intransigence, steel-like hardness, and sure faith in one's ideals with an external rationale, an appeal to purely hypothetical historical laws and principles (all symptoms of insecurity).

The admiration and respect for the Russian Revolution that some of the most intelligent and lively fascist writers have expressed, however ambivalently, is a direct result of their aesthetic repulsion for some of the attitudes that prevail in today's Italy. They cannot help but admire the Russian communists' revolutionary confidence, the intransigence with which they present themselves, their unwillingness to rely upon more or less immortal principles from the past.

Ours is a revolution: a people's revolution, as the Duce has repeatedly proclaimed. It is not the revolution of pseudo-aristocrats or of cloak-and-dagger knights. It is a true revolution: an action deeply carved into the present, animated by the necessities of the present moment, averse to summoning back to life the residues of remote historical times.

A modern people's revolution, a true revolution, is a revolution distinguished by both European and universal characteristics. Misreading fascism as a reactionary movement that would seek to overturn the Risorgimento — a deeply European phenomenon, if there ever was one — is especially dangerous in this context, for it interferes with the spread of fascist ideals abroad. Caution must be exercised here, because the very principles that yesterday were being used to mock the League of Nations, the ideals of European collaboration, and the existence of a European moral unity today are being bandied about in support of these very positions. For many, naturally, such stances are simply ideological gambits to be freely altered according to current tactical needs. So, one encounters people who celebrate European unity so that they may all the more vigorously criticize other nations for their scarce sense of — you guessed it — European solidarity. What they forget is that such ideological manipulations bear dangerous consequences: they breed confusion, skepticism, and deep uncertainty, especially among the young (who watch intently, read more than one newspaper, and retain a lot and thus are led to simplistic but basically sound conclusions). The damage is even greater to our international reputation [*propaganda*]. It confirms the impression that the Italian press is semi-official and that it always awaits instructions from the powerful, thereby facilitating confusions between the utterances of this or that irresponsible journalist and the government's views. This provokes, in turn, greater rigidity in our approach to propaganda, all to the benefit of those who confidently (and arrogantly) proclaim that whoever does not share their ideas is not a fascist. A highly effective (not to mention overbearing) system for the most brazen: a system that corresponds to the well-known tactic of threatening an opponent right from the start with the harshest insults and the worst possible accusations because of one's full confidence that one's own position is moral, just, and true, while the opponent's position is immoral, antinational, and so on.

Fascism's European character may be analyzed from a number of independent standpoints. It may be understood as a pragmatic effort to gain advantage by participating in plans for a European union and to avoid being caught unprepared with respect to some sudden diplomatic action. (A natural reaction involving the ideal and ideological actions that make up the field of political culture. The time is past when those on the outside can presume to pass judgment on a government's diplomatic actions.) Second, fascism's European character can be understood — many have somewhat reductively understood it in this way — in the obvious sense that Italy belongs to Europe and to the world. A great deal of chattering has been heard to this effect, but it is of little consequence. Many commentators assume as their first axiom that a revolution cannot be a true revolution unless it possesses a universal ideal value. They then set out to determine the value in question. Two principal forms of Europeanism surface in this context: a reactionary-conservative one and a revolutionary one. The former regularly trumpets its revolutionary identity for reasons that we have already explicated: in modern Europe it feels "revolutionary" to celebrate the Counter-Reformation, European "Catholic" unity, the descendants of the duke of Alba, Metternich, and so on. It relies upon pseudo-aristocratic, snobbish opposition to concepts firmly established in European public opinion and is animated by the restless, youthful Romantic minority within groups championing these sorts of ideas. It casts the future united Europe in the mold of the old Holy Alliance: a Europe of peaceful subjects, treated with kindness by fatherly rulers; a return to the elegant life-styles once lived by absolute monarchs, all related to one another . . . The sentence pronounced by the former king of Spain to the king of Italy comes to mind. Introducing Primo de Rivera in the context of a visit to Italy, he is reported to have said, "Here is my Mussolini." Many foreign "sympathizers," be they reactionaries and/or absolutists, view fascism in precisely this manner!

The fate of Primo de Rivera has been dealt with. But fascism's Duce and governmental head is no reactionary Spanish general. He is the leader of a great revolution entrusted with the task of bringing to term the national revolution begun by the Risorgimento, launched by the Savoy monarchy, and supported by the Italian populace: a revolution against the Holy Alliance and the Restoration. The fascist revolution was not born to uphold a medieval, reactionary mystique or to replace a Parisian Europe with a Roman Europe (wherein the adjective "Roman" refers to a pale imitation of Vienna at the time of Metternich, Berlin at the time of Wilhelm, or Paris under the ancien régime). While it may be understandable that many young people are today attracted by the sweet smell of such beautiful old things, they bear no relation whatsoever to fascism's revolutionary character. Sure, some will opt for the simple lineaments and consistent logic of such nostalgic alternatives when confronted with the bourgeois pan-Europeanism of the present. But this means nothing. One is reminded of Prince Bülow's communist friend who could find no merit in the German social-democrats but recognized the prince as one of the last "great gentlemen" [*grands seigneurs*], to the great satisfaction of the evil Bülow. We are not after these sorts of satisfactions, because we are not the descendants of a beautiful, dated world. We belong to fascism, a European revolutionary movement. The actions of the fascist government must not be interpreted on the basis of ideas that have no meaning for fascism itself.

The Risorgimento was aware, in the best of its men, of its Europe-wide significance. It sought its roots in the revolutionary triumph of the city-states: the cradles of Renaissance culture and of modern European civilization. Fascism represents the continuation and the renewal of this action, and it is, therefore, revolutionary. If it were not, the *Osservatore Romano* would be right in declaring that a European union achieved thanks to intermarriage among princely families and diplomatic plotting might well have succeeded were it not for the Risorgimento, which it accused of accelerating the political fragmentation that led, in turn, to the current "European anarchy."[12] The Vatican's newspaper is at least consistent, something that cannot be said about most of our reactionaries. The latter appeal to nationalistic myths that openly conflict with the fact that dynasties and aristocracies are inherently supranational. (Of course, national feelings and a national and state conscience are one thing; nationalist myths are quite another.)

The fascist corporative revolution has nothing to do with these forms of political melancholia. For years we have been talking about fascism's European quandary and about its need to achieve a consciousness that, fully aware of European political and cultural problems, permits it to make its revolution felt in its own backyard. We also need to do away with some myths: the myth of an Italy that has withdrawn into self-admiration; the dangerous myth that, even as our government pursues a politics of recovery and solidarity, our propaganda never transcends the limits of chauvinistic (not national) self-aggrandizement; the myth that Italian youth is totally indifferent to events on the global or European stage. Fascism must put itself forward as the dialectical synthesis of the demands made by both the revolutionary and the reactionary extremes: in the social sector, a synthesis of genuine (not just propagandistic) importance known as the corporative system. In the diplomatic sector, the international community is just beginning to follow the solutions to which the Duce has been pointing for a very long time. We must not underplay these social, economic, and diplomatic successes of our government and our regime by dressing them up in reactionary and pseudoconservative clothing, ornamented with rickety historical recurrences and racist Gnostic-heretical or pseudohistorical myths à la Gobineau, de Lagarde, Rosengarten, William II, or Friedrich Schlegel.[13] Otherwise, one of our flanks will always be exposed to the weapons of antirevolutionary, bourgeois hypocrisy. We must not simply scorn and negate the political life of other European nations, however different it may be from the one that, due to distinctive historical and political conditions, the fascist revolution has bestowed upon Italy. We must understand their needs and satisfy them as others cannot. And, as we have already started to do, we need to broaden our horizons, make our Europeanism and our fascism one, and cast aside the false belief that one can deny the value of another nation's heritage on the basis of ideas that were never held by living Italians.

translated by Maria G. Stampino and Jeffrey T. Schnapp

Notes

1. The word *schermistica* refers to the sport of fencing and alludes to the notion of a "screen," or *schermo*.

2. Cantimori is alluding to Mazzini's Giovine Europa movement, founded in April 1834 with the publication of an "Act of Brotherhood": a document, printed in Italian, German, Polish, and French, advocating the values of liberty, equality, and humanity on a supranational scale.

3. The reference is to the Spanish general and dictator Miguel Primo de Rivera (1870–1930) and not his more radical son, José Antonio, whose Falangist politics would surely have received Cantimori's approbation. As dictator between 1923 and 1930, Primo de Rivera was noted for his ultraconservatism.

4. Founded in 1915 as an umbrella under which the activities of various lay Catholic groups were coordinated, Catholic Action (Azione Cattolica Italiana) was an avowedly apolitical organization that represented the interests of the Church in Italian society. Up through the time of the 1929 Lateran agreements, Catholic Action managed to expand with only limited interference from the fascist authorities, though there were frictions in key areas such as education and control over youth groups. Tensions accelerated in the course of 1930 and 1931, fed by a heated press campaign and actual physical conflicts between fascists and Catholics, who prompted a fierce confrontation between the Holy See and the National Fascist Party over the activities of Catholic Action. The crisis was resolved in September 1931 by restricting the latter's initiatives to the religious sphere and altering its leadership structure. In the midst of the 1930–31 crisis, Pius XI pronounced the sharply critical encyclical *Non abbiamo bisogno* despite his mostly warm relations with the regime during the duration of his papacy.

5. Cantimori is alluding to the myths that were elaborated in anti-Risorgimental circles regarding Camillo Cavour (1810–61), the principal architect of Italian unification.

6. In his political writings Mazzini had envisaged the destiny of a newly unified, republican Italy in terms of a Third Italy to follow the First Italy of the ancient Romans and the Second Italy of the Renaissance. Much like the medieval Guelphs, who advocated the supremacy of the Papacy over the Holy Roman emperor, Vincenzo Gioberti's "Neo-Guelphism" envisaged a newly unified federal Italy under papal oversight.

7. The Piedmontese diplomat and politician Clemente Solaro della Margherita (1792–1869) was a major opponent of Camillo Cavour. An ardent antiliberal and advocate of a Catholic monarchism, he served as King Carlo Alberto's first secretary of state and between 1826 and 1834 as minister plenipotentiary to Spain, where he was an avid supporter of the Carlist party.

8. The allusion is to the concordat with the Catholic Church signed by Ferdinand, king of the Two Sicilies, in which the Holy See renounced its political claims

over the kingdom in return for, among other things, control over education and powers of censorship. The concordat provoked both dissension and revolt within the kingdom.

9. The Soviet GPU (United Department of Political Police) took the place of the Cheka in 1922 and lasted until 1934, when Stalin absorbed it within the People's Commissariat. Its responsibilities included prison and labor camp oversight, espionage, uncovering "enemies of the people," and political re-education.

10. By the 1930s Giovanni Papini's revolt against analytical reason, positivism, and democracy had led him far from his earlier pro-Futurist allegiances and into the Catholic fold. This is the context within which the writings of Joseph de Maistre came to assume importance for his followers.

11. Oberdan, Sauro, and Battisti were "martyrs" of the nationalist cause. Guglielmo Oberdan (1858–82) was executed by the Austrian forces for planning the assassination of the Emperor Franz Joseph. Nazario Sauro (1880–1916) and Cesare Battisti (1875–1916) were World War I heroes, executed by the Austrians. Giuseppe Garibaldi (1807–82) was the leader and hero of the Risorgimento.

12. Founded in 1861, the *Osservatore Romano* was the more or less official newspaper of the Holy See. Its overall stance toward the fascist regime would remain favorable until the late 1930s, though it published sharply critical editorials on issues regarding Catholic education and youth groups.

13. The list includes the racial theorist Joseph Arthur de Gobineau (1816–82), the biblical scholar and Orientalist Paul de Lagarde (1826–91), William II (1859–1941), and the philosopher Friedrich von Schlegel (1772–1829). The allusion to "Rosengarten" is unclear and may result from a melding of the names of German National Socialist leader Alfred Rosenberg (1893–1946) with the philosopher Alexander Gottlieb Baumgarten (1714–62).

CHAPTER 11

Corporativism as Absolute Liberalism and Absolute Socialism (1932)

Ugo Spirito

A prolific philosopher, corporativist theorist, and university professor, Spirito (1896–1979) was long a follower of Giovanni Gentile, his teacher and mentor at the University of Rome. With degrees in law and philosophy, he worked under Gentile as editor of the economics, law, and philosophy sections of the Enciclopedia italiana. During the 1920s he taught at a number of universities and edited numerous publications, including Educazione nazionale (1923–24) and, the source of this piece, Nuovi studi di diritto, economia e politica (1927–35). The 1930s saw him break with Gentile's thought and propose the skeptical doctrine of "problematicism" (problematicismo). But his most controversial contribution to period debates was his advocacy of an "integral" conception of corporativism that called for the fusion of labor and capital in large industries to insure that first the corporations and then the workers would gradually become the proprietors of the means of production, thereby ending all class struggle. His proposal drove a wedge between so-called Left and Right fascists, receiving support from the former (who viewed it as a recommitment to the progressive social agenda of the 1919 program) and criticism from the latter (who viewed it as a philocommunist assault on private property).

✻

To understand corporativism's essence and make its original meaning and revolutionary value clear, one must begin by studying its relations to liberalism and socialism. Many such analyses have been attempted, yet they have never yielded the sort of definitive results needed if one is to place the matter on a sound theoretical and practical footing. This is perhaps attributable to the fact that leading scientists and economists still betray disbelief and uncertainty regarding the corporativist system, a system that they suspect (or are firmly persuaded) is a cloudy hybrid, incapable of developing principles that spell out its historic role. According to this view, corporativism consists in little more than the empirical effort to remedy the shortcomings of the liberal system and to stem the consequences of socialist ideology. Born as an immediate reaction to postwar anarchy, nourished both by liberalism and socialism, corporativism has not only failed to deepen its roots but has also, by and large, allowed its actions to be governed by negative considerations. Thus, rather than providing a model for how one might build up an entirely new system, corporativism has mostly reduced itself to antiliberalism and antisocialism, that is, to a fight against forces of social disintegration.

The context has changed, and it has now become necessary to move from abstract negation—the first phase in every revolution—to a deeper understanding of the world that is to be overcome (and overcome it we can, if only we rise to another plane and avoid dismissing ill-satisfied needs). A positive instance must thus be added to the negative one; synthesis must follow antithesis; and corporativism understood as antiliberalism and antisocialism must be replaced by corporativism understood as true or absolute liberalism and as true or absolute socialism.

It is clear a priori that this new positive definition of corporativism can represent liberalism and socialism in their absolute nature, if the latter are conceived of as abstractly opposed to one another. The complication that arises, however, is that there are so many varieties of liberalism and socialism (including intermediate or eclectic forms) that it is far from easy to choose a model upon which to base our argument. For purposes of defining the antithesis to be overcome, I will therefore consider liberalism as synonymous with individualism and socialism as synonymous with state control. Admittedly, such equations are arbitrary. But this cannot jeopardize the conclusions that I wish to draw because it is not my intention to do battle with specific thinkers or specific liberal and socialist regimes. I wish instead to delineate precisely the opposing demands that are to be resolved in our new synthesis. The fact that (at least in theory) certain forms of liberalism and socialism have overcome the abstract antithesis that once opposed them demonstrates their movement in the direction of a concrete solution: the corporativist synthesis.   ✳

Since the eighteenth century, political and economic liberalism has defended the freedom and personality of the individual against a transcendent and autocratic state that makes a citizen's activity depend on elements imposed from without. Freedom has meant choosing and pursuing an autonomous goal, not one that has been chosen by somebody else. Freedom has meant that instead of turning an individual's work and goods into instruments for someone else's pursuit of wealth, one dedicates them to the individual's own pursuit of wealth, free from restriction. It is to these ends that liberalism negates the state or gradually reduces it to the smallest possible unit, especially in the economic domain. The individual is the absolute arbiter of the economic world. For liberals, the highest ideal is a society where the state no longer has a reason for existing.

At the negative and abstract revolutionary stage little thought is given to the meaning of the reality that is about to be destroyed. But if one were to have the courage to fully consider the logical consequences, the result would be a call for a return to the state of nature. The freedom of each and every individual can only be fully achieved by sundering all bonds, destroying all relations with other individuals, releasing men from their obligations to society and law. A man who is not accountable for his actions cannot expect anybody to come to his assistance. He must be self-sufficient in finding food to nourish himself, a resting place, and weapons to defend himself from wild animals. He becomes a sort of wild animal, since he can only see the animal in himself and in those to whom he is similar. Man raises himself out of the animal world when he encounters another human and speaks. He becomes himself by abandoning his state of disconnectedness and establishing intersubjective bonds on the basis of a discipline, the discipline of human language.

One talks in order to make oneself understood; one makes oneself understood in order to collaborate. No longer satisfied with wild life, man unites with other men to create together what he cannot create alone. The cave is replaced by the hut, the hut by the home, the home by the palace, and along with the home and the palace comes the whole civic world of which they are an expression. As men form reciprocal bonds and organize themselves according to their tasks, the goals that they set themselves become larger and more complex, and the progress of civilization becomes real. But civilization brings limitations on the individual's free will in the form of increasing norms and bonds. Society acquires the appearance of a machine ruled over by the chronograph. The higher a man's position is, the more important his social function is, the more numerous and complex are his social bonds and the more subject to chronometrical discipline. This is the rule of civic life. It is stupid and useless to try to remove oneself from it out of fear that the mechanism has no value.

This mechanism represents the very condition of true freedom. The more rigorous it becomes, the richer and fuller an individual's freedom. The reason that I am able to spend so many hours at my desk thinking about these problems and living such a rich, serene, and unfettered spiritual life is because I am embedded within a social setting [*un organismo sociale*] that imposes upon me ever more rigorous forms of discipline but *frees* me from natural necessities by virtue of the same discipline. It is this social mechanism that frees me from the need to go out and hunt the animals that I consume at every meal. It frees even the humblest of men, the one who butchers the animal that will feed us, from an infinity of other tasks so that he too may be lifted to a higher spiritual plane. The development of social mechanisms and of spiritual freedom is thus closely intertwined.

Yet social mechanisms liberate us and distance us from matter in a second significant way, one that derives from the first and is intrinsically connected. The links that bind us to society replace activities of an inferior character with superior pursuits endowed with social value. In other words, we are freed down below in order to bind us up above. But higher bonds are hardly shackles. They are instruments of emancipation. They link us to others, widen our horizons, grant our actions an effectiveness that transcends our individual existence, and shape our social duties such that they express our interrelations with every person and with the entire society to which we are bound. When I inhabit the will of an isolated man, the absence of ties might seem to free me from any dependency upon others. On a deeper level, however, it prevents me from acting upon other people and from endowing my actions with spiritual value, which is to say, with true freedom. The more I am linked to others, the more I can influence them, convince them, convert them to my ideals, the more I can gain the recognition required to confirm my actual value. True, if I were a hermit I might carry out arbitrary actions that are prohibited by society. But with no purchase on the world, such actions simply run their course and vanish within the confines of the hermitage. Connected to the world to the point that I become one with it, my word can instead resonate throughout the universe. The louder it echoes, the greater the personality expressing it becomes. My enslavement is the precondition for my freedom. The very mechanism that appears to attenuate the individual's action also multiplies and strengthens its power and effects.

✶

Laissez-faire liberalism proclaims freedom of thought and of action, free competition, private enterprise, and, above all, the sacred and inviolable character of private property. But it ends up realizing, more or less consciously, that these don't add up to genuine freedom. Freedom is founded upon collaboration, that is, upon a choice of social goals and the social discipline required to achieve them.

The field of economics provides us with compelling evidence that pure individualism is fruitless. Upon the bedrock of primitive atomism are built businesses of ever increasing dimensions: first a company, then a joint-stock company, then a cartel, a trust, a cooperative, a syndicate, and so on. Within these entities men freely join up with one another and subject themselves to the collectivity's laws. That such alliances are entered into *freely* permits liberals to endorse these nonindividualistic economic forms, designed as they are for purposes of competition. If they come into being and prosper, the liberal assumes that they respond to actual needs and that their scale is governed by economic laws. There is but one thing that he cannot tolerate: that the state monitor these economic forms by means of mediating and transcendent actions. In the liberal imagination the state remains the same old entity that revolutions have abolished, an entity whose interventions necessarily disrupt social life and whose regulatory actions cannot avoid violating the spontaneous and self-regulatory laws of economic development.

At this point in the argument, liberalism is approaching its solution to the problem: neither the suppression of law, discipline, and collaboration nor placement of the individual's untrammeled will above the law but instead affirmation of the positive and necessary character of the economic order. (Liberalism's opposition to the state remains firm, but for other reasons and according to another logic.)

Once a liberal acknowledges the legitimacy of trusts and other conglomerates, reason dictates an extension of his arguments regarding individuals to economic groups. He must recognize that the same spontaneous (and, hence, legitimate) law that drives individuals to sacrifice their free will in the name of the group can (and should) induce groups to leave their arbitrary and fruitless particularity behind and bind together within a single economic order. The rationalization process must be consistent and thoroughgoing if it is to remain true to its ultimate rationale. If the individual's freedom is strengthened (not weakened) by forming groups, the same ought to be the case of groups coming together within a single state. The concept of freedom as unlimited free will having been thereby overcome, the fulfillment of liberalism's needs becomes a synthesis of freedom and law, a totalitarian solution. It becomes impossible for economic actors not to will, freely and spontaneously, a state-controlled economy. Lastly, the individual must come to realize that in his pursuit of true freedom, intermediate or hybrid forms of liberty will not do. They merely tend to replay the battle among individual wills at a higher (which is to say, grander, more dangerous) level, when what the individual must instead seek out is a sense of absolute identity between his goals and the goals of a state to whose formation he freely and rationally contributed. Once liberalism reaches this juncture, there is no more need to exalt private enterprise and property. Public and private have become one and the same. Liberalism's needs are no longer opposed to the needs of the state, because the state is no longer conceived of as transcendent vis-à-vis the individual. On the contrary, the state becomes a necessary precondition for achieving liberalism's aims. Liberalism becomes absolute and assumes the new name of corporativism.

✷

In the nineteenth century, socialism rose up against liberalism, understood in its initial abstract sense. It arose not in opposition to the demand for freedom but against liberalism's false interpretation of that demand (evidenced by capitalism's rapid development). The economic struggle that liberalism preached had from the very start pitted the strong against the weak or, to echo the harsh polemics of yore, the exploiters against the exploited. The process of capitalization was meant to reward merit, but the institution of inheritance caused it to rigidify, reinforcing social inequities. The latter prompted socialism's rise. In true dialectical fashion, it put on liberalism's original mantle and proclaimed itself the defender of freedom against capitalist dictatorship. Through socialism, the class of the ruled organized against the ruling class in order to found a state that would recognize equal rights and give everyone what he deserved.

Socialism subordinated individuals to the state and endowed the latter with precisely those functions that it wanted to deny capitalists (i.e., powerful individuals acting on the basis of personal whim). But socialism's concept of the state was still cast in a liberal mold (which it simply reversed). According to the liberal laissez-faire model, individuals are meant to defend their freedom by negating the authority of the state; according to the socialist model, individuals look to the state for protection from other individuals. In both cases the state maintains its transcendent position vis-à-vis individuals, functioning as an external regulating body that is fundamentally different from the society that it disciplines. What this means is that the socialist ideal is a bureaucratic and paternalistic state, a state that acts in the name of individuals by effectively replacing them. Such a state cannot in any way reciprocate the trust that one places in it, nor can it defend freedom or administer justice due to one simple reason: it is merely a part of society, not the whole, and, as such, cannot *know and want* the common goal.

One of the commonplaces of liberal economic writing is the claim that the state is a bad manager and that, consequently, state management is inherently uneconomic. If one already envisages the state in liberal terms, the criticism is irrefutable, as is the assertion that a bureaucrat's care and competence in managing the common wealth [*cosa pubblica*] will always be inferior to that of an individual managing his own affairs. The point is irrefutable even in the case of truly exceptional bureaucrats because of the way bureaucracies are formed and act upon the nation. Bureaucrats make up a social class, a minority, the center. They represent centrality even when they expand into the outskirts, because their very presence creates a new center in the outskirts. It is a well-known fact that from the center one cannot see and know things with the same immediacy and concreteness that one can from the periphery. Moreover, only a few can occupy the center, while the great multitudes stand outside. So even if the few represent the elite of the nation, each of them cannot simultaneously know and observe as many things as the multitudes individually know and observe. From the perspective of the center individual problems lose their specificity, become subsumed within larger problems, and, when resolved, the solution is utterly generic (which is to say, inadequate).

The abstract prevails over the concrete. Overarching directives end up being emptied of their meaning through their mechanical application to life's rich and manifold variety.

Let us assume that it were possible to do away with this mismatch between the part and the whole, between the state and the nation. Let us assume that it were possible (through improved organization) for the state to attain true knowledge of even the nation's smallest, most remote events. This knowledge would still not be readily translatable into leadership and discipline of a spiritual sort. It would remain abstract because outside known reality; it would generate laws that correspond only to the knower's will. The state would still function as a bureaucracy, setting goals for the entire nation and, therefore, reducing the nation to a kind of mechanical instrument. The organism's life would be that of a machine: to each man an assigned place, to each worker an imposed job, all according to the scheme's rigid necessity. Each individual would be a cog lost in the overall machinery. Freedom, personality, and individual enterprise would become meaningless terms. The hoped-for social justice would translate into a general leveling, and the individual would vanish in the eyes of the state.

✳

In all truth, the best socialist theorizations do not advocate this sort of crude state-worship, nor does their critique of liberalism fall back upon such rigid materialism. Principles of collaboration and solidarity become embodied little by little in social institutions of various kinds and political stripes: cooperatives, leagues, and unions all represent a first attempt to create a convergence between the individual will and that of society. Just as within liberal theory the abstract cult of atomistic individualism eventually requires an account of concrete forms of collaboration and association (albeit of a capitalistic character), so abstract socialist statism also yields social theories and forms better suited to individual needs and morality [*personalità morale*]. The latter will prove crucial in overcoming the gap between state and individual. Individuals must be encouraged to spontaneously unite, to discipline themselves, to organize without waiting for rules and laws to be handed down from above. By this means, the state's reality and society's unity can both be experienced in a more immanent way that grants each individual's efforts greater value and, in so doing, transcends our initial crude statism. Thus come into being those socialist theories that have been accused of liberalism: theories that oppose the rhetoric of revolution as miracle, insist on the need to respect historical conditions, and are not afraid of fusing contradictory needs and bestowing on socialism attributes that before had seemed antisocialist.

An eventuality, this, that socialism could not (and will not be able to) avoid. Socialism must realize that the state that will bring about social justice is not the same state against which liberalism fought its battle and won. It cannot assume the form of a part that doesn't coincide with the whole or of a bureaucracy that rigidifies into a ruling caste, replaces the nation's will with its own, and places all individual action in a subordinate relation to itself. Socialism must realize, in short, that the state cannot violate an individual's freedom because the state cannot be disjoined from the individual. Its goals must be the goals of the very individuals that it must discipline. For the state to fulfill socialism's promise and bring about justice, individuals must find their reason for being and the necessary context for self-assertion within the state. Then and only then can the state reveal its true universality. Then and only then can socialism become absolute and assume the new name of corporativism.

⋆

Once the problems with liberalism and socialism are laid out in this fashion, the historical duty of corporativism comes into focus: its point of departure must be recognition of the innate needs of all individuals—freedom, personhood—and of the state—authority, social order [*organismo sociale*].

In fascism's precorporative phase, when nationalist and liberal ideologies still had the upper hand and when fascism's economic program corresponded nearly verbatim to the one the nationalists had devised at the third convention of the Nationalist Association (in May 1914), this double need found expression as a juxtaposition. The individual and the state were both to be respected in their reciprocal autonomy, though the former would be subject to the latter in cases of conflict. What was envisaged was a middle way between two extremes in the form of an eclectic solution.

Needless to say, such an eclectic solution was doomed to be illusory and contradictory inasmuch as the extrinsic convergence between individual and state that it envisaged amounted to little more than a combination of liberalism and socialism, preserving both of their flaws and abstract qualities. The individual was granted the freedom of private enterprise, an autonomous sphere of action in which the old individualism could live on, undisturbed. The state was also granted its own domain of action, above the individual's and replacing the latter whenever necessary. On one side stood the individual, on the other the state. The individual was mostly left on his own. The state, also on its own, was occasionally free to *intervene* in the individual's life, overriding with its own the individual's will. Thus, the deeper meaning of fascism's two objectives went unacknowledged, and, seeking compromise, fascism fell short of both liberalism and socialism. By partially adopting the liberal conception of individual freedom, the fascist compromise entailed a partial negation of that freedom, thereby falling short of liberalism's promises. By partially adopting the socialist conception of the state's absolute value, the fascist compromise curtailed the state's power over the partially autonomous individual sphere. Far from enriching one another, fascism's two objectives ended up impoverishing one another in the sort of pragmatic modus vivendi that liberalism has always endorsed.

I repeat, fascism was attempting to overcome the old dualism by subordinating one half to the other. But the split between transcendent state and individual remained all too firmly in place, so much so that the latter was subordinated to the former by means of an arbitrary, exceptional act. The state was still outside the individual and pitted its goals against the other's goals, its will against the other's will. This theoretical eclecticism could hardly avert clashes among individual interests or compensate for the imbalances resulting from occasional acts of state intervention.

✶

Fascism's true corporative phase—begun with the 1930 institution of the National Council of Corporations and fully under way at the present moment—involved the gradual abandonment of compromise solutions and a more logical and radical approach. The prior antinomy is now overcome by means of a concept that transcends both liberalism and socialism, a concept more liberal than liberalism and more socialist than socialism inasmuch as, instead of borrowing, it subsumes both in their absolute being.

Corporativism replies to liberalism by confirming that every person's individual freedom [*l'esigenza di personalità dell'individuo*] is sacred. Corporativism proclaims itself antiliberal only because the individual under liberalism is not a true individual, nor is his will truly free. It points to the fact that liberalism ends up denying individuals the very rights that it purports to defend. Corporativism's antiliberalism is thus not meant to deny or to curtail freedoms. Rather, it aims to strengthen them as much as possible and to achieve liberalism's highest aim.

Corporativism replies to socialism by confirming that the desire to seek true liberty and justice within the state is incontrovertible. Corporativism proclaims itself antisocialist only because the state under socialism is not a true state, that is, it does not coincide with the organized nation and, therefore, cannot achieve the solidarity for which it was established. Corporativism's antisocialism thus aims at conceptualizing and realizing the state that socialism itself cannot create because it is still not absolute socialism.

In this way liberalism and socialism are both embraced and their innermost consequences are brought to light by demonstrating how each moves from the individual to the state and vice versa, how law becomes identified with freedom, and how the organic whole of society encompasses the multiplicity of people that make it up. In response to the competing abstract claims of the individual and the state, corporativism puts forward *the individual*, who, in all his concreteness, freely recognizes his purpose and reason for being in the state, and *the state*, which, in all its concreteness, is endowed with spiritual value only to the degree that it is alive in each citizen's mind and will. Theory posits such an identification in absolutely rigorous terms, terms to which, in its historical unfolding, political life must strive to conform. The fascist revolution's greatness lies in its commitment to achieve such an ideal conformity by creating and continuously improving the corporative system.   ✱

In order to achieve the identification just discussed, corporativism understood that it was necessary to overcome the dualism of state and individual and to fill the gap separating these two terms. This it sought to accomplish by devising a dialectical middle term that would establish a continuous and concrete interconnection between the two extremes, a point of convergence where extremes could meet and be born into a true spiritual life. The middle term in question was the corporation, a grouping suspended between the state and the individual, a partial community but one readily amenable to fusion with the socioeconomic totality.

There are two ways of understanding social groups, and only by ex-amining the disjunction between them can one fully appreciate the fascist corporation's mediating role. If all social groups are imagined as equals, occupying the same intermediate level, halfway between the state and the individual, then our earlier problem has been displaced but not resolved. The dualism that we wish to overturn remains firmly in place. Disjoined the same way individuals are disjoined, groups stand like atomized individuals vis-à-vis the state, and conflicts among them can only be solved through the state's transcendent action. In order to avoid this, a dialectical step needs to be taken: it is necessary to stop envisaging these groups as lined up side by side but instead to think of them as one within the other—to think of them *hierarchically*. In other words, each group should be one of a kind (whether a current unity or a state-run union). Rather than having to compete or fight with others, it coordinates and subordinates its activities. Only in this manner can we overcome the need for a higher power that imposes justice from outside in the case of a dispute. In its place, we substitute a new kind of higher power, one that expresses the organizational structure of inferior groups immanently and thereby refutes the fundamental premise of classical (or individual) economics.

In the chain of interconnected groups, the state starts at the center and radiates outward from link to link. It ends up coinciding with the entire nation. No longer a transcendental being, a party, class, or bureaucracy, the state doesn't impose its will or laws upon a passive citizenry. Instead, it expresses the very will of the nation in the structure of its system [*organismo sistematico*]. Materialistic conceptions of democracy identify the will of the people with *majority opinion*, while corporativism sees majority domina-tion as but another avatar of the old dualism of ruling and ruled classes. The corporativist solution is the totalitarian state, within which everybody has his place from which to express his will, thus contributing directly to governing the overall system.

The individual proceeds link by link, from periphery to center, through the state hierarchy. His freedom to act, no longer restricted to the sphere of private interests, can now assert itself within the entire social system. Even at the lowest, most peripheral rung of the ladder, the individual's contribution not only shapes the group to which he belongs but also, however infinitesimally, the system as a whole. As his merit becomes recognized, he ascends the ladder step by step. His sphere of action widens, and he can ever more directly imprint his personality on the nation's life. His freedom becomes unlimited with the very organism to which it is strictly bound.

Such is corporativism's essence. It is a hierarchical communism that denies both a leveling state and an anarchic individual, that opposes bureaucratic management but bureaucratizes the nation (turning every individual into an official), that resists private management and assigns a public value to the work performed by individuals. Wills unite to form a single will; multiple goals coalesce to form a single goal. All social life is rationalized. The economic world moves in the direction of unitary organization, which makes possible the realization of a dream: a planned economy that can overcome the chaos produced by liberal economics.

This is an ideal rationalization, a rationalization never fully achieved or achievable. But it can serve as a light that illuminates the path that men of good will in the fields of science and political action must take. Science and politics must devote all their energies to creating institutions, methods, and structures that can gradually close the gap between reality and this ideal.

✳

The distinctiveness of the new corporative concept vis-à-vis liberalism and socialism can perhaps be seen best in the international arena. If the term *international* is concretely understood as meaning *the relationship between nations,* one can confidently assert that only under corporativism can one speak about a true "International." The liberal and the socialist International were in reality only an *antinational.*

The truth of this assertion can be readily demonstrated in economics, where the specific problem has emerged and various solutions have been attempted. Traditional liberal economics has refused to recognize frontiers, which is to say, nations. In the domain of economic life, where each citizen's most concrete and visible interests are at stake, the nation is presumed to have no meaning. One of the most famous and most consistent liberal economic theorists has written: "International trade is carried on by *individuals,* not by *nations; individuals are debtors* or creditors of other *individuals.* A *country* or a *nation* is not a *debtor* or creditor of *another country* or of *another nation.*"

Individuals are authorized to pursue their own private extranational interests in order for economic life to truly prosper. No other outcome is conceivable given liberalism's abstractly individualistic negation of the state.

Yet the opposing statist stance of socialism yields the same result. The state upon which one relies to achieve justice and freedom levels all individuals, just like it levels all nations. The socialists shout, "Proletarians of the world unite!" — that is to say, "Deny your fatherland on behalf of humanity, renounce your individual states in the name of the state that will bring you redemption."

In contrast, fascism recognizes the value of the universal urge that lies at the heart of liberalism's and socialism's so-called Internationals. It proclaims the need for a true International on the basis of corporative principles.

Moving from the individual to the state and from corporation to corporation, we reach the national corporation. But confronted by a short-sighted naturalistic nationalism that asserts the dogma of economic independence — last vestige of liberalism's individualistic and anarchical concept of freedom — and readily wields the weapon of protectionism, fascism has understood that corporativism's true triumph can only be achieved by insuring the triumph of the corporative idea throughout the world. Contemporary market conditions leave it with no choice but to make use of protective import duties, yet it combats custom barriers and all egoistic efforts to limit international trade. It goes without saying that this is done not to promote laissez-faire liberalism but rather to establish a system of collaboration among nations in which every country, when engaging in economic planning, takes into account the organization of other countries and agrees to coordinate planning efforts. Corporativist development does not and cannot stop at the nation's frontiers without contradicting its very nature. Instead, the move must be made from national to international corporations in which all nations find ideal conditions for economic and spiritual development. Not a leveler of individuals, corporativism can never become a leveler of nations. Just as it recognizes the individual's work and right and duty to affirm his personality freely within the nation, so internationally it recognizes each country's distinctive contribution to the creation of a new civilization.

translated by Maria G. Stampino and Jeffrey T. Schnapp

Address to the National Corporative Council (14 November 1933) and Senate Speech on the Bill Establishing the Corporations (abridged; 13 January 1934)

Benito Mussolini

✶

Corporativism was the central article of faith among those who saw in fascism a "third way": an alternative road to industrialization that combined the advantages of the "first way"—laissez-faire capitalism—and the "second way"—communism. It sought to bring together representatives from labor and capital within state-sponsored corporate entities, each responsible for a given sector of the national economy as well as for coordinating their policies at the level of an advisory economic parliament called the National Council of Corporations (founded in March 1930). A feature of fascist thought from early on, the implementation of corporatist ideas began in the mid-1920s and reached its peak in the early 1930s, particularly in the wake of the government shakeup of July 1932, after which Mussolini assumed the helm of the Ministry of Corporations. In the following speeches Mussolini addresses, first, the National Council of Corporations and, second, the Senate on the occasion of a vote on the legislation that established twenty-two separate corporations. Despite its progressive pretenses, the system ended up granting little real power to worker representatives and became highly bureaucratized in the course of the second half of the decade.

✶

Address to the National Corporative Council

The applause that greeted the reading of my resolution yesterday evening made me ask myself this morning whether it was worthwhile to make a speech illuminating a document that had already been grasped by your minds, interpreted by your convictions, and touched by your revolutionary sensibility. It may nevertheless be interesting to know what line of meditation and thought led me to formulate the resolution.

But, first of all, I wish to congratulate this assembly and to express my satisfaction with the debates that have been held here. Only a moron could be surprised that divergent views and shades of opinion have arisen, for this is as inevitable as it is necessary. Harmony is harmony; discord is another thing. Moreover, in discussing a problem as delicate as that before us, it is perfectly logical and inevitable that each of us should bring to it not only his doctrinal preparation, not only his state of mind, but also his personal temperament. The most abstract of philosophers, the most transcendent of metaphysicians cannot entirely disregard or set aside his personal temperament, whatever it may be.

You will remember that on 16 November of Year X [1932], in the presence of the thousands of fascist party officials assembled in Rome's Piazza Venezia for the decennial celebrations [*decennale*], I asked, Is this crisis that has held us in its grip for the past four years — we have now begun the first month of the fifth year — a crisis within the system or of the system?[1] A grave question, a question to which it was not then possible to give an immediate reply.

Today I can answer it: the crisis has penetrated so deeply into the system that it has become a crisis of the system. It is no longer an injury, it is a constitutional disease. We can now assert that the capitalist mode of production has been superceded and with it the theory of economic liberalism that illustrated and defended it.

I wish to trace for you, in its main lines, the history of capitalism in the past century, which can be defined as the century of capitalism. But, first of all, what is capitalism? Capitalism must not be confused with the bourgeoisie. The bourgeoisie is quite another thing. The bourgeoisie is a mode of being that can be great or petty, heroic or philistine.

Capitalism, on the other hand, is a specific mode of production, a mode of industrial production. When capitalism attains its highest expression, it is a mode of mass production for mass consumption, financed en masse through the national and international issuance of joint stock capital. Capitalism is therefore industrial and has had little impact upon the field of agriculture.

Periods of Capitalist Development

I would single out three periods in the history of capitalism: the dynamic period, the static period, and the period of decline.

The dynamic period is that extending from 1830 to 1870. It coincides with the introduction of the power loom and the appearance of the steam engine. The factory arises. The factory is a typical creation of industrial capitalism. This is a period of enormous [profit] margins, during which the laws of free competition and of the struggle of all against all rule supreme. Some fall by the wayside, others die and the Red Cross picks them up. This early period also has its depressions. But they are cyclical depressions, neither long nor global. Capitalism still has such vitality and such power of recovery that it can get over them brilliantly. It is the period in which Louis Philippe exclaims, "Get rich." Urbanism develops. Berlin, which had a hundred thousand inhabitants at the beginning of the century, reaches one million. Paris grows from 560,000 (at the time of the French revolution) to near the million mark. The same can be said of London and the Transatlantic cities. During this first period of capitalism natural selection really works. There are also wars.

Those wars cannot be compared to the world war [World War I] we ourselves have lived. They are short wars. The Italian one of 1848–49 lasts four months during its first year and only four days during the second; that of 1859 lasts but a few weeks. The same holds true for the war of 1866. Nor are the Prussian wars of longer duration. That of 1864 against the Danish duchies lasts a few days; that of 1866 against Austria, a continuation of the former one, lasts a few days and ends at Sadowa. Even that of 1870, which saw the tragic days of Sedan, doesn't outlast even two seasons.

It would be tempting to say that, to a large degree, those wars stimulated the economic development of the nations in question, so much so that barely eight years later, in 1878, France is once more on her feet and can organize the Universal Exposition, an event that gives Bismarck pause for thought.

I will not call what was going on in America heroic. That word should be reserved exclusively for events of a military nature. But there can be little doubt that the conquest of the Far West was arduous and adventurous and meant risks and victims (just like a great conquest).

This dynamic period of capitalism begins with the advent of the steam engine and closes with the building of the Suez Canal. It is a period lasting forty years. During those forty years the state looks on and remains inactive. The theorists of liberalism declare to it: you, state, have but a single duty, that of acting in such a way that your existence is imperceptible in the economic sector. You will govern all the more successfully the less you concern yourself with problems of an economic nature.

Economic activities in all their manifestations are, therefore, limited only by the penal code and by trade laws. But after 1870 the situation shifts. The struggle for life, free competition, the survival of the fittest no longer determine everything. The first symptoms of fatigue and of deviation appear in the capitalist world. The era of cartels, syndicates, consortia, and trusts begins. I won't linger over the differences between these four institutions. But they are insignificant, or nearly so, like that between rates and taxes. Economists have not yet defined the distinction. But the taxpayer who confronts them sees no point in discussing the matter. Whether they are rates or taxes, they must be paid.

Economic Liberalism and Tariff Barriers

It is untrue, as an Italian economist of the liberal school has claimed, that a trustified, cartellized, syndicated economy is a consequence of the war. No: the first coal cartel arose in Germany, in Dortmund, in 1879. In 1905, ten years before the world war broke out, there were sixty-two metals cartels in Germany. There was a potash cartel in 1904, a sugar cartel in 1903, ten cartels in the glass industry. During that period the direction of industry and commerce in Germany was divided up between five hundred to seven hundred cartels. In France, in 1877, the industrial office of Longwy was opened to deal with the metals industry. In 1888 another was opened to deal with petroleum. Already in 1881 all the insurance companies had coalesced. The Austrian iron cartel dates back to 1873.

International cartels grow up alongside the national. The glass bottle syndicate dates back to 1907. The plate and looking-glass syndicate, which brought together French, English, Austrian, and Italian manufacturers, is from 1909. In 1904 the rolling mills formed an international cartel. The zinc syndicate started in 1899. The British-Chilean nitrate cartel was started in 1901.

I have here before me a complete list of national and international trusts, the reading of which I will spare you. It is safe to say, however, that there is no sector of the economic life of Europe and America in which these characteristic manifestations of capitalism are absent.

But what is the consequence of all this? The end of free competition. As [profit] margins were reduced, capitalist enterprises deemed it better to come to an understanding rather than to fight. They formed alliances, amalgamated, divided up the markets, and distributed the profits among them.

Even the law of supply and demand is no longer a dogma, for it is possible through cartels and trusts to act upon both demand and supply. In the end, the coalesced, trustified, capitalist economy turns to the state. What for? Customs barriers.

Free trade, which is only one of the founding principles of the doctrine of economic liberalism, free trade receives a death blow. Indeed, the first nation to raise almost unsurpassable tariff barriers was America. And now, for some time, England herself has rejected all that which seemed until now traditional in her political, economic, and moral life and has adopted protectionist measures of an increasingly aggressive kind.

Supercapitalism and the Standardization of Humankind

The war came. After the war and as a result of the war came capitalist inflation. The size of enterprises began to be calculated not in millions but in billions. Seen from afar, these so-called vertical constructions give the impression of something monstrous, like the tower of Babel. The dimensions of business enterprises come to exceed the possibilities of man. Formerly spirit dominated matter; now matter bends and subdues the spirit.

What was physiology becomes pathology. Everything becomes abnormal. Two personalities — in all human vicissitudes representative men crop up on the horizon — two personalities can be identified as typical of the new situation: Krueger, the Swedish match-man, and Insull, the American business speculator. (With that brutal frankness that is our fascist custom let me add that there have also been manifestations of this kind in Italy; but, on a whole, they have not reached the same heights. . . .)

At this stage, supercapitalism finds its inspiration and its justification in a utopia: the utopia of unlimited consumption. Supercapitalism's ideal is the standardization of the human race from the cradle to the grave. Supercapitalism wants all babies to be born exactly the same length so that cradles can be standardized and all children persuaded to like the same toys. It wants all men to don the very same uniform, to read the same book, to have the same tastes in films, and to desire the same so-called labor-saving devices. This is not the result of caprice. It inheres in the logic of events, for only thus can supercapitalism make its plans.

When does a capitalist business cease to be an economic phenomenon alone? When its size transforms it into a social phenomenon. It is then that a capitalist enterprise, when difficulties arise, throws itself like a dead weight into the state's arms. It is then that state intervention begins and becomes ever more necessary. It is then that those who once ignored the state now seek it out anxiously.

Things have now gone to such lengths that if all of Europe's governments were to go to sleep for twenty-four hours, that parenthesis would suffice to precipitate a disaster. At the present time there is no branch of economic activities in which the state is not called on to intervene. Were we — it's merely a hypothesis — to give in to this latest phase of capitalist development, our path would lead inexorably into state capitalism, which is nothing more nor less than state socialism turned on its head. In either event, [whether the outcome be state capitalism or state socialism] the result is a bureaucratization of the economic activities of the nation. This is the crisis of the capitalist system considered in its universal significance. But our concern here, both as Italians and Europeans, is with a more concrete crisis.

Why Europe Is No Longer at the Head of Civilization

There is a European, a typically European crisis. Europe is no longer the continent that guides civilization as a whole. This is the dramatic fact that those whose duty it is to think must recognize and point out to others.

There was a time when Europe dominated the world politically, spiritually, economically. Politically, through her political institutions. Spiritually, through all that the European spirit has produced over the ages. Economically, because Europe was the only highly industrialized continent. But, beyond the Atlantic, a great industrial capitalist business world has developed. And, in the Far East, Japan, after coming into contact with Europe during the war of 1905, is advancing rapidly toward the West.

Here the problem is a political one. Let us talk politics, for this assembly is also an exquisitely political body. Europe can still try to reassume her place at the lead of world civilization if she can achieve a minimum of political unity. The policies we have steadfastly adhered to should continue to be followed. But a European political entente cannot come about unless grave injustices are first repaired.

The Four-Power Pact

We have now reached an extremely serious juncture.[2] The League of Nations has lost all that could confer upon it political significance and historical weight. Even the very country that invented the league has remained outside it. Russia, the United States, Germany, and Japan are all nonmembers.[3] The very idea of the League of Nations originated as one of those maxims that, when first pronounced, sounds very beautiful but that, when afterward carefully considered, anatomized, dissected, turns out to be absurd.

What other diplomatic deeds are there that could reestablish ties between Europe's governments? Locarno? Locarno is a different matter.[4] Locarno has nothing to do with disarmament. The way out doesn't lie in that direction.

Of late, a great silence surrounds the Four-Power Pact. No one mentions it, but it's on everyone's mind. For this reason, I do not intend to take any new initiatives or to try to accelerate the unfolding of a situation that must logically and fatally ripen.

Is Italy a Capitalist Country?

Let us now inquire as to whether Italy remains a capitalist country. Have you ever asked yourselves that?

If by capitalism we mean that complex of practices, customs, and forms of technological progress that are now common to all countries, we may declare that Italy is indeed capitalist.

But if we delve more deeply into the matter and examine the economic status of several demographic groups on the basis of statistics, the data suggest that Italy is not a capitalist country according to the meaning now conventionally assigned to that term. On 21 April 1931 farmers farming their own lands numbered 2,943,000, while tenant farmers numbered 858,000. There were 1,631,000 crop-sharing farmers and peasants and 2,475,000 other agriculturists, farm hands, wage workers, and occasional agricultural laborers. The total population directly and immediately dependent on agriculture numbered 7,900,000.

There were 523,000 manufacturers; 841,000 traders; 724,000 craftsmen working on their own account or for others; 4,283,000 industrial wage earners; 849,000 domestic servants and porters; and 541,000 persons enrolled in the armed forces (including the police). The liberal arts and professions accounted for 553,000 individuals; public and private service industries employed 905,000. Which gives us a total, thus far, of 17,000,000.

Few Italians earn their living exclusively as landlords: only 201,000. There were 1,945,000 students and 11,244,000 women minding their homes. Another 1,295,000 Italians belong to other nonprofessional categories, a figure that can be variously interpreted.

Why Italy Must Retain a Diversified Economy

This picture makes it self-evident that the economic activities of the Italian nation are varied and complex and cannot be said to belong to a single type of economy. All the more so given that the great majority of Italy's 523,000 manufacturers—an impressive figure—are small or medium-sized concerns. I'm defining small businesses as those with a minimum of 50 and a maximum of 500 workers. Those ranging from 500 to 5,000–6,000 workers are medium sized. Next comes large-scale industry, which sometimes overlaps into the category of supercapitalism.

This compendium also shows just how mistaken was Karl Marx when, elaborating upon his apocalyptic beliefs, he claimed that society can be divided into two social classes, clearly divided and eternally irreconcilable.

In my opinion, Italy should remain a country with a diversified economy. A strong agricultural sector must remain no less the foundation of its economy than it is at present. (In the unanimous opinion of those who understand such matters, Italy's slight recent industrial upturn is attributable to the fairly good harvests of the past year or two.) Upon this base must stand a healthy industrial sector made up of small and medium-sized firms, a banking system that does not fall prey to speculators, and a trade sector that delivers commodities rapidly and rationally to consumers.

The Corporations

The declaration that I submitted to you yesterday evening defined corporations as we understand them and as we want them to take shape. It also defined their objectives. The corporate system, the document states, is founded with the aim of expanding the wealth, the political power, and the well-being of the Italian people. These three objectives are closely intertwined with one another. Political strength creates wealth, and wealth, in turn, invigorates political action.

I would like to call your attention to the third stated objective: the well-being of the Italian people. It is essential that the institutions we are in the process of establishing should be felt and perceived by the masses themselves as instruments for improving their standard of living. At some time in the future, the worker or the tiller of the soil must be able to say to himself and to his family, If I am really better off today, it is due to the institutions created by the fascist revolution. In all national societies there is a residuum of poverty that is unavoidable. A certain number of people live on the margin of society. Special institutions attend to their needs. But what distresses our spirit, on the contrary, is the poverty of strong, capable men, feverishly hunting for jobs but finding none. Our hope is that Italian workers—individuals who concern us at once as Italians, as workers, and as fascists—will feel that we are establishing new institutions not only to give expression to our doctrinal views but also to yield positive results. Concrete, practical, and tangible results.

I will not dwell on the reconciliatory functions that the corporations can exercise. I see no drawback to the practice of conciliation. Whenever the government has to make an important move it already consults with the concerned parties. If consultation on certain specified matters were to become obligatory tomorrow, I would not disapprove. Everything that brings the citizen into closer contact with the state, everything that integrates the citizen into the machinery of the state, serves the social and national goals of fascism.

The Fascist State

Our state is not an absolute state. Still less is it an absolutist state, far removed from men and armed only with laws, inflexible as laws should be. Our state is an organic, human state, striving to adhere to the realities of life. To "adhere" ever more closely because the bureaucracy is no longer (and, in the future, will be ever less desirous of) acting as a buffer between the state's sphere of activity and the concrete interests and effective needs of the Italian people. I feel quite certain that the Italian bureaucracy, which is admirable, will cooperate with the corporations in the future as it has done in the past so as to find better solutions to problems when and as they arise.

The point, however, that has most keenly interested this assembly is that which proposes to confer legislative powers upon the National Council of Corporations.⁵ Some have already spoken of the end of the present Chamber of Deputies, but they are looking far down the road. Let me clarify. As this year's legislative session is now drawing to a close, the present Chamber of Deputies will have to be dissolved. The time is lacking to fully set up the new corporative institutions, so the new chamber will be chosen by the same procedure as in 1929.

A Constitutional Reform

But a time will come when the Chamber of Deputies will have to determine its own fate. Are there any fascists tempted to weep at the prospect of its replacement? If there are, let them know that we will not be drying their tears. It is eminently conceivable that a National Council of Corporations may replace in toto the present Chamber of Deputies. The Chamber of Deputies has never been to my taste.

Even the label "Chamber of Deputies" has now become something of an anachronism. It is an institution we inherited from the past and that is foreign to our mentality and to our fascist passions. The chamber presupposes a world that we have demolished. It presupposes a plurality of parties and, not infrequently, impediments to the efficient functioning of government ministries. Since the day on which we abolished this plurality, the Chamber of Deputies has lost the essential reason for which it was created.

With hardly any exceptions, our fascist deputies have been transported to new heights of faith, proving that the blood coursing through their veins remains very pure (so long as it hasn't been poisoned by that environment where everything exhales the stale breath of the past).

But all these are future developments. We see no reason for undue haste. The important thing is to establish the principle, because from that principle inevitable consequences are sure to be drawn. When, on 13 January 1923, the Fascist Grand Council was set in place, it seemed to superficial observers that little more than an institution had been founded.[6] They were wrong. On that day political liberalism was buried. When the Militia, the armed guard of the revolution, was created in tandem with the Grand Council, supreme organ of the revolution, the death knell was sounded for the theory and practice of liberalism.[7] We set out definitely along the path of revolution. Now we are burying economic liberalism.

The corporations' impact upon the economic field is comparable to the impact of the Grand Council and of the Militia upon the political field. The corporations mean a regulated economy and, therefore, also a controlled economy, for there can be no regulation without control.

The corporations supercede socialism and liberalism. They provide a new synthesis.

One fact is symptomatic, a fact that has perhaps not been adequately understood: that the decline of capitalism coincides with the decline of socialism. All of Europe's socialist parties are in a shambles. (I'm referring not only to Italy and Germany but to other countries as well.) I am not, of course, claiming that the two phenomena depended one upon the other from a strictly logical standpoint. Rather, the link joining the two together is one of simultaneousness.

It is for this reason that the corporative economy arises at a juncture when the two concomitant phenomena, capitalism and socialism, have already given all that they could give. We inherit from both that which was vital in each.

A Step Forward along the Path of Revolution

We have rejected the theory of economic man, the liberal theory. And we have risen in indignation every time we have heard labor spoken of as a commodity. Economic man does not exist. Man is integral, he is political, he is economic, he is religious, he is saint, he is warrior.

Today we are taking a further step forward along the path of revolution. Comrade Tassinari was right in stating that for a revolution to be great, for it to make a deep impression on the life of a people and on history, it must be a social revolution.[8]

If you look into things deeply you will observe that the French revolution was eminently social, for it demolished all that remained of the Middle Ages, from tolls to corvées. It was social because it brought about a vast upheaval in the landed property system and created the millions of landowners who were and remain the bedrock of modern France.

Were this not so, anyone could carry out a revolution. A revolution is a serious matter, not a palace conspiracy, nor a change of ministry, nor the rise of one party that displaces another party. It is laughable to read the advent of the Left to power in 1876 described as a revolution.

In conclusion, let us ask ourselves, Can the corporatist solution be adopted in other countries? We must pose this question because it is being asked in all other countries. Everywhere the matter is being studied and efforts are being made to understand corporatism. There can be little doubt that, given the general crisis of capitalism, the corporatist solution will increasingly come to the fore. But if corporatism is to be implemented fully, integrally, with revolutionary results, three conditions must be met.

Single party rule is necessary. Necessary so that economic discipline may be accompanied by political discipline and so that, rising above contrasting interests, all may be bound together by a common faith.

But single party rule is not enough. In addition there must be a totalitarian state, which is to say, a state that absorbs all the energies, all the interests, all the hopes of a people in order to transform and unleash them.

But even a totalitarian state is not enough. The third and final, the most important condition that must be met is to live during a period of high ideal tension [*alta tensione ideale*].[9] The latter explains why it is that we are sure to strengthen and consolidate all our achievements step by step, why we will successfully translate into action the entirety of our doctrine. Who can deny that the present fascist period is a period of high ideal tension? No one. Ours is an era in which arms have been crowned with victory, institutions renewed, the land redeemed, new cities founded.

Senate Speech on the Bill Establishing the Corporations

If the topic weren't inexhaustible, I would willingly have refrained from speaking to you today. For the bill submitted for your approval has been slowly and thoroughly prepared. It is the result of no sudden birth. Its precedents can be traced back to what may be described as the protohistory of the regime: the first meeting of the Fasci di Combattimento held in Milan fifteen years ago. After the March on Rome, the first tentative moves toward establishing the corporations took the form of the Palazzo Chigi and the Palazzo Vidoni Pacts.[10] Then came the bill of 3 April 1926, followed by the regulations of 1 July 1926.[11] The Labor Charter dates from 21 April 1927. The first corporative law was passed in March 1930.

The bill now before you was first examined by the Central Corporative Council. The chrism of the Fascist Grand Council was conferred on it after long and detailed debates. It has been revised by the Council of Ministers, and it has been presented to you accompanied by a report from the Ministry of Corporations. To this has been added a report, solid in substance and fervid in faith, by the Quadrumvir de Vecchi.[12] . . .

This bill is not an expression of doctrine alone. Doctrines should not be unduly despised, for doctrine enlightens experience just as experience tests doctrine. Twelve years of experience have shaped it. Twelve years of living, practical, daily experience confronting the problems of national life viewed from an economic standpoint, problems always prismatic and complex. I have had to face them, and, not infrequently, I have had to solve them.

Capitalist Economy

What are the premises of this bill? The fundamental premise is the following: there is no such thing as an economic fact that is exclusively private and individual. From the day on which man resigned or adapted himself to living in the company of his peers, from that day forward not one of his actions has been limited in its development and consequences to himself. All actions have reactions that transcend the individual.

The phenomenon of capitalism, the economic model known as the capitalist economy, must also be viewed in its historical context. The capitalist economy is a phenomenon of the last century and of the present one. It was unknown in antiquity. . . . Nor was it known in the Middle Ages, with its craft-based economy of varying magnitude.

Capitalism implies machinery, and machinery implies factories. Its growth is bound up with the rise of industrial machinery. Capitalism expands with the long-distance transmission of electrical power and when the circumstances are ripe for a rational and universal division of labor. (Our present situation is quite different.) It was this division of labor in the latter half of the nineteenth century that led the British economist Stanley Jevons to state: "the prairies of North America and Russia are our wheat fields; Chicago and Odessa are our granaries; Canada and the Baltic States are our forests; Australia raises her flocks for us, America her cattle; Peru sends us her silver, California and Australia their gold; the Chinese grow tea for us and the Indians coffee; sugar and spices come to our ports; France and Spain are our vineyards; the Mediterranean our market-garden."

Of course, all this had, as its counterpart, the production of coal, cotton goods, machinery, and so on. During this first phase of capitalism—on another occasion I defined it as the "dynamic" or even "heroic" phase—economic facts could be conceived of in predominantly individual and private terms. Theorists were thus emphatic in ruling out state intervention in the economy. All they required of the state was that it be quiescent and that it provide the nation with safety and order.

Industrial Dynasties

It was also during this period that industrial capitalism was characterized by the rule of families, a feature that, wherever and whenever it has been preserved, has proved of the utmost value. Great industries transmitted from father to son in dynastic fashion ensure not only that factories change hands but also the preservation of a feeling of family pride and a sense of honor. In his book *The End of Capitalism*, [Ferdinand] Fried, though limiting his remarks to Germany, notes that already in the years between 1870 and 1890 these great dynasties of manufacturers declined, broke up, dispersed, revealed their inadequacy.[13]

During this time frame joint-stock companies appear on the scene. The joint-stock company must not be thought of as a diabolical invention or as the product of human malevolence. (Gods and demons are usually best kept out of our affairs.) Joint-stock companies arise when capitalism can no longer rely on the wealth of families or small groups. As a result of its growth it finds it necessary to appeal to impersonal, undifferentiated, gelatinous capital through the issuance of stocks and bonds. The manufacturer's proper name now comes to be replaced by company acronyms. Only those who have been initiated into the rites of this financial mysteriosophy [*misterosofia*] know how to read beneath "the veil of the strange verses."[14] . . .

When an enterprise seeks capital on the markets, it relinquishes its private character. It becomes a public or, if you prefer, a social fact.

State Intervention

. . . These sorts of changes accelerated during and after the war. State intervention was no longer deprecated, it was solicited. Should the state intervene [in the economic sphere]? There can be little doubt as to the answer. But how to intervene? Government intervention, of late, has assumed varied, contrasting forms. Most have been disorganic, empirical interventions, interventions on a case-by-case basis, as the need arises. This has occurred in all countries, including those that until recently flew the flag of economic liberalism.

There is another form of state intervention, that practiced by communist regimes, with which I have no sympathy whatsoever. . . . For my part, I would argue that if communism had been applied in Germany it would have yielded no better results than it has in Russia. Little does it matter. It's clear the German people will have nothing to do with communism. In some of its expressions of immoderate Americanism—the extremes meet—communism amounts to a form of state socialism. It amounts to a wholesale bureaucratization of economic activities. I believe that none of you wish to bureaucratize, which is to say, to freeze the realities of the economic life of the nation. The realities in question are complex and changeable. They are bound up in world events. They are of such a nature that when they give rise to mistakes, those errors have unforeseeable consequences.

The American experiment should be followed very closely. In the United States, government intervention in business is direct. Sometimes it assumes a peremptory form. The [trade] laws are nothing more nor less than collective contracts to which the president compels both parties to submit. It's still too early to pass judgment on this experiment. My opinion on one point, however, can already be sketched out. Monetary maneuvers cannot bring about real and enduring price increases. If we wish to delude mankind we can have recourse to what used to be known as "clipping the coinage." But, except among slaves to economic and social empiricism, there exists a clear consensus that the path of inflation leads to catastrophe. After all, who really believes that the multiplication of monetary instruments can actually increase a nation's wealth? This sort of thinking is akin to imagining that by printing one million copies of the same photographic negative of the same person, the population is increased by one million. Moreover, what of our prior bitter experiences in this domain, from the *assignats* of revolutionary France to the postwar German mark?[15]

A fourth approach is that advocated by fascism. If the liberal economy is an economy of individuals in a state of more or less complete liberty, the fascist corporative economy is an economy of individuals, of associated groups, and also of the state. What are its characteristics? What are the characteristics of a corporative economy?

A guild or corporative economy respects the principle of private property. Private property completes the human personality. It is a right and, if it is a right, it is also a duty. So true is this that property must be viewed from the standpoint of its social function. Ownership must be active, not passive. It entails more than merely enjoying the fruits of wealth, for such fruits must be developed, increased, and multiplied.

The corporative economy respects private enterprise. The Labor Charter specifically states that only when private enterprise is deficient, lacking, or inadequate does the state intervene.[16] It is obvious, for instance, that government alone, because it alone possesses the necessary means, could undertake a project as vast as the reclamation of the Pontine marshes.[17]

Corporatism brings order to the economy. If there is one aspect of the nation's life that requires regulation, one aspect that needs to be guided toward certain pre-established goals, it is precisely the economic domain, for it concerns the nation as a whole. The need for regulation extends not just to the industrial sector but also to agricultural, trade, banking, even craft production. How should such regulatory processes be carried out? In the first instance, by means of self-discipline on the part of the concerned economic parties. Only when the concerned parties fail to agree and to achieve the proper balance should the government intervene. It has a sovereign right to do so, in this field as in others, for the government represents the other side of the equation: the consumer, the anonymous masses who, because unorganized, must be safeguarded by a representative of the collectivity.

Here someone might be tempted to interject, "And what if the depression were to end?" My reply is that, in the unlikely event that this were to come to pass, change is needed more than ever. We mustn't nurture illusory hopes of a rapid end to the present depression. It will leave behind enduring legacies. And, even if there were to be a general economic revival and we were to return to the favorable business conditions of 1914 (alluded to earlier), regulation would remain every bit as necessary. "Necessary" because men have short memories and would commit the same foolish acts, repeat the same follies.

The bill before you, honorable senators, has already permeated the consciousness [coscienza] of the Italian nation. In the last few days, the people's actions have spoken volumes to this effect. This admirable, hardworking, indefatigable, thrifty people has cast eight billion votes of one lire each in favor of this law. While you have been holding your debates, the populace has shown that this law is not a threat but a guarantee, not a danger but a supreme safeguard.

The stages of implementation? As soon as the law has been passed we will proceed to set up the corporations. The Grand Council has already examined and discussed the text of the bill and has defined the character and composition of the corporations. Once these are established we will examine their operations, which must be efficient and not weighed down by red tape. As is the case in evaluating all institutions, costs will have to be analyzed alongside the resulting benefits. Some increase in bureaucracy, however modest, need not be feared. (It is important to recall that no human organization is imaginable without a minimum of bureaucracy.) Only when we have had the opportunity to fully study, track, and check the practical workings of the corporations will we have reached the third stage, that of constitutional reform. Only when the third stage is reached will the fate of the Chamber of Deputies be decided.

As you can gather from all that I have previously said and from these brief remarks, we are moving forward calmly. Far from wishing to produce immediate results, we are sure of ourselves. Sure because we embody the fascist revolution. We have the whole century before us.

anonymous translation revised by Jeffrey T. Schnapp

Notes

1. Following the precedent of the French republican calendar (which had set the year I as 1792), the fascist calendar began counting years with the October 1922 March on Rome. November 1932 was, accordingly, the tenth year of the revolution. Roman numerals were employed to designate the years of the fascist calendar.

2. The Four-Power Pact (or Patto Mussolini) was a document drafted in the first half of 1933 in the wake of the Geneva Disarmament Conference. Developed by the Italians and made the centerpiece of Mussolini's foreign policy, it declared that Italy, France, England, and Germany would continue their peaceful coexistence but make necessary adjustments in the World War I peace treaties (particularly as concerned the delicate issue of re-arming Germany). The pact was signed in mid-July 1933 but went unratified except by England and Italy.

3. Political and economic disputes led to a number of temporary or permanent defections from the League of Nations, including Germany's in October 1933 and Japan's in 1932 (over its invasion of Manchuria). The USSR was offered admission only in September 1934.

4. The allusion is to the Pact of Locarno, a series of treaties drawn up in 1925 in Locarno, Switzerland, by Germany, Italy, France, Belgium, and Great Britain in which these powers promised to maintain the peace, and Germany promised to submit its territorial disputes with France, Belgium, Poland, and Czechoslovakia to arbitration. Mussolini was a signatory to the pact.

5. The National Council of Corporations was founded in March 1930 as a sort of

economic parliament made up of representatives of the major employer and worker organizations in all sectors of the national economy. Though it never replaced the actual Parliament and it played a largely advisory role, its powers over collective contracts were substantial.

6. The Fascist Grand Council was the highest organ of the fascist regime and state and included among its members the Quadrumviri, top ministers in the government, the leaders of the National Fascist Party, and the presidents of both houses. Though its juridical status was only resolved at the end of 1928, both before and after this date it provided Mussolini with a powerful political tool for consolidating and enforcing his dictatorship.

7. The actual foundation date of the Militia (Milizia Volontaria per la Sicurezza Nazionale, MVSN) was 1 February 1923, some three week after the creation of the Grand Council.

8. The agriculturalist Giuseppe Tassinari (1891–1989) served in Parliament between 1931 and 1934 and was Italy's minister of agriculture and forests between 1939 and 1941.

9. Though opaque in English, the phrase "high ideal tension" alludes to Mussolini's oft-repeated notion that human potential is best realized in high-pressure settings, such as on the battlefront, particularly when the source of the conflict is "ideal," that is, ideas, ideologies, ideals. Tension is viewed as a positive factor by fascism, opposed to the liberal-democratic ideal of the easy life. Likewise, the fascist dedication to "ideal" concerns is to be contrasted with the materialism of socialism and liberal democratic thinking.

10. The first of these two pacts between Italy's major industrialists and the fascist labor unions was negotiated on 19 December 1923, the second on 2 October 1925. Both claimed to promote industry/worker cooperation but, in reality, represented victories for industry and defeats both for the independent (socialist-led) labor union movement as well as for the more socially progressive elements within the fascist unions, led by Edmondo Rossoni. The fascist syndicates were granted exclusive rights to negotiate collective contracts on behalf of workers, but they were stripped of many of their most powerful organizing tools as well as denied the right to index wages to the cost of living.

11. The bill in question was that implementing the fascist labor union laws, drafted by Alfredo Rocco and known as "The Law for the Judicial Regulation of Labor Disputes." The regulations refer to the newly founded Ministry of Corporations.

12. As indicated in Volpe's history, the *quadrumvirs* Cesare Maria de Vecchi, Italo Balbo, Michele Bianchi, and Emilio de Bono were appointed in the days immediately preceding the March on Rome as the supposed directors of the seizure of power. Their actual role was more honorific than otherwise, though they all held positions on the Fascist Grand Council.

13. The work Mussolini is referring to is Friedrich Zimmermann's *Das Ende des*

Kapitalismus (Jena: Diederich, 1931); translated into Italian by Angelo Treves as *La fine del capitalismo* (Milan: Bompiani, 1932). Both books were published under the pseudonym Ferdinand Fried.

14. The allusion is to canto 9, verse 63 of Dante's *Inferno* ("sotto il velame de li versi strani") in which Dante's pilgrim is called to decode the oracular words of the citizenry of the city of Dis, who threaten him by invoking Medusa and her powers to petrify.

15. *Assignats* were the units of currency issued under the French revolutionary regime between 1789 and 1797. As in the case of the postwar German mark, their issuance was associated with inflation and devaluation.

16. For the Labor Charter, see chapter 23. The reference is to article IX.

17. The allusion is to the reclamation projects in the Pontine Ager region, outside of Rome, one of the showpieces of the regime's land reclamation (*bonifica*) program.

CHAPTER 13

Three Documents on Race

The Manifesto of Race (1938), Critique of The Manifesto of Race (1941–42), and New Revised Draft of The Manifesto of Race (1942)

★

The Manifesto of Race *was published anonymously in* Il Giornale d'Italia *on 14 July 1938, having been so substantially revised by Mussolini and by officials within the Ministry of Popular Culture that two of the ten original signatories (Nicola Pende and Sabato Visco) demanded that their names not be listed among the authors. A National Fascist Party memorandum ignored their wishes and published the names on 25 July. With its proclamation that Italians were racially Aryan and biologically distinct from such non-Europeans as Jews and Africans, the manifesto was clearly designed to please Nazi Germany in the immediate wake of Hitler's May 1938 visit to Italy. (The importance of the German alliance had vastly increased due to the political isolation and economic sanctions imposed on Italy by the League of Nations in retribution for its 1935 invasion of Ethiopia.)*

Though motivated by political opportunism, fascism's embrace of racism was facilitated by a range of factors, including the increasing importance of imperialist ideology (racial vocabulary had crept into the antimiscegenation laws in Ethiopia), the presence of vocal anti-Semitic minorities in the National Fascist Party and Catholic Church, an anti-Jewish press campaign carried on in 1936, and Mussolini's fears that Hitler was emerging as the true figurehead of international fascism. This said, the manifesto was inconsistent with Mussolini's prior positions (which had been unambiguously antiracist) as well as with prevailing Italian political traditions. Its inordinate emphasis on the role of Jews in Italian public life appeared at odds with reality since they represented only one tenth of 1 percent of the population. As a result, the manifesto met with substantial resistance both inside and outside the party even as it became official policy and was translated into a corpus of laws. The sorts of objections that it was still eliciting two years after its publication are documented in "Critique of The Manifesto of Race," *an internal report regarding debates within the*

*Higher Council of Demography and Race. The result of these debates led the
council to draft a revised version of the manifesto on 25 April 1942.*

The Manifesto of Race

1. *Human races exist.* The existence of human races is not an abstraction of
   our spirit but corresponds to phenomenal, material reality. It is perceivable
   with our senses. This reality is embodied by impressive masses of millions
   of men who share similar physical and psychological characteristics that
   were inherited and continue to be passed on. To say that there are human
   races is not to imply a priori that there are superior and inferior races but
   simply that there are different races of men.
2. *There are "large" races* [grandi razze] *and "small" races* [piccole razze].
   It is not enough to acknowledge that there are major systematic groups,
   commonly called races and identified by a very limited set of characteristics.
   One must also admit that there exist minor systematic groups (for example,
   Nordics, Mediterraneans, Dinarics, etc.) distinguished by a greater number
   of common characteristics. From a biological point of view, the latter groups
   constitute true human races, and their existence is a self-evident truth.
3. *Race is a purely biological concept.* The concept of race is based on other
   concepts than those of a "people" or a "nation," both of which are primarily
   founded on historical, linguistic, and religious considerations. Underlying
   differences between peoples and nationalities, however, are differences of
   race. If Italians are different from Frenchmen, Germans, Turks, Greeks,
   and so on, it is not simply because each group has a different language
   and a different history. It is also because the racial constitution of each
   of these peoples is distinct. Since very ancient times, the proportions of
   different races that have gone into forming various peoples have themselves
   varied. They have varied to the point that sometimes one component race
   has exerted absolute dominion over the others; at other times they have
   all become harmoniously fused; while at other times still, the different
   component races have persisted in an unassimilated state.
4. *The population of Italy today is of Aryan origin, and its civilization is Aryan.*
   This population and its Aryan civilization have inhabited our peninsula for
   many millennia. Very little remains of pre-Aryan civilization. The origins
   of modern Italians may be principally traced back to components of those
   same races that made up and continue to make up the living fabric of
   Europe.

5. *The notion that, during the historical epoch, great hordes of men made a contribution to the formation of Italy is a legend.* After the invasion of the Lombards, there were no other remarkable movements of populations in Italy capable of influencing the racial character of the nation. Thus, while the racial composition of other European nations has varied considerably even in modern times, the racial composition of Italy today is mostly the same as it was a thousand years ago. An absolute majority of today's 44 million Italians dates back to families that have lived in Italy for a millennium.

6. *A pure "Italian race" has by now come into existence.* This statement is not based on the confusion of the biological concept of race with the historico-linguistic concept of a people or a nation. Rather, it confirms that the purest of blood ties unite present-day Italians with the generations that for millennia have populated Italy. This ancient purity of blood is the greatest symbol of the Italian nation's nobility.

7. *The time has come for Italians to openly declare themselves racists.* All the regime's efforts up to this point have been founded upon racism. Appeals on the basis of race have always been a recurrent motif in the speeches of our leader. In Italy the question of racism must be approached from a purely biological point of view, without philosophical or religious preconceptions. Italian racism must be conceived of as essentially Italian and as tendentially Aryan-Nordic. In no way does such an assertion imply either that German racial theories can be introduced into Italy without modification or that Italians and Scandinavians are identical. It merely singles out for Italians a distinctively European physical and, above all, psychological model that stands entirely apart from all non-European races. All of which means infusing Italians with an ideal state of higher self-awareness and a deeper sense of responsibility.

8. *A clear distinction must be made between Mediterranean Europe (populated by Occidentals), on the one hand, and the Oriental and African Mediterranean, on the other.* We should be wary of dangerous theories that assert that some Europeans are of African origin and count the Semitic and Hamitic populations as part of a common Mediterranean race, claiming ideological relations and sympathies that are absolutely unacceptable.

9. *Jews do not belong to the Italian race.* Nothing substantial remains of the Semites who have landed on the fatherland's sacred soil over the course of centuries. Even the Arab occupation of Sicily left nothing apart from the memory of a few names. Besides which, the process of assimilation has always been very rapid in Italy. The Jews represent the only population that was never assimilated in Italy because it was comprised of non-European

racial elements absolutely different from the elements that gave rise to Italians.

10. *Italians' purely European characteristics, both physical and psychological, must not be altered in any way.* Unions are allowable only within the European racial fold. In such cases one cannot speak of a true hybridism because the races in question belong to a common body [*corpo comune*], differing only in a few characteristics while remaining equal in many others. The purely European character of Italians is altered by their crossbreeding with any non-European race that brings with it a civilization different from the ancient civilization of the Aryans.[1]

✶

Critique of *The Manifesto of Race* Elaborated within the Higher Council of Demography and Race

1. The caption is naive.[2] The illustration defies logic and avoids putting forward a concrete definition. Everything is reduced to common physical and mental characteristics that are hereditary and inheritable among large human groups (millions of men). The assertion could also be used to define the human species. It follows that if we wish to attain a better understanding of the word "race," we must first establish the more or less numerous physical and mental characteristics that are involved when one moves from the concept of species to that of race. The a priori denial of a hierarchy of race is at odds with a racial standard that recognizes the differing historical fortunes of human races.

2. Here, evidently, the authors wished to describe the great subdivisions of the human species into white, black, and yellow groups, each characterized by somatic aspects that readily strike the senses, even if they have no absolute scientific value as regards the definition of race. Given this premise, it would be improper to speak of the minor systematic groups as "races" in the true sense; rather, they ought best be considered subvarieties of the larger races.

   So, for the purposes of a politics of race, must we refer to larger or smaller groups?

   Furthermore, this definition implicitly excludes the existence of racial compounds (Aryan Italian, etc.) that are mentioned in number 6.

3. It is absolutely correct to assert that the concept of race cannot be extended beyond the domain of biology. Morphological characteristics, as well as physiological and psychological ones, are transmitted from man to man via the mechanisms of heredity. The point is that such characteristics can be

modified over time by endogenous and exogenous factors. The hereditary legacy thus presents new characteristics that either enrich individuals or cause them to degenerate.

When the study of large human groups demonstrates that there exist certain shared characteristics that are common to all individuals in a given group and are susceptible to genetic transmission, then we can embrace the biological concept of race.

The authors state that the concept of a "people" or of a "nation" is founded essentially on historical, linguistic, religious, and so on considerations. Yet they also assert that differences between one people and another or between one nation and another are based on racial differences. This appears to be a contradiction in terms.

Aware of this, the authors retreat to arguing that peoples are differentiated by the proportions of different races that make them up. But this still implies that the concepts of "people" and of "nation" are essentially racial concepts.

4. The notion of an Aryan "race" is the byproduct of modern linguistic studies of idioms documented in an extremely vast territory that extends from the Tarim Basin, from India, and from Persia to all of Europe.

Obviously, a language always presupposes the human community that produced it. Nevertheless, it does not provide us with any criterion for a biological definition of the corresponding human type.

Consequently, when one speaks of an Aryan race, one must assume that the reference extends to white human groups but that it does not encompass all white humans, because some whites (Basques, Caucasians, Finns) can in no way be traced back to an Aryan origin.

To assert, then, that very little remains of the civilizations of pre-Aryan peoples on our peninsula constitutes an unjustified and indemonstrable denial of the anthropological, ethnological, and archeological discoveries that continue to be made.

The civilization of Italy's population is supposed to be Aryan. But it has been proven that numerous exotic influences were exerted by different races and made their impact on our peninsula's indigenous population, just as they did on Hellenic civilization.

It is difficult to understand why Aryan civilization, which is supposed to have been perfectly autonomous, would have developed so precociously on the Greek and Italian peninsulas while it lagged behind, remaining primitive, in the Scandinavian, Anglo-Saxon, German, Slavic, and Celtic countries.

This said, there are obvious differences between Hellenic civilization and Italian/Roman civilization, differences that are surely attributable to the prevailing influence of indigenous human groups.

5. The lead sentence is accurate. But when one speaks about "ancient times," it is necessary to look back far beyond the barbarian invasions in general and the Lombard invasions in particular.

Modern scholarship has demonstrated that the invasions that took place after the fall of the Roman Empire were carried out by numerically modest groups. One need only remember that a few thousand Byzantine mercenaries, guided by the eunuch Narsete, were able to expel all the Goths from Italy. The Lombards themselves (outside of Pavia) consisted of little more than scattered groups of feudal warriors who were rapidly absorbed by the Italian population and disappeared without leaving a trace of their influence.

It should be noted as well that here the authors state that the population of modern Italy is comprised of descendants of the families that inhabited our peninsula a thousand years ago, while in point number 4 they assert that an Aryan population has inhabited our country for various millennia.

Although the authors do not say so explicitly, one might also point out that the statement implicitly grants the barbarian invasions a formative influence on the Italian race that is surely disproportionate to the number of the invaders and to their capacity for biological predominance.

What is certain, on the contrary, is the biological dominance of Italian peoples over all the groups of foreign extraction.

6. There is an Italian "race," but not a "pure" Italian race.

Moreover, there are no pure human races on earth anymore, and, on this issue, there is universal agreement among scholars.

The fact remains, however, that today's Italian race is a descendant of the generations that for millennia and millennia populated the peninsula, whether due to the purest of blood ties or simply very close kinship.

Here too the authors rightfully assert, as in point number 4, the antiquity of our race. But by claiming for it the span of several millennia, they contradict the single millennium claimed in point number 5.

7. While there is nothing to object to in the first and second sentences of this statement, the final section is plainly inconsistent.

The authors assert that Italy's conception of racism must be essentially Italian, but . . . "tendentially Aryan-Nordic." This means that Italian racism must be based on Aryanism [*nordismo*], which, as everyone knows, resolutely denies any virtue to Mediterraneans, deemed a population of slaves.

This would require, likewise, the repudiation of all of Italian civilization, which the Aryanists [*nordisti*] accuse of having brought cultural barbarism and decadence to pure Nordic civilization. Thus, despite their supposed superiority, the Nordic peoples would have been enslaved by Mediterranean civilization in general and Italian civilization in particular. An odd contradiction in terms that Aryanists have neglected to eliminate from their writings.

Nevertheless, according to the authors, the Aryan-Nordic linkage need not entail the wholesale adoption of German racist postulates or assertions that "Scandinavians and Italians are identical."

Just how Aryan-Nordic racism differs substantially from German racism remains a mystery. The authors explain only that they want to provide Italians with "a distinctively European physical and, above all, psychological model that stands entirely apart from all non-European races." This makes their subsequent assertion that they wish also to "infuse Italians with an ideal state of higher self-awareness" elusive, if not self-contradictory.

The fact of the matter is that a physical model can be shown to an artist and a psychological model shown to an educator. But it is useless to show it to a man and a woman for purposes of procreation. It is almost as if the authors aimed to promote sexual couplings between individuals with Nordic morphological and psychological characteristics. The result would be an implicit devaluation of the Italian physical and psychological type. So just how might this infuse them "with an ideal state of higher self-awareness and a deeper sense of responsibility"?

It is useless to dwell on the patriotic aspect of these guidelines and on how little these are in agreement with the claimed purity of the Italian race.

8. In a scientific forum one can expound objectively on the African or non-African origins of European peoples without this representing a danger. Far more dangerous, however, is the omission of any reference to Mediterranean unity, achieved politically under the aegis of Rome. In any event, the authors confuse racial origins with ideological relations and sympathies within the fold of a single sentence.

We could, for instance, feel strong ideological-political affinities and sympathies for the Arab struggle to gain independence from the Anglo-Saxons without, however, having to invoke a common racial origin.

Mediterranean Africa is different from the rest of Africa. From a racial perspective it is best to push aside the confusion created by the geographical label Africa.

This continent's history differs markedly depending on whether one is considering the area north of the Sahara, the equatorial region, or southern Africa.

Mediterranean Africa has maintained continuous and documented relations with all Mediterranean peoples, more than any other region. Such contacts were rare with the true blacks of equatorial Africa.

This is easy enough to understand when one considers the segregating effects of the Sahara Desert.

9. This statement is self-evident; no one has asserted a racial commonality between Jews and Italians.

However, the authors make two contradictory assertions. On the one hand, the Semitic Jews are said to remain unassimilated because they are comprised of non-European racial elements (absolutely foreign to the ancestors of modern Italians) whose alterity seemingly breeds a reciprocal sexual repugnance. On the other hand, they assert that nothing remains of the Semitic Arabs, since "the process of assimilation has always been very rapid in Italy."

Thus, they imply that the Semitic race was subdivided into two groups: one assimilable and the other unassimilable by the Italian race.

The authors do not tell us how such an assertion can be justified on scientific grounds.

10. While the purity of the Italian race is declared in point number 6, here the authors acknowledge that the Italian race has crossbred with other European races. According to them (but not according to the German racists), such crossbreeding does not lead to true hybridism, since these races belong to a "common body," a novel phrase whose meaning could use some clarification.

It is impossible to prove that all European races belong to a single stock or "common body" on the basis of scientific data since racial groups in Europe have origins that are Uralo-Altaic, Mongol, Aryan, Caucasian, Iberian, and so on.

So the Europeanism espoused by the authors ends up granting legitimacy to Aryan/non-Aryan pairings, pairings that, one would have every reason to expect, give rise to the formation of true hybrids. If, instead, pairings are limited to so-called Aryan groups, this would entail granting legitimacy to pairings with non-European races: races that, contrary to what the authors claim, are bearers of a civilization not at all "different" from ancient Aryan civilization.

✶

New Revised Draft of *The Manifesto of Race* Approved by the Superior Council on Demography and Race on 25 April 1942

Races must be regarded as variations on the human species, distinct in their physical-mental characteristics, of which cultures and civilizations are concrete manifestations. Such characteristics are inscribed into our hereditary patrimony and, for this reason, are transmittable from generation to generation.

Environmental influences and contact with other groups have contributed throughout the millennia to shaping the character of current civilized human societies.

The distinctive features that identify a given ethnicity [*una realtà etnica*] thus derive not only from its basic genetic components but also from characteristic creative forces actualized and revealed in the course of generations. These forces are shaped through interactions with the environment, through contact with human groups of varying proportion, and by the progressive unfolding of actions on the part of each group (a process in the course of which elective affinities play the decisive role).

The presence of man on the Italian peninsula dates back to the very dawn of humanity. The peninsula is circumscribed on land by the Alps, a barrier against the great invasions of hordes. It is bounded as well by the sea, another hindrance to invasion. At the same time, it facilitates trade and cultural exchange.

Man has indeed inhabited Italy from the time when he first appeared in Europe. His existence in the remotest Quaternary Period is demonstrated by certain Paleolithic tool-making activities. Even if his physical characteristics are unknown, he constitutes the "Proto-anthropos of Italy."[3]

In the Middle Quaternary Period, the existence of man is documented by groups to whom the men of Saccopastore and of the Circeo belong. The discovery of the fossil remains of these men can be considered the first documented chapter of human history on Italian soil.

Today's population finds its ancestors in the very ancient men of the Upper Quaternary Period who can rightfully be called Italic proto-Mediterraneans. They appear in great numbers in the Ligurian grottos, in Tuscany, in Abruzzo, and in Sicily, and they left clear traces of their skills up and down the entire peninsula.

So the most ancient culture of Italy is contemporaneous with that of other European countries. It would be reasonable to suppose that its development in Italy was partially autonomous with respect to the higher forms of Neolithic civilization.

From the Upper Paleolithic on, we can thus postulate the existence in Italy of a race endowed with great creative and assimilative capacities, a race destined to impose its physical type and its ethnic and cultural genius on others. Out of these indigenous groups emerged a prehistoric race, the creator of Neolithic civilization, formed for the most part of human types still widely distributed on the peninsula.

Much later in Europe and thus also in Italy, a new ethnic order arose with the arrival of human groups that spoke so-called Aryan or Aryan-European languages. That these Aryan groups must have quickly developed modes of coexistence with Italian proto-Mediterraneans, as occurred everywhere in Europe and on parts of the Asian continent, is proven via analysis of the Aryan-European languages. The latter preserved an essentially Aryan phonetics and morphology but began to show ample traces of the substratum's influence in their lexicon.

These Aryan groups influenced the cultural development of early Italian civilization and were able to do so because of the favorable circumstance that the latter and the former had achieved comparable levels of sophistication. If conditions had been otherwise, *one couldn't explain why, for many centuries, the Aryan groups that spread out across the rest of Europe were unable to create a civilization even remotely comparable to that of our peninsula.* The civilization that arose in Italy at the beginning of history fused two ethnic elements and two forms of cultural genius into a unique whole, permeated with undeniable Mediterranean influences.

Our distinctive prehistory assumes the form of a long and grand unified process whose defining attributes are best considered indigenous (an incomparable mark of noble origins).

Already at the threshold of history, the numerous peoples that are present on the peninsula's ethnic and cultural map vary in their features. Sometimes they demonstrate greater adherence to the traits of our endogenous tradition. Other times they demonstrate a syncretism in which the Aryan factor prevails.

By the time of the Iron Age [*l'epoca dei metalli*] Italy forms a cohesive cultural and ethnographic whole. As is the case with all unified phenomena, more or less backward groups and local aspects provide the necessary backdrop against which the first historical cultures delineate themselves, tangibly differentiated by the existence of a tradition of memories committed to writing. The civilizations in question are those of the Etruscans and of the Hellenic colonies of southern Italy and of Sicily.

With the appearance of the Etruscans, a unique ethnic identity arises in Italy: an identity that is Italy's own and no other people's, informed by common characteristics shared by the peninsula's peoples; an identity that thrives and radiates outward from its place of birth.

Far from marking a breach in the ethnic unity of Italian peoples, Hellenic colonization reinforced this unity. It did so by transforming a vast portion of Italy into a forge where the most illustrious historical civilization of the Mediterranean—the Greek—was modified and melded with Italian elements, so that its compass could then be expanded through the political unity of Rome.

The presence of Celts in Italy did not extend much beyond a century and a half. There can be little doubt that it contributed to strengthening the basic characteristics of the preexisting population.

A typical and magnificent expression of deep ethnic and cultural interpenetration between preexisting populations and more recently arrived Aryan elements can already be found in ancient Rome. The uniformity of the latter's population and civilization makes it very difficult to accurately distinguish native traits from those that represent Aryan contributions. This is the result of the profound syncretism governing relations between the proto-Italic peoples (who, over the course of many centuries, developed an advanced civilization) and other peoples (who brought with them a variety of instincts [*impulsi vari*]).

So, even at time of its first appearance on the stage of history, the Italian people assumes a unified form. This proves that certain *select genetic characteristics, whether physical or mental, have shaped the syncretic absorption of different elements* (elements bound by elective affinities), giving rise to a superior human type. The Italian race owes its irreducible originality, never lost during millennia of varied adventures, to the genetic principles embodied by this human type. These principles are expressed *physically* in the face's nobility and in the solid and harmonious architecture of the body, always responsive to environmental conditions. They are expressed *spiritually* in the intellect's proclivity to achieve a clear and direct vision of reality, in a marked sense of ethics, and in the instinctual political and legal perspicacity that creates and informs our civil organization.

A synergy between race and overall natural environment has always made the Italian element stand out distinctly within the sweeping landscape of European life and civilization. This helps to explain the successive presence on the peninsula of four different civilizations, each endowed with a universal character and distinguished by soaring and harmonious accomplishments in the domain of thought; each able to engender human personalities of global importance, makers of historic epochs. A majestic example is the fascist epoch: the creation of Mussolini's genius.

When the Emperor Octavian set up regional administrative institutions in 28 B.C., the realism of the Roman spirit led him to adapt them to the geographic individuality of each Italian province. But his enterprise also reflected a conviction that Italy's (ever growing) ethnic unity was founded upon the remote fact of the original unity of its primitive populations.

The invasions that, after the fall of the Roman Empire, followed one after another with varied intensity during the course of the Middle Ages did nothing to alter this homogeneous adamant block of humanity, so thoroughly tested and strengthened [*collaudato*] by Rome. By now this constitutes one of the most widely accepted conclusions of modern scholarly inquiry. With the end of the invaders' ephemeral political function came their demographic dissolution or even elimination, a case in point being the Arabs in Sicily, who remained encamped and separate from the local populations until they returned to Africa, leaving in their wake scarce cultural remains (remains that very soon disappeared).

The Jews, an unrelated ethnic group, dispersive by nature, always constituted a scanty minority. They didn't corrupt the biological and spiritual unity of the Italian race in any way for they had not even the slightest effect upon it.

The ethnic unity of Italy, resulting from this long millennial process, becomes distinct at the moment at which Augustus institutes the Roman imperial state. Nearly two millennia later, this order expresses the fundamental structure of today's Italy.

translated by Olivia E. Sears

Notes

1. The manifesto initially appeared without any signatories, but a subsequent party memorandum revealed the following list of authors: Lino Businco (assistant professor, general pathology, University of Rome), Lidio Cipriani (visiting professor, anthropology, University of Florence), Arturo Donaggio (director, Neuropsychiatric Clinic, University of Bologna), Leone Franzi (clinical assistant, pediatrics, University of Milan), Guido Landra (assistant professor, anthropology, University of Rome), Senator Nicola Pende (director, Institute of Pathology, University of Rome), Marcello Ricci (assistant professor, zoology, University of Rome), Franco

Savorgnan (professor, demography, University of Rome), Sabato Visco (director, Institute of General Physiology, University of Rome), and Edoardo Zavattari (director, Institute of Zoology, University of Rome).

2. Note that this document follows the unfolding of the 1938 manifesto and dismantles its arguments point by point. The numbers, therefore, refer to those employed in the 1938 manifesto.

3. A reference to *Homo erectus*, it appears.

CHAPTER 14

Twenty Years of *Critica Fascista* (1943)
Giuseppe Bottai

✳

From his editorship of Roma Futurista *in 1919–20 through* L'Archivio di Studi Corporativi *in 1930–33 to* Primato *in 1940–43 to A.B.C. in 1953–59, Bottai's intellectual career was largely built around journals. And, from the standpoint of the era's political and cultural debates, none was more important than* Critica Fascista, *a review Bottai founded in June 1923 and employed (with mixed success) as an instrument to advance a vision of fascism that valued intellectualism and debate over repressive violence, an elite technocratic vision of the National Fascist Party, cultural cosmopolitanism, and corporativism as the fascist "third way." Though the review became a key rallying point for technocratically inclined young intellectuals, its ability to actually shape the regime's policies and practices was limited. The following bittersweet and disenchanted reminiscences regarding the review's history attempt to combat the forces of reaction and repression within the party. They were published in* Primato *on the twenty-year anniversary of* Critica Fascista *in May 1943, only months before Bottai, Dino Grandi, and Luigi Federzoni led the 25 July coup against Mussolini that led to the setting up of the Badoglio government. (See also the introductions to chapters 6, 16, and 24.)*

✳

1. First Part: Action

I must confess: an autobiographical temptation seizes me when I hold in my hands and weigh this slim bundle of proofs, soon to become the pages of a book. Newspapers . . . are not always associated with private events, with particular aspects of this or that person's temperament. The link is more frequent in the case of magazines: small reviews—the products of a man's youth. Not a pretext to get into print but a reason for living: such was *Critica Fascista*. Born on 15 June 1923, the first year of the regime, *Critica Fascista* was inspired not by bookishness but by an urge to action, an action whose motives and goals could only come to light in the course of its realization. Since fate reserved for me a central role in this action, let me probe its

secret origins with the benefit of hindsight, for the passing of time allows
our experiences to ripen and take on added importance.

We were in the eighth zone. (Fascist Italy had been divided into large
areas referred to as "zones" at the end of the March on Rome; that is,
at the end of the armed insurrection that had lasted for four years.) We
were at a bivouac in Tivoli, between the roaring waterfall and the silence
of the Este villa. My command had found temporary housing at a small
hotel near the waterfall's steep rocks. I had cantoned the volunteers from
Abruzzi and the Tiber region at the Este villa, with desperate warnings
that they pay attention to the freshly painted wall. But the silence of the
Este villa proved too solemn, too bland for men excited by the action they
had undertaken. Days went by, one after the other. We reached the end of
the month amidst unconfirmed reports and rumors: the candid, heartfelt
rumors of an innocent season, the source of legends, songs, or myths (but
never, as would happen later, of wicked or scurrilous tales). In any case, my
men could not keep quiet any longer. For a couple of days they had taken
turns observing Rome from the terraces of the villa under a gray thundering
sky. Now they wanted to be there. They would not take "no" for an answer.
I tried my best to invent rites and inspections to distract them, even to
entertain them. But they wanted to *march*. This verb, which Mussolini had
just endowed anew with a revolutionary meaning that is now apparent to
all, had taken hold of their souls. The same was true of [Ulisse] Igliori in
Monterotondo and [Dino] Perrone Compagni in Santa Marinella.[1]

One of them sent me a messenger on the twenty-ninth in the middle
of the night. We gathered together to read the words inscribed on a small,
crumpled, wet piece of paper. It stated that they couldn't take it any longer
at the other bivouac. Since no order was forthcoming, they had decided to
move on the following morning of their own initiative. After thinking over
the situation, I summoned Mario Mazzetti, my aide-de-camp, and dictated
an answer: "Your letter finds me and my men in the same spiritual condition.
My men want to march and to enter Rome. I am with them. However, I want
to point out to you that such a move could gravely compromise the outcome
of the current political negotiations that are going to obtain for us an even
larger victory. . . . Can we arrogate to ourselves the power to act *against
the leaders of the party, who are about to become the leaders of the nation?*
This is the troublesome question that I ask myself and you. In any case, I
want you to know that earlier tonight, before your messenger had arrived,
I had already decided to move toward Rome. In point of fact, tomorrow
morning I will be looking for a new place to bivouac. By noon I will be

around Mammolo bridge and from there I will contact you. . . . In this way, we can be closer to Rome as we await the order that *Mussolini as head of the government* will certainly issue. It is my conviction that we should wait for orders from the supreme command; by this I mean, definitive orders."

2. Armed Criticism

In the previous lines I find traces of that temperament that I mentioned in my exordium. These are lines written in an atmosphere charged with passion, an atmosphere in which invocations and curses sometimes rang out thunderously among rowdy men in arms. I had the good fortune to recall the moment, six years after that revolutionary October night, for the comrades of *L'Assalto* (a Bolognese review): "There is nothing in my life that belongs to me alone, because my life is so thoroughly intermingled with the era of Mussolini. Nothing, except a tendency to arrange the facts in my spirit, to order my ideas, to place things in perspective." I also mentioned an inner "effort to coordinate." I may be wrong, but I think that the true roots of *Critica Fascista* . . . are to be found here, in the power to experience an action while observing it, to study an action as it unfolds. This is a power bestowed by nature, often against one's own will, and perfected through education. It is the power to see oneself in action, to see oneself act under the sway of feelings, thoughts, and interests. It is the power to test oneself not solely on the basis of a momentary and fractured action, episode, or phase but rather over a stretch of time within which are already embedded the action's outcome. The origins of *Critica Fascista* are therefore to be found in action and not in a criticism that dissects completed actions and formulates postfactum historical or scientific judgments. The "criticism" [in the journal's title] consists, rather, in the thought process that accompanies action, that illumines action and provides its substance.

I must insist upon this point, even twenty years after the first issue hit the stands, in order to underscore the fact that *Critica Fascista* was not the product of philosophical habits of mind or of intellectualism. My purpose here is not to defend myself against the accusation of being—God forbid!—a philosopher or an intellectual. Spiritual illiterates seem ever more prone to hurling these sorts of accusations at anyone who struggles to reflect upon his experiences, even though, in my case, I never had the chance to become a philosopher or to sharpen my intellect. In the course of my years, action greatly exceeded study, especially between January 1915 (when, not yet twenty years old, I volunteered for the army) and June 1923. The little studying that I did was never concentrated, systematic, or continuous since it was always interrupted by battles, insurrections, and punitive sorties. I studied the philosophy of law on the cliffs of the Tombolin di Caldenave in the Val Sugana. The same goes for all the other subject-matters, not just for me but for my entire generation. Our studies were mingled with action. This rendered us immune to the bloodless pallor of intellectual hysterics, still very much in vogue among culture lovers. Our rifles [moschetto] were literal, not figurative bookmarks.[2] "Criticism" was for us the desire to understand and investigate the reason behind our actions. If you wish to understand this you need to consider that for four years our criticism assumed the form of a war waged both within and without the Italian context; a war that was resumed during the ensuing four years of armed insurrection and waged internally. Ours was an armed criticism [una critica in armi]. For the great majority, the war was, of course, waged exclusively with assault weapons. But for a small vital core group of men, scattered among various units on the wartime and revolutionary battle fronts, the war was also fought with weapons of the spirit, of the mind, of a new intelligence. In their acute minds, these weapons had already assumed an immaterial value as dialectic, polemical, critical instruments. Every period of intense action, unless it proves historically inconsequential, is characterized by this sort of critical ferment.

3. From Insurrection to Revolution

Let me back up for a moment to that message on the Tiber. In its italicized lines ("*against the leaders of the party, who are about to become the leaders of the nation*"; "*Mussolini as head of the government*") you can see the man of action in action, bowing to the eternal laws of politics, following the instinctive motion of his soul and intellect. Whereas for him politics once marked the boundary between insurrection and revolution (a revolution in the process of being recast as a new category and new method), he now undertakes a course of action that could not have been foreseen the previous day, not to mention an hour earlier. Before our very eyes, Mussolini the subversive, the same Mussolini who for four years we had followed as the leader of an insurrection, was becoming the head of government and the builder of a new order. This metamorphosis seems so self-evident today that my insisting on it may appear superfluous. Not so back then. It passed unnoticed and remained so during the many months of that two-year period of transition from revolution to power that has been rightly labeled "the conquest of the state." The sudden transformation of party leaders into national leaders received even less attention. In the course of political action, circumstances arise that the majority fails to perceive at the right moment (or indeed ever), thereby condemning itself to act on the basis of yesterday's formulas and trends. The great challenge faced by political parties is, thus, the overcoming of a temptation, the temptation always felt by a majority of its membership (reflected in turn in the ruling minority) to live off the past, to rely on principles that were fruitful yesterday but not today, to launch appeals for insurrection when the people clamor for revolutionary laws, to systematically misplace one's emphasis.

On the night of 29 October, fascism changed its emphasis. Not only did it cease being a rebellion . . . but it also elaborated a new concept and vision of revolution, a revolution in power, armed with the instruments and organs needed to exercise power, fully in command not only of existing laws but, more importantly, of the laws to be enacted. To quickly and immediately grasp this fact in the midst of the swirling forces, passions, and interests that demand our attention is akin to discovering within oneself the critical powers that make up what we today understand as a revolution: intrinsic power; certain fatal, unavoidable consequences that one can neither fight nor shoulder passively; certain features of continuity that demand assiduous and shrewd interpretation on the part of a revolution's head. Vincenzo Cuoco in his "Essay on the Neapolitan Revolution of 1799" warns us that

> the history of a revolution is not a history of facts as much as a history of ideas. A revolution is but the effect of a people's shared ideas. Only he who has understood the course of such common ideas on the basis of sustained observation can be said to have profited from his studies of history. For every individual the history of facts is the same as the history of one's own ideas (self-contradiction being impossible). But when nations act en masse such as in the case of revolutions, then contradictions and uniformities, resemblances and dissimilarities must necessarily arise. They determine the slow or rapid, good or bad outcome of revolutionary events.

The duty of a true revolutionary criticism is to look deep into history in the very act of making history. It is authentic because it is born of the revolution or, better still, it itself embodies the revolution in its unfolding.

4. Revolutionary Crisis and National Crisis

When we first came up with the unusual coupling of the noun "criticism" with the adjective "fascist," a great many people objected that the two were contradictory terms. The adjective, they thought, implied the refusal of criticism and acritical celebration of what was already at hand. Of course, there was little or nothing that was "already at hand": a fact lost on those who, because of their commitment to nineteenth-century revolutionary canons, could not see beyond the fact of insurrection. Mazzini had admonished: "Insurrection is but a negative principle; insurrection ends when a revolution begins." But who was in a position to recognize Mazzini as the genuine master of our national political thought, given that Italy had cast him as a partisan? Only Mussolini. He set about elaborating Mazzini's thoughts, thoughts that anticipate the modern concept of revolution. "Insurrection," he declared in a speech to the party leaders on 17 October 1932, given in commemoration of the ten-year anniversary of the March on Rome, "is to revolution what tactics are to strategy. Insurrection is but a moment in a revolution. The totalitarian revolution must begin afterward." Beyond the more or less catastrophic episode with which it opens, a revolution displays its true inner effectiveness when, endowed with all the complex technical and economic tools necessary to transform a modern society, it operates on the marrow itself of this society, precisely monitoring shifts in vital tone [*tono vitale*] with the precision that control over the entire state apparatus alone makes possible. This is the point at which a revolution is transformed from an extraneous device into an effect (as per the Cuoco quotation). No longer viewed as something imposed from without by an audacious, strong-willed minority, it becomes integrated into the people's shared ideas.

Two months after the March on Rome and six months before the first issue of *Critica Fascista*, I wrote in *Il Giornale di Roma* (31 December 1922):

> The year about to end offers us . . . the clearest example of what our fascist revolution is and aspires to become: a slow, inexorable movement that involves, interests, and permeates the entire old order [*organismo*] and that strips away with admirable precision all those elements that the rhythms of modern life have rendered outmoded. Destruction and reconstruction proceed at the same time. It is a slow but sure revolution.

A thoroughly journalistic sentence, to be sure. But, written in a context in which many were already launched on a different course, it bespeaks a new vision of revolution that emphasizes the need to harmonize the nation's totality of interests as a function of the need for change. In the journal's first issue I admitted that there existed a crisis within fascism: a crisis due to the fever for renewal that was sweeping through the entire party organism. I added:

> It is useless, not to say malicious, *to view fascism's crisis as a free-standing phenomenon with no impact on the nation's life* (something our adversaries

do all too readily). To this we reply decisively that *the thorny problem of the definitive shape that fascism should take is an Italian problem, and a fascist problem only as such.* It was natural that the inner forces driving fascism should come out into the open once we acquired power. In a way, one might be tempted to say that *it is not fascism that is in crisis but rather Italian life, whose crisis is synthesized by fascism: a crisis involving growing pains and the struggle to shape and define values.*

Here the coincidence is fully explained: the crisis of the revolution and the national crisis are one and the same. From this one crisis, as from fertile soil abounding in ferments and vital juices, criticism springs forth. . . . This criticism is an indomitable force that places everything under review and that insists on measuring and remeasuring the very institutions that it founded to replace old or unnecessary ones so that they may become stepping stones to future creations.

5. How Revolutionary Criticism Works

It is this sort of criticism and creative energy that we have tried to provide during the past twenty years. If, in order to abide by this ideal, we have often had occasion to hark back to the squadrist experience (which, along with its immediate predecessor, the experience of assault troops, we consider the defining experience of the entire Mussolini generation), it is only because we have wished to visibly anchor our ideal where it belongs: in the realm of action. Action and action alone is our calling.

Those pondering the themes represented in the twenty-year index that accompanies this essay will notice a scattering of topics as well as recursions and rhythms. Just like a person takes action in the real world, so revolutionary criticism draws its strength from momentary attractions and fleeting temptations. It sniffs out and explores; it follows one trail, then abandons it for another. This very restlessness brings nourishment, breath, and energy; it revivifies. We have frequently touched upon the need for debate, defended the critique of inert discipline, championed the more difficult grassroots approach to appointments against choices that rain down like manna from above. In short, we have sung the goodness of the corporative principle beyond even its strict institutional limits in order to affirm it as the only means by which our era can hope to "deparliamentarize" inorganic democracy and forge a society of organically conjoined individuals. We have denounced the dispersion of authority among hundreds of lesser authorities who have sometimes instituted a crippling, blood-letting authoritarianism, as if this were the last word in "law and order." (It is, according to some tried and true idiots—after all, idiots too can be tried and true.) In its place we have defended the moral prestige that authority gains by descending directly from a single leader. At all times and in all these stances, our sole aim has been to preserve action, an action that dwells within the organs that will become its executors well before it surfaces in the public realm of the visible and that communicates conviction (without which action is little more than bustle).

Ours is not criticism for its own sake, as some imitators [*orecchianti*] claim or fear. If these political imitators were a bit more literate, we could put their minds at ease: first, by citing the advice of the Tuscan writer who declared that "human militancy has abused the term criticism, stretching it to mean blame, censure, and accusation," and second, by reassuring them that we speak without malice. Exercises in criticism do, of course, often give rise to actual criticisms. But let us assume that the order in place is so ideal that it is not susceptible to any sort of criticism, rebuke, or reprimand because everything takes place according to plan, in perfect observance of rules and laws. Even in such an ideal setting, as a result of government actions, the internal connections between component institutions, and their reciprocal action upon one another, forces will necessarily be unleashed that tend to modify an order's structure and functionality. One passes laws, for example, that govern collective work contracts, paying heed to that objective alone. What is easily forgotten is that effective enforcement of such laws must necessarily extend beyond the immediate work sphere. Once the collective contract is in place, and it begins to be enforced, first in one factory, then in all factories in the system, people become aware that its mere existence creates additional needs and problems that require, in turn, a shift in attention from work relations to economic ones. In other words, though the notion of the "collective" originally referred to a particular feature of economic life, it ends up raising questions about that economic life, even criticizing it globally. Once instituted, the principle of the "collective" contract thus acquires critical powers of its own. A revolution can disregard criticism. It can choose to disallow criticism during sensitive moments in its fateful unfolding. Sometimes it must be able to suffocate criticism. Yet a revolution cannot avoid fatal interruptions and fatal errors if it neglects that critical force from which it arose and that continues to propel it.

6. Why One Party Is Necessary

I mentioned scattering, something inevitable in a magazine like ours that has never limited its horizons to its editors' ambitions. Rather, our aim has been to fully and openly record the varied life of a regime in the making and to provide an outlet for critical energies whose revolutionary temper is beyond dispute. In so doing, we have deliberately embraced a certain eclecticism (and somewhat perilously so): a favorite target of detractors who understand neither our critical method nor our generous goal—an eager search for men and motives, for character and direction.

On one front there never was any real scattering: the party. This was, after all, our overriding theme. Certain long-standing polemics had convinced many people that because fascism was born as an antiparty, it should never constitute itself as a political party. (To recall the ardor of the debate, think only of the congress of the Fasci held at the Augusteum in Rome on 7–10 November 1921.) The transition from antiparty to party was, nonetheless, made, and we were among its strongest supporters. Once constituted, the party had to evolve toward becoming a sort of "hyperparty" [*iperpartito*]. Subject to an inescapable inner law of growth, it had to gradually enfold the lives of the nation, state, and regime within itself; it had to integrate them within its own development. Whether one retraces the party's entire history from 1921 to the present or instead scrutinizes recurring debates about its role, two alternating and contradictory concepts always surface: the antiparty and the hyperparty. The first aims to do away with even the slightest traces of division within the body politic (by building upon the changes wrought by great national events like the conquest of power or a war), so as to attain true unanimity within the fold of the state's venerable authority. The second aims to embrace the totality of the citizenry and to actualize unanimity through the power of its organization and leading organizations. Thus, ours is a partly antiparty, partly hyperparty, party. The alliteration might seem to reduce this formula to a mere play on words. It is not. On this very basis, one could retrace the history of Italian political parties from liberalism to totalitarianism. But this is not our goal.

Rather, our aim is to identify . . . the precise place within a modern regime that the party occupies in all of its *necessary* singularity. We believe neither that the party should be dissolved nor that it should splinter into various parties. Without a *single* party to represent them, the masses would be unable to express their will within the immense collective structures that characterize our era's economic organization. For them, the party is an indispensable instrument for achieving cohesion and coordination. Even less would they be able to do so if one restored the party system, based as it is on coalitions formed from political minorities. The masses' needs are less distinct and differentiated than those of political minorities. Uniform in character, they are best represented by a uniform organization; not by

parties, opinion groups [*sindacati d'opinione*] (often barely distinguishable), and special interest groups [*sindacati d'interessi personali*] (for whom
doctrine is simply a cover-up), formations that proliferate only among
minorities who have emerged from out of the masses thanks to culture or
wealth. To return to a multiparty regime today would be antihistorical. It
would be tantamount to overturning the unitary leadership that the masses
require in order to fulfill their shared interests. It would unleash dispersive
and destructive forces that would undermine the social and national unity
of the people. So, against the antiparty and against the multiplication of
parties, we turn to the party. The single-party model represents the summit
of modern political development. Such development might someday lead
to other forms of diversified expression. But what is the use of far-flung
predictions? Better to focus our attention on the moment of history that
is ours to live and to shape: a moment in which single-party rule remains
one of the necessary elements [*passaggi*]. That we were among the first to
reach the summit, that we did so in such an original manner, is to Italy's
enduring credit.

7. Criticism's Functions within the Single Party

We must not squander or dissipate this credit. On the contrary, as stated
earlier, we need to identify the precise place within modern states and
societies occupied by the single ruling party. This has been our constant
overriding concern. More than any other review, ours has made a massive contribution to the party literature—if not qualitatively massive, then
quantitatively so—on the topic of slowing the drift toward the hyperparty
model. Single-party rule is a natural aspiration in an era that calls itself
the fascist era; just as multiple-party systems were natural expressions of
the era of liberalism. The multiple-party system degenerated because of
parliamentarianism. The latter encouraged splintering and specialization
of interests to such an absurd degree that then-operative distinctions came
to include, for example, that between social democratic liberalism, liberal
social democracy, and liberal-democratic socialism. Similarly, single-party
rule can degenerate into totalitarianism, which carries the pursuit of unity
to such an extreme that all powers, functions, and tasks are so centralized
and concentrated that initiative progressively dwindles and vanishes. This
danger is far from imaginary. To combat it the ruling party must safeguard
its flexibility as an interpreter of the masses that it organizes, whether
directly or through subordinate or affiliated institutions. Its goal must be
to keep alive the dialectical process from which the party itself took shape

and drew its strength. The dialectical process must always be open to small changes in pitch, to sudden disagreement and unexpected agreement over ideas, evaluations, and judgments. It is driven by masses who, because of differing life-styles, social identities, economic conditions, degrees of cultural refinement, and age groups, provoke change. And provoke change they must if they are to remain a people, like today's Italians, rich in historical values and revolutionary passions.

The ruling party must exercise a critical function precisely in the sense that I have tried to define. Criticism is revolution in its continuous unfolding [*nel suo corso continuo*]. Criticism is action. And what is the party if not action? It is in action's dynamic progress from one field to the next, from occasion to occasion, from problem to problem, that party and criticism meet and are grafted onto one another, blessing new generations with new branches, leaves, and fruits. It is action that men and institutions incessantly renew in their work; action that tests laws, rules, and characters, confirming or altering them, reshaping norms so that they always reflect ever-changing reality. It is with criticism that the party can reach out to new generations, inviting them to become intimate collaborators in the revolutionary process, to step inside our formulae and institutions, to assimilate and not just accept (because only by assimilating do men acquire the sort of deep, enduring beliefs that engender decisive forms of intransigence, the sort of intransigence that gets performed on the stage of the world).

This is not the place to explain how this grafting ought to take place, because there are so many possible solutions. Once there is agreement regarding our objective, your solution might be just as valid as mine, his just as valid as someone else's. Learned disputations about the technical details of rules or statutes leave me utterly cold, whether in this particular area of party policy or in any other. But, unless I am mistaken, there should be absolute agreement at least on one matter: a party defined by the combination of action and criticism—one might be tempted to risk adopting the hybrid label "criticism-action"—must necessarily be understood as an *association*. The party does not consist in its management or its central and peripheral apparatuses, nor is it reducible to its several thousand leaders and officials. The party is you and me and all of us, joined together by a common faith. Aware of our presence within its fold, it makes its presence felt within us when we obey its officials and leaders but have the feeling—even the certainty—of obeying our own destiny and conscience. In this association—the word evokes the ever more prestigious name of Mazzini—criticism unfolds in authorized and acknowledged ways, in the meeting and clash between needs, aspirations, and ideas. A Fascio is also an "office" in the technical-bureaucratic sense of the word: an "office" that acts and makes people act (whose functional necessity ought not be denounced as long as it is rationally adjusted to the desired ends). Yet a Fascio is above all an "office" in the sense of collective political service, one that assures sustained contact among spirits, intellects, souls; one that channels their singularity into the common energy of the association. The party is defined by its oneness, but a oneness that is always being formed and reformed. In the perfect circle of our faith, it is as much the point of departure as of arrival. It is a premise that points to a conclusion that points back to a premise.

8. Mussolini's Faith in Criticism's Creative Power

We must not use Mussolini's words as crutches on which to support our short-term or long-term musings. But how can we avoid recalling to memory the many assertions of his that reveal his inexhaustible critical genius and his faith in criticism's creative powers in the enlivening realm of action? This is the Mussolini that we encounter in "Foundations and Doctrine of Fascism," masterfully tracing the reciprocal interplay of doctrine and men's activity, as well as their mutual reactions, transformations, and adaptations; appealing elsewhere to "restless and pensive spirits"; inviting "fascists to get in contact with each other" so "that their activity is also doctrinal, spiritual, and thought-related"; asserting that "a philosophical process" subtends fascism's "political process"; recognizing that there exist reciprocal relationships between doctrine and experience: "doctrine sheds light on experience, and experience puts doctrine to the test."[3] This is the Mussolini that we love the most. (Each one of us loves in him an ideal type, as is always the case with a great man whose accomplishments can be measured in work and thought.) The Olympian Mussolini, supremely confident that he has anticipated and brought about a new dispensation [*secol nuovo*], always on the lookout, with his incredible historical instinct and farsighted gaze, to launch in new directions and seize new forms of universal life.

This is the Mussolini to whom we have dedicated all our work: the Mussolini whose party wields the weapon of criticism with ease, dexterity, and agile foresight as it clears the path for a revolution that can no longer be restricted to its initial ideological intuitions or first topographical site. When necessary (and it frequently has been), *Critica Fascista*'s writers have proven capable of moving from polemics to *pòlemos*: from the clash of words to the clash of weapons. The transformation was easy because they had learned from Mussolini that words are not just figurative weapons and that there are times when one must defend the words of one's faith with weapon in hand, animated by a will to die that purifies the very necessity to kill. Yet we have never forgotten, and we never will, the opposite lesson, also learned from him: that there are other times when the heroic impetus must find its way into the realm of words by means of our mind's assiduous critical labors. And that word is action.

translated by Maria G. Stampino and Jeffrey T. Schnapp

Notes

1. Igliori and Perrone Compagni were leaders of individual columns of Black Shirts.
2. Bottai is alluding to the symbol of the fascist university groups (Gruppi Universitari Fascisti, or GUF), the book and musket. The symbol represented not only the ideal of merging intellectual training with military training but also that of infusing the domain of thought with the sort of activist, militant ethos that Bottai evokes throughout the essay.
3. See chapter 5 in this anthology for the overall context of this patchwork of excerpts.

CHAPTER 15

The Manifesto of Verona (1943)

The Republican Fascist Party was created in the wake of the 1943 coup by an extremist core group that included Roberto Farinacci, Alessandro Pavolini, and Renato Ricci, all of whom had sought refuge in Germany during the months of Mussolini's imprisonment (July–September). Upon his release Mussolini retained his titular role as leader, but Pavolini, who enjoyed strong German support, emerged as the prevailing policymaker of the Italian Social Republic. Proclaimed party secretary in mid-September 1943, Pavolini issued the Manifesto of Verona two months later, on 14 November, at the first Republican Fascist Party congress (at which Mussolini was not even present). The document's eighteen points are indicative of the elitist, socially progressive, and totalitarian course upon which the new republic would embark. Among other things, it calls for a return to the 1919 roots of fascism, for an anti- or postcapitalist economy with a single union to represent workers, for the formation of a European community, for continued Italian exploitation of Africa, and for a more vigorous official embrace of anti-Semitic racial politics. In addition, Pavolini's manifesto demands the creation of a special tribunal to investigate the "traitors" responsible for the July 1943 coup. (The latter led to the Verona trials, in which all but one of the accused were executed by firing squad, including Mussolini's own son-in-law, Galeazzo Ciano.)

The Eighteen Points

As concerns internal constitutional issues, we propose:

1. That a constitutional assembly (whose sovereign power derives from the people) be convened in order to declare the demise of the monarchy, openly condemn the treasonous last king (now in flight), proclaim the Social Republic, and name its head.
2. That this constitutional assembly be made up of representatives from all labor unions and administrative districts and also include representatives from invaded provinces in the form of delegations of evacuees and refugees residing in free territories.

   This constitutional assembly must also include representatives of servicemen, war prisoners (represented by those sent back due to disabilities), Italians abroad, the judicial bench, universities, and any other body or institution whose participation contributes to designating this constitutional assembly as a synthesis of the nation's values.

3. That this republican constitution grant to citizens, be they soldiers, workers, or taxpayers, the right to audit and criticize the public administration's actions, so long as this right is exercised in a responsible manner.

   Every fifth year citizens will be called upon to name the head of the republic.

   No citizen will be held for over seven days without a warrant from the judicial authorities irrespective of whether he was arrested in the act or detained for preventive reasons. A judicial warrant will also be required to carry out searches of homes, except in cases of flagrante delicto.

   The judicial branch of government will operate with complete independence while carrying out its functions.

4. That an intermediate solution be adopted in the electoral domain given Italy's bad prior experiences with elections and its partially negative experiences with too rigidly hierarchical methods of appointment. A mixed system seems the most advisable, one, for example, that would combine popular election of deputies with appointments of ministers made by the head of the republic and government. Within the party, it would probably be best for elections to be held on the Fascio level, with approvals for appointments to the national directorate being made by the Duce.

5. That the organization responsible for politically educating the people be one.

   The party, an order of fighters and believers, must become an organism of absolute political purity, fit to be the caretaker of a revolutionary idea.

   Party membership is not required for any job or position.

6. That the republic's religion be the Roman Catholic apostolic one. Respect is assured for other religions so long as they do not violate the law.

7. That those belonging to the Jewish race be considered foreigners. During the war they belong to an enemy nation.

As concerns foreign policy issues, we propose:

8. That the key aim of the republic's foreign policy be the unity, independence, and territorial integrity of the fatherland. The territory in question comprises maritime and alpine borders marked in nature as well as borders consecrated by bloody sacrifice and by history. Both are now threatened by the invading enemy and by their promises to the governments that have

sought refuge in London.[1] A second key aim will be to achieve recognition of the fact that a 45-million-strong population living in an area that cannot sustain it has certain indispensable and vital spatial needs.

This foreign policy will also strive for the creation of a *European community* made up of all those nations that accept the following fundamental principles:

a. elimination from our continent of the century-long British intrigues;

b. abolition of the internal capitalist system and combat against world plutocracies;

c. exploitation of Africa's natural resources for the benefit of Europeans as well as natives, with full respect for those peoples, particularly Muslim ones, who have already shaped themselves into civilized nations (such as Egypt).

As concerns social issues, we propose:

9. That the foundation and the main goal of the social republic be work — manual, technical, intellectual — in all its manifestations;

10. That the state guarantee private property, which is the fruit of individual labor and savings as well as an extension of the human personality. Private property, however, must not be permitted to have a disintegrative effect on the physical and moral personality of other individuals by way of the exploitation of their labor.

11. That in the domain of the national economy, the state's sphere of action encompass everything that extends beyond individual interests out into the domain of collective interests, whether due to scale or function.

    Public services and, in most cases, defense industries must be managed by the state through state-controlled corporations.

12. That in every factory (whether industrial, private, state-controlled, or state-owned) representatives of technicians and workers collaborate closely — to the point of having direct knowledge of the factory's management — in setting fair wages and in equitably distributing profits between reserve funds, stockholder dividends, and worker profit shares.

    In some factories this measure will be implemented by expanding the powers of the existing factory commissions. In others, the current management will be replaced by a managing council made up of technicians, workers, and a state representative. In others still, a union-controlled cooperative will be set up.

13. That in the domain of agricultural production, landowners' freedom of enterprise be curbed whenever and wherever the spirit of enterprise is lacking.

Expropriations of idle farms may lead to their being parceled out among field workers (who thereby become farmer-landowners). Similarly, badly managed factories may be transformed into union- or state-controlled cooperatives, depending upon the needs of the agricultural economy.

Since current laws already provide for these sorts of measures, the party and various trade unions are now hard at work on their implementation.

14. That farmer-landowners, craftsmen, professionals, and artists be fully entitled to pursue their vocations individually, as a family or other nucleus. However, they are subject to legal requirements governing mandatory contributions to government stockpiles or to regulation of fees for services.

15. That home ownership be treated not just as an extension of property rights but also as a right. The party's platform proposes the creation of a national agency for popular housing that will absorb the existing institute and greatly enhance its effectiveness. Its aim will be to make home ownership available to families of all categories of workers via the construction of new homes or the gradual repurchase of existing ones. To this end, the general principle that rent payments ought to go toward purchase of a home, once capital and interest have been paid off in full, must be adopted.

    The first duty of this agency will be to address the war's detrimental effects on housing by expropriating and distributing empty buildings and by erecting temporary structures.

16. That workers automatically become members of the union regulating the category to which they belong, but that this membership must not preclude transfer to another union if all requirements are met. All the trade unions are gathered together under the umbrella of a single confederation comprising all workers, technicians, and professionals (but excluding landlords, who are neither managers nor technicians). This umbrella organization will be named the General Confederation of Work, Technics, and Arts.

    Like other workers, employees of state-controlled industries or public services are integrated into unions as a function of their category.

    The imposing complex of social welfare institutions created by the fascist regime over the past twenty years remains intact. Consecrated by the 1927 Labor Charter, its spirit will inform all future developments.

17. That the party considers a salary adjustment for all workers an urgent necessity. This can be effected by adopting a nationwide minimum wage (with prompt regional adjustments). The need is particularly great among lower- and middle-echelon workers, both in the public and private sectors. Part of the salary should be paid in foodstuffs (at official prices) so that this measure not prove ineffective or harmful for all parties concerned. This can

be accomplished by means of cooperatives and factory stores, by expanding the Provvida's responsibilities, and by expropriating stores that have broken the law and placing them under state or cooperative management.[2] This is the best way to contribute to a stabilization of prices and of the lira's value as well as to the market's recovery. As concerns the black market, speculators must be placed under the authority of special courts and made subject to the death penalty, just like traitors and defeatists.

18. That with this preamble to the constitutional assembly the party offers proof that it is not only reaching out toward the people [*andare verso il popolo*] but also one with the people [*stare col popolo*].

As for the Italian people, it must realize that it only has one way to defend its past, present, and future conquests: to reject the slavelike invasion of the Anglo-American plutocracies whose sole aim, confirmed by a thousand signs, is to make the lives of Italians more modest and miserable. There is only one way for us to accomplish all our social goals: to fight, to work, to triumph.

Necessary Premise

In this manifesto, broadcast to the entire nation, the party congress established the program that will serve as the basis for the new republican state.

The document goes back to the premises that first gave life to the Fasci di Combattimento, premises to which we often turned when the revolution's future became clouded due to the seepage of base elements into our ranks, to the bourgeois propensities [*l'imborghesimento*] of many comrades, and to constant bureaucratic obstructionism.

In what did our simple but profound 1919 program consist?

a. a constitutional assembly to determine the organization of the state;

b. abolition of the Senate;

c. expropriation of large estates and creation of small farms;

d. labor legislation and participation of workers in management;

e. nationalization of defense industries;

f. a one-time tax on capital, review of all contracts for war supplies, and the sequestration of 85 percent of war profits;

g. condemnation of the Treaty of Versailles.

From that moment on we organized ourselves along strictly socialist lines. We were on the [socialist] high road over and against the Leninist theories that were intoxicating the masses; over and against Marxist socialism with its celebration of class hatreds and struggles and animosity toward patriotism; over and against the capitalist banking system controlled by the Jewish international and run with unabashed egotism.

So no one can accuse the program recently approved by the congress of the Fasci (and soon to be debated and deepened by the constitutional assembly) of demagoguery.

The password is: to reach out toward the people, toward manual and intellectual laborers. But it is essential to insist that our embrace must be reciprocated. Just as there are rights, so there are duties. Our common goal must be to create the preconditions necessary for the wholesale fulfillment of the republican party's proclamations. It would be absurd for Italians to hope for prosperity unless Italy is united, free, victorious, and powerful. At present the fatherland is threatened by Anglo-American plutocrats and Stalin's communists. Both would like nothing better than to enslave us. And, all the same, we find among our citizenry conservatives and communists who would look with favor on the United Nations' victory. The first hope that England will save them from Bolshevism. The second are convinced that an Anglo-Saxon victory would permit the Soviet Union to impose its law over our country.

Italy must be liberated and freed from the enemy. Only one solution is available: to rejoin the army so as to run off and fight alongside our courageous and generous German comrades whose aims are the same as ours. By this means alone can proletarian peoples be assured their right to life and can we cast asunder, once and for all, the oppressive encirclement that was ever increasingly suffocating us.[3]

The poisonous words of Pietro Badoglio are still eating away at many Italians, who remain impassive and fearful when confronted by the rush of recent events.[4] Perhaps they are unaware that they will be held responsible by the people and history.

One thing is perfectly clear: the Italy of tomorrow will not belong to traitors, deserters, absenteeists. It will belong to those who believed, obeyed, and fought.

It is especially to the young that we now speak. It will be impossible for them to claim their rights unless the rights in question have been earned by means of combat and sacrifice. Such is also the conviction held by the hundreds of thousands of veterans who will return from the front with their flesh torn apart by Anglo-American and Soviet lead or return from concentration camps with firsthand experience of the cruelty and hypocrisy of the so-called defenders of liberty.

translated by Maria G. Stampino and Jeffrey T. Schnapp

Notes

1. The allusion is presumably to the French government in exile formed around Charles de Gaulle, leader of the French Resistance forces.
2. The Provvida stores, sometimes referred to as Liverani shops, had since the early 1930s offered big-city consumers the possibility of purchasing merchandise directly from producers at what amounted to wholesale rates. Their diffusion was limited, but they were celebrated in the regime's propaganda as exemplifying corporativist ideals.
3. The reference is to Corradini's concept that Italy was a "proletarian nation" engaged in a struggle against bourgeois nations like Britain.
4. Although Marshall Pietro Badoglio (1871–1956) was not a fascist supporter at the time of the March on Rome, he assumed a series of highly influential positions during the fascist decades that included army chief of staff, chief of the Supreme General Staff, governor of Tripolitania and Cyrenaica, and (briefly) viceroy of Ethiopia. He was selected by King Victor Emanuel III to replace Mussolini in the wake of the 25 July 1943 coup led by Dino Grandi and set about negotiating both the "short" and the "long" terms of the armistice agreements under which the Italian government surrendered to the British and American forces over subsequent months.

PART 3

FASCISM AND CULTURE

CHAPTER 16

Nine Selections from
the Debate on Fascism and Culture
Critica Fascista (1926–27)

✳

The fascist regime devoted the first years after the March on Rome to absorbing new political blocks (such as the nationalists) and consolidating its hold on power by weakening or eliminating the most resistant liberal-democratic institutions. With the proclamation of Mussolini's dictatorship in January 1925, the question of reshaping the state and molding new political subjects became the order of the day. This was the context in which on 7 October 1926 Mussolini issued the following call to the students of the Academy of Fine Arts in Perugia: "We must not remain solely contemplatives. We must not simply exploit our cultural heritage. We must create a new heritage to place alongside that of antiquity. We must create a new art, an art of our times: a fascist art." The call was picked up by Bottai's Critica Fascista, *which solicited the comments of some of fascism's liveliest cultural figures, men such as Marinetti, Soffici, Maccari, Bontempelli, Malaparte, Oppo, Pavolini, Rocca, Puccini, Bragaglia, and numerous others. Their responses were published over several months and followed by a concluding essay (authored by Bottai himself) that makes a number of concrete proposals regarding fascist cultural politics. The debate reveals a wide spectrum of opinion, extending from the radical avant-gardist redaction of fascism (Bragaglia) to the synthetic mythic redaction of the* novecentisti *(Bontempelli, Soffici) to a range of conservative, nationalist, or radical populist trends (Pavolini, Puccini, Malaparte). It attests to a recurring nervousness about matters of cultural-political precedence (vis-à-vis Soviet Russia) and foreign influence (Hollywood) and acknowledges—albeit negatively—the antifascist opposition (Benedetto Croce and the prodemocratic and internationalist forces). The debate proved seminal to the degree that the regime's actual cultural policies and patronage practices would remain eclectic over the course of the ensuing decade, integrating everything from avant-gardism to neo-Roman iconography.*

The following brief anthology is made up of abridged versions of contributions to the Critica Fascista *debate. A brief biographical sketch precedes each essay.*[1]

✳

Ardengo Soffici

✳

A Florentine painter and writer, Soffici (1879–1964) was cofounder, with Giovanni Papini, of the influential review La Voce. *He subsequently became a Futurist and founded the review* Lacerba. *His post–World War I turn against the Futurist cult of the new led him to argue for a cultural "return to order" and for the adoption of the Novecento movement, championed by Massimo Bontempelli and Margherita Sarfatti, as the fascist regime's official art. In 1939 Soffici was elected to the Royal Academy. The following piece was originally published in* Critica Fascista *4.20 (15 October 1926): 383–85.*

After having struggled for several years over this question of the relation between fascism and art, I recently swore to throw in the towel, as the commoners say: to let things run their course and avoid further discouragement, considering the lousy turn the whole business was taking. In short, I swore to wash my hands of it and return to busying myself with my own art-without-adjectives and peacefully so.

The reasons for my decision were many, so numerous that it would be too long and boring to enumerate them. I will tell you, though, that among the principal reasons were the superficiality [*superficialismo*] and confusion [*confusionismo*] with which our party's press addressed such an important issue and the stupefying incongruence of all the acts that the organs of the regime in charge of such matters were carrying out. The same goes for all the initiatives they have embraced since the March on Rome.

I do not believe it would be an extraordinary revelation to say that slovenliness, ignorance, and vulgar social climbing have been encouraged in these years . . . and that the most foolish representatives of prefascism have been reevaluated by the new authorities and by the self-styled "new" journalism. Still worse, fascism has always chosen its men from among those whose mentality, aesthetics, and forms of artistic expression were in essence and in derivation not only foreign but, more precisely, barbarian, anti-Italian, liberal, Judaic, Masonic, democratic—in a word, antifascist par excellence.

I won't name names, because that seems to me superfluous, nor will I cite old or recent examples. But is it somehow not obvious . . . that between base academic vulgarity, archaizing or primitivistic dilettantism, romantic, anarchic Germanizing and Americanizing utopianism, and artistic internationalism (completely discredited everywhere and resurgent among the diehards of artistic liberal democracy), fascism has never known what path to take? The same goes for the pure elements of fascism's autochthonous character, which might be analogous to those that form the living nucleus of its political make-up. . . .

Things being as they were . . . I thought it best to wait and see how it would all end. . . . But here you are, taking advantage of what our Duce has said to the students of the Academy of Fine Arts of Perugia, coming to me and begging me to express my opinion on the very same question of art and fascism. . . .

Very well, then, I accept the challenge, especially since I will only have to make a minimal effort to satisfy you—that is, to copy over here an old piece of writing whose relevance will seem corroborated by the recent speech of our venerated leader. . . . I am referring to an article entitled "Fascism and Art" that I published in the September 1922 issue of *Gerarchia*. . . . I cite the text:

> Let me begin by declaring that fascism, which is not (strictly speaking) a party as much as a movement aiming for total regeneration, for the clarification of values and the restoration of the hierarchies of the Italian fatherland . . . needs more than any other party to tackle this problem and to resolve it. I mean that while its adversaries—all Italian parties are naturally its adversaries or will become them—may handle themselves regarding this subject as they handle themselves relative to so many others (that is, contradictorily, illogically, and, indeed, stupidly . . .), fascism cannot afford to do so because it . . . tends necessarily toward a vision of the whole where political facts spontaneously merge with spiritual facts, philosophy mixes with action, reality with imagination, and thus poetry with politics. For fascism, consequently, the work of Dante—which is like the gospel and the paradise of our race, as well as the ledger where all of its rights have been recorded . . . —cannot be a matter of little interest. . . . Nor can it be unimportant whether one type of poetry or art triumphs over another.
>
> . . . What, then, is the kind of art that fascism should defend and strive to exalt?
>
> This question might well stir up a suspicion that I wish to clear up right away: the suspicion that we are asking for a kind of political control over the free expression of the creative genius of beauty; or, what would be even more grotesque, an art of the party or of the state, a political art! Let me say, once and for all, that no idea horrifies me more. . . .
>
> We are now able to address our prior question. We may declare that

fascism, for example, must never embrace literary forms that are best described as philistine. This is the case because, reflecting a state of mind that is alternately vulgar, materialistic or theatrical, or redolent of a petty bourgeois or socialist sentimentalism, such works guide the spirit toward prosaicism, unrefined sensualism, or democratic cowardice. Similarly, the movement's preferences cannot lead to forms that, even if less bestial, have a foreign derivation. . . .

But what matters most is a further question: that is, which among the various artistic tendencies . . . fascism ought to support, according to our argument. And since these tendencies at the present time are, roughly, two, the reactionary and the revolutionary, which of these do we believe best corresponds to fascist theory and practice? Will it be that tendency put forth by those who hold that the art of the most distant past is infinitely greater and purer than it has been ever since and who aspire to that art and attempt to connect themselves to it . . . via an audacious backward move that must signify both protest and disdain toward every modern tendency? For obvious reasons, this cannot be. Fascism, which respects and can even adore the past and antiquity, is not reactionary or regressive . . . and it is not the enemy of modernity.

Will it be, then, the art of those who lean emphatically toward the future, renouncing the past and cursing it, discarding all principles in a revolutionary overturning of all recognizable values . . . ? We have already seen how this Futurist tendency has been followed and glorified, logically enough, by Russian Bolshevism. The fact alone suggests that this cannot be the optimum manner to achieve the general goals of fascism. Fascism, which is a revolutionary movement but not a subversive or extremist one, does not tend toward the overturning of values as much as toward their clarification, does not accept anarchy or whim but rather desires that the law be stabilized and reinforced.

. . . I think the literature and art that fascism should and indeed must sponsor is that which lends itself less to simplistic definition because it more fully embodies the spiritual essence of fascism and whose excellence is less apparent in the present state of total confusion. Such literature and art can call itself neither reactionary nor revolutionary because it unites the experience of the past with the promise of the future. It is a literature and art of equilibrium and integrity; a literature and art that can call itself both materialistic and idealistic because matter and spirit both participate in it as essential terms of life. It is a literature and art that, neither new nor traditionalist, neither romantic nor classical, neither heavy nor light, neither cultural nor completely instinctive, tempers within itself the extremes of every experience, and in this way it tends toward the sincere expression of the soul of the artist—that is, toward style, toward perfection. I would venture to say that it is a realistic literature, a realistic art, in the sense that this term can have when applied to the poetry of Alcaeus or Sappho or the sculpture of Phidias or Praxiteles.

In a word, it is an *Italian* literature and art. . . .

Fascism, which means Italy, has implicitly placed the principles of this art among the principles of its program. Perhaps it should articulate them explicitly.

So I wrote four years ago. And if you compare my words to those of the president when he envisaged the new Italy, the fascist Italy, "a great art . . . that embraces and in turn gives a unitary meaning to all manifestations of life, an art that must be traditionalist and at the same time modern, that must look to the past and at the same time look to the future," you will agree that, to use a colorful but accurate expression, you'd have to be nuts to expect a meeting of the minds more absolute.

If I were to add anything to my earlier words, I would further clarify that I did not then use the term "realist" with the intention of designating the proposed art of the regime. Since then I have used it elsewhere, most recently in the preface to a catalog of an exhibit of my paintings, wherein I insisted upon appending to the word "realism" the adjective "synthetic." By such a phrase I meant to describe an art that is not objectively "realistic" [*veristica*] but which, in the representation of the truth, reveals the lyrical spirituality and the stylistic will of the author.[2] I did not mean to evoke an art that abstracts from visible reality and experiments with the senses (as do all the schools of decadence of idealistic-romantic origin, from Cubism to Dadaism, through Neoclassicism and Futurism). Rather, I intended an art that draws its inspiration and its elements from the observation and the study of living, current, functional reality; an art that elaborates these elements until, having undergone a higher synthesis, they fuse in a creation that evokes the poetic qualities of nature . . . the splendor of the world as it shows itself to us as moderns and as Italians, as men who live with their spirits open to the present but who do not negate or disdain the national tradition to which we owe our exquisiteness of feeling and of taste. I meant, in brief, an art that evades idiotic and foggy theory mongering, snobbish and rebellious aberrations, the monstrosity of all vulgar primitivisms and charlatanisms . . . an art that would, instead, bring back a sense of concreteness, of measure, of order, and of authentic creative genius.

One further point, however, will help me to express my thoughts better than all of the preceding; namely, that in order to understand my views one need only contemplate the true essence and substance of fascism as it presents itself in our historical reality and to refer all the characteristics and virtues of the fascist movement to the type of art I have outlined. For the fascist movement finds its justification and its reason to be in reality and in the restoration of the lost values of our race.

Now, the Duce has done precisely this. Henceforth for us there is little more to do than to wait for his words to become facts. I am not hiding from you . . . the fact that this waiting is not—at least for me—without a certain perplexity and apprehension. Has it not been proven that many of the excellent ideas expressed by our leader have come upon stumbling blocks and deformations of every kind as soon as they have been handed down to those whose responsibility it is to translate them into active and fruitful realities?

Let's hope that such will not be the case this time around. Otherwise we would really have to retreat each to his own little burrow, from which not even your courteous solicitations might be enough to dig us out. . . .

Alessandro Pavolini

✶

After an early career devoted to journalistic and literary pursuits, Pavolini (1903–45) rose rapidly through the ranks of the National Fascist Party to become minister of popular culture between 1939 and 1943. In the wake of the July 1943 coup, he was appointed party secretary of the Republican Fascist Party and spearheaded the republic's efforts to return to the violent but socially progressive politics of 1919. The following piece was originally published in Critica Fascista *4.21 (1 November 1926): 393–95.*

. . . is it conceivable that certain historico-political conditions can have a profound and beneficial influence on art? Does it make any sense whatsoever to expect an artistic rebirth to derive from a political rebirth? Can the work of a politician, however exceptional, influence that most intimate, personal, and jealously guarded thing that is artistic creation?

Counter to every romantic prejudice, our answer to these questions is *yes*.

What stands out in the minds of those who are conversant with the great classical centuries of Italian art—the fourteenth, fifteenth, and sixteenth centuries—is more than the great faces of the creators and, next to them, the great works of art, unforgettable profiles, fixed on canvas or in marble, of terrestrial and heavenly muses, of human and divine men, of heroes of the common people and of myths. At the feet of the creators and their masterpieces stands without fail a choral presence: the people.

Behind Giotto, as behind the irascible Michelangelo, entire citizenries burn with passion. The artist paints and carves, the people are present at the work that they have commissioned. They give advice, admire, discuss face to face with the artist, who always comes up with a reason for what he is doing. They know each other well, people and artist; they are friends. Florentines and foreigners stream by the model of the miraculous door for the Baptistery, invited by Ghiberti himself, each offering his own opinion. This was enough, Vasari assures us, for Ghiberti to bring forth a work without a single defect, thus winning the competition over Brunelleschi, Donatello, and the Sienese Jacopo della Quercia.

The dome of Brunelleschi is born and grows dramatically in a ruthless and universal debate between the architect, his rivals, the city magistrates, and the chorus of the people: a magnificent drama with a happy ending.

The base of Benvenuto's *Perseus*, as soon as it was uncovered in public, was totally covered over again with notes of praise in prose and verse.

But why go on enumerating examples, when everyone is familiar with them? Art is of general interest in these great centuries. Townspeople are artists on the same level as lords. If there is reason to go down to the town square or to fortify the city walls, the artists are first to heed the call. If it is time to celebrate a carnival or a wedding, to cheer up the people by moving multitudes or improvising shows, the best artists are there to stage masquerades, processions, and displays.

In a healthy climate works of art simply flourish. They do not have the stuffiness of the academy, nor do they arise out of romantic solitude. They are brimming over with health, human laughter, and human pain. Besides the style of the artist, the style of one's ancestry stamps the art. It is not those estranged from the public who create works of art but commoners of genius—this one can sense at first glance. The souls of the creators and the souls of the people bring to mind the image of communicating vessels, some larger and some smaller, through which rushes the same wave of fervent feeling, faith, and thought.

The work of art is the work of an individual, not a collective. But in our (Italian) works of art, one can sense that the artist, while his mind was reasoning on its own and his arm was moving freely in the ardor of his work, had his feet resting on solid reality, on a precise plane of reference.

That plane of reference was his understanding of the people, of the thirst for beauty shared by men of the same race, with all their limitations yet with all their incomparably fresh and deep intuitions.

The understanding surrounding them was an element that our grand masters held in the highest esteem through an instinct that we might call one of preservation. . . .

But this is not enough. Everyone knows that the works of the artists of our golden ages were in large part commissioned. Reference on the part of the artist to the common people, to their genius and characteristics, was therefore necessary, humble, assiduous, and loving. Those characteristics are expressed in the faces of the men and women portrayed, in the outline of a piazza or church in which the monument is to be set or of the landscape in which a villa is placed.

The teachings of the Romantic school would have one believe that the imposition of such obligations on the artist necessarily does great harm to an artist's inspiration because his liberty is thereby limited. What a mistake!

If liberty is the unfolding of individual energies — creative energies, in our case — in conditions favorable to the fulfillment of their ends, it is easy enough to ascertain that artistic creativity was never freer than in those eras in which the majority of works were commissioned.

Artistic liberty is like political liberty. It is only conceivable when it has limits; it cannot exist without law.

Within the extrinsic limits imposed by the dimensions of a wall for which a painting is to be done, of a chapel to be frescoed, of the necessity of a harmonious environment, and so on, within those limits the inspiration of our painters was powerfully stimulated. They were moved to arrive at "that certain idea," as Raphael would have said, that shone in their souls. Similarly, the inspiration of our old poets, when love "dictated within their souls," instinctively found its freedom in the rigid laws of rhyme, of verse, of traditional lyric composition.[3]

The originality of each artist was derived from tradition, just as naturally as the fruit tree rises from the earth.

The progressive alienation of the artist from the popular matrix coincides with our artistic decline.

Slowly that spontaneous sense of tradition, the depth of human meanings, and the classical values of our art vanish, drowned by the flood of decadence. . . .

Barbarians rule supreme. Romanticism, announced by a thousand heralds, approaches, a romanticism that will gouge out an abyss of mutual incomprehension between artist and people.

Pure art, accursed poets, angels in exile, bohemia, pride in garret rooms and Wildean intentions, the cult of Nietzsche's superman picked up in art studios, Rollandesque idolatry of more or less misunderstood geniuses, the ultramodern usage of bourgeois, middle-brow, and other respectable attributes, the jealously guarded, secret jargon of avant-garde cliques, the quest for artificial paradises: these are some of the typical signs of romantic times.[4]

In the modern liberal-democratic state, the romantic artist finds the position most suited to him, which is to say, no place at all. Any sympathy toward politics, toward the life of the nation is blocked off for him. He has all the isolation, the disdain, and the misery that he needs.

So, shabby, anarchical, and desperate, he stoops to wretched trysts with shady ladies, shuts himself up in dark chambers where the smoke of cigarettes and theories is asphyxiating. He aims to provoke those who will look at his paintings. His paintings show he has entirely lost sight of the concept that art is pure decoration and that a painting is, above all, an object designed to nobly decorate the walls of men's houses.

Glaring mistakes are made about the nature of art. Ravings about a "fusion of the arts" are their symptom.

In the name of "pure art," they ban from the work of art its content, its subject, its substance and preach against craft, technique, and formal grace.

Little by little, between flashes of grandeur and of the silliest insanity, through episodes of heroism and of wearisome imbecility, through enormous waste of talent, perversions of intelligence, the abandonment of instinctive traits, we arrive at aborted attempts that, though logical from an historical point of view, are aesthetically absurd and of value to the healthy only as a tragic document of decadence.

To the hundred "internationals" is added that of artists, of recluses in ivory towers who speak to each other in their latest jargon, above the fray and beyond national borders, playing catch with the innumerable "isms" of the modern intellectual movement.

Around them, a whole bastard world, equivocal and parasitic, takes shape, a world that the people do not even know exists: critics who speak in mysterious tongues, editors of unfindable and unreadable journals, impostors and perverts, lazy intellectuals and idiotic wheelers and dealers, merchants who buy for five and resell for a thousand after the death of the "misunderstood artist."

A certain snobbish bourgeoisie (on the order of Proust's Verdurins), attentive to "previews" but whose interest in things related to art does not foster any link whatsoever between artist and people (as did certain aristocracies in the past), is delegated by democratic society to maintain an oscillating and unproductive contact with artists.[5] In the drawing rooms of this plutocratic international bourgeoisie, artists escape from their own exhausting cliques only to shut themselves up in new, worldly cliques whose cloistered distance from the people is just as jealously guarded.

Meanwhile, the people, left to its own devices, uneducates itself, turns into rabble, and finally does not even recognize real art, which, though timid and gone astray, continues to flourish all the same.

Only those incapable of any artistic endeavor, the most brazen quacks and the least enlightened scholars of the state academies, are left to serve the architectural and decorative needs of the people and the state.

Then democratic ugliness is born, hatched in the ministries of the fine arts and in government-sponsored competitions. Art Déco is born to the tune of the Excelsior Ball. The obscene tastes of Masonic lodges overrun defenseless cities.

. . . Every time that we take a mental trip into our artistic past and every time we contemplate the present, we arrive at the same conclusion. To wit: if there is one cause to which we can attribute the current drying up of the wellsprings of creativity, it is the progressive schism between the people and artists, between the nation and the creators. If, beyond our hope that providence will see to the birth of artistic geniuses among us, we may entertain yet another hope for our artistic rebirth, that hope would be that the romantic abyss between artist and people be filled in and overcome.

Three recent phenomena seem to aspire to the realization of that hope: Futurism, the war, and fascism.

We see the Futurist movement in art as a brief and salutary bridge between two long eras: between that era that we hope has passed and a new era that we hope has finally been inaugurated.

Since Italy had completely lost touch with her own personality and proud autonomy as a leader in the field of art . . . those currents that Futurism conveyed, to which it gave a name and whose energies it multiplied, appear to have been providential. Such currents were destined to enter Italy via the same wretched road that others had traveled for over half a century, a road from which there is no exit save that of continuing to the bitter end.

With Futurism . . . we caught up and passed from the rearguard to the avant-garde. Nearly all the epidemic spiritual sicknesses that our young artists would have fatally contracted (and could have recovered from only with great difficulty) were prevented and overcome thanks to the atrociously violent Futurist vaccination, often lethal to weak temperaments yet sometimes leading to fruitful convalescences. The vaccine was imposed through the generous activity of Marinetti and his friends and their doses of this obligatory prophylactic.

This was the negative liquidating function of Futurism, its romantic side, through which we were able to perceive the extreme limit of our decadence. But there is another side to Futurism, in decided contrast with the first—a contrast at once historical and logical. This second side identifies the Futurist movement with the beginning and end of a transitional phase, that is, as a brief hinge between two long eras.

In fact, if, on the one hand, with Futurism the romantic schism between the people and artists . . . became wider than ever before, on the other hand, through Futurism artists began once more to search out the masses and feel a need for them. They began to leave the stuffiness of their little schools and to bring the people together in theaters and public squares. Even if the aim was only to insult them and the dialogue was a heated one, this was after all a sign of a love that was being reborn.

Artists thereby appeared who had political programs to expound, who struggled to do everything possible to be in the forefront of the national scene and of popular life.

It seems significant that this instinctive and unconscious aspiration of young Italian artists for close contact with the Italian people should occur on the eve of the war.

It might seem that the war should have brought about . . . a reconciliation of artists with the masses, with their faith and aspirations. In reality, the mere fact of having fought, of having engaged in war was not enough in itself to profoundly alter the spiritual destinies of individuals and of warring peoples. For a spiritual bounty to be reborn, combat alone was not enough. Only by interpreting the war and understanding its value, only by uncovering its true essence could new ideas and new myths be engendered.

As it happens, such an interpretation was not arrived at by all nations and veterans. . . .

Now, the Italian people not only waged the war, but they also interpreted it. Their grand, all-comprehending, realistic, and religious interpretation—whose universal value is now becoming more widely accepted—is fascism itself.

The war, as regards artists, had the effect of breaking up their asphyxiating cliques and dragging them down from their ivory towers, thereby immersing them in popular reality—a magnificent baptism in the trenches. Yet this experience might have vanished or been erased in the postwar atmosphere of fatigue and uncertainty . . . were it not for fascism, which, in our case, held off the forces of dispersion and false interpretation. Moreover, fascism perpetuated and continues to perpetuate the wartime experience.

In conclusion, fascism—even in its errors and occasional confusions (which have not ceased and which we must not forget)—is increasingly bringing Italian artists to the spiritual conditions most befitting their work and faithful to our Italian tradition.

Judging from this daily recovery from the romantic infection, a recovery of which fascism is the catalyst, it is reasonable to hope that art in Italy is destined to flower again, to rediscover its own nature, its own sanity, its own classicism.

There are, in fact, signs that might lead us to be optimistic, others that might lead us to be pessimistic. We will see. In the meantime, we have faith not only in those artists whose integrity, capabilities, and intelligent adhesion to the new Italian spirit we already know but also in Mussolini, this great provocateur of will and inspirer of faith who even in the field of art can do much. For art, as every other human endeavor, is the fruit of will and faith and not only of a certain inclination or of uncontrollable inspiration.

If our art will find such a renewal, then this art will be "fascist art." . . .

Massimo Bontempelli

✳

Bontempelli (1878–1960) was one of the leading novelists, playwrights, and critics of the fascist decades. Founder of the Novecento movement and its review, associated with the ideal of "magic realism," he was elected to the Royal Academy in 1930. During the late 1930s he began his break with fascism that led to his eventual election to the Senate as a communist deputy (though he was not seated because of his prior profascist activities).

The following piece was originally published in Critica Fascista *4.22 (15 November 1926): 416–17.*

. . . "Fascist art." There you have it. If "fascism" were only the name of a party or a political preference (however victorious and flourishing), art would have absolutely nothing to do with it: they would be two independent and incommunicable worlds. But by "fascism" we mean a whole orientation of life, public and private: a total and perfected order that is practical and theoretical, intellectual and moral, application and spirit. We all agree on this (and those who don't simply don't count).

And so it is evident that one can legitimately speak of "fascist art" just as one can properly speak of "classical art" or "romantic art."

The latter examples are not simpleminded ones. . . . They spring from a not-too-recent fixation of mine, and one that is ever more deeply rooted. I will restate it gladly, because up to now it has always been received (at best) as an amusing paradox. But by sheer repetition it is possible that even the most unwilling listeners could end up understanding its seriousness. (Habit engenders truth.)

I will affirm then, once more, that the history of Mediterranean-European-Western civilization (that is, of Greece-Rome-Europe-America) has evolved in two great periods up to the present: the *classical* period, extending from Homer up to (but not including) Christ, and the *romantic* period, extending from Christ to the Great War . . .

The Great War reopens, between one era and another, the same gaping abyss that, twenty centuries earlier, resulted from the appearance of Christianity. Of course, every era has certain foundations and certain precursors in the era that precedes it. Magnificent precursors: the second epoch had Plato, as ours has Friedrich Nietzsche.

Fascism, a specifically Mediterranean phenomenon, is the precise historical event that inaugurates the latest era: the third epoch of human civilization. It was not for nothing that fascism was born as the correct interpretation of the Great War.

Such is its historical stature. As for fascism's geographic necessity, it corresponds to that mysterious logic of fate that ordains that civilization's new beginnings and periods of renewal should always come from the Mediterranean basin. . . . Therefore, Italy is forever destined to serve as a reflective and civilizing force; and the Mediterranean must be eternally vigilant if it is to avoid its own downfall (should the balance of power suddenly shift).

And here today is fascism: a phenomenon at once spiritual and temporal (like the double dominion of medieval Catholicism through which the universality of the Roman world was saved). Without that double nature, neither the Catholic Church nor fascism could have come into being or become a reality.

As you can see . . . we have taken a rather long detour, and perhaps you think I have strayed and lost sight of our goal. But at the last bend we unexpectedly stumbled upon our topic. For *art* is the sensitive instrument that must at once mark off and foster, express and bring to maturation the fecundity of the third epoch of civilization: the fascist era.

And here, if you were to insist that I enumerate the modes and forms, the attitudes and colors of the new art that is slowly but surely preparing itself in Italy and Europe, I would refuse: it is in the nature of prophecy to remain generic. So much the more so since art, no matter how reflective, intelligent, and self-conscious, must always maintain a reserve of the spontaneous, unpredictable, and instinctive elements that are its life. If this epoch is truly fascist to the core, all that is of lasting value and is accomplished during its course will bear the visible imprint of fascism. But it will be up to future historians to define such interconnections and signs; for us to do so would be useless, compromising, and even ridiculous.

Of course, we must impose some restrictions. We must negate all that which, in the art that surrounds us, is not a glorious heritage but rather the sterile and tired vestiges of the century that preceded us. For twenty-five years now we have been desperately seeking something salvageable from among those leftovers: rotting leftovers of psychological analysis, of naturalism, of aestheticism, of petty bourgeois tastes, of nauseating and fraudulent sentimentalism that would like to make us to believe that it is "human art."

The new art must be entertaining, even when its roots are in suffering; it must cover with smiles the saddest of things and with wonder the most banal. It must be a miracle rather than a chore, an act of magic rather than the bustle of official business. It must rediscover a sense of mystery and the equilibrium between earth and sky.

We are emerging from a period of restless, arid, wretched dispersion—the last debris of the last leftovers of great romantic art. The forms taken by this worm-infested flotsam and jetsam were the love of impressions, of fleeting shudders, of suggestive fragments, of lyrical moments. Against this anemia we invoke a cure by imagination. Today, out of reaction and the necessity to begin rebuilding, inventive qualities must come to the fore. Above all, we must learn over again how to tell stories, to combine new myths and new fables, to invent characters and plots. We must build things and not just put together words or sounds or colors. . . .

Anton Giulio Bragaglia

✳

Bragaglia (1890–1960) was Italy's leading avant-garde theater director during the fascist decades, though his activities included play writing, set design, experimental photography, and filmmaking. Long associated with the Futurist movement, a prolific critic and theater historian, his Teatro degli Independenti received government financial support during the mid- to late 1920s. Despite this early support, Bragaglia was a frequent critic of the regime's cultural policies during the 1930s. The following piece was originally published in Critica Fascista *4.22 (15 November 1926): 417–18.*

As the coming to power of fascism was being prepared, we all agreed on the necessity of dismantling the old conservative milquetoast Italy. These were the words of Marinetti, our first master. We felt the spirit of Futurism invading other areas, as well as artistic ones, and you can easily understand how pleased we were. . . . For our groups, the word "revolution" referred to the artistic field, then as now. To foment a revolution meant to bring about what we had been talking about since 1911 and what Marinetti had been repeating since 1909. A revolution in the worlds of banking, industry, agriculture, or what have you had nothing to do with our problems. To each his own business. We had to skin the cat of Apollo—hardly a mild-mannered beast, even when half dead. Having envisioned only a revolutionary program for the arts, we greeted with enthusiasm the formation of the first nuclei of political revolutionaries who intended to struggle not with words but by means of decisive actions. In Rome, the extremely violent meetings of this period were held at the Casa d'Arte Bragaglia, whence the director of this journal [Bottai] departed for the first protests with banner in hand.[6]

I was present at sessions when Futurist periodicals were edited and was summoned frequently by the police commissioner to present to him, as a representative of the artists and Futurists, the nature of every action organized in the Casa d'Arte by Bottai, Enrico Rocca, Calderini, and the other Futurists.[7] We [artists] then conceived of such parallel efforts to impose modern reforms in the administrative and political fields as an infallible path for our own claims.

We believed that national purification, the supreme goal of the revolution, would also force some fresh air into the academies, halting the tyranny of outdated ideas, the practice of excluding youth, the fear of all modern points of view.

. . . We thought, then, that our brothers fighting for a national rebirth would make artistic dignity a top priority, since it is the ornament of every great revolution and the pride of our tradition in every age. This had nothing to do with profit or with the usual dash to hoard lucrative positions or practical advantages. Ours is another kind of chase; that's why they call us cloud-chasers. If we were just left to chase these clouds, we would be satisfied. Our battle is more for form than for substance! Hence the divergence between us and the appointed governing boards, commissions, academies, consortiums, and other official troughs where what should be the goal of every study is an afterthought, namely, the creation of a style for this, our shameful, artistically corrupted era. . . .

All that is merely rehashed from historical styles will not figure into our plan: this is not the work of our contemporaries. . . . The revolution, as we see it, should have insured the adoption of a specific artistic style. It should have sealed the matter once and for all. Instead of resigning oneself to ancient laziness like historico-maniacal copycats, this should have been understood right away.

They tell us, "The geometric style was adopted by the Soviets: how could fascism, therefore, adopt the same style as the communists?" Just one moment! The geometric style *was* adopted by the USSR, but only after Mussolini and *Il Popolo d'Italia* had fostered its growth, supporting the creators of this eminently Italian style whose influence now extends throughout the entire world. When Mussolini was a Futurist, Lenin was still in exile and only dreaming of the Bolshevik revolution. To speak of "precedents," then, is hardly proper (the Russians themselves, in the person of Lunacharsky, admit that their art was influenced by Italian Futurism).[8] To be modern instead of neo-antique seems legitimate to me when, in any case, both are equally Italian; what seems strange is to disdain a contemporary style . . . merely because it has succeeded in becoming an international style. Despite the fear of this word "international," one ought not to forget that had modern Italy officially adopted this style as the distinctive sign of our century instead of becoming an international style, it would have been viewed in every nation as an Italian import. Here, then, is the way to brand with Italianness an "international" geometric style that is in no real sense "international" because it is one of *our own* Futurist creations!

What could this "fascist art" be that the head of the government evoked in his speech at Perugia? When Mussolini had Marinetti, Papini, Soffici, Palazzeschi, and the other Futurists as collaborators, he would not have hesitated to declare the art of the Futurists the logically fascist art, for fascism itself arose in the Futurist intellectual atmosphere. In the beginning fascism and Futur-art were but a single language. Today there are so many ignorant newcomers (as Gentile would say) that we barely keep in touch with our childhood friends. Today it can no longer be said that Futurist art . . . fulfills the needs of a style *for our times*. But, by necessity, such an art would have to take into account new conquests in the expression of new sensibilities. Such an art could not be founded, in any event, on the exhumation of historical styles. . . .

As for theater, I see my own well-known theory of performance (to which I have dedicated innumerable articles) as the theatrical art of our time. "Theater Italian-style" would fuse in a modern manner the vivacity of improvisation with as much premeditation as possible (without, however, drowning out the freshness of improvisation). With the help of old devices [*macchine*] that are now perfected, we can be in step with the new times in this "era of cinematography."

Born during the moment of its final decline, cinematography was a terrible omen for dramatic theater. Nonetheless, the former will prove the latter's salvation. The musical theater has not been harmed by the advent of film because it has remained true to its own canons. The case of dramatic theater (theme theater, theater of thoughts, theater of poetry, etc.) is different: film has served to remind it of its fundamentally sensory nature. . . . Movies thus have nothing to fear from the theater, nor will a theater that is genuinely theatrical (as it well ought to be) have reason to envy film. The medium of each, powerful but quite opposite, gives the theater of images [film] wonderful and miraculous possibilities while yet preserving for the living theater its own unique and powerfully original means of representation. This will become clear when the yokes imposed by current theatrical organizations (both bureaucratic and financial) are sundered and the theater has the means to develop organs in harmony with its true nature. . . . The meetings, conferences and orders of the day, the issues of wages, unions, economic and class interests, the formation of corporations are all extremely useful actions, yet in the end they ignore the core problem and solution. Theater is theatrical *art*: this is what needs to be protected at all costs.[9] Any cure will have to keep the latter in mind; otherwise, it will be little more than a palliative. . . .

The public is waiting for the theater to be reformed, rejuvenated, brought up to date. As soon as it knows that one of the stock thirty-six dramatic situations is not being rehashed, it will return to the theater. Neither organizing class groups nor the splendid chatter of conferences will bring the public back. This crisis is similar to that of the national motion picture business. There is a lot of shouting back and forth, but where are the Italian directors who know how to make films like the Americans? There might be some out there. There probably are! But they are certainly not the creators of the "psychological film," that wondrous Italian innovation that, with the gracious help of star worship and a pervasive drunken megalomania, has helped to sink our film industry.

The group now championing the cinema and organizing the rebirth of national production is precisely that responsible for the disaster and that, therefore, ought to be strictly excluded. It is clear that a small handful of spirits representing the various branches of this complex art should be sent off to America to study the new techniques, photographic media, and chemicals; only after two years of schooling should they be allowed to venture out. Our venerable directors have their own work habits, which they will not change. They are spoiled and callous; nothing can be done with them. Let them shout.

Obstacles to the creation of an "art of our times" or a "fascist art" arise whenever an artistic discipline finds itself personified by the same old crew who administers every opportunity in every branch of the arts. Musical theater is in the hands of the last imitators of the nineteenth century. So is the [dramatic] theater. . . . So are the plastic arts, degraded by a commission of "old fogies of the Apocalypse," immortal by divine punishment. They remain the same. Nor has fascism rid itself of these fossilized guests. Such was the intent of our complaints soon after the March on Rome, when we began to fear that art was not going to be revolutionized at all because its concerns seemed trivial. Now the leader of the government has brought us hope again. Let us hope that political matters will not distract him again from our problems. Now that young artists are better established, we can still encourage "fascist art," which means the art of young people. The first thing to do is to push aside those who still look to the light of the last century for their inspiration and, with them, those who look to the light of the centuries even before the last. Let us rejuvenate and support the young, who must bring forth this art of the new times and who are the only ones who can do it. Open the windows! Those who catch pneumonia will die, it is true.

But only the old will catch it. Finally the appointed hour will have arrived for the poor rascals; we have been patiently awaiting the moment since 1919 and had hoped it would have come earlier.

Curzio Malaparte

✳

Malaparte (1898–1957) was a noted novelist, journalist, and newspaper editor whose intransigent squadrist loyalties rendered him something of a gadfly during the fascist decades. By the late 1920s Malaparte had emerged as a

*leading advocate of the radically populist, antimodern Strapaese movement,
one of the period's prevailing cultural strains. The following piece was originally
published in* Critica Fascista *on 15 November 1926 (421–22).*

Surely you jest? A fascist art? Just what might that mean, a fascist art?
We must get this straight, even if it means risking our reputations and our
health. If by fascist art you mean an art that agrees unqualifiedly with official
tastes in vogue with the Fascio, the institutes, and the agencies . . . ; if by
fascist art you mean that art that is proposed, defended, advanced by push
and by shove, imposed upon us in showers of pamphlets, of exhortations,
and veiled threats, glorified in the speeches of all the Sunday Ciceroes and
rhetoricians, crammed down the throats of all the oh so highly disciplined
sheep who would accept a fist in the eye as art, as long as it were handed
down to them via the proper hierarchical channels; if by fascist art you mean
the art of bureaucrats and trouble-makers, of academics *in pectore*, of hog
catchers and ball busters stuffed with goose fat, of swamp-rats who dive in
the marsh of the innumerable profiteers of fascism, crab-infested low-down
hypocrites, philistines in top hat and gloves, Franciscan extremists, raving
duck-billed platypuses, or, in short, old farts and hecklers, well, then . . . if
that's what you mean by fascist art, then I say it's hopeless. . . .

   But if by fascist art you mean a profoundly and essentially Italian art
that has roots in our true, classical, and most Italian tradition; an art that
is popular (in the true sense) rather than academic and insolent, up-to-
date rather than old hat, rural and provincial rather than dottardly; an art
that, to be more precise, would have not only our own home-grown virtues
but also our own home-grown defects rather than home-grown virtues
and foreign defects, or maybe even only our own defects rather than only
foreign virtues. (As far as this is concerned, it's better to get this straight
once and for all: European art has always lived and still today lives off the
interest accumulated by the enormous capital of our artistic and literary
defects.) If by fascist art you mean a truly Italian art, then . . . it's a different
story. But, in that case, we must first begin to clear the field of all that which
claims the right to call itself *fascist* art. . . .

   For what happens in politics often happens in art: when Mussolini
says, "This is fascist," he means that it is Italian, purely and traditionally
Italian, that it has in it the essential characteristics of our authentic and
virile spirit, rather than that incredibly polluted and decayed spirit by
which the preceding political climate lived and breathed and that we of the
Mussolinian generation have repudiated and against which we battle for the

good of all. But the idiots who always constitute the majority misunderstand this, and when they declare, "This is fascist," they hope to pass off as fascist the expression of their own mediocrity, of their bad taste and spiritual and intellectual poverty, believing in good faith in the thaumaturgic, protective, and constraining powers of party badges. It never occurs to them that it's not enough to be fascist to be able to create fascist things, and that you can have been a member of the fascist party for forty years (as especially the most recent recruits tend to claim) and still have preserved a contaminated, decayed, and degenerating spirit. That spirit is, in politics, democratic and liberal and in art, boorish or romantic or neoclassical or cosmopolitan or French or foolish or convenient—take your pick.

Would you like an example . . . ? Benedetto Croce is, politically, a liberal, which is to say, an antifascist. But his *History of the Kingdom of Naples* is a fascist work, the most fascist of all works to appear in Italy in the last few years. It is pervaded by a spirit that is completely fascist. And yet Benedetto Croce is not a card-carrying fascist but, on the contrary, an adversary of the regime. Would you like more examples, more names? . . . I think that it would be useless to cite them. But it is not useless to warn that many of the manifestations and expressions of so-called fascist art, whose authors or initiators are authentic card-carrying members of the party, are merely expressions of the commonest boorishness, of the most incurable bad taste, and of the solidest ignorance. In other words, they are the expression of the most organic antifascism. I won't name names, especially since they're always the same ones.

The truth is . . . that it suits many people (and especially those who stand to gain) to misunderstand the words pronounced by the Duce in Perugia. The Duce, as Soffici has made remarkably clear, meant to allude not to an art of the regime or of the party or to an official state art but to a "new art that would be the most excellent sign of these new times." It's so clear. You really have to be proud of your imbecility to misunderstand the Duce's crystal clear words. Therefore, we're talking about an art pervaded with the spirit of the revolution. That's the point. And on this point we all agree. I am absolutely certain . . . that Mussolini's faith in us, the Mussolinian generation, will not be betrayed.

For the moment, the only original and powerful artistic expression of fascism is Mussolini himself. He has the same all-encompassing and conclusive value for our time and our spirit that the greatest artistic creations of the Italian spirit have always had for their times. Nevertheless, we must point out that we, the Mussolinian generation, have contributed nothing to the creation of Mussolini as a work of art. Quite the contrary: it is to him that we owe what is artistic and original in us. We must, in conclusion, declare that the artistic masterpiece of Mussolini is not fascist Italy but Mussolini himself.

Mario Puccini

✳

Puccini (1887–1957) was a prolific and well-known novelist and critic whose writings straddle the divide between the realism of Giovanni Verga and post–World War II neorealism. The following piece was originally published in Critica Fascista *4.23 (1 December 1926): 435–36.*

. . . it's all a question of the will. For just as, politically and morally speaking, few European nations are today on a par with us, so we soon could be, if not in the lead artistically and literarily, then at least not at the rear of the pack and could give to the world a remarkable example of health, of moral, civil, and intellectual strength. But only if we will it. Other peoples have, at least for the most part, lost that sense of virile stability and that contact with reality from which, and solely from which, a lasting and deep art may be born. Now, it seems to me that they have lost this sense and this connection because they are eager and anxious for novelty at any price. In pursuing novelty, they first strayed from and then lost connection to their true inner life (whose laws and equilibrium cannot be betrayed without incurring difficulties and losses). . . .

I said "if we will it" because I, and fortunately the Duce before me, believe that, as in other fields, it is possible in ours, the least disciplined of fields, to arrive at robust artistic manifestations by means of internal discipline. No one can or should impose it, but each artist must find it for himself, by himself, and in himself. But to obtain this, and in order that the religious and active spirit of fascism improve our artistic, literary, and cultural life, isolated cases of integrity are not enough. All men called to this vocation must feel themselves, before artists or writers, to be sons of a strong and healthy race, citizens of a nation that knows its worth and what it *wills*: these are rings in a single indissoluble chain. I, for example, am not one who condemns immorality in art because of some a priori decision, but when I find before me profoundly immoral books that have nothing to do with art, banal vulgar books, then . . . I cannot help condemning those who write them, those who print them, and (forgive me) the prefect or chief of police who gives his permission for distribution. I am not speaking only of books that flaunt their brazen immorality. There is an immorality that is even more dangerous: the immorality that hides and crouches between the lines of false artistic and even noble beauty, the immorality of books that present a reality that does not exist and that causes the weak-spirited to fall into frivolous and melancholy dreams that weaken all desire for struggle and all good instincts toward action. If I (may God forgive me) were the Duce, I would be ruthless with this false, affected art (and perhaps even more ruthless than with brazenly immoral art) as well as with dewy empty rhetoric, tidbits of poetry, of the plastic arts, of music, and of all the other arts and pseudo-arts.

It may be that a fascist art will be born, since the spirit of the race is, by now, essentially fascist. But in order that it find an appropriate and fertile terrain, the young must not read adulterated books, see adulterated paintings, nor hear adulterated music so that, from the very start, they breathe in a healthy, honest, ardent, and fibrous atmosphere in both the artistic and practical life of the nation. No . . . the coming of a fascist art (that is to say, an art that improves the race and at the same time expresses it) is not possible as long as thousands and thousands of young people find short stories and novels in nightclubs or in theaters: ignominious operettas and even more ignominious fox-trots. I'd like to say the same for a certain kind of patriotic but not virile literature, as well as of certain examples of false aestheticism that some god of the ancient Italian Olympus offers every day, examples that Italian newspapers then publish with an exaggerated abundance of boldface and italics. Quite a different example is to be found in him who surpasses us all in intellectual and moral stature: the Duce. I do not understand how, with a leader who lives so austerely and writes and speaks with equal austerity, so many who claim to be his faithful followers and whose words and gestures are in the public eye, can show themselves to be anything but austere, virile, and moral. A fascist art cannot and will not be born as long as we breathe the same air as before the war, the heavy artificial air of fine words, all hot air dominated by insincerity, no matter how expressed or presented. Unless I am deceived, now is the time to pull in our sails in order to become simple, homey, provincial, realistic, perhaps even crudely and roughly realistic.

In a period of a little over twenty years, France has given us a patent example of the moral decadence that the artistic spirit may reach when it yearns after goals of unattainable originality. And today we can readily see the consequences of attempts at novelty and love of the eccentric: a literature that believes it has attained the apex of art by representing nothing less than the cult of pederasty. But be it pederasty or Satanism, ultraism or surrealism, I condemn all these physiognomies of a single ill that consists in insincerity toward oneself and others, the abandonment of solid ground, of one's own feelings and nature. All those who love Italy and her frontiers, her ethnic and spiritual character, a healthy, peasant, municipal, and earthy Italy should join me in this condemnation.

Pay no heed . . . to those who would claim that in this way we are marking time and will lag behind all other peoples. I know, in spite of all the attempts that artists of all times have made to find novelty at any price, that true art is always born of suffering and human dramas, and that every time that art has been suffocated by either fine but empty words or contrapuntal caprice, the human heart has condemned and forgotten it. It is impossible that you not believe, along with me, that an art that is colored only by our suffering and by our living joy, an art that mirrors the life of our country and of our Italian spirit, has a right, tomorrow, to universal citizenship. There will perhaps be some delay in its appearance. It will reach others after a slow and difficult journey, but it will arrive and will be a deeply moving art. I believe, then, that a fascist art, in order to be born, must take nourishment from our healthiest and most intimate life. It must despise all external trappings and fads and firmly believe in the substantial, if not glittering, qualities of our nature as Italians. And above all, we are, let us be, virile. For the model of masculinity and seriousness has great power over youth, and when they are called by the phantasms of art, they will neither embroider songs and lyrics with feminine intonations nor chatter on about the same old love affairs with call girls and maids, nor fiddle around with words to come up with the same old descriptive morsel. Just as in fascist life we must all be active and energetic, so in art we must interrogate only our deepest feelings. He who lacks a strong heart eager to express itself, he who, in a word, lacks an imperious and glorious vocation should be able to find neither editors who publish him nor newspapers that invite him to collaborate nor friends who protect him even if, as a fascist and a citizen, he can boast of noble titles and undeniable seriousness.

If I am not mistaken, this was the spirit of the words pronounced by the Duce in Perugia and at the Society of Authors. It is impossible to think that by fascist art he meant an art into which fascist ideology enters just any old way, an art in which I could not believe except for extremely rare cases. No. Like the Duce, Turati too has a literary past and culture, and Turati too asks, in his recent book, for "integrity every day, every hour, every minute." He battles against every form of intellectual snobbery and empty rhetoric. He orders us to be simple and to take pride in that simplicity.

I think then . . . that I am not deceived when I say that a fascist art must be synonymous with human art, art of substance, simple art, virile art. For no other political ideology has ever offered proof of so much humanity, of such substance and virility, as has fascism. A capricious and incoherent, a gossipy and academic art, false in spirit and in form, would really make no sense in this era. It would contrast not only with the spirit of the Duce and of the Fascist Party but also with the will that our race today demonstrates to return to simple and primitive feelings that yesterday were easily forgotten if not completely derided.

Antonio Aniante

Aniante (1900–1983), a minor playwright and novelist with connections to the novecentisti, *was best known as a journalist and as the editor of* Tevere. *The following piece was originally published in* Critica Fascista *5.2 (15 January 1927): 23.*

. . . Yesterday hand-to-hand struggle with our enemies drove us from our fields. Today, upon returning, we find the garden overgrown and thick with democratic literature. We must cut it out and burn it. This labor of demolition will mold the fascist writers, those who will give Italy a new style.

. . . The democratic era gave us democratic writers; the fascist era must give us fascist writers. We must give to the latter a political content that can dominate even the moral content. "Fascist writers" will not only be those whose artistic production follows the fundamental canons of our thought, demonstrating intense love for the nation, respect for the principles of discipline and hierarchy, repulsion for the demagogic forms of literature that exalt class struggle, internationalism, and every principle of disgregation in the race. Rather, above all they will be those who draw their inspiration from fascism, who will create to insure the evolutionary continuation of fascism.

Ours is a policy of intransigence because we want literature and art to develop in an atmosphere clearly and decidedly favorable to the ethical principles that animate fascism and Mussolini's government. . . . The writer must stop seeing himself as a superior being above and beyond the state and the nation. The will of the race calls him back to his duty as a faithful soldier to the national cause, so that he may serve the great idea that animates contemporary Italians both with passion and with sincerity. (Always keep in mind that one can forget art for the sake of the fatherland but not the fatherland for the sake of art.) This is the banner under which the intellectual forces of fascism are organizing in preparation for the attack.

To give Italy a style is the phrase that synthesizes the platform of restless spirits forged in new times. Fascist style, like fascist politics, will have to achieve supremacy in the field of literature and art by means of great tenacity. Expressions of the contemporary spirit must translate into symbolic form the influence of the vast political movement led and conceived of by Mussolini.

Fascist politics can be defined as a "new" politics because it does not respect the so-called immutable rules that have regulated and oriented prior social movements. "This comes first and that next" is a dogma that fascism has obliterated. In earlier times the Muses, dressed in flimsy romantic veils, were invoked to lead revolutions, exerting such a profound fascination over the masses that historians immortalized them in their handbooks as the sole creators of revolt. The fascist revolution, on the contrary, does not have literary roots. Its legacy will not include a single anthology of rhetorical lyrics. . . .

. . . Departing from tradition, fascism appeared without being preceded by literature. Today, battle is fought so that Italian art can become a shining reflection of the new politics. It is Mussolini who cuts the ribbon of the Mostra del Novecento.[10] Mussolini, our head of state, encourages us and leads us into the difficult battle of fascist art, which will be correctly called an art "of the state." Today he is the only brilliant and commanding fascist artist, but around him there will soon grow an army of strong intellectuals who feel his spirit reverberating even in the most distant trenches.

The enemies of fascism take refuge in art; it is through art that they would strike at us. We will drive them out of even this sacred temple, and we will crush them so that they can no longer act with such cowardice against fascism.

In the imperial dreams of Mussolini, he who creates a great Italian art will occupy the place of honor. This is what drives so many pure poets to fight as brave storm troopers on the fascist lines, as simple storm troopers, because muscles are also needed to impose poetry. . . .

Cipriano Efisio Oppo

★

Oppo (1890–1962) was a painter, illustrator, and art critic associated during the late 1920s with the Novecento movement. He served as a deputy between 1929 and 1934 and remained an influential figure in fascist cultural circles through the early 1940s. The following piece was originally published in Critica Fascista *5.3 (1 February 1927): 44.*

. . . The fad for novelty and shock, devastating to the old scholarly and theoretical structures, has created a truly anarchic situation in European artistic circles and provoked a revolution by successfully appealing to the snobbery of the once-skeptical. But the ever shifting avant-gardes of the young no longer know where to seek out originality. With every possibility for future-oriented abstraction seemingly exhausted, they logically turn to the earliest link in the chain: to the art of savages, children and, in general, of all primitives. This mixture produces . . . an international physiognomy with a false intellectual depth, a dreamless and imaginationless adventure, a bitter and inescapable artistic atheism. It cannot be taken for granted that such changes have come about as the result of simple experimentation or that they reflect the predicaments of modern life and the rapid spread of mechanical progress. No, today's international art is merely a decorative fashion.

Fascism . . . must have the courage to bear the weighty crown—not chain, as the Futurists have called it—of our great artistic heritage with the ease of an old gentleman wearing a monocle. The glorious past of Italian art is a requisite finishing line toward which foreign ignorance and presumption must be driven. In Italy there can be no neoclassicism simply because classicism has never grown old. In Italy one is either a classicist or nothing, just as here neobarbarism, which is the natural and logical art of other races, could never endure.

With fascism, therefore, one can hope for the advent of a different sort of classical period, one limited to the eternal values of the race, with an Italian face and spirit. The old cannot be copied. Those who see fascism as a good vehicle for a new imperial art (with Roman attributes) should remember the result of such artistic assumptions under Napoleon: academies, false grandeur, rhetoric, stylization two to three times removed. We believe, in any case, that those things were consistent with the French character but were and remain unnatural to the Italian character. Thus, the festive multicolored vivacity, subtle irony, and theatrical ceremony that typify French art in this period—a logical outcome of the sophomoric spirit of the tribunals of the French Revolution—could not have been accommodated within Italian art.

The fascist revolution arose from the deepest roots of the race and nourished itself on long-suffocated natural drives. It armed itself with the most brilliant and pure self-love and with the healthiest common sense, cultivated a sense of sacrifice recovered thanks to the war, resurrected the magnificent Italian seed of voluntary discipline and active obedience. Fascist art must mean Italian art in this same traditional sense. Italian art is that of Giotto, Dante, Masaccio, Jacopo della Quercia, Leon Battisa Alberti, Brunelleschi, Michelangelo, Raphael, Giorgione, Titian, Ariosto, Caravaggio, Palestrina, Rossini, Manzoni, Leopardi, Verdi, and a thousand others, revolutionary and traditional at the same time, new and old together like the magnificent contradiction that is the history of Italian art.

Italian art is primarily order, tough discipline, good faith, and awareness, hermetic art that does not need to proselytize. It is joyous candor and sincere anguish, not born of intoxication or intellectual and artificial torment; roughness, not frivolity and pedantry; simplicity, not verbosity and foolish luxury. It is intelligence, not cleverness and theory; originality of substance, not originality of form; technical jealousy of every art, not the unnatural coupling of painting, music, poetry, and so on. Finally, it is the ambition to be of the people and universal, in contrast with the spirit of elites and schools.

But since fascist art means Italian art, it follows that fascism will become a *way of life*. Of course, one cannot pretend that the old carrion will change their way of life as quickly as they changed the badges on their lapels. And the Italian art world is still far too filled with (or, indeed, *crammed full* of) these old carrion who in the time-worn fashion assist, feed, and give life to their carrion progeny, hoping for the eventual shipwreck of this fresh wave of faith and hope in the fortunes of our Italy.

We must have the courage to consult with young artists and not with the toadies of the old professorial and bureaucratic regime or with those despicable Masons.

Outcome of the Fascist Art Inquiry

✶

At the conclusion of its half-year-long open forum on fascism and culture, Critica Fascista *published a summation— authored by Giuseppe Bottai— in which the review's own modernizing stance was put forward. "Outcome of the Fascist Art Inquiry" was originally published in issue 5.4 (15 February 1927): 61–64. (On Bottai, see the introductions to chapters 6 and 14.)*

What Fascist Art Should Not Be

. . . It is not yet possible to pass judgment on the essence of fascist art. Nonetheless, it is ready to burst forth from the deepest roots of the consciousness of the new Italian: the fascist Italian. . . . But if something must be said in favor of fascist art, we might say that it manifests itself, for the moment, as a simple tendency, generated by the same tendency at work in the political sphere, toward more solid, more full, more powerful constructions. This it does along the lines of the great autochthonous traditions of Italian art, which can be found alive and well, despite the superimpositions and incrustations of foreign artistic movements. One must not simply reproduce this great thriving tradition . . . but rather ought to carry on those characteristics that have remained constant throughout the centuries with a specifically modern sensitivity, culture, and taste.

To return to tradition means to continue it, enriching it with new energy and materials furnished by the perennial flux of life. Tradition is not preserved only in libraries, picture galleries, exhibition halls, museums, and lecture halls. It lives insofar as its germs are found in living men.

All this makes it easier for us to say what fascist art should *not* be, rather than what it *should* be. It should not be fragmentary, syncopated, psychoanalytic, intimist, crepuscular, and so on, because these artistic forms are nothing but diseases of art. They are clinical-aestheticizing rebellions against the great Italian artistic tradition, which is reappearing today in all of its grandeur (despite the fact that, before and during the above-mentioned disease, Raphael was called a superficial colorist, Verdi a drum-beater, and Foscolo a mere rhetorician).

First Signs of Fascist Art

This point settled . . . the rest remains the work of free creation. We cannot give decalogues, formulas, maxims, or recipes that would contain the exact doses of the various ingredients that make up fascist painting, sculpture, music, or literature. The creation of fascist art now requires only artists: sincere and authentic artists . . . artists who possess creative genius. To *proclaim* yourself as such, an unfortunate but fashionable practice in recent times, is simply not enough.

One need only leaf through a political newspaper or an art or literature journal each day to discover a worrisome quantity of "fascist" artists. Reading the definitions and judgments proffered by these so-called fascist writers upon this or that other artist or writer and the attestations of greatness they often publicly exchange with an impudence that would be exhilarating if it were not so painfully grotesque, we must ask ourselves if it is not time to propose to the responsible authorities a practical plan for forceful intervention so as to put an end, in the name of the dignity and success of our national art, to such degrading and pernicious habits. It might be necessary to impose a stiff law against those who defame and mystify art; a law that states, for example, to all pseudowriters and pseudo-artists, those convicted of having outraged Italian good taste and of attributing to themselves false qualifications, it is, during their natural lifetime, formally forbidden to write books and articles, compose symphonies and sonatas, paint pictures, sculpt statues, erect monuments in the squares, or hang wingèd victories on the walls of public buildings in memory of the fallen. . . .

But, in spite of this, fascist art will not be lacking, because fascism already has proof of such an art. At the moment, the only great artist of the regime is its founder, Mussolini. He has given as many speeches and written as many political articles and essays as are necessary to make him our only great contemporary prose writer. From an artistic viewpoint, his recent circular to the prefects constitutes the most illustrious piece of Italian prose of the past few years, the masterpiece of fascist literature.[11]

Reactions to Fascist Bad Taste

In the fascist state . . . the problem of art cannot be resolved by leaving art to free creation. . . . It remains, then, to examine the most important side of the question: what can the state do for art?

First, we assert that the state must intervene in artistic problems in support of their resolution. Agnosticism toward the subject is a liberal-democratic tic. It belongs, that is, to that antiquated social doctrine that leaves everything up to the individual's libido. We must now look to specific ways in which the fascist state can intervene to foment the growth of art. But before taking a stand on this matter, we wish to argue that the various fascist organizations, the party, and the unions ought to put into immediate effect certain forceful and necessary public measures. The headquarters of the Fasci, of local governments, associations, and unions are all brimming over with horrid pseudo-artistic objects. Similarly, all of the celebratory and propagandist rallies of the above bodies take place among grossly ostentatious material emblems of the crassest bad taste. Incredible painted wall decorations, horrible tinted-chalk busts in every corner, signs and banners in garish colors in the place of tapestries, gilt stucco lictor's fasces that look like bundles of kindling, chromaliths of the Duce in absurd poses, sabers and lances painted black: these are the headquarters of the Fasci, unions, and many local governments. They would be better off as stage props for some vaudeville company. And then there are those same old fogies who now under fascism have somehow landed on their feet. At every ceremony and before the astonished eyes of the population, they trot out plaques befitting mountain cemeteries, Roman scenes from suburban cinematography, ugly calendars, horrendous book covers, ridiculous trifles and knickknacks, all bringing great disgrace to our artistic civilization.

Enough of this! We must strip our cities of these ambulatory monuments to bad taste. We must discredit the calling-card printers and pseudo-artists who have sold or given them to us by exploiting the ignorance of the local leaders.

The State and the Art Problem

This said, we understand that state intervention on the behalf of art is an action that must be undertaken with great wisdom and prudence.

First, the state must provide economic assistance for artists, be they excellent or mediocre, accomplishing this through the respective artists unions. But simple union assistance will not be enough, because artists unions cannot be considered capable of evaluating individual artistic worth. Nor will it be conceivable, in this century of heavy industry, to adopt any model of patronage in conflict with the principle of state intervention in the sphere of artists and art.

By now the artist of the good old days — or, rather, the bad old anarchic, bohemian days — who lived according to moral laws contrary to those of the people has ceased to exist. Every period of civilization has an art corresponding to its own moral substance, and fascist civilization cannot allow artists to exist as a group morally severed from the national collectivity. By organizing artists into their respective unions like all other producers, the corporative system will doubtless succeed in convincing artists that, once they have left their rooming houses, studios, libraries, and academies behind, they will perhaps find the best artistic inspiration by participating fully in the life of the people. Therefore, artists do not need the simple economic assistance required by other classes. The period of patronage and of bohemianism is over. Artists need the state, and, above all, they need artistic, moral, and spiritual assistance (especially to the most gifted artists). Since such support must be extended on the grounds of precise and particular evaluations that are in practice extremely difficult to make, the necessity of creating an appropriate branch in Italy's Academy looms very large. One cannot object that the Ministry of Public Education has always served this purpose. The ministry — the name explains its function — essentially provides for extensive, not intensive, culture and even less for the development and perfection of artistic culture. We maintain, therefore, that this latter function must be assumed by the Italian Academy.[12]

The Anti-Academic Academy

The Italian Academy must be anti-academic. It must be antiparasitic and antistatic, dynamic, working, creative. We believe that the Italian Academy must be the fascist revolution's organ in the domain of art. Thus, as a general duty, it must shoulder the task of defending and illuminating the Italian spirit by means of precise and effectual actions in all matters involving our nation's culture (understood as the sum of every intellectual and artistic tradition). Such defensive action must be construed as the judicious spiritual and material preservation of the artistic patrimony of our race, which must be protected—as it is not today—not only from the harmful effects of time upon all vulnerable works but especially from foreign influence and contamination of that which is the distinctive aesthetic, philosophical, religious, and moral essence and style of our race. Since shedding light on the latter spirit complements the defense of our patrimony, it ought to be favored by every endeavor and every initiative. Particular encouragement should be given to manifestations and forms of intellectual and artistic expression that are, in the opinion of the academy, in keeping with the immutable historical character of the Italian genius. . . .

Once the appropriate organ for such a complex function has been created in the Italian Academy, it is conceivable that the material defense of our artistic patrimony would then consist in keeping a watchful eye on every public and private body that might intend (whatever its goals or motivations) to diminish, destroy, or distort the essential character of monuments, the appearances of sites precious because of their antiquity or historical associations, cultural or artistic training institutions, picture and exhibition galleries, and libraries. The state authorities would then be alerted to these dangers.

Thus, the academy must make its solemn voice heard every time a branch of the great historical, cultural, and artistic national body is endangered by mercantile greed, by ignorance, or by the presumption of philistines and bastards infatuated with fashion or intellectual and aesthetic aberrations of a foreign and barbaric nature.

The Italian Academy can accomplish its ideal function of defending our artistic civilization by deprecating . . . all of those literary, mystic, artistic, moral, and other manifestations that plant in the mind and spirit "seeds" of error and degeneration contrary to the openly creative national genius or spirituality. Thus, the academy . . . would combat every form of decadence in the Italian spirit with the very characteristics and strengths that are traditionally, historically, and innately its own.

The essential nature of the Italian language must first and foremost be protected with vigor. Spoken as well as written language must be free of the pedantry of Italianized foreign terms, which are more harmful to Italy than imports. Italian must be considered a living and continually growing thing. But it can no longer be contaminated with impunity . . . according to the whims of the journalists and publishers who control the literary field.

To this same end we say "enough" to all the so-called festivals honoring saints, artists, and heroes that consist in little more than speeches, articles, monographs, and essays overflowing with the frills, fillers, and fatuous rhetoric of a language that is ungrammatical, bombastic, and contorted—a language that no Italian could recognize as his own.

And "no more" to much of the intolerable bad prose of the pseudofascist writers of the past few years, found in newspapers and books that pretend to contribute to the formation of fascist literature while they suffocate the style of our great language beneath an immense wave of unintelligible, barbaric, and puerile terminology.

The Ministry of Italian Culture

The Italian Academy, then, in order to proceed with its evaluation of the merits of individual artists . . . ought to create incentive awards as well as to facilitate artistic publications and manifestations that have a clearly Italian stamp. It also ought to have its own periodical so that it can offer to those (besides the academicians themselves) deemed worthy an opportunity to publish their ideas and artistic expressions.

In short, the Italian Academy ought to represent a type of *Ministry of Italian Culture.* . . .

In order to avoid territorial conflicts with similar state institutions, the academy's primary function would be advisory (except in those cases in which the government assigned to it specific tasks that needed to be accomplished). By this method one could not only achieve an admirable unanimity in the direction and style of everything pertaining to the ideal cultural and artistic life of the nation but also could reassemble the foundations of that global spiritual empire that Italy is destined to build anew. Recently, for instance, there have been cases in which the Italian Academy could have been quite effective. Not long ago a ship filled with Italian art works was sent abroad. These works of art, chosen by people who either were incompetent or had their own interests at heart, could not have been less interesting or less representative of the current Italian genius. If the academy had existed then and had consulted its artistic wing, the choices and the criteria would have been different, and an embarrassing fiasco could have been avoided.

Furthermore, I would cite as evidence the truly barbaric and dishonorable undertakings that have been attempted and/or completed in cities such as Rome, Bologna, Florence, and Vicenza: the demolition of buildings, the transformation of streets and squares, the completion of ingenious architectural works left unfinished by their designers, the erection of horrid galleries and bridges, and so on.

The Italian Academy could have (or, better, will) put in a timely word about all of this with immeasurable benefit.

The Paths of Culture

It is clear that the academicians are to be selected from among the nation's most lively, distinguished, Italian, fascist personalities in the arts. Hybridism within the new academic body would be deleterious, and the intrusion of the superficial, the dilettantish, the agnostic, the decadent, and so on would be inauspicious. The spiritual empire of fascist Italy must be founded by artists openly and traditionally Italian, that is, fascist. Awhile back the Duce announced his intention to transform Rome into a great modern metropolis, not unworthy of its imposing traditions. Which organ of the state could be better suited than the Italian Academy to indicate the path to be followed . . . and contribute to the effective realization of such a magnificent idea?

The Italian Academy—ideal artistic and intellectual synthesis—would imprint its Italian character and stylistic unity, its stamp at once traditional and modern on all that the new Italy is readying itself to create in every field: from science to art, from literature to architecture to theater.

Just as the Great Council sets the tone and indicates the path to be followed in our political life, just as the corporative system will set the tone and indicate the paths to be followed in our economic expansion and forging of a new social order, so too will the Italian Academy set the tone and indicate the paths to be taken by Italian culture (a phrase to be understood in its broadest sense as nearly synonymous with civilization itself).

> *translated by Barbara Spackman, Jennifer Roberts, and*
> *Elizabeth Macintosh; revised by Jeffrey T. Schnapp*

Notes

1. An earlier version of this anthology appeared as "Selections from the Great Debate on Fascism and Culture: *Critica Fascista* 1926–1927," co-edited with Barbara

Spackman, in *Stanford Italian Review* 8.1–2 (1988): 235–72. New introductions have been added, the translations have been revised, and one selection (by Marinetti) has been dropped.

2. The allusion to an "objectively realistic" or *verista* art points to Verismo, an Italian literary movement of the latter half of the nineteenth century that, much like French naturalism, sought to employ scientific methods of observation in the pursuit of objectivity.

3. The reference is to the famous definition of the "sweet new style" (*dolce stil nuovo*) found in canto 24 of Dante's *Purgatorio*: "I' mi son un che, quando / Amor mi spira, noto, e a quel modo / ch'e' ditta dentro vo significando" (vv. 52–54).

4. Romain Rolland (1866–1944) was, in addition to being the Nobel Prize–winning author of *Jean-Christophe*, the author of a series of widely read biographies of figures such as Beethoven, Tolstoy, Mahatma Gandhi, Michelangelo, and Péguy.

5. The Verdurins are one of the families whose activities are chronicled in Marcel Proust's *A la recherche du temps perdu* (1913–27).

6. The Casa d'Arte Bragaglia was Bragaglia's personal base of operations in Rome. It served as a gallery and gathering place and published a bulletin (the *Bollettino della Casa d'Arte Bragaglia*).

7. Bragaglia's reference is to the period between September 1918 and January 1920, when, amidst violent clashes, the editors of the review *Roma Futurista* included Bottai, Rocca, and Guido Calderini.

8. The dramatist and critic Anatoli Vasilyevich Lunacharsky (1875–1933) was a leading figure in the early Bolshevik regime, serving as commissar of education between 1917 and 1920. A participant and advocate of the cultural avant-gardes, he harbored sympathies for Marinettian Futurism, despite his political opposition.

9. Bragaglia is here reprising a long-standing polemic of his in favor of what he referred to as the "theatrical theater" (*teatro teatrale*). Throughout the world, but in Italy especially, the enormous success of the cinema threw the theater into a crisis from which it could emerge, Bragaglia argued, only by turning away from the pursuit of cinematographic effects: away from the pursuit of realism and verisimilitude toward a new magical, experimental hypertheatricality.

10. Thanks to the influence of Margherita Sarfatti, Mussolini had in fact attended the February 1926 opening of the Mostra del Novecento (Exhibition of the Twentieth Century), which included works by major artists such as Mario Sironi, momentarily raising expectations that the Novecento movement might become the regime's official style.

11. Mussolini's January 1927 circular to the prefects explained to these regional agents and representatives of the central government the expansion in prefectural powers that was entailed by the legal reforms of 1926. The circular described squadrism as part of the movement's past and insisted upon the party's subordination to the authority of local prefects, who were now to be viewed as strong and active representatives of the state.

12. It is worth underscoring the fact that the foundation of the Royal Academy had only been announced a year before Bottai's concluding essay, that its statute was not officially approved by the Council of Ministers until January 1929, and that its inauguration took place in October 1929. So Bottai was entirely free to speculate about the academy's future responsibilities.

CHAPTER 17

Art and Fascism (1928)

Margherita G. Sarfatti

Sarfatti (1883–1961) was a leading art and culture critic. In her youth a socialist and feminist, she contributed to Avanti, Rassegna Femminile, *and* Difesa delle Lavoratrici, *which she cofounded. She and her husband, the socialist lawyer Cesare Sarfatti, left the Socialist Party along with Mussolini in 1914 and joined the fascist movement in 1919. Sarfatti served as art editor for Mussolini's newspaper* Il Popolo d'Italia *from its inception in 1915, directed* Gerarchia *from 1921, and wrote the widely celebrated biography,* Dux, *in 1926. A defender of modernism in the arts, she cofounded the Novecento movement and helped it obtain government patronage. This selection appeared in* La civiltà fascista, *edited by Giuseppe Luigi Pomba. After the racial laws went into effect, Sarfatti (who was Jewish) left Italy for Argentina in 1938, only to return after the war.*

✶

It is true that reality inspires art. But life is even more inspired by art. It follows in art's footsteps because creations of the spirit are far more adaptable and farsighted than material creations. An ideal (yet very real) unity in the spirit, in the words, and in the genius of Italy's poets existed long before Italian unity was achieved in life and in history. Only gradually did life and history adapt themselves to the form prescribed by poets; only gradually did their slow and dense matter fill in the overall contours of the poets' design, animated by the irresistible yearning of an astral creature, marked out in luminous points, that "wanted" to become reality.[1]

Art was fascist before there was fascism. Art first brought about the fascist climate that now directs art's own development. All three of our great poets can claim an inaugural role. In Carducci, it is the fiery Italian spirit, the sense of patriotism and of reverent union with our classical antiquity that today reawakens in us, who were once the humiliated servants of "German science," the pride of being Rome's genuine descendants.[2] Admittedly, this Roman spirit is not entirely free of the dross of rhetorical pedantry. But thanks to Carducci, thanks to his intolerance, to his reproaches, to his invectives against the Umbertine little Italy [*Italietta*], we maintained a pugnacious awareness that we belonged to a people and nation for whom "Rome" provides a universal watchword, a warning, and a command that greatness alone is a worthy pursuit.

The contribution of Giovanni Pascoli is less obvious but more profound.[3] It was he who first introduced into the Italian lyrical tradition two themes neglected by all prior poets: the agitation of an impassioned humanity and the thrill of brotherhood with unknown multitudes, packed shoulder to shoulder over the horizon. Pascoli was deeply concerned with the fate of the humble, deeply haunted by the struggles of labor and by the thorny difficulties encountered by immigrants in Europe and across the Atlantic. He gave the bound and gagged giant that was beginning to misrepresent itself under the factious label of "the proletariat" a voice and a right to artistic citizenship. The "proletariat" in question was in reality nothing more than our people, the Italian people. That is how Pascoli referred to them, that is how he loved them. He understood the people. He knew how to speak to them and how to make them speak in works of genuine, enduring poetry.

Everything in fascism is corporation, labor, and people; the appreciation of workers; the will to uplift them; respect for the people's dignity; respect for the sentimental and patriarchal family values of unassuming common folk who form the core of Italian life, its source of well-being and civility. Giovanni Pascoli felt all of this in the very depths of his soul. He prophesied it and praised it before the conscience of the nation. He brought to light treasures that lay dormant in the neglected humus, revealing their beauty, making them shine in the rays of his incomparable genius. His also is our feeling for the land and for the countryside, for that authentic Italian soil that is crust, plow, joyous sunshine, open sky, and toil, toil, toil. In the *Poemetti* [Short poems] and *Nuovi poemetti* [New short poems], modern georgics composed without an Augustus to command them or a Maecenas to pay for them, Pascoli's inspiration was Virgilian. And not by chance, because even in his solemn *Poemi conviviali* [Convivial poems], the section entitled "Poema degli iloti" [Poem of the Helots] formulates an explicit program for an art drawn from the wellsprings of the earth. This at a time when people were fleeing the land, flocking to the cities, or deserting Italy in swarms due to the mirage of overseas societies where they would be sacrificed to the great Moloch of the factory, the God machine that rules over all labor as well as all recreation and pleasure.[4]

As for Gabriele D'Annunzio, we all know how deeply we are indebted to him. Emblem of velocity, modernity, extreme urbanity, of a heroic vision of life, of daring, hope, greatness, and limitless faith, he was the poet who prophesied, preached, and fought the war [World War I]. The young bard of the *Odi navali* [Naval odes] became the protagonist and poet of the Beffa di Buccari twenty years later.[5] Blessed with the rare privilege of possessing a twofold—Dionysian and Apollonian—gift, the author of the *Laudi* [Lauds] and *Forse che sì forse che no* [Maybe yes, maybe no] glorified imaginary feats of aviation whose grandeur could not compete with the flight over Vienna, conceived and realized by him [in August 1918]. D'Annunzio's warlike octosyllabic lines are unequaled in their ability to capture a certain arrogant, knightly, derisive, fascinating, and cruel spirit that belongs to the immortal youth of fascism (to its organic, not chronological, youth):

> With one fate, we are thirty men
> And with death, we're thirty-one.[6]

Don't these verses echo regularly through the popular refrains whose rhythms accompanied the preparation and fulfillment of the March on Rome? Aren't their coarse and anonymous melody, their spirit and form, their thoughts, words, and music the same as those that marked the fascists' joyous fervor and youthful sacrifice? The squadrists sing [*canta lo squadrismo popolaresco*]:

> I don't give a damn about Bombacci,
> and about tomorrow's sunrise. . . .
> I don't give a damn about Dronero,
> I don't give a damn about death.[7]

They march, threaten, and sing in double time:

> To arms, fellow fascists,
> Terror of the communists.
> We will struggle to our death
> We will fight with all our strength
> As long as blood courses through our veins.[8]

To the lord of Fiume, to the commander who presides over the border of the Nivôse (which he himself embodies), to the magnificent Grand Master [D'Annunzio], we owe the honor of having provided the Arditi with many of their characteristic rites, rites that, under fascism, became an art form and a national way of life; rites that figure significantly within a new ritualism that is at once gay and austere, carefree and pregnant with religious and moral content.[9] It is he who improved upon the nine traditional Muses, all ragged with use, by adding a new Muse, a Muse that represents fascist efficiency and everything that is ultramodern and electric—Energy.[10] Without her, the others are but pale rhetorical images. They inspire desires and not results, hazy dreams and coffee chatter, not concrete works.

It is D'Annunzio, in short, who deprovincialized Italy's spirit and culture, as well as its social and political aspirations.

He granted her an imperial gaze that crosses borders with unfailing bravery. He exalted the "Odyssean man" [*ulisside*]: the explorer and founder of distant colonies, the hero of seafaring adventures, he who "mans the prow and sails out into the world." He taught her to look beyond the Alps, as well as to look beyond the Adriatic (which Giosuè Carducci had viewed as the final Thule). Rather, he taught her to project herself outward from the Adriatic toward still vaster seas—a key measure to insure her security.

I still remember the first performances of *La nave* [The ship] in prewar Venice.[11] "Man the great ship named The-Whole-World"—"O God who measures and renews the races at sea, oh God who destroys them—Make all the oceans our own sea."[12] These words and gasps were sounded facing Trieste and a Venetian shore widowed from the tricolor flag amidst the torpor of a listless and hesitant Italy. They preceded fascism's famous Roman salute by the span of a full generation. They resonated across Trieste's beautiful sea, but only in passing: this was but the initial phase of their journey, not their destination. They traveled beyond with an entirely new and proud consciousness.

The renewal of Italian culture in the world; promoting the influx of currents of thought and modern art into Italy; and, conversely, promoting Italy's distinctive but universal presence within currents of thought and modern art: all these achievements may be largely credited to Gabriele D'Annunzio. This imperial expansionism of Italian culture, which, like a river that never stagnates but is fed by other rivers, gives and takes, universally assimilates and is assimilated, is a spiritual attitude characteristic of fascism and its ever intensifying revival of the universal and imperial ancient tradition.

We should not hide timidly behind comfortable old habits or settle into ruts or always travel the same streets. We must instead breathe the air of grander horizons—however turbulent it may be—and go down unfamiliar roads with quiet daring. To face others on the battlefield does not mean slavishly imitating them. We must get to know them and their weapons so as to develop other weapons with the same range or better. And it may very well be that sitting around a rural tavern in shirtsleeves playing cards or, at most, throwing a few punches among close friends and enemies is an enviable and superior way of life. It is certainly a comfortable one. But such a choice means giving up competing in the spiritual conflicts of a world where people are armed with cannons, tank-mounted machine guns, and other long-range deviltry.

Today more than ever, the life of nations is all combat without truce in every sphere of culture and technology. What sort of general or minister would, "in the spirit of patriotism and Italianness [*italianità*]," refuse to study Moltke's campaigns or to use torpedoes, dynamite, and submarines because they are not Italian enough? Yet some zealots demand or even order our publishers not to publish books translated from foreign languages under penalty of excommunication from fascism. But who authorized them to speak in the name of fascism?

Anyone who cowers in his own domestic corner, clinging to his familiar truncheon [*manganello*], cannot expect parties involved in ferocious worldwide competition to consider him their equal.

We have begun (though with great difficulty) to cast aside the rotten mediocrity of so-called folklorism: the lazy cult of local color that provides foreigners with entertainment and with a reason to scorn us. Folklorism is not part of our true tradition but rather is the legacy of our century-long serfdom and of the sad customs to which it gave rise. In the wake of the Risorgimento came a feeble generation of imitators, so it was with the rise of socialism that we first began to raise our gaze and to broaden our (hitherto too narrow) horizons: socialism understood as the aim of improving the people's miserable material lot and as a stimulus to raising the no less miserable moral standards of the ruling elites. The interventionist movement, the world war, and, finally, fascism served as the crucible and testing ground for the new governing aristocracies [*aristocrazie-guida*]. Fascism is their conquest and their determining experience. The Italy for which they strive will not withdraw behind a great wall of China or barbed-wire fences but rather will be a contender in every field of international competition: if not an equal among equals, possibly first among equals.

When D'Annunzio appeared, he in no way renounced the Italianness [*italianità*] of his literary and artistic identity. But his native thought was rich and universal. It was nourished by a universal culture and directed toward universal problems. It was Italian, and precisely because Italian, nonprovincial.

So throughout the world they hushed in order to hear his words. Nothing is less fascist than provincial parochialism, which must not be confused with ruralism. No one is less provincial and more "universal" than the farmer, just as nothing is more "universal" and less provincial than the soil [*zolla*] upon which his life depends.

✱

Carducci—Pascoli—D'Annunzio: in these three authors' pursuit of our nation's highest aspirations, they longed to rid us of the vestiges of empty form. And so has fascism, whose battle is not just one of longing but of longing and effort transformed into action, action that seeks to free us from forms that were once necessary to clothe the master's sentiments but became empty and fluttering rhetorical drapery in the hands of followers.

Cases in point: the triumphal display of athletic musculatures or of learned classical togas by Carducci's followers; the simpering and swooning childishness of Pascoli's imitators; and, more widespread and nauseating still, the affectation and the archaizing contorted sonority of the Dannunzians.

In order to find someone who can free us from these stale remnants and sweep them away with a powerful broom (or, better, with the sweeping action of an airplane's wing), one must turn from poetry to politics and from lyrics to polemics. (It is true that Carducci was a fierce polemicist not just in prose but also in meter and rhythm as demonstrated in his *Versaglia* [Versailles] and *La consulta araldica* [The heralds' college], so perhaps Carducci the polemicist was Mussolini's teacher to an unsuspected degree.) One must turn from Gabriele d'Annunzio to Benito Mussolini. One must turn from the former's set of parchment quartos emblazoned with a title derived from astronomical myth and ornamented with Bodonian rubrics to the latter's thin rag, printed on bad cellulose, with characters from a shabby, worn-out rotary press, entitled *Il Popolo d'Italia*.[13]

The fascist style, all the qualities and prerogatives that distinguish fascist art, is recorded in the exemplary prose of the writer Benito Mussolini. Here is a man who has taken Carducci's lesson to heart: "Whoever can say something in three words and says it in four is dishonest." Adjectives are scarce, epithets are austere, verbs are sober. His sentences are dry, crisp, and resolute, mostly composed of verbs and nouns. Synonyms are banished. Description takes the form of great and clearly delineated, shadowless masses of color laid down as in a fresco painting. Verbs are naked and direct yet not schematic.

Like Carducci (but even more so than Carducci), this great stylist writes with his nails when engaged in polemics. He writes with nails untamed by the art of manicure, nails that tend to grow into claws that rapaciously hook all adversaries. No humor. Irony and sarcasm without subtle undertones so as to better jump on the opponent, to smash him with insolence after the debate, and to bring the scoffers over to one's own side.

Held back like the tears of a strong man, feeling shines forth from this subdued prose with greater effect thanks to constraint. No elastic rounding out of the sentence. It remains squared off, with all its sharp corners, solid at its base, but airy at a summit made up of arches and lancet windows that burst open to the sky or reflect the capricious lightness of the clouds.

The style of Mussolini the journalist, orator, and writer is simple, highly distinctive, and spontaneous. It is animated by an immediate and direct sincerity and is therefore interesting.

This fact helps to explain the powerful hold that Mussolini's personality has exercised over the Italian populace, especially over the youth who make up the new class of intellectuals. That his propriety and probity of thought and form should become a style is well and good. That it should also become a fad driven by snobbery, so much the better. Fashion and snobbery play no small part in the evolution of new aristocracies toward perfection.

Revolutions in every domain of religion, society, philosophy, and art are made by altering the watchword. They are made by launching a new watchword first within the governing elites [minoranze-guida] and then by extending it to the mob: a watchword that stops them, surprises them, makes them reflect, and places them under the spell of action.

Simplicity, concision, and clarity of thought and expression are the great watchwords for the artistic style of a new regime, of a renewed nation.

✳

These matters of new and renewed artistic creation involve slow and gradual preparations. But when the solution arises, it reveals itself, all of a sudden, like an explosion. They are matters of atmosphere and, like the blooming of bud into flower, they unexpectedly burst out.

Futurism was in certain regards the progeny of Gabriele D'Annunzio. But it was also his opponent, which is to say, it was his genuine and legitimate son. Every generation rebels against the preceding one in order to reconquer tradition and continue it in revised form. Futurist aesthetics celebrated a heroic vision of modernity that, though previously reviled as monstrous, was first exalted by D'Annunzio. More thoroughgoing and bolder, Futurism rejected D'Annunzio's antiquarian and archaeological side. It rejected all that was antithetical to the dynamism of risk and of machines, worshiping only the inexorable geometric fetish.

Futurism thus contributed to the creation of a new rhetoric. And

D'Annunzio's recent books demonstrate that, like every good young father, he was the first to learn from his child.

In the insular, mildewed environment of prewar Italy, Futurism shattered some windows, and violently so. It adapted a good many new ideas.

The renovation of Italian culture initiated by Gabriele D'Annunzio was completed by two conflicting forces and temperaments: on the one side, by Futurism; on the other, by Benedetto Croce and by the cultural movement that gave rise to the reviews *La Voce* and *Lacerba*.[14] Within the spheres of the spirit and of culture, both contributed (though in contradictory ways) to creating the great Italy of today: an independent Italy, able to stake out firm positions, planted right at the center of international life. Tomorrow, after the war and thanks to fascism, she will be greater still.

However unlike one another, *La Voce* and Futurism were working so single-mindedly toward a common goal that a moment of convergence and collaboration was inevitable. It occurred within the fold of Ardengo Soffici's and Giovanni Papini's review *Lacerba* at a time when Soffici was busy importing from France to Florence the poetry of Rimbaud and the paintings of the post-Impressionist and Cubist schools. At this same time, *La Voce*, *Lacerba*, and the Futurist groups found themselves fighting side by side—hardly a minor detail—for Italy's intervention in the war.

With its stormy gladiatorial attitudes, its defiant challenges, its extremist and paradoxical outcries, Futurism was deeply romantic at its origin. It stressed the analytic and fragmentary dissolution of artistic representation. But through Cubism it eventually turned classical, at least as regards the visual arts.

This is the case, firstly, because Futurism renounced all weepy nostalgias for a confused and contradictory pantheism. Instead, it placed modern man and modern life—all the pursuits, creations, and concerns of today—at the center of the universe, like some sort of heroic giant. It once again made him the central focus.

Second, pictorial Futurism rejected fragmentary, casual, and eclectic "sensations" and other fleeting material impressions, even though it had recourse to deformations and to fairly arbitrary recompositions. It again began to build, to compose, and to create with a conscious will: a methodical, reasoning will that is not exclusively instinctive or chaotic.

✶

The point is crucial if one is to gain an understanding of how a fascist artistic atmosphere and climate took shape. Thanks to a thousand interesting and contradictory experiences—principally in the field of the plastic arts—something began to ripen. To call it a "fascist art" would be saying too much at the present time. Perhaps it would be more accurate to affirm that fascism and this form of art are born of a single rootstock. Both have been nurtured by the recovery of strength and energy; both are expressions of a will to action, a will to greatness, and a will to power on the part of the Italian nation and civilization.

In the domain of literature, the signs are murky at present. New forces have yet to appear, forces that can cut a definite and distinctive profile against the horizon.

Pirandello's marvelously subtle theater is not a fascist creation. Nor can it be said that the work of Grazia Deledda flows out of the spiritual movement that is fascism.[15] Nevertheless, it is no accident that the world's attention is riveted on these two writers. And never more so than in recent times, when Deledda has been granted the Nobel Prize and Pirandello's plays are receiving ever greater acclaim on stages throughout the world.[16] That Italy and things Italian are now held in far greater respect worldwide has surely benefited the work of these two great geniuses.

Within and outside Italy, whatever is daring and Italian is admired and encouraged. Italian spiritual values are no longer systematically debased and trampled upon.

The foundation of the Italian Royal Academy has been solemnly announced, to be housed in a magnificent location: Rome's Palace of the Farnesina. Authorities speak of instituting annual prizes for the best works of literature and grants for artists. The Royal Theater of the Opera is set to open in Rome and to become our national operatic stage. The government is no longer an agnostic in cultural matters; it no longer stands aloof from literary and artistic competitions.

Our young composers will no longer knock in vain on the doors of the most sought after or exclusive concert halls. Among them, Pizzetti, Respighi, Malipiero, Casella, and de Sabata are names that show promise as composers for the opera.[17] An Italian melody wells up spontaneously (though deeply) in their pensive souls.

✳

But it is in the domain of the visual arts—architecture, sculpture, and painting—that a distinctive period style has begun to emerge. The style of the classic Novecento, the fascist style, has set off from Italian shores and is sure to conquer the world.

The committee on the Novecento Italiano gathered these forces together, providing them with a sense of direction and of collective consciousness.[18] The Duce inaugurated their first exhibition in 1926 in Milan and sponsored many other exhibitions, both within and outside of Italy: exhibitions in which, far from dead, the ancient power of summoning up ever new apparitions of beauty was on display.

The world's painters, sculptors, and architects look upon us with joyous anticipation. They had become accustomed to regarding us as makers of figurines, as slavish reproducers of the past's great creations, and as profiteers, incapable of penetrating the past's banal surface or renewing its spirit.

With the Duce's encouragement and under his direct authority, the regime and the national government have devoted a great deal of energy to reshaping the urban fabric of Rome.

Benito Mussolini is carrying out a gargantuan task that in France required the combined efforts of a great dynasty and of many men of genius (from Louis XI through Richelieu, Mazarin, Colbert, and Louis XIV through Napoleon I, Haussmann, and Napoleon III). By mobilizing every possible means and all the nation's forces, he is making Italy aware of its unity and moral greatness through her capital's architectural unity and material greatness.

It goes without saying that the work of centralization imposes painful sacrifices, defacements, and decapitations on the other cities of the "Italic folk endowed with many lives" [itala gente dalle molte vite].[19] But these are necessary and fruitful.

Rome is on the road to becoming a truly great capital, a great, unique city of ancient and modern beauty. Air, light, space, and solitude — in short, respect — surround the monuments of the past. No faking or refacing them, just the pick, the broom, and a good cleaning to sweep away the parasitic mold that has clung for centuries to majestic ruins. Reinforcement so as to insure their preservation.

Thus the Temple of Virile Fortune, the Augustan Forum, the Theater of Marcellus have been luminously resurrected. Next in line are the thermal baths of Paulus Emilius. All this within the framework of the brilliantly devised new city plan for Rome, drawn up by the architect Brasini under the personal guidance of the Duce.

My heart goes out to those who worship picturesque filth. The supposed folklorism of Italy, with its bandits, mandolin players, and street urchins doing cartwheels and shoving spaghetti in their mouths with their fingers, is a lurid pseudo-aesthetic myth. The sooner the myth collapses, the better it will be for the dignity and true beauty of our beloved land.

The Temple of Victory, a commemorative monument being built in Milan, will be one of the regime's magnificent works. The architects Ponti, Muzio, and Buzzi will work on it with the help of many sculptors, from Adolfo Wildt, who is preparing the statue of Sant' Ambrogio, to Libero Andreotti, Rambelli, Saponaro, and several other young artists.[20]

We have at our disposal a group of architects: in Rome, Brasini, Piacentini, Limongelli, and others; in Milan, Muzio, Buzzi, Ponti, de Finetti, Rava, and others elsewhere.[21] We have at our disposal a remarkable group of sculptors and a truly outstanding group of painters who inspire hope and faith in contemporary art.

Now all they need is to be able to work nobly and with dignity in Rome. Every century and every epoch of civilization has left its clear and substantial imprint on Rome: the Etruscans, the Republic, the Empire, Byzantium, the Middle Ages, the popes, the Renaissance, the Baroque, the Jesuits, rococo, neoclassicism. Even Pius IX and Umbertine Italy left their mark in the form of the Palace of Justice and the monument to Victor Emanuel II. Both are extremely ugly monuments, but at least they are monuments, monuments that document the struggle for greatness and the civilization of the epoch that produced them.

But the Palace of the Lictor is little more than the ancient Vidoni Palace with Raphael's facade.[22] The head of government and fascism's Duce currently sits at Chigi Palace in his role as foreign minister. He sits at the Viminale, a building in the style of Giolitti, in his role as interior minister. And the gothic Palazzo Venezia is being prepared for his work as prime minister.

All of which underscores the point that courage, audacity, and greatness must at last assert themselves in the form of a truly imposing architectural project for the year VI [1928] or VII [1929]: a building that can become the principal edifice of the regime, our fascist edifice, an edifice in the fascist style.

translated by Olivia E. Sears and Jeffrey T. Schnapp

Notes

1. Sarfatti's conceit involves an imaginary constellation, much like the eagle that Dante's pilgrim sees in the heaven of Jupiter in cantos 18–20 of his *Paradiso* that serves as a kind of celestial prefigurer of the palpable reality of the monarchy.

2. The poet, critic, and scholar Giosuè Carducci (1835–1907) was one of the towering figures of the second half of the nineteenth century in Italy. A liberal republican with strong anti-Catholic convictions, he stood in opposition to the Romanticism of his era, calling for a return to pre-Romantic and classical cultural models. He was awarded the Nobel Prize in 1906.

3. The poet and critic Giovanni Pascoli (1855–1912) was, alongside Carducci, one of the most influential Italian writers at the turn of the century. The author of numerous and voluminous verse collections, including *Myricae* (1891) and the *Canti di Castelvecchio* (1903), his work is distinguished by its remarkable melding of classical echoes and rhythms with a lexicon encompassing dialect forms, rural slang, archaisms, and even Italian-Americanisms. Pascoli was a brilliant Latinist and the author of several prize-winning collections of Latin verses, including *Carmina* (1914).

4. The reference is most likely directed at emigration to the United States. Moloch was the title of the Canaanite deity to whom the men of Judah were wont to sacrifice their sons and daughters in Old Testament times.

5. The February 1918 Beffa di Buccari (hoax of Buccari) was one of D'Annunzio's heroic World War I actions (known as the *colpi di mano*) that rendered him the symbol of Italy's victory and set the stage for the march on Fiume.

6. The original text reads "Trenta siamo ad una sorte / E trentuno con la morte."

7. The original text reads "Me n'infischio di Bombacci / E del sol dell'avvenir. . . . / Me n'infischio di Dronero, / Me n'infischio di morir."

8. The original texts reads "All'armi, a noi fascisti / Terror dei comunisti. / La lotta sosterrem fino alla morte / E pugneremo tutti forte forte / Fin che ci resti un po' di sangue in cuore."

9. During the occupation of Fiume, D'Annunzio devised a series of elaborate rituals, some of which became standard features of everyday life under fascism. Among them were ceremonies involving the regalia and relics of the Arditi; ritual roll calls of "martyrs" to the cause; and use of the Homeric war cry "Eia eia alalà."

10. The allusion is to the section of book 1 of D'Annunzio's collection *Maia* (1903) referred to as "The Tenth Muse" (*La decima Musa*): "E la nomata nel grido / Euplete Eurètria Energèia." Cited from *Versi d'amore e di gloria II*, in *Tutte le opere di Gabriele d'Annunzio*, ed. Egidio Bianchetti (Milan: A. Mondadori, 1950), 163.

11. The year referred to is 1908.

12. The final section of the quotation from D'Annunzio's drama puns on the secondary Latin name of the Mediterranean (and sometimes Adriatic) sea as Mare Nostrum: "Fa di tutti gli Oceani il Mare Mostro."

13. "Astronomical myth" is a reference to *Alcyone*, the third book of D'Annunzio's *Laudi*. The book draws its title from the Alcyone of Greek myth, one of the Pleiades.

14. One of the most influential reviews of the pre–World War I years, *La Voce* was directed by Giuseppe Prezzolini from the time of its foundation in December 1908

to its demise in December 1916 (if one exempts the brief tenure of Giovanni Papini between April and October 1912 and the addition of Giuseppe de Robertis in 1914–16). The review served as a lively political and literary forum and featured contributions from many of the period's leading intellectual figures, such as Giovanni Amendola, Giuseppe Antonio Borgese, Benedetto Croce, Gaetano Salvemini, Riccardo Bacchelli, Umberto Saba, and Aldo Palazzeschi. In 1913 Papini and Soffici abandoned *La Voce* (which they deemed inadequate as a tool for provoking a cultural revolution) and founded their own militant review entitled *Lacerba*. Initially a bimonthly, *Lacerba* became a weekly in early 1915, ceasing publication later that same year. During the middle year of its existence it momentarily allied itself with the Futurists and featured Futurist words-in-freedom poems, graphics, and manifestos. Harshly polemical in its approach, *Lacerba* was a ferocious critic of the contemporary Italian scene and was regularly subject to government censure.

15. The Nobel laureate Grazia Deledda (1871–1936) was the author of a large body of novels, including *Naufraghi in porto* (1902), *Elias Portolu* (1903), *Cenere* (1904), *L'edera* (1906), *Canne al vento* (1913), *La madre* (1920), and *La fuga in Egitto* (1925). Although much celebrated after her 1926 Nobel Prize, Deledda remained apolitical and distant from fascism.

16. Sarfatti could, of course, not have known that Pirandello too would be awarded the Nobel Prize for literature six years later, in 1934.

17. The core of Sarfatti's group of promising composers is made up of the so-called generation of 1880 (*la generazione dell '80*): Alfredo Casella (1883–1947), Ildebrando Pizzetti (1880–1968), Gian Francesco Malipiero (1882–1973), and Ottorino Respighi (1879–1936).

18. The Novecento (Twentieth Century) movement encompassed all of the arts (including architecture) and was led by Sarfatti herself, with Massimo Bontempelli as her closest collaborator. In line with the various returns to realism and classicism that characterized the 1920s cultural scene both in Italy and abroad, it advocated a fusion between properly modernist and classical elements.

19. The violence of Sarfatti's lexicon derives from the fact that Mussolini's urbanistic plans were referred to as the *sventramento* (disembowelment) of Rome. Indeed, numerous medieval residential districts made up of narrow and dark passageways through the city's "belly" were demolished and excavated in order to construct new avenues such as the Via dell'Impero (now Via dei Fori Imperiali).

20. The list includes the distinguished architect and designer Giò Ponti (1891–1979), the sculptor and Mussolini portraitist Adolfo Wildt (1868–1931), the Novecento and Futurist architect Giovanni Muzio (1893–1993), and the painter Libero Andreotti (1875–1933).

21. Sarfatti's list includes the dean of Italian modern architects Marcello Piacentini (1881–1960), Tommaso Buzzi (1900–), and Giuseppe de Finetti (1892–1952).

22. The Palace of the Lictor (Palazzo del Littorio) was the headquarters of the National Fascist Party. As Sarfatti indicates, the Vidoni Palace had served this purpose for some years, though discussions were already under way to incorporate a new Palace of the Lictor into plans for the completion of the Via dell'Impero. In 1933–34 an architectural competition was held that included the participation of many of Italy's foremost modernist architects, including Giuseppe Terragni and Adalberto Libera.

CHAPTER 18

Excerpt from
The Ideal of Culture and Italy Today
(1936)
Giovanni Gentile

Gentile (1875–1944) was the regime's foremost philosopher and an important arbiter of fascist cultural policies. His teaching career included positions at the universities of Palermo, Pisa, and Rome. His philosophical contributions included the doctrine of actualism and the theory of the ethical state (which validated the regime's totalitarian concept of politics). Between 1902 and 1922 he was co-editor with Benedetto Croce of the important review La Critica, *though the two split over ideological differences, with Gentile going on to become the principal signatory of the 1925 Manifesto of Fascist Intellectuals and Croce the principal author of the antifascist response. As minister of public instruction between 1922 and 1924, Gentile instituted a number of major reforms in the national educational system. He also served on the Fascist Grand Council between 1923 and 1929. A member of the Royal Academy, his influence was extensive as founder and president of the National Institute of Fascist Culture, general editor of the* Enciclopedia italiana, *and director of the* Giornale Critico della Filosofia Italiana. *In political seclusion from 1929 on, he delivered a final political speech on 24 June 1943, calling upon Italians to support the fascist government; he went on to endorse the Social Republic. Both these gestures may have led to his assassination by partisans in April 1944.*

*

When one speaks of an "ideal," it is essential that the term be clearly understood. The ideal is not, nor can it ever become, an actual reality, because if the ideal were ever achieved, our reason for living and so life itself would be lost. Those with careless habits of mind who tout superficial solutions that easily resolve all awkward problems are eager to spread another untruth, namely, that if an ideal is true, concrete, and rational, it will be achieved at some time or other and that, once achieved, another ideal will take its place and provide new challenges and sustenance. This is false for two reasons.

First, because ideals are interconnected and converge in a single global ideal that gradually evolves and attains completeness, a global ideal that assumes forms ever more in harmony with the fundamental principle from which it derives and with the ultimate purpose toward which it is directed. Conclusion: a specific and transitory solution is never a real solution to the problem of life. Second, because every ideal, even when it assumes the particular lineaments that distinguish it from other ideals, derives its essential ideal nature [*idealità*] from the impossibility of a perfect equation between idea and reality, between principle and action, between value and deed. Much as it may seem to embody some exemplary perfection or an ineffable divine model to which one ideally adapts, the ideal always remains distinct from the principle that generated it and looms in the distance like something one can outdo, like a boundary beyond which the human spirit will always feel the need to push itself. Hence the dissatisfaction and sublime melancholy that surprises great minds as soon as they complete any dazzling work of human genius, that melancholy that, in contrast to the vain arrogance and bliss of mediocre minds, is the surest sign of greatness. Hence the law of "the limit of the ideal" that Francesco de Sanctis, the greatest of our historical thinkers of the past century, invoked so often in his meditations on history: the law that holds that the abstractness of all sought-after ideals confers upon them a distinctive vacuity; they are all light without shadows, absolute and divine perfection without those limitations that make of the divine something real and operative in the lives of men.[1]

On the other hand, it must be borne in mind that "limit" does not equal negation. In other words, by shunting aside the utopia of absolute perfection, one does give up on one's lifelong pursuit of perfection or effort to put into practice the ideal nature [*idealità*] of values. The word "limit" marks a practical turn. It means conferring upon the ideas that govern our conduct that practicality they will always lack as long as they remain abstract. It means that ideas intended as norms of life and ideals of action are false if unrealizable. It means that the concrete value of ideas derives from the dialectic reconciliation of positive and negative elements that are both essential to the life of the spirit as actualized by men through their tireless struggles to improve both themselves and the world in which they work. A tireless struggle that can never cease because man's dignity resides in work and in disdain for the idleness that would result from reaching the summit of perfection. So the "limit" of the ideal is not some defect. Rather, it is the ideal's virtue, its immortal quality, the mark of its convergence with the immortal life of the spirit.

Such considerations are hardly superfluous when talking about an ideal (which is to say, a conception of human activity, irrespective of its form or of the field in which it unfolds). A political party, an artistic trend, a church, a school: each has its own program that translates into an ideal, an ideal that corresponds to a given conception of political reality, art, divinity, education. But now we see party supporters acting against the program's maxims; artists deviating from the style championed by the group to which they belong; priests violating the essential precepts that they preach; teachers and students lagging behind and demonstrating at final exams that everything that should have been achieved was not. At this point skepticism creeps in, and one is tempted to deny any foundation and efficacy to programs and ideals. Instead of emphasizing what is positive, lively, vital, true to the ideal, one sees only defects, without understanding that a defect is actually nothing other than the limit of the ideal, the limit that is the condition of the ideal's fulfillment. Which all goes to say that we must avoid irrational and corrosive skepticism if we want to understand life and to maintain our faith in life's value. Notwithstanding its defects, life is a monumental edifice built by generation after generation so that the reign of the spirit may be brought about.

Culture . . . lies at the very heart of this existence in which the immortal spirit strives to realize its world. Spirit's world is a civilized [*civile*] world made up of science and art, an ethical society and state. It is made up of religion, which offers man the possibility to reach out beyond the succession of forms and the rush of all living beings toward death and to embrace a superior principle with which his intellect can unite and in which his spirit can find repose. It is also made up of physical nature (which must be treated, investigated, and discussed as something human: as an instrument of human industry and as a function of technology that man himself creates and determines so as to bring about a world that is always more submissive to his desires and more respondent to his needs). Is it not the case that this entire civilized world in which and from which every one of us lives, in which freedom battles every variety of rigid determinism [*meccanismo*] is encompassed within the domain of thought, if by this word we mean to indicate every spiritual activity with which man constructs his world? Take away thought, its struggles to resolve problems, the passions with which it colors the universe with the light of our soul and warms it with the fire burning deep within us, the illusions it offers in which everything becomes beautiful with the quiver of life sprouting again in our hearts, and all is idealized and eternalized in the immortal life of art; take away thought and life would vanish all at once like the shadow of a dream. So to live is to participate in the constant becoming of the world and to maintain a relationship between the external and internal that preserves and sustains the center that we occupy, a center from which we reach out into the periphery from which we draw the treasures of our being. To live is to feel, to think, to want. It is to center the universe's infinite rays in our person, to unify them in our conscience, to strengthen them with the powerful energy that we radiate in order to create ever new conditions of life and thus the very reality that we require in order to live, the reality that is our reality. Man does not live in ignorance. Unlike plant life, he is not absorbed by the circuit of material exchanges between self and environment, nor does he find fulfillment in those rudimentary forms of reaction to the external world with which animals begin to affect exterior circumstances and modify them to suit their own needs. From the moment he opens his eyes to the light, man locates his world within himself, in his consciousness. He sees it, he longs for it, he measures and ponders it, he thinks about it, he continuously constructs and reconstructs it, always striving to place its inner structure in the brightest light. Either he praises the world just as he finds it and exalts it in his heart, or he judges the world inferior to his conception and attempts to free himself by destroying it. But one way or another, he always strives to bring into existence the world that is most in keeping with his goals. Man affirms his human essence, in short, when he frees himself from all external forms of subjection and internalizes that external reality already known and subjugated by his will. This is how he becomes free, creative, solitary, infinite.

When man feels shut out of an alienating reality, a reality that conditions him and imposes its iron-clad law, he is quick to flee the tyrannical and mechanical world that surrounds him, driven by a fundamental urge that scientific inquiry and practice are unable to satisfy. He is quick to flee from the world as best he can: by means of art. He thereby freely creates for himself a world that is entirely subjective but that, for the artist, retains the solidity and stability of the real. A world that is completely coherent and rational, not to mention transparent, in which man cleaves only to himself and need go nowhere because his chest is filled with the infinite breath of the divine being. If art seems to suddenly lure the human spirit away from an autonomous reality that would impede the freedom of the subject, this is because art is the most striking primary manifestation of the spirit's life.

The experience of developing an intellectual identity [*personalità mentale*] and of the obstacles and conflicts encountered in the course of testing and educating one's will confronts the human spirit with a world that is foreign and heterogeneous, a world that must be absorbed, placated, or subjugated within one's inner being. Even when this operation has been accomplished, the subject will have mastered only that which he has been able to represent to himself and what the inner workings of his knowledge and will have managed to make his own, so that when he turns his attention to an absolutely superior and transcendent Being, he will be unable to sunder the bond with this Being's presence within himself, his representations, and his moral stance of religious worship. It follows that the subjectivity of the world, brought to universal attention through candid artworks, is actually the constant and insuperable form of the world whether conceived theoretically or practically, scientifically or religiously, the world, that is, in relation to which the spiritual life of man unfolds.

This is the reason why I stated that culture occupies the center of the world that interests us. To master the world, to make use of it, to strengthen life, man has no more powerful tool than culture. The world turns and is organized around culture. Civilization itself (which I would define as the complex of forms through which man's power asserts itself as a triumph of liberty or, rather, the domination of spirit over nature) has its base and beginning in culture. Civilization is the effect; the cause is culture. Barbaric and uncivilized peoples possess no history because they neither evolve nor develop their fundamental attitudes into ever more complex forms of economy, art, religion, science, law, government, and custom. In them humanity remains numb, enclosed in the primitive shell of a conscience that is unstimulated, unnourished, uninformed by culture. Spirit mechanically repeats traditional customs and beliefs, enforces social forms that are servile and deaf to the moral demand for the free development of personality, transfers the material superstitions (treated as inviolable) that children receive from their fathers and pass on to their own children. Where there is no progress, there is no civilization. Progress is synonymous with thought, culture, and the formation and development of what makes man human: personality and self-awareness. Unlike natural formative processes, self-awareness affirms individuality, innovation, absolute originality, the miraculous, which is to say, freedom.

You seek proof? Look at the highest and at the humblest expression of the self-awareness with which man distinguishes himself from the world: by asserting himself, saying "I," and speaking. Look at the greatest artistic geniuses, admired by everyone (be they learned or ignorant), able to recast the simplest words in a tone that captures our spirits, that stirs and moves us like the sound of words never before heard but resonant like a secret voice that manages to express what is already astir in our very hearts. Look at the humblest creatures: babies who form their first words by babbling, who always surprise and amaze with observations brimming over with an intuitive truth that forces mature and self-absorbed minds to reflect and leads Jesus to assert the natural closeness between small children and his divine wisdom. The original, the unforeseeable, the miraculous: these are habitual domains occupied by the human spirit when pursuing the sound and vigorous development of its nature. Stagnation, imitation, psittacism, rote memorization, fixity, every purely or passive conservative tendency: all are signs of the spirit's decay and of a renunciation of its privileges. . . .[2]

✳

. . . Character! It is intuitively self-evident that man is man, acquires significance, and acts as he must so as not to be "lived through" but rather to live a life of his own: a life with purpose, . . . a life of the mind [*ingegno*] filled with studies and work to the greatest degree possible, lived with honesty and in good faith toward others and especially himself and with the will to take himself and everything seriously. All this, however, is nothing without character. The character of man is the golden seal of his spiritual nature. Character means unity, and to speak of spirit means to speak of that unity that spirit alone is capable of imprinting on a material world otherwise fated to disperse into atomized elements. Spirit consists in the unity of parts that harmonize and converge in the synthesis that is an individual's life, a life that is unanalyzable without killing it. This is the case with words, sonnets, and long poems in which every word's accent echoes the theme that binds everything together into a single flowing life form. This is the case with every concept, system, soul, and individual conscience. Without unity there is no spiritual life. And without character man fails as artist, philosopher, scientist, apostle, warrior, or man of state. He fails as a man, as that work of art he must always be in order to be someone.

The primordial work of art that every artist must create is his own personality, which must take the form of a melody dominated by a fundamental theme that recurs in the course of all its variations from beginning to end. It is untrue that poets and writers sound different during the various phases of their development or in the various songs or stories in which, from time to time, they pour out their hearts and say everything they have to say. And just as in each artistic work, so in the totality of the poet's life through which his personality is fulfilled. What applies to every poet also applies to every individual, whose utterances — whether understood as a single sentence, a speech, or everything spoken over the course of an entire life — are also suffused with a personality.

True, there are men who are inconsistent, scattered, and ineffectual, but only in the course of a single day or in the beginning, middle, and end of a single speech, not throughout their entire lives. Otherwise, they would be failed men.

Unity of character consists in more than the "longitudinal" unity by means of which every man can be judged only after death (as the proverb has it). This is the most readily accessible aspect of character and, hence, the easiest to recognize. But another unity defines the essence of character: the unity of every instant, recognizable before a man's demise. Here resides character's deepest unity. Even fragments evince a unity: a distinctive tone, spirit, beauty, worth, character that makes the old adage true that "it is enough for a man to open his mouth and he can be judged." We all know how to prick up our ears and to determine in an instant whether a speaker is serious or unserious, sincere or insincere, single-minded or duplicitous, whether he is an actor putting on a show or a man who lives and breathes his own thoughts. Sure, we can deceive ourselves if we judge only on the basis of tone, gesture, and gaze. But what does this potential for deception demonstrate except that our minds rush to judgment and strive to surmise everything about a man? Our every judgment, however considered and cautious it may be, is subject to error. But the lance that wounds is also the lance that heals. And if we were to judge friends only after their deaths, all our friends would be the inhabitants of graveyards.

True character is simply the character of a constant and tenacious subject who is always ready to face the consequences of his ideas, not because he is hard as stone and resistant to seductive new aspects of reality previously unseen or unknown, but because he has at his disposal the nucleus of living ideas that make up his personality. The personality in question can adapt to new exigencies, suggestions, and considerations. It can grow progressively larger and richer without interrupting the course of its own development, without starting anew, falling into self-contradiction, or failing in its commitment to fulfill an entire life plan. The only thing that matters is that nucleus or "content" of personality, that distinctive point of view with which every living man enters and views the world and that corresponds to a certain way of feeling and reacting. This distinctive perspective confers an unmistakable individuality upon a person: an individuality made up of features, a tone of voice, an expressivity, and a carriage that permits us to single out a familiar person in a crowd even without seeing his face.

So character is the presence of that individuality that informs everything we think, say, or do. It is our very soul and thus also the soul of the art we create, the thoughts we formulate, the faith we profess, and, more generally, the culture to which we give rise. Without character all culture would devolve into dilettantism, and, reduced to frivolity and games, life would become a comedy in the worst sense of the word.

The new Italy does not interpret life as a comedy. Her cultural ideal is not dilettantism but, rather, character, the same character inaugurated by Mazzini but now fully mature. A warning (that should be unnecessary but isn't): I do not mean to suggest that all the Italians of today must become Mazzinis to the second power. Not even Mazzini was always Mazzini. Despite the fact that, historically speaking, he lived his ideal to the fullest extent, even he spent a few sad hours in his own garden of Gethsemane, assailed by doubts and dismay. So let it be perfectly clear that we are speaking of an ideal, not an empirical, observable, and verifiable reality. The new era of Italian history initiated by fascism conceives of culture in Mazzinian terms but with a difference: it maintains the old ideal of Italian culture but adds a new twist.

Mazzini strained to see beyond his era's most distant horizon. The issue of his time was resurgence [*risorgimento*]: the independence and unity of Italy and the transformation of the Italian nation into a state. Aside from the need for national boundaries, he envisioned a federation of peoples and an abstract humanity that guaranteed the brotherhood of all peoples (much like contemporary French humanitarians). Though Mazzini conceived of the life of the spirit as a struggle sanctified by martyrdom, even he longed for the peaceful co-existence of peoples and for something like an end to history's dynamic unfolding, an end that, once and for all, would provide a definitive solution to spirit's immanent problem. Fascism's roots place it in direct opposition to Mazzini's eschatological vision. Fascism is not about bringing Italy into existence, because Italy already exists. The last war saw the young nation, for the first time in its history, enter the field of international competition where national strength and vitality are put to the test. Italy fought, shed rivers of blood and triumphed, but to no avail. Her victory and contribution to the common victory were disregarded.

The prize to which her victory entitled her was withheld. And so she fell back upon herself, exhausted by the enormous effort. She needed to rouse herself anew, but Mazzini's goal of forming the state would no longer do. Instead, she had to forge ahead, to create a strong state, to gain the spoils denied her in the wake of the war (the first great testing ground for her powers). In short, her goal was now to achieve true victory by asserting herself and achieving the recognition beyond her borders indispensable to her life (crucial because to live is to develop, to progress, to grow, to advance). The means to this end was an internal discipline that Italians had never known: strict forms of organization, however harsh; moral and military training; international prestige; self-assertion as proud and warlike both on the national and international fronts; a demand for a revision of treaties and of the status quo; appeal to a higher justice; a constant state of readiness for war (which is to say the development of military forces capable of bearing down heavily on the enemy). This is of course a sketch, not an exposition. Everyone knows our era and is aware that the ideal fascist man is the Black Shirt. He is the soldier ready to risk everything, who, unlike his Mazzinian counterpart, is no longer content with merely a fatherland or with yearning for a third Rome where a new lay gospel — a generous utopia but a utopia all the same — is preached. He aspires instead to become Mussolini's new Italian: a human subject to whom corresponds a great, dynamic fatherland, conscious of its rights in the world, powerful and thus vibrant, victorious in mortal conflicts and in the clash of interests. The state has changed: its horizon has broadened, and man has attained a deeper self-awareness. Man lives with the awareness that he is the citizen of a state that, no longer circumscribed within a static and stagnant structure, is active, dynamic, open to the future, predisposed to embrace its existence and to conquer all circumstances on its own.

The Italy of today, our Italy, is obviously no longer that of the Risorgimento. It finds itself surrounded, on the one side, by wealthy nations (some of which became rich in the course of the war) that are content to sit at the sumptuous postwar banquet; on the other side, by nations under the sway of their more fortunate counterparts. Together the two rally together to defend the status quo and to frustrate Italy's demands, break her will, and drive her to resignation and inaction. It would be naive to marvel at this fact as do those Quakers and good Samaritans . . . who are always scandalized by the so-called politics of aggression. But reality is what it is: life is a struggle, to acquire something is to conquer it, even God cannot bestow his graces without taking man's merits into account. The state is not a state if it is not an expression of the universal will. And this will can only be self-limiting, because any external limitation upon it would lead to its destruction.

So what about war? War is a necessary sacrifice: "necessary" when one wishes to live, act, and desire with seriousness, because without obstacles to overcome and enemies to defeat, the will ceases to exist. Sooner or later all peoples who aren't resigned to perishing must wage war. The logic of events and an immanent historical necessity demanded that fascist Italy face a war as a function of the coalition of political principles and interests that it uprooted: Freemasonry, radical democratism, pacifism, corporate deceit, communism. As harbinger of a new civilization, a new style, a new humanity, and a new Europe, fascist Italy could not escape the fate of all the great innovators, namely, martyrdom (in the majestic etymological sense of the word). And hence the need for a battle to serve as the chrism of our revolution: a sacramental anointing whose meaning and honor are enhanced by the number of our enemies and the imperial power and prestige with which they embody the principles the fascist revolution rebels against.

Today's Italy is proud of its war. So every time that foreigners try to drive a wedge between the people and their Duce or attempt to disarm or to subdue her, Italy rallies with ardent enthusiasm around her leader, the very symbol of her faith and reason for existence. Such threats and abuses of power have shaped the Italian people into a single unbreakable block and eliminated all traces of passive opposition and national discord. They have endowed our resistance to the economic siege with a religious form and tone, as is befitting a religious war, one of those wars in which compromise is impossible because the outcome is a question of life and death for all combatants.

That foreigners sometimes misunderstand the soul of today's Italy is not wholly surprising. But this very incomprehension reinvigorates and strengthens our commitment to insure that a new Italy arises from out of fascism: an Italy finally free to call the shots in the world of nations, a modern state fully aware of its being, its dignity, and its needs. A tragedy, yes, the tragedy of a life lived with high seriousness, fully in keeping with the fascist ideal.

✶

Our present ideal is to create a culture that produces men aware of this great tragedy of life: life as the struggle to make one's way not selfishly or for oneself but for everyone. For everyone, because the life of Italy also informs the life of Europe and the rest of the world. Our culture is not crudely or narrowly based on doctrines of race [*razzistica*], nor is it geographically landlocked; rather, it is intelligently universal and human. This is the Italian ideal of which I have provided only a thumbnail sketch that emphasizes the special importance of character within this new culturally grounded conception of the spiritual life.

Indeed, character formation must be the highest goal of contemporary Italian culture, the best starting point being the reorganization of the school system. The regime has devoted a great deal of attention to this matter, constantly revising the first school regulations it established, always wanting to do more and better, afraid of not having done enough or well enough. This excessive concern is probably attributable to the uneasy critical spirit of our educators, who never cease expressing their doubts and dissatisfactions. But sooner or later the schools will resume a course consistent with the ideals of modern culture, which is to say, with fascism's own ideals. We must safeguard this ideal, the spirit of culture.

Dangers abound and, if we wish to avoid them, our eyes need to be wide open. Let me touch upon two dangers here that seem to me worthy of our attention.

One is a danger inherent in the discipline that the regime imposed upon the Italian people, one of its most remarkable, important, and praiseworthy achievements. If caution is not exercised, discipline can easily be transformed from self-submission to an authority capable of interpreting one's inner needs into merely formal, external obedience, a corrupting falsity that encourages hypocrisy and destroys character. This is a very grave danger for a rigid mass organization whose knowledge and control over individuals are usually fairly cursory.

A second danger is linked to the religious restoration that fascism has promoted in the name of developing a sense of civil conscience and moral institutions, a restoration that, for the most part, may amount to little more than a resurgence of Catholic traditions. As a result, our national culture may again fall prey to empiricist and mechanical forms of external piety and to a resulting loss of inner spiritual freedom (won after centuries of struggle). All this is in striking conflict with the openness, sincerity, and spontaneity that foster an authentic life of the spirit. It is also in conflict with the energy of character upon which we found our ideal of culture.

Dangers and difficulties dishearten only the weak. The strong draw from them grounds for vigilance and combat, for firmly maintaining their own positions. And fascism has always stood its ground. It has always kept an eye on all internal enemies and has defeated them, which is why today this wonder of the civilized world and source of pride for an ancient but always youthful people stands firm against its external adversaries and will defeat them.

translated by Olivia E. Sears and Jeffrey T. Schnapp

Notes

1. The essayist and literary historian Francesco de Sanctis (1817–83) was the author, among many other studies, of *Saggi critici* (1867), *Saggio critico sul Petrarca* (1869), the classic *Storia della letteratura italiana* (1870–71), and *Nuovi saggi critici* (1872). A Hegelian in his vision of history, de Sanctis merged a concern with human history as the ideal unfolding of spirit with passionate civic and political commitments that included stints as minister of education in 1861–62, 1878, and 1879–81 during the course of a distinguished academic career.
2. The arcane word "psittacism" literally means "parroting" and is based upon the Latin word *psittacus*.

CHAPTER 19

Two Excerpts from *Futurism and Fascism*
The Florence Address (1919) and
The Italian Empire (1923)
Filippo Tommaso Marinetti

✶

Born in Alexandria, Egypt, Marinetti (1876–1944) was the founder and leader of the Futurist movement. A prominent late Symbolist poet by the time he was in his twenties, Marinetti founded the review Poesia *in 1905 through which he brought the leading modern poets to the attention of Italian audiences. In 1909 he published the* Manifesto and Foundation of Futurism *on the front page of the Parisian daily* Le Figaro, *calling for a revolt against the cult of history and its institutions (libraries and museums) and for a radical renewal of cultural forms, after which time he emerged as the world's leading proselytizer for cultural modernism. An active participant in the interventionist movement, Marinetti took part in the Fiume occupation and ran unsuccessfully for Parliament on the fascist ticket in 1919. As testified to in the first of the following documents, Marinetti's intransigent anticlericalism and antitraditionalism led to early tensions and even an open split with fascism mended only in 1924. Despite the tensions with antimodernist fascists, Marinetti remained close to Mussolini and was a tireless defender of the regime, both at home and abroad. He was rewarded for his loyalty by being elected to the Royal Academy and by numerous public charges.*

✶

The Florence Address

De-Vaticanization [*Lo svaticanamento*]

In the name of Futurism and the Italian Futurists, I unconditionally approve the entire program of the Fasci di Combattimento, set forth for you by my friend [Sileno] Fabbri.[1] There are, however, some serious gaps in this program to which I wish to draw your attention.

Fascists! Italy faces no greater danger than the black peril. The Italian people dared to bring to term the enormously heroic and successful war effort, thereby insuring, in turn, the victory of inspired and resilient

Futurism over square and pedantic Teutonic traditionalism [*passatismo*]. Their mission will have failed, however, if we do not now turn our energies to freeing our beautiful peninsula, agile and pulsating with life, from the plague of the papacy. We must will, demand, and order the expulsion of the papacy. Or, better yet, to coin a more precise expression, we must pursue the de-Vaticanization of Italy. (Applause, ovations.)

The Agitatorium [*L'eccitatorio*]

I return to my analysis of the program of the Fasci di Combattimento, which proposes replacing the Senate with a national technical council. I wish to state that, however important, the concept of technicity [*technicità*] is inadequate. In the history of nations, senates embody an eternal deference to the wisdom of old men, old men whose role is to rein in power, slow the maturation of plans, steer decisions in prudent directions. The concept of the Senate, like that of the chorus in a Greek tragedy, has single-handedly weighted down, bureaucratized, and slowed the spiritual and material progress of humankind.

Legislators and philosophers, concerned exclusively with preserving, improving, and consolidating the status quo, have found in the Senate an ideal guarantor of order and tradition, a powerful check (founded on lived experience) on the potential folly of governments.

Those who do not worship at the Senate's feet are so audacious as to propose perfecting it by instituting senatorial elections. You wish to abolish the Senate but seem unaware that the technical council you have devised in its place will inevitably be rife with the same premature senility, cowardly prudence, bureaucratic pedantry, decrepitude, and chronic hatred for youthful innovation and daring. The technical council should instead be a council made up of a few very young men and ought therefore to be called an Agitatorium.

Legislators have always dreamed of checking the power of government, unaware that power means restraint and that a government is always more or less a policeman. Nothing could be more absurd than expecting one policeman to guard another. Let us instead place at his side a subversive, a rebel, an agitator. And thus is born the concept of the Agitatorium: an animating, simplifying, and accelerating device that will defend youth and guarantee the progress and spirituality of a race full of precocious geniuses. I dream of a future Italy governed by technicians energized by a council of very young men to take the place of our current Parliament of incompetent orators and decrepit experts, held in check by an ever more moribund Senate.

The technical council that will replace the Senate must be composed of men younger than thirty years old. The point is of crucial importance because, in a country where a man of fifty-five is considered young and virile, it is all too easy to celebrate the coming to power of "youth." Salandra cries, "Long live youth!" but, like his peers, he is terrified of youth.[2] He and his peers quarantine forty year olds as if they were cholera carriers, treat fifty year olds like terrorists, and consider sixty year olds daring but almost mature enough for membership in the Italian government!

We must avoid this new plague: a technical council made up of old people who, having neglected their technical skills for so long, know only how to die technically.

Italian life is still reducible to the inane cohabitation of senile legions without authority and without prestige and a filthy servant girl. The former, enshrouded in the usual dreary gloom, spread pessimism, pedantry, professorial austerity, and patriotic drivel while sprinkling around the dust of ancient Rome. The latter wanders among them. Mean, provincial, and slovenly, she does everything wrong, keeps house very poorly, resists any and all improvements. She wastes her day checking the kitchen accounts, always afraid to spend money and to be ruined. Her idea of triumph is a minestrone that is cheap and not too salty.

The senile legions mutter, "Remember the Roman legions, the Eternal City . . . the fathers conversing along the sacred Tiber. . . ."

The servant girl feverishly explains how she upholds her master's prestige by gossiping with merchants and by being obstinate, how she keeps on good terms with the doctor, and so on. She boasts that she is a courageous freethinker because she mocks [fa le corna] the priests behind their backs. Yet she goes to church, is chummy with her representative [delegato], and knows just how to choke a dreadful economy. The servant girl and the senile legions rebel ferociously against the idea of moving. They also wholeheartedly agree that dust, woodworms, mice, mold, prefects, and so on must all be scrupulously preserved.

The senile legions bear the names of Boselli and Salandra; the servant girl bears the name of Giolitti or Nitti.[3] (Ovation.)

Against the senile legions and the servant girl, we propose an Agitatorium of students and Futurist Arditi.

Arditismo: Schools of Physical Courage and Patriotism

A third gap in the program of the Fasci di Combattimento regards schooling. Our Futurist friend Fabbri has brilliantly described a complete overhaul of the school system.

I believe, however, that we could achieve all this and more (leaping far beyond what is today imaginable into a miraculous new realm) by means of an absolutely strict, even fierce, imposition of exercise in the schools.

In addition to practical and technical training both in workshops and on farms, we will also have to found itinerant schools—schools where travel itself provides the foundation for education—as well as schooling in physical courage and patriotism.

Games must have absolute priority over reading, as must the joys of outdoor life. Every day we must tell Italian children about our divine Italy and relentlessly teach them physical courage and contempt of danger, rewarding reckless daring and heroism.

Schools of physical courage and patriotism must replace our nearly prehistoric and troglodytic Greek and Latin curricula.

We Futurists are convinced that this is the way to forge a new kind of heroic citizen able to defend himself, capable of free thinking and free fighting; a citizen who will render police, police headquarters, carabinieri, and priests utterly useless.

With my Futurist friend Mario Carli, captain of the Arditi, and Captain [Ferruccio] Vecchi, the renowned assailant of *Avanti* and head of the Association of Arditi, I have seen Arditismo arise from out of Futurism and the war and assume the form of a new heroic and revolutionary patriotism.[4] Vecchi's newspaper *L'Ardito* is a forceful newspaper that should be commended to all Italian youths. (Ovation.)

Perhaps the day will come when Italy will be filled with the *schools of danger* that I proposed ten years ago in the earliest Futurist manifestos, an ideal first realized in the wartime training schools of the Arditi (where soldiers advanced on their hands and knees under grazing machine gun fire; where they waited, without even closing their eyes, for girders to sweep overhead, etc.).

The Proletariat of Geniuses

I wish to fill another gap by turning now to the only proletariat that remains forgotten and oppressed: the vitally important proletariat of geniuses.

It is indisputable that our race surpasses all others in the large number of geniuses that it produces. Even the smallest Italian group, the smallest village, can claim seven or eight twenty year olds who are brimming over with creative fervor, youths of overweening ambition as revealed in volumes of unpublished verse and in eloquent outbursts in the public squares and at political rallies. Admittedly, some (though they are few in number) are little more than foolish dreamers who will probably never attain true genius. But there is genius in their temperament, which is to say that, encouraged in the right manner, they might well contribute to the nation's intellectual dynamism.

In that same small group or village it is easy to find seven or eight middle-aged men above whose heads hovers the melancholy halo of failed genius, a halo that accompanies them throughout their lives as petty clerks or professionals, in neighborhood cafes, and with their families. Remnants of a genius that never found a propitious environment in which it might thrive, they were quickly laid low by economic and sentimental necessities.

I founded the Futurist artistic movement eleven years ago in order to brutally modernize the literary-artistic milieu, to deprive it of authority and destroy its ruling gerontocracy, to debunk pedantic professors and critics, and to encourage the reckless outbursts of young genius. My aim was to create a fully oxygenated atmosphere, a healthy, encouraging, supportive atmosphere where all of Italy's young geniuses might prosper. I sought to encourage all of them, to increase their pride, to clear a path for them, to swiftly reduce the proportion of failed and worn-out geniuses.

It is sometimes difficult to recognize, appreciate, and encourage young geniuses. In part this is because instead of viewing their homeland as a vast malleable mass to be molded spiritually, these youths regard it as an idiotic network of abuses of power, criminal rackets, corrupt authorities, and asinine rules. And, of course, they are right. Everywhere in our country, genius is undervalued, derided, imprisoned. Only mediocre opportunists and over-the-hill, one-time geniuses are celebrated and crowned.

Futurism gathered together many of these young geniuses. Among them, the following shone like giants in the Futurist blaze: Boccioni, Russolo, Buzzi, Balla, Mazza, Sant'Elia, Pratella, Folgore, Cangiullo, Mario Carli, Mario Dessy, Vieri, de Nardis, Pasqualino, Funi, Sironi, Chiti, Jannelli, Nannetti, Cantarelli, Rosai, Baldessari, Galli, Depero, Dudreville, Primo Conti.[5] [To these names one must add] the creative geniuses of the Synthetic Theater (Bruno Corra and Settimelli) and the courageous and skillful Futurist writers of *Roma Futurista* (Rocca, Bottai, Federico Pinna, and Volt), not to mention Bolzon, the noblest banner of Italian culture in America.[6]

Passing from art to political action with extraordinary elasticity, these young men were always at my side during our earliest demonstrations against Austria and at the battle of the Marne. They accompanied me in prison during the interventionist campaigns and into battle.

Many other youths—dynamic, impetuous young men, intoxicated with spiritual heroism and revolutionary patriotism—have now swollen the

Futurist ranks. But a great many others remain ignorant or depressed, stifled by the atmosphere of small ultrapasséist cities. Thanks to the vast wave of stormy soirées and demonstrations that swept up and down the Italian peninsula, Futurism came into contact with nearly everyone. But the nation's political forces will have to undertake a more systematic campaign if we are to save, re-ignite, and tap the vast energies possessed by the proletariat of geniuses.

I propose the construction in every city of a number of buildings that bear a title like the following: Free Exhibition of Creative Genius. In these facilities:

1. works of painting, sculpture, graphics, architectural drawings, machine drawings, and designs of inventions will be on display for a month at a time;
2. musical works, small or large, for orchestra or piano, in any genre, form, or size will be performed;
3. poems, prose, scientific writings of all kinds and lengths will be read, displayed, recited;
4. all citizens will have the right to exhibit free of charge;
5. works of any kind or any value, even if seemingly judged to be absurd, inane, crazy, or immoral, will be displayed or read without a jury.

With these free and open exhibitions of creative genius, we Futurists wage war against an ever present danger: the danger of seeing the spirit shipwrecked on the ideological seas that swirl around the formulas of communism and the dictatorship of the proletariat.

Let Us Defend the Mind!

Everywhere one encounters pathologies brought about by the exhaustion produced by the war, by a mania for plagiarism, by provincial myopia, by journalistic verbosity, and by conservative cowardice. Everywhere attempts are under way to glorify the manual laborer and to raise him above intellectual work.

I am firmly persuaded of the bad faith of gentlemen such as Anatole France and [Henri] Barbusse, who, descending from the highest peaks of skeptical irony and from the golden summits offered by best-selling novels, pen manifestoes addressed *to manual and intellectual laborers.*

No, Italians! Political Futurism will tenaciously oppose every attempt at leveling. Let everything, everything be granted to the manual proletariat [*proletariato manuale*] but without sacrificing the spirit, genius, the great guiding lights.

Let us sacrifice the entire parasitic plutocracy of the world to the oppressed classes and to the workers who barely eke out a living.

But let the intellectual laborers and intuitive creators plainly rise up above their manual peers, for they alone can invent, discover, renew; they alone can increase the sum total of earthly happiness.

You fascist interventionists know that our victory in the great revolutionary war was the result of the daring, will power, and tenacity of a minority of intellectuals who were the best, the least traditional, the most Futurist. While the entire nation was still slumbering in a pacifist stupor, they felt the need for war and violently diverged with all those pedantic, cultural, reactionary, quietist intellectuals, endowed only with the negative qualities of the spirit. Unlike the latter, these pure, lyrical, and creative spirits led the way. They hurled themselves into hails of gunfire emanating from old professorial and cowardly intellectuals of the ilk of Benedetto Croce and [Giacomo] Barzellotti and from the captious and pettifogging [*avvocatesco*] intellectuals like Treves and Turati.[7]

Among these higher spirits was Gabriele D'Annunzio, who flew over Vienna and presented Fiume as a gift to Italy.[8] Among them was Benito Mussolini, the great Italian Futurist, who from the trenches of his *Il Popolo d'Italia* fearlessly defended our front-line soldiers against the waves of internal enemies, guiding our cities from the gruesome horror of Caporetto to the ideal glory of Vittorio Veneto. (Applause.)

Glory to the Italian people who fought and won the war, but glory also to the geniuses who inspired it. In June 1910 I delivered a sensational ultra-Futurist speech on the necessity and beauty of violence at the Neapolitan Trades Council, the Parma Chamber of Labor, and the Milanese Theater of Modern Art. In it I foresaw the energetic and decisive entry of artists into Italian political life, a prediction magnificently fulfilled by Gabriele D'Annunzio's conquest of Italian Fiume.

In the end, artists will transform the art of government into a disinterested art, to replace the pedantic science of theft and cowardice that it has become today.

But already I hear you speak of our inexperience.

Come on! Do not forget that the Italian race excels above all else at producing great artists and poets.

I believe that parliamentary institutions are destined to collapse. I also believe that the Italian political system is fated to go under, unless it is renewed by the animating force of Italy's creative geniuses, and unless it rids itself of those two scourges of Italian society: lawyers and professors.

Once unshackled by the dynamic drive of an Agitatorium, by the patriotic spark of Arditismo, by schools of physical courage and heroism, by open exhibitions of its creative genius, and by the proletariat of geniuses, Italy will finally fill the world with its peak output of Italian light.

Creative genius, artistic elasticity, synthetic practicality, improvisatory speed, and lightning-like enthusiasm: these are the beautiful forces that account for our victories of 15 June on the Piave and at Vittorio Veneto. (Applause.)

Improvising like mirthful students, tapping their creative artistic powers, the Arditi brought about their own slaughter on the Grappa in order to deceive and cheat the old Austrian bull with their bloody demise, drawing him in by the horns where there was nowhere to break through. A colossal chess game. Thousands of Casanova assassins on the footbridges of the Piave, under the daring flight of the Cagliostros of the sky, masters of the wind.

From the bow opposite them, extending from the Astico to the sea, the arrow shot out from Montello, at the center, in the direction of Vittorio Veneto. Not to the left (on the Grappa) or to the right (Cervignano) but to the center! The most daring target and the least expected. Against that target, an arrow in the form of twenty-two divisions! With bloodless wings, the heart swollen with blood and fire surged and conquered.

Improvising like an artist, the speedy troops, cavalry, bicycle sharpshooters, and armored cars elegantly taunted and choked the retreating Austrian army.

Improvising like an artist, tapping its creative genius, my beautiful armored car (belonging to the eighth squadron under the command of Captain Raby) forded the swollen torrents like a torpedo boat. Then it swooped down from the Carnic Mountains with the frenetic flashing plunge of a fascist dagger into the immense swollen belly of the defeated Austrian army and shot out the back against Vienna.

The creative genius of D'Annunzio conquered Italian Fiume artistically. In Italian Fiume I recently experienced a spasm of joy equal to none when I crumpled a bundle of Austrian crowns whose value had depreciated to a few pennies, thanks to our victory.

What a wild joy to finally crush the financial, military, passéist heart of our traditional enemy between my hands, still throbbing from the pulsations of the machine gun that I held at Vittorio Veneto! (Ovation.)

✶

The Italian Empire

To Benito Mussolini, Head of the New Italy

For fourteen years we have been teaching Italian pride, courage, daring, the love of danger, the habit of energy and recklessness, the religion of the new and of speed.[9] Aggressive movement, feverish insomnia, running, the mortal leap, the slap, and the punch.

War as the world's only hygiene, militarism, patriotism. A firm belief in our racial superiority.[10] Obedience to Italy, absolute sovereign.

The defense of Italian creative genius against traditionalism in all its forms: archaeology, academicism, senility, quietism, cowardice, pacifism, pessimism, nostalgia, sentimentality, erotic obsession, crafts for foreigners. Youth's seizure of power against the bureaucratic and skeptical parliamentary mentality.

Our teachings were successful, but they did not bear all their potential fruit. Today we must loudly repeat our famous manifesto introduced at Italian Tripoli in October 1911:

> We Futurists who, amidst the boos and hissing of cripples [*podagrosi*] and paralytics, have been glorifying for many years the love of danger and violence, patriotism and war, sole hygiene of the world, are happy to experience Italy's great Futurist hour. Let the filthy race of pacifists agonize, holed up again now in the cellars of their laughable building in The Hague.
>
> In Italy's streets and public squares we have recently had the pleasure of coming to blows with the most feverish adversaries of war, screaming our firm principles in their faces:
>
> 1. Let all freedoms be granted to the individual and to the people except that of being a coward.
> 2. We proclaim that the word ITALY must prevail over the word LIBERTY.
> 3. Let the tiresome memory of ancient Rome's greatness be erased, and let Italian greatness exceed it one hundred–fold.
>
> Italy today has for us the form and power of a beautiful dreadnought with its squadron of torpedo-boat islands. Proud that the bellicose fervor that animates the entire nation now equals our own, we call upon the Italian Government (which, at last, is also Futurist) to expand its national ambitions, to disdain the stupid accusations of piracy, and to proclaim the birth of Pan-Italianism.
>
> As of today, this prophetic manifesto must become a reality!

Yes! Yes! We must march and not rot [*marciare e non marcire*] in the name of our sacred ambitions! Italian youth is more than prepared, whether in the muscular or the spiritual sense, so let us propel them toward the conquest of an Italian Empire! "Italian" because if it were "Roman" it would simply restore or plagiarize the past.

An Italian empire, because our slender peninsula—elegant backbone with a hard head of heavy and domineering Alps, epitome of all the beauties of the earth and bursting with creative genius—has the right to govern the world. The imposition of this right will be an act of faith-force, a defiant youthful improvisation, a work of art miraculously blossoming.

Italy's ancient greatness is obscured by the flash of the Carso![11] We are the sons of the Isonzo, of the Piave, of Vittorio Veneto, and of four years of fascist rule: impressive credentials [*blasoni*]! The idea of empire springs from our blood and from our Futurist muscles, that is, victorious, innovative, tireless muscles.

Hostile both to a timid, anti-artistic, antiliterary, socialist-sympathizing, and traditionalist monarchy and to an antiwar, humanitarian, renunciatory, and mediocritizing republic, we are preparing our alternative: an empire of genius, art, strength, inequality, beauty, spirit, elegance, originality, color, fantasy. . . .

The Italian Empire will be antisocialist, anticlerical, antitraditional, with all the liberties and technical advances inscribed within the circle of absolute patriotism. The right to criticize, check, oppose will be denied only to antipatriots. The Italian Empire belongs in the fist of the best Italian. He will govern without Parliament, with a technical council of young men.

This concept-will of an Italian Empire will seem absurd to the weak but no less absurd than did our definitive victory at Vittorio Veneto and the shattering of the Austro-Hungarian Empire in the trembling eyes of the old Italy. If anything, our ambitions may prove too modest once the future of Italians is placed on a footing of war and conquest!

This is what the living dead heroes of our great war were shouting when Futurism speedily interviewed them one Easter on the Carso. As they pressed close around our fantastic automobile they battered us with fervid violent enthusiastic words:

By means of war, sole hygiene of the world, make our Carso the iron pedestal, the dynamic pivot, the unbounded capital of the Italian Empire!

The red sun did not set between the green sky and the white sea. Rather, it swooped across the sky like the flight of a machine-gunning airplane. All the crosses in the cemetery of Redipuglia suited up quickly and presented their arms to Futurism like eager soldiers, each brandishing some engine of war: shrapnel, grenade, bomb, bayonet, pipe bomb, airplane propeller, flame thrower, machine gun, rifle, or rotary motor still drunk with the sky.

Thus the round hill of Redipuglia, planted with crosses, works day and night like a pulsating factory of war. And if the wind thick with heroes attacks it, that cemetery rushes all its armed crosses to the attack, with polyphonies and noises [*rumorismi*] that are imperious and imperial.

translated by Olivia E. Sears and Jeffrey T. Schnapp

Notes

1. This is an excerpt from an impromptu speech given at the Fascist Congress in October 1919.

    Fabbri figured alongside Mussolini and Marinetti on the 1919 fascist electoral list. In *Marinetti e il futurismo* (1929), Marinetti lists him as a member of the Rome futurist Fascio, even though the Futurist leader is here engaged in a critique of Fabbri's presentation at the 1919 Congress of the Fasci.

2. Antonio Salandra (1853–1931) was one of Marinetti's favorite emblems of the old regime and its political gerontocracy. As prime minister between March 1914 and June 1916, Salandra was instrumental in Italy's entry into World War I and was tolerant of fascism up through the proclamation of Mussolini's dictatorship.

3. The national coalition government that immediately followed Salandra's was led by Paolo Boselli and lasted only one year.

4. Carli (1889–1935) was a key member of the *Roma Futurista* group in the immediate wake of World War I (in which he participated as a captain in the Arditi) and a founding member of the Futurist Fasci, the association of the Arditi, the Futurist Political Party, and Fascio of Rome. An intransigent and radical nationalist, he directed the influential (but controversial) newspaper *L'Impero* between 1923 and 1929. The Ardito commander Ferruccio Vecchi (1894–) was indeed the leader of the assault of fascists and Futurist's on the *Avanti* headquarters. Trained as an engineer, he became a writer and novelist during the 1920s, only to start a career as a sculptor in the following decade, capped by a 1941 Italo-German exhibition attended by Mussolini himself.

5. Always fond of similar lists, Marinetti here names most of the major figures belonging to the first decade and a half of the Futurist movement, covering the domains of painting and sculpture (Boccioni, Balla, Sironi, Rosai, Conti), graphic arts (Depero, Dudreville), literature (Cangiullo, Folgore, Buzzi), architecture (Sant'Elia), and music (Russolo, Pratella).

6. In addition to Enrico Rocca and Giuseppe Bottai, the journal's editorial group included the Fiuman legionnaire and poet Federico Pinna Berchet and Count

Vincenzo Fani Ciotti (alias Volt), author of numerous Futurist synthetic theatrical pieces and of a Futurist manifesto of fashion (1919). The Ardito Piero Bolzon (1883–1945) was an early collaborator of Marinetti and Mussolini who went on to serve in several significant party positions in the course of his career (including serving as member of the Directory and the Grand Council). Before World War I he had traveled widely in Latin America.

7. Another favorite Marinetti target, Senator Giacomo Barzellotti (1844–1917) was the author of a wide range of learned studies, including *La rivoluzione e la letteratura in Italia* (1875), *Santi, solitari e filosofi* (1886), *Studi e ritratti* (1893), *La Philosophie de H. Taine* (1900), and *Dal Rinascimento al Risorgimento* (1909).

8. In August 1918 D'Annunzio and a fellow pilot accomplished one of World War I's most celebrated gestures by flying over the Alps in order to "bombard" the city of Vienna with pamphlets printed in the colors of the Italian flag.

9. This piece was cowritten with Mario Carli and Enrico Settimelli (*L'Impero*, 25 April 1923).

10. It is worth noting that Marinetti's notion of race and racial "superiority" is not founded upon eugenic concepts. "Race," rather, functions as an all-embracing term associated with both culture and context and is better understood as anchored in the concept of nationality. This said, when confronted, during the late 1930s, with the regime's new racial policies, Marinetti's attitude was somewhat equivocal. But his motives were pragmatic: he was intensely loyal to Mussolini and did not want to relegate his movement to the margins by opposing one of the Duce's new directives.

11. During 1916–17 Italian troops had engaged in a series of successful battles against the Austro-German troops along a limestone plateau called the Carso that extended from the Isonzo to Fiume and from Vipacco to Trieste. But the enemy offensive of October 1917 — the so-called Battle of Caporetto — reversed their fortunes and inflicted a resounding defeat upon the Italian troops.

CHAPTER 20

Four Excerpts from
Pagan Imperialism: Fascism before the Euro-Christian Peril (1928)

Julius Evola

Though Evola (1898–1974) was an outsider who never occupied any official positions during the fascist decades, his Nietzschean brand of fascism, saturated with esoteric elements borrowed from Gnosticism and the ancient mystery cults, proved influential. Initially a painter affiliated with Futurism, Evola subsequently moved on to become a leading Italian exponent of Dadaism. The 1920s saw his definitive turn to philosophy and to links to hierarchs such as Bottai and Roberto Farinacci. A "spiritual" racist who repudiated the narrowly "materialistic" racism of the Nazis, Evola attained his greatest prominence after the proclamation of the 1938 racial laws. He remained an active philosopher in the postwar era, influential in neofascist circles.

European Decadence

Present Western "civilization" awaits a substantial upheaval [*rivolgimento*], without which it is destined, sooner or later, to smash its own head.

It has carried out the most complete *perversion* of the rational order of things.

Reign of matter, gold, machines, numbers; in this civilization there is no longer breath or liberty or light.

The West has lost its ability to command and to obey.

It has lost its feeling for contemplation and action.

It has lost its feeling for values, spiritual power, godlike men [*uomini-iddii*].

It no longer knows nature. No longer a living body made of symbols, gods, and ritual act, no longer a harmony, a *cosmos* in which man moves freely like "a kingdom within a kingdom," nature has assumed for the Westerner a dull and fatal exteriority whose mystery the secular sciences seek to bury in trifling laws and hypotheses.

*maybe — phenomenon of why fascism.
philosophes approved*

It no longer knows *Wisdom*. It ignores the majestic silence of those *push for philosophes* who have mastered themselves: the enlightened calm of seers, the exalted reality of those in whom the idea becomes blood, life, and power. Instead it is drowning in the rhetoric of "philosophy" and "culture," the specialty of professors, journalists, and sportsmen who issue plans, programs, and proclamations. Its wisdom has been polluted by a sentimental, religious, humanitarian contagion and by a race of frenzied men who run around noisily celebrating becoming [*divenire*] and "practice," because silence and contemplation alarm them.

It no longer knows the state, the state as value [*stato-valore*] crystallized in the Empire. Synthesis of the sort of spirituality and majesty that shone *positive on empire building* brightly in China, Egypt, Persia, and Rome, the imperial ideal has been overwhelmed by the bourgeois misery of a monopoly of slaves and traders.

Europe's formidable "activists" no longer know what war is, war desired in and of itself as a virtue higher than winning or losing, as that heroic and sacred path to spiritual fulfillment exalted by the god Krishna in the *Bhagavad Gita*. They know not warriors, only *soldiers*. And a crummy little *war itself has changed* war [*guerricciola*] was enough to terrorize them and drive them to rehashing the rhetoric of humanitarianism and pathos or, worse still, of windbag nationalism and Dannunzianism.

Europe has lost its simplicity, its central position, its life. A democratic plague is eating away at its roots, whether in law, science, or speculation. Gone are the *leaders*, beings who stand out not for their violence, their gold, or for their skill as slave traders but rather for their irreducible qualities of life. Europe is a great irrelevant body, sweating and restless because of an anxiety that no one dares to express. Gold flows in its veins; its flesh is made up of machines, factories, and laborers; its brains are of newsprint. A great irrelevant body tossing and turning, driven by dark and unpredictable forces that mercilessly crush whoever wants to oppose or merely escape the cogwheels.

Such are the achievements of Western "civilization." This is the much ballyhooed result of the superstitious faith in "progress," progress beyond Roman imperiousness, beyond radiant Hellas, beyond the ancient Orient— the great ocean.

And the few who are still capable of great loathing and great rebellion find themselves ever more tightly encircled.

✳

Fascism as Anti-Europe

Can fascism be the source of an anti-European restoration?

Is fascism powerful enough today to take on such a task?

Fascism arose from below, from confused needs and brutal forces unleashed by the European war. Fascism has thrived on compromises, on rhetoric, on the petty ambitions of petty people. The state organization that it has created is often uncertain, awkward, inexpert, violent, cramped, riddled by ambiguities.

Nevertheless, if we look around us today and note the demise of the only two states—Russia and Germany—that had preserved remnants of hierarchical values (however distorted and materialized), we must draw the conclusion that fascism is the West's best hope.

For better or worse, fascism has developed a *body. But this body is still lacking a soul.* It is still lacking the superior power [*atto*] needed to justify it, complete it, make it rise to its feet as a *principle* opposed to all of Europe. The soul in question can achieve these ends only if fascism manages to resurrect a distinctive system of meta-economic and metapolitical values by means of a radical, profound, absolute upheaval [*rivolgimento*], a new leap ahead and away from the politics of "normalization" and bourgeois compromise [*imborghesimento*] that is beginning to pervade contemporary fascism.

But let's not misunderstand one another.

The breeding ground of fascism were youthful, resolute forces, ready for anything, immune to the *evils* of "culture." To this day they represent the vital nucleus of fascism, while those who worry about developing a "philosophy of fascism" and a "fascist culture" are themselves symptoms of degeneration or, at the very least, of a turn away from the path leading to something really new: a true *revolution* (not one regarding which one can conclude "plus ça change, plus c'est la même chose").[1]

No. Fascism must remain *antiphilosophical.* Decisively and crudely so. Tapping into its purest core of force, it must sweep away the filthy film of rhetoric, sentimentalism, moralism, and hypocritical piety with which the West has clouded and humanized everything. There is an irrefutable need for someone to break into the temple—perhaps even a barbarian—to drive out the corrupters of "civilized" Europe, the monopolistic preachers of the "spirit," good and evil, science, and the divine who actually *know only matter* and what human words, fear, and superstition have layered over matter.

To all this I reply, "That's enough!" My negation is meant to allow a *few* men to rediscover the long paths, the long danger, the long gaze, and

the long silence, to unleash the wind of the open sea—the wind of the
MEDITERRANEAN TRADITION—so that it may revive the enslaved men of
the West.

Antiphilosophy, antisentiment, antiliterature, antireligion: these are the
premises. *No more* aestheticisms and idealisms: not a single one! *No more*
thirsting of the soul for a hallucinated God to pray to and adore. *No more*
acceptance of the common ties and mutual interdependencies that bind
beggars together on a foundation of lack.

To soar beyond and above with *pure forces*. Forces that will have to meet
a challenge that transcends politics and social concerns, that recoils at the
clamorous gesture and superficial resonance, a challenge so great that the
material forces vibrating out in the world of people and things can no longer
have any effect.

In silence, under conditions of strict discipline, inflexible self-control,
seriousness, and simplicity, with the brisk and tenacious effort of individuals, we in Italy must create an elite in whom *Wisdom* comes to life again.
By "wisdom" I mean that power [*virtus*] that does not allow itself to speak,
that rises up out of a hermetic and Pythagorean silence, that comes into
being by subduing the senses and the soul, and that manifests itself not by
means of arguments and books but through powerful actions.[2]

We must reawaken to a renewed, spiritualized, bitter *feeling* [*sensazione*]
for the world, not as a philosophical concept but as something that vibrates
in the rhythm of our very blood: a feeling for the world as *power*, as the agile
and free rhythmic dance of Shiva, as a sacrificial act (Veda). This feeling
will breed strong, hard, active, solar, *Mediterranean* beings; beings made
up of force and eventually *only* of force; beings infused with a sense of
freedom and nobility whose *cosmic perspective* [*respiro cosmico*] has been
much stammered about but little understood by Europe's "dead."

Science today is profane, democratic, and materialistic. Always relative
and qualified in its truths, a slave to phenomena and to incomprehensible
laws, it remains mute with regard to the profound reality of man. To debunk
it we must reawaken in the new elite a sacred science, a science that is interior
and secret and gives rise to *initiations*, a science of self-fulfillment and self-
dignification that taps the occult forces that govern our being and subdues
them so as to permit men to be actually (not mythically) reborn as beings
superior to the laws of the body and of space and time.

So *a race of leaders it will be*. Invisible leaders who do not rattle on or
parade about but who act irresistibly and are capable of *anything*. A center
will thus exist in decentered Europe.

The problem of hierarchy can only be addressed by creating leaders, a strictly individual and internal problem, resistant to external solutions. Hierarchy can come into being only when there are leaders and not vice versa.

The empire cannot be built on economic, military, industrial, and even "ideal" foundations. The *imperium*, according to the Iranian and Roman conception, is *transcendent*. It can only be attained by those who have the power to transcend the petty lives of petty men and their petty appetites, patriotisms, "values," "nonvalues," and gods.

The ancients understood this when they deified their emperors, joining together royal dignity and spiritual dignity. Have the young barbarians who have dared to resurrect the eagle and the fasces learned this lesson? Have they understood that *there is no alternative*, that this is the only way to transform their "revolution" into the first light that pierces the thick fog of European decadence? Rather than amounting to little more than the small contingency of a small nation, they could plant the seed for a resurgence of Rome throughout the world, the seed for a *true* restoration.

★

Mediterranean Tradition against Christian Tradition

Anti-Europe is anti-Christianity.

Christianity is at the root of the evil that has corrupted the West. This is the truth, and it does not admit uncertainty.

In its frenetic subversion of every hierarchy; in its exaltation of the weak, the disinherited, those without lineage and without tradition; in its call to "love," to "believe," and to yield; in its rancor toward everything that is force, self-sufficiency, knowledge, and aristocracy; in its intolerant and proselytizing fanaticism, Christianity *poisoned* the greatness of the Roman Empire. Enemy of itself and of the world, this dark and barbarous wave remains the principal cause of the West's decline.

Christianity—take note—is not to be confused with what passes today for the Christian religion: a dead stump cut off from the initial profound impulses. Having disrupted the unity of Rome, Christianity first infected the race of blonde Germanic barbarians, thanks to the Reformation, and then penetrated so deeply, tenaciously, and invisibly that it infused current European liberalism and democratism and all the other splendid fruits of the French Revolution up through anarchism and Bolshevism. Christianity today informs the very structure of modern society (typified by the Anglo-Saxon model) as well as modern science, law, the illusory faith in technology's power. The latter are permeated by the will to equalize, the will to numbers; by the hatred of hierarchy, quality, and difference; and by a collective and impersonal vision of society, a society based upon bonds between mutually inadequate men, worthy of a race of slaves in revolt.

There is still more. Christianity's root sense of "passion" and orgasm was shaped by the promiscuity of the Imperial plebes in an atmosphere of messianism and millenarianism. Opposed to the serene superiority of Roman rulers, to the Doric beauty of the Pindaric hero, to the harmonious, chaste intellectuality of philosophers and pagan initiates, Christianity has resurfaced today in the irrational cult of the "élan vital," in the chaotic impetuosity of contemporary activism and Faustianism. The latter are crude entities that overwhelm the individual and drive him toward what he wants least. Already theologized by Calvin as the equation between God's will in action in the world and the absolute predestination of beings, today this cult has become a *religion*: the religion "of Life," of "becoming," of the "pure act."

I have alluded to a *Mediterranean tradition*. This is no myth but rather an archaic reality whose existence the profane historical sciences have only recently begun to suspect. The epic and magical legacy of an affirmative and active civilization, a civilization strong in knowledge and strong in science, this tradition first imprinted itself on the elites of Egyptian-Chaldaic civilization, of ancient Greece, of Etruscan civilization, and of other more mysterious civilizations whose echoes can be found in Syria, Mycenae, and the Baleares. Infused with the spirit of paganism, it was then borne by the mystery cults of the Mediterranean basin until, against the Judeo-Christian tide, it became Mithra: Mithra, the "ruler of the sun," "killer of the bull," symbol of those who, reborn in the "strongest force among all forces," are able to go beyond good and evil, lack, longing, and passion.[3]

Two destinies, two indomitable cosmic forces thus appeared, clashing over the legacy of Roman splendor.

The tradition of the mysteries, apparently overwhelmed, assumed a more subtle existence. It was passed from flame to flame, from initiate to initiate, in an uninterrupted though secret chain. Today it surfaces here and there (albeit in a confused manner) in figures such as Nietzsche, Weininger, Michelstaedter who feel crushed under the weight of a truth that, although it is too strong for them, will triumph with the advent of a new being who will brandish it, hard and cold, against the enemy in the great revolt and coming battle in which the West's fate will be determined.[4]

Anti-Europe means anti-Christianity. And anti-Christianity consists in the

Mediterranean, classical, and pagan tradition that is our own. This must be perfectly clear.

Without a return to such a tradition, no liberation will be possible, no true restoration, no transfer of spirit, power, and empire into the realm of values. But let not our "anti" give rise to misunderstandings. *They*, not we, are forces of negation. They are the ones who sapped Rome, contaminated Wisdom, and destroyed aristocracy in the name of a reign of sentimentalism and humanitarianism, ruled by "enemies of the world." And they did so in order to exalt a superstition according to which God is an executed man and enslaver of other men whom he condemns to damnation unless "grace" intervenes on their behalf. No more foolish or absurd fable has ever been devised than that which treats paganism as a synonym for materiality and corruption, while Christianity is, instead, associated with purity and spirituality. Yet this superstition still manages to inform so much contemporary thinking!

No. The living and immanent spirit, spirit actualized as initiatory knowledge and power, glory of kings and conquerors, was unknown to the Semitic contamination. But not to the Roman, Hellenic, and ancient Oriental races. And he who rebels against Christian corruption, against all that plagues today's Europe, is alone in knowing the meaning of affirmation. He is not a denier but an affirmer.

So today in Rome we bear witness to the pagan tradition and invoke the restoration of Mediterranean values in a *pagan imperialism*. The person who speaks and who is joined in this same spiritual reality by others—isolated, impassive, and rigorously aristocratic souls opposed to this world of merchants, shut-ins, and deviants—dissolves into this higher reality, conveyed through him to the one in whom the fascist movement is today resumed.

Will we manage to feel that this is not about words, utopias, or romantic abstractions? Will we manage to believe that the most positive and most powerful realities are waiting to be unearthed by beings capable of anything and everything (realities that will dwarf everything fascism has accomplished to this point)? Can we persuade ourselves that all this is truly *possible* and that a thousand forces hover in the darkness waiting for an outlet?

The identification of *our* tradition with either the Christian or Catholic tradition is *the most absurd of errors*.

Roman spirit is pagan spirit [*Romanità è paganità*], and the imperial restoration of which I have spoken would be meaningless if it is not, above all else, a pagan restoration. Nothing could be more contradictory than to proclaim the resurgence of Rome without remembering that Christianity was one of the principal reasons for Rome's downfall, or to invoke the empire without realizing that the entire Christian vision of life negates the empire's premises.

So will fascism dare to take up the torch of the Mediterranean tradition *here* where the imperial eagles began their conquest of the world under the Augustan, solar, and regal power? Will fascism dare to take up the torch here in Rome where the ironic vestiges of the only hierarchy Christianity was ever able to devise (through self-deception) remains present?

Better neither to hope nor to despair. Time will tell. Hegel said that "the idea does not hurry," and what already is cannot be transmuted by what is not.

The values that we affirm are that circumstances and men present themselves such that they can shape a given period of contingent historical and temporal things; that such an event is of less interest to us than to those whose truths are impeded by this historical contingency.

Fascism against Christianity: The Great Liberation

Let us conclude.

Today we must absolutely put a stop to Christianity.

Everything in it is incompatible with and contradictory to the ideals, the morals, the vision of the world and of man that would enable a race to bring about the resurrection of the empire.

Our sleep has lasted long enough. All the possible compromises and variations have been exhausted. It is time to say, "*Enough!*" No more of Christianity embraced *as a whole*, in the totality of *all* its forms! The Latin race in particular must bitterly disavow any descent from this dark object that emerged from the Jewish slums of Palestine to contaminate us. Thus:

On an ideal and moral level, it is time to unmask Christianity's enormous doctrinal bluff and to refuse to allow it to continue to parade around loaded up with all the values that have been superstitiously and unconsciously attributed to it.

On a practical level, it is time to become aware of the *European danger* and the *decline of the West* and to respond by reviving in the modern world the political and sapiential values characteristic of the Mediterranean tradition.

Ethical and religious Christianity today is nothing more than a name and a habit, absolutely external to conscience; but nobody, or nearly nobody, has bothered to abolish the name itself and to put its content on trial again, so as to start right back at the beginning, rejecting the "fact" of Christianity, its "tradition," and all the rest.

This is precisely my intent: to hold such a trial, demanding that every account be scrutinized with inflexible severity, that all cards be placed openly on the table, and that every way out and every compromise be barred in advance. At stake are not more or less anticlerical polemics but rather a serious, objective examination, unbiased by feeling and belief. A cool-headed examination should suffice to blunt the ecstatic thrill and to unmask the true poverty and inferiority of the Christian vision of the world and of man.

With regard to *fascism*, I declare:

Fascism . . . will blaze the path toward breaking up the monstrous political connivance with the Catholic Church, abetted by the intrigues of that secret and illicit association, the Society of Jesus. It will become aware that it has fallen prey to a suckers' marketplace [*marché de dupes*]. The petty political advantages to be gained are *trivial* when compared to the Church's devious efforts to achieve monopoly control over Italy's conscience by means of public education and clever sophistries that polarize the fascist regime against everything that is not Catholic. To have agreed that a crucifix should be placed not in the universities, not in the coliseum, but *on the Campidoglio* in place of the eagle and the fasces is a blot without precedent that it will take a lot to wipe away.[5]

This transpired because fascism still lacks a spirituality and culture of its own, as fresh and vibrant as the warrior forces that brought it into being. The result was that fascism's political triumph was unaccompanied by a spiritual-cultural triumph. This transpired because fascism is still crippled by a definition of empire as a simple political, economic, and military organization, based on the industrial-capitalist system and cast in the mold of British and German *bourgeois* and material imperialism. But such a definition has nothing in common with true imperialism, that spiritual, sacred, and heroic imperialism of ancient Rome, Byzantium, and Persia. The real explanation for the success of Catholic infiltration lies in fascism's actual (though concealed) indifference to spiritual questions, whereby it did not hesitate to embrace new members who could solidify the material structure of the new regime, even at the cost of accommodating the most strident of contradictions.

Once fascism transcends the bourgeois-industrial definition of empire, once it embraces imperiousness [*imperialità*] in the true, traditional sense, the problem will be resolved. Fascism will find its soul within itself, a fact that will paralyze all efforts to apply external pressure and render ever more acute the incompatibility between state and Church. "Incompatibility" not as understood by demagogic, anticlerical, or secular ideologies but in the sense that the empire would become the true spiritual reality, the immanent, powerful religion that ousts the dead hierarchies and empty devotional forms that have survived in Catholicism.

So if the "daring" that fascism regularly exalts is more than rhetorical bluster, here's a first task: deride the arrogance that did not hesitate to call the king of Italy a *usurper* from on high at the Vatican and reaffirm the complete dominion of the state over the Church. The Church must be directly controlled by the state. Its every organization must require state approval and sanction. . . . Above all, it must be denied any role in the education of souls during the period in which the will is not yet formed and the conscience is not yet clear. (Though its continuing presence can be tolerated as a feature of popular belief, but only on a temporary basis, until such a time as the Mediterranean and imperial sense of life has fully revitalized everyone's spirit, thanks to pedagogical training carried out over several generations.)

So much for Catholicism, which on a practical plane must be distinguished from Christianity. The latter is mostly to be identified with the forms of Protestantism active in Anglo-Saxon liberal democracies. Here lies the true *European danger* from which we must protect ourselves, reacting ruthlessly to all the international, unionist, Masonic, anti-aristocratic, anti-Roman, socialist, humanitarian, moralist ferments with which it would seek to infiltrate Italy.

In the properly cultural field, fascism ought to begin by promoting critical and historical studies, not partisan studies but cold surgical analyses of the essence of Christianity akin to Louis Rougier's work in France, published in his collection, *Masters of Anti-Christian Thought*.[6] At the same time, fascism ought to promote studies and research on the spiritual side of paganism (and work to diffuse such knowledge), studies extending from paganism's true vision of life to rigorously appropriate (because many are not) explorations of the Mediterranean tradition in its primitive and metaphysical nature.

Let the following be stated firmly, absolutely, and unambiguously. *We are not destroyers but restorers. When we appear to be destroying we are in fact rearranging and replacing what is on the wane with higher forms, forms more vibrant and glorious. We possess a complete, total, positive system of values, developed in close connection with the forms of contemporary civilization, a system that provides us with a firm foundation and frees us from any fear of the void as we demolish all the negatives of European decadence.*

From the standpoint of its praxis, fascism must not betray itself, which is to say, it must deeply embrace those values of affirmation, activity, will to power, antisentimentalism, and antirhetoricism whose imprint it bears (especially in its purest manifestations). Values that are essentially anti-Christian. Values to be raised to a higher internalized and spiritualized form and freed from the inferior and provisional approach based on mere violence and material domination.

And here there is a precursor, a misunderstood man, who waits in the shadows: *Friedrich Nietzsche.* The Nietzschean experiment is not yet exhausted because it hasn't even truly begun. What is worn out is the aesthetic-literary or firebrand [*baionettista*] caricature of Nietzsche found in characters like Corrado Brando, Stelio Effrena, or William II.[7] But very much alive are the values that Nietzsche heroically propagated despite no end of suffering, despite the rebellion of his entire being, which, after having given everything without complaint, simply collapsed. These values transcend his philosophy, his "humanity," even himself. They are of cosmic significance, reflecting the power of the Aeion, the *Ur*, the terrible fire of magical initiations. These are the values that are still waiting to be understood and taken up. They encompass the sounding of an alarm, an appeal for disgust, the call for an awakening, and a summons to participate in the great struggle in which the destiny of the West will be decided, whether toward twilight or toward dawn. Fascism must begin here: by beginning the slow, tenacious construction of a new and wondrous race.

Accordingly, education will be reoriented toward pagan and Mediterranean values.

The "myth" of the crucified God-man who suffers and loves will be opposed that of the man-God, a being radiating light and power, the summit of an imperial ethos. To a dualistic and transcendental worldview will be opposed a vision of free and immanent unity, withdrawn into itself, matter for domination. To Christianity's race of "slaves and children of God" will be opposed a race of liberated and liberating beings who interpret God as a supreme power that one may freely obey or do battle against in manly fashion with one's head held high, immune to the taint of feelings, vacillations, and prayers. To feelings of dependence and lack will be opposed a feeling of sufficiency; to the will to equality, the will to difference, distance, hierarchy, and aristocracy. To the mystical communist promiscuity will be opposed firm individuality; to the need for love, happiness, peace, and consolation, the heroic contempt for all this and a law of pure will and absolute action. To Christianity's providential vision will be opposed the tragic conception whereby man stands alone facing the contingencies of nature such that either he must redeem himself or redemption will forever elude him. Do away with "sin" and "bad conscience," brashly heap all responsibilities upon one's shoulders, bar the door to any escape, fortify the innermost spirit.

No more "brothers" or "fathers" but instead fully autonomous individuals, self-enclosed as if each were a separate world, rock, or peak, individuals clothed only in their strength or in their weakness, each and every one operating like an independent combat post that defends a distinctive quality, life, dignity, unequal strength, indomitable force. No more subjection to the need to "communicate" and to "be understood" or to fraternal bonds or to the sensual pleasure of loving and of feeling loved as equals. All are subtly corrupting and violent forces that weaken aristocracy and individuality. On the contrary, incommunicability must be celebrated in the name of absolute purity and respect. Stronger forces and weaker forces, the one alongside or against the other, loyally, coldly acknowledging one another thanks to the discipline of a spirit that burns within but produces an exterior rigid and tempered like steel, forces magnificently infused with the immeasurability of the infinite as found in feats of war and on the battlefield: [this is the ideal]. A state of absolute justice, interrupted by conflagrations in which fulgurant acts of absolute generosity and absolute cruelty insure that some men and races ascend, while others fall with a thud. Nothing "infinite." Precise relations, order, cosmos, hierarchy. Solar and sufficient beings, masters who are far-sighted, fearful, distant, and solitary; who, instead of taking in, *give out* an overabundance of light and power; who resolutely incline toward ever more dizzying intensities within a hierarchical chain of being that comes not from above but from the dynamic natural interconnection between their natures.

"How beautiful they are, how pure are these free forces not yet corrupted by the spirit!" wrote the young Nietzsche after an ascent during a storm. In the place of Nietzsche's "not yet," I would substitute "*no longer* corrupted by the spirit" in the present context, the word "spirit" meaning the *unreal*: an outer crust of feelings, hopes, doctrines, beliefs, "values," sensations, words, sensual pleasures, and human emotions. But the meaning remains the same. The world is to be cleansed, returned to its *pre-Christian state*. It is to be returned to a free, overabundant, essential state within which nature is not yet nature or the spirit, spirit; in which "things" and "forms" do not exist except as powers; in which every instant of life is a heroic event, made up of acts, symbols, commands, magical gestures, and rituals, accompanied by great waves of sound, light, and terror.

This is our truth and this is the threshold of our *great liberation*: the end of *faith* and the world's emancipation from God. No "heaven" will hover over the land, gone will be "providence," "reason," "good," and "evil," masks for the terrified, pallid escapes for pallid souls. At last, those who think themselves men, unaware that they are *sleeping gods*, will be left to themselves: everything, all around, will return to a state of freedom; everything will finally *breathe*. The weak will collapse. The strong will assert themselves and will be rekindled as the "holy race of the kingless" of the ancient Gnostic oracles: the race of "those who are," of the unchained and the unburdened, of redeemed justifiers of the world, lords of necessity and suffering.

This is our truth. This is the "myth" that we pagans oppose to the superstition of Galilee, the myth that we affirm today as central to the values of our race and to the restoration of the empire in the West.

translated by Olivia E. Sears and Jeffrey T. Schnapp

Notes

1. The proverb is best translated as "The more things change, the more they stay the same."
2. Evola's usages of terms such as "wisdom" and "power" are meant to carry far broader meanings than is conventionally the case. The first refers to the entire tradition of pre-Christian "wisdom literature" with its stock of traditional doctrines and proverbs emanating from ancient Babylonia and Egypt but assimilated within various early Mediterranean and Levantine traditions (tied to Neoplatonism and the mystery cults). The word *virtus* (or power), on the other hand, retains magical/metaphysical connotations, even if it relies upon ancient Roman usage. Derived from *vir* (man), *virtus* is at once the "virile" possession and manifestation of "power" (whether literal or figurative) and moral virtue.
3. Mithra was a cultic god in the Zoroastrian tradition who in the fifth century B.C. became the chief god in the ancient Persian pantheon. From Persia the cult spread throughout Mediterranean Europe and Asia, becoming one of the principal mystery cults of the Roman Empire. As had been the case with Nietzsche and Schopenhauer, Evola was attracted by Mithraism's anti- and ante-Christian attributes: its sacramental rituals, cult of secrecy, and emphasis upon a rigorous ethics.

4. The triad formed by Friedrich Nietzsche (1844–1900), Otto Weininger (1880–1903), and Carlo Michelstaedter (1887–1910) was an important one for Evola's philosophy. Weininger was the author of *Geschlecht und Charakter* (1903), an influential work that attempted to prove that the moral "deficiency" of woman was of a bodily nature. Michelstaedter was the author of *La persuasione e la rettorica* (1910) and of numerous philosophical dialogues and poems. Both were avid readers of Nietzsche and committed suicide at an early age.

5. Evola's indignation is driven by the fact that the Campidoglio (or Capitolium), which lies right at the heart of ancient Rome and towers over the forum, is a symbol of Rome's imperial might. The fact that numerous state buildings are located either on the Campidoglio or in the vicinity, including Palazzo Venezia, city hall, and various ministries, may have seemed to reinforce the point.

6. The philosopher and logician Louis Rougier (1889–1982) was perhaps the leading representative of neopositivism in France and authored numerous studies on the theory of cognition (*La Structure des théories déductives* [1921]) and on pagan and early Christian religion as well as mysticism.

7. The barb is aimed squarely at D'Annunzio, who, in the wake of his discovery of Nietzsche's writings (via their French translation) in the mid-1890s, composed a series of novels with Nietzschean heroes, including Stelio Effrena, the playwright-protagonist of *Il fuoco* (1900), and Corrado Brando, the superman-hero of *Più che l'amore* (1905).

PART 4

DOCUMENTS

CHAPTER 21

Manifesto of Fascist Intellectuals (1925)

✳

On 29–30 March 1925 the first Conference on Fascist Culture was held in Bologna under the leadership of Giovanni Gentile. Over four hundred profascist intellectuals lent their names to the event, though actual attendance was more modest. Its aim was to rally Italian intellectuals behind the regime in an effort to enhance the image of the newly declared dictatorship both at home and abroad. One of the congress's immediate results was the following manifesto, largely drafted by Gentile, in which fascism's political and cultural legitimacy was defended, albeit in rather generic terms. (For further information on Gentile, see the introductions to chapters 5 and 18.)

✳

Origins

Fascism is a recent yet ancient movement of the Italian spirit. It is intimately linked to the history of the Italian nation, yet it is not devoid of meaning and of interest for other nations. Its immediate origins must be sought in 1919, when a handful of veterans from the trenches gathered around Benito Mussolini, determined to combat vigorously the then-dominant democratic-socialist [*demosocialista*] politics. Democratic socialism was blind to all but one side of the great war from which the Italian people had emerged at once weary and victorious: the side of immediate material consequences of this war. It squandered the war's moral value when it did not resort to outright denial. It presented the war to Italians in a crudely individualistic and utilitarian light. The war, it claimed, had been little more than the sum of individual sacrifices, sacrifices for which each and every party was to be repaid according to the precise degree of suffering. The results were an arrogant and menacing opposition of individuals to the state; neglect of the state's authority; a lowering of the prestige enjoyed by the king and the army (symbols of a nation that transcends individuals and individual social categories); the unleashing of base passions and instincts; the fostering of social disintegration, moral degeneration, and a self-centered and mindless spirit of revolt against all forms of discipline and law.

Pitting the individual against the state is the characteristic political expression of a soul so corrupt that it cannot abide by any higher life principle that would vigorously channel and contain the individual's feelings and thoughts. Fascism was, accordingly, a political and moral movement at its origins. It understood and championed politics as a training ground for self-denial and sacrifice in the name of an idea, a training ground from which the individual derives his reason for being, his sense of freedom, and all his rights. The idea in question is that of the fatherland. The fatherland is an ideal that is in the process of being historically actualized but that remains inexhaustible. It represents a distinct, singular historical embodiment of a civilization. But it also represents a living tradition. Far from lingering like a dead memory of the past, it assumes the form of a personality attuned to the end toward which it strives. The fatherland is, therefore, a tradition as well as a sense of mission.

Fascism and the State   *government = Church*

This explains fascism's religious character.

This uncompromising religiosity is illustrated by the fighting tactics that fascism adopted from 1919 to 1922. Fascists were a minority, both in the country and in Parliament (a small nucleus of deputies was seated after the 1921 elections). The constitutional state was antifascist and necessarily so, inasmuch as it was the state of the majority. Fascism was opposed by precisely such a liberal state whose liberalism was of the agnostic and renunciatory sort that attends only to outward freedoms. "Liberal" because it considered itself extraneous to the conscience of its free citizens and because it was indifferent like a machine toward the actions of individuals. It goes without saying that this was hardly the state the socialists had dreamed of, even if the representatives of a hybrid socialism, daubed in democratic values and parliamentarianism, . . . were making their peace with its individualistic conception of politics. Nor was this the state that had proved such a powerful ideal during the heroic period of our national resurgence [*Risorgimento*], a state engendered through the efforts of a small minority, animated by the power of an idea to which individuals had variously submitted; a state founded with the grand plan of making Italians, now that it had granted them independence and unity.

This was the state that fascism, armed with the power of its vision, took on. Any religious idea inviting to sacrifice exerts a special fascination, and the fascist idea was no exception. It attracted a growing group of young supporters and became the party of the young (much as Giuseppe Mazzini's Giovine Italia movement arose out of the riots of 1831 to satisfy similar political and moral needs).[1]

The party even had its own anthem to youth that the fascists sang with joyful, exultant hearts![2]

Like Mazzini's Giovine Italia, fascism became the faith of all Italians who disdained the past and who longed for renewal. It was a faith like other faiths that confront a fully constituted reality that must be destroyed, melted down into a crucible of new energies, and forged according to a new, ardent, uncompromising ideal.

It was the very faith that had ripened in the trenches and in intense reflection on the sacrifice accomplished in the course of battle, a sacrifice for the only worthy goal: the vigor and greatness of the fatherland. It was an energetic, violent faith, unwilling to respect anything opposed to the fatherland's vigor and greatness.

This is how squadrism arose. Determined youths, armed, organized in military fashion, and dressed in black shirts, placed themselves outside the law in order to institute a new law. They fought the state in order to found a new state.

Squadrism's targets were the proponents of national disintegration, whose activities culminated in the general strike of July 1922. On 28 October 1922, fascism finally dared to mount an insurrection as, after occupying public buildings in the provinces, its armed columns marched on the capital. The March on Rome (whether in its execution or its preparatory phase) was not without casualties, particularly in the Po Valley. Like all courageous actions inspired by the highest moral goals, it was greeted with marvel and admiration, followed by universal acclaim. To many it seemed that the Italian people had recovered the unanimity it had felt on the verge of war but now redoubled by its awareness of the nation's recent victory and by the invigorating conviction that the victorious nation was now on the road to recovering its financial and moral integrity.

The Fascist Government

Squadrism and outlaw activities ceased, and the components of the fascist regime began to come together. On 29 and 30 October, the fifty thousand Black Shirts who had marched on Rome departed the capital in orderly fashion, but only after parading before His Royal Highness, the King. They were following the orders of the Duce, now the head of the government and the soul animating the new Italy that fascism had willed.

Was the revolution over? In part yes, in part no. Certainly squadrism no longer had a place. The MVSN was founded in order to absorb ex-squadrists into the ranks of the armed forces.[3] Then there was the matter of reshaping the government. If fascism already enjoyed the support [*consenso*] of the large majority of the population that was convinced that it alone had the capacity to tap and discipline all the nation's forces, it still faced the challenge of making the legislative changes needed to insure that the state closely mirrored the social currents and spiritual exigencies of today's Italian populace.

This transformation is currently under way within a setting where law and order reign supreme. The government has put in place a rigorous fiscal policy that, after years of deficit spending, has managed to balance the national budget by reorganizing the army, the judicial system, and the schools (while avoiding shocks and uncertainties). Public opinion has ebbed and flowed, the inevitable result of a national press whose violent opposition and desperate urge to turn the clock back lead it to seize upon every mistake and every incident in order to rally the citizenry against the new government's tenacious work of rebuilding.

Foreigners who have come to fascist Italy have had to pass through the ring of fire and prohibitions created by the Italian and non-Italian protagonists of a violent campaign that aims to isolate the peninsula from the rest of the world. Italy has been calumnied as being a nation where the most violent and cynical whims rule unchecked, where all legal rights and guarantees of justice have been abrogated. But those who have made the journey and have seen the new Italy with their own eyes, heard the new Italians with their own ears, and shared the citizens' material lives have come to envy the new public order. They have become intrigued by the spirit that every day strengthens its hold on this well-oiled machine and have discovered that, however intransigent is fascism's patriotism, its heart is filled with humanity. After all, for fascism the fatherland is not an external appendage. It lives and beats within the chest of every civilized man. Reinvigorated by the tragedy of the latest war, the fatherland within is ever vigilant in its effort to protect the nation's sacred interests, whether after the war or due to the war.

Such a fatherland also consists in the reconsecration of all those traditions and institutions that continuously inform a civilization, beyond the flux and perennial recurrence of tradition. It also teaches the law of subordination of what is particular and inferior to what is universal and immortal. It teaches respect for law and discipline. It teaches freedom, but a freedom that must be conquered through the law, gained by renouncing everything that is capricious, unreasonable, and wasteful. It is an austere concept of life. It is religious seriousness that does not divorce theory from practice, speech from action, that doesn't devise magnificent ideals so as to relegate them to an other world while we live like cowards and beggars in this world. It consists in the onerous effort to idealize life and to affirm one's beliefs in one's very actions or via words that are themselves actions. These are words that bind the speaker, and, in so doing, they bind the world of which he is a living and responsible part at every moment and in every secret flicker of consciousness.

This ideal is indeed an ideal, but one for which people do battle in Italy today: fierce and serious battle waged by spirits who are filled with faith. Like all great individual movements, fascism is becoming stronger all the time, more able to attract and to absorb, more effective and integrated in the complex of souls, ideas, interests, and institutions that compose it (the vital merger of the Italian folk). For this reason, it is now beside the point to count and measure mere individuals. The time has come to look at the idea itself and to evaluate it. Like all true ideas, this one is alive and powerfully vibrant. It is not made up *by* man but made *for* man.

State and Unions

Fascism has been accused of being a reactionary, antiliberal, anti-working-class movement. The accusation is false. Fascism represents, on the contrary, the spirit of progress that drives all of our nation's forces. Fascism wants to demolish the fallacious incrustations that the old liberal political establishment has layered over the actual activities of every citizen through the atomizing effects of universal suffrage. The latter annihilated the real interests that give individuals a feeling of involvement in the overall system of economic forces. The old order turned the people over to professional politicians controlled by a coalition of ever more powerful special interests whose aims were in conflict with the nation's common interest.

Fascism, whose leaders, from the highest on down, have all gone through a socialist phase, aims at reconciling two elements that always appeared irreducibly opposed: the state and labor union organizations. The state is to be understood as the juridical force of the nation in its organic and functional unity. The labor unions are to be understood as the juridical force of the individual in his economic activity, protected by the law as a socially distinct activity linked to a given social category. The state is to be understood as the organizer of all individual activities in their organic and concrete dimensions. This hardly marks a retreat from the constitutional state. Rather, it marks a forward step that permits both a higher degree of intrinsic cohesion and more effective popular representation in the legislative branch of government. And they accuse the fascist government of imposing police measures that curtail the freedom of the press!

These are factual matters more than matters of principle. In even the most liberal states constitutional liberties have been suspended when made necessary by special circumstances. All of liberalism's theorists and defenders have recognized the legitimacy of such suspensions. The question then becomes one of judging the government recourse to such police measures. Is it true that portions of the press (whether inadvertently or not) placed the nation at the mercy of extremely serious public disorders? Did the government, acting as it did on behalf of the nation, defend the very freedom that such disturbances would have compromised? The truth of the matter is that the great majority of Italians feels that the government acted appropriately. Proof may be found in the quiet indifference with which the citizenry looks upon the opposition's fiery protests and complaints. This because it is fascism, not antifascism, that today strives for the nation's freedom in the world. It is fascism that laboriously strives to erect upon sound foundations the edifice in which the citizenry's free activities can unfold, guaranteed by a law that is the true expression of their real, organic, concrete will.

Today in Italy souls are drawn up on two opposing sides. On the one side stand the fascists; on the other, their enemies: democratic forces of all hues and tendencies. The two form mutually exclusive worlds. Yet the great majority of Italians remains aloof and senses that the source of conflict, as defined by the opposition, lacks the political substance required to hold the people's interest. Those outside the opposition know well just how elastic is the meaning of the word "freedom," which so many parties freely bandy about.

The Opposition to Fascism

A second point needs to be made. This small-scale opposition to fascism (made up of holdovers from the old Italian politics [*vecchio politicantismo*], whether democratic, reactionary, radical, or Masonic) is irrecuperable. Condemned to stand at the periphery of the political forces actually building the new Italy, it will die a slow death due to internal attrition and inaction. This because it can put forward no counterprinciple that is not inferior to fascism's principle. History's judgments are unwavering in such matters. When two equal but opposing principles confront one another, a higher principle triumphs: the synthesis of two divergent vital elements from which each draws its inspiration. But when two unequal principles confront one another, one inferior and the other superior, one partial and the other total, then the first must necessarily succumb because it is already contained within the second and because its opposition is simply negative. It is built on nothing.

This is how fascists feel with regard to their adversaries. This is why they have an unshakable faith in their triumph and cannot compromise. They can patiently wait for their opponents to come to the inevitable conclusion that they must cease illegal combat just as before they abandoned the legal terrain of parliamentary fights. In the process they will come to recognize that whatever residual vigor and truth their program retains, it is already fully encompassed within the fascist program but in a bolder, more complex form, better adapted to the realities of history and to the needs of the human spirit.

The current spiritual crisis of Italy will be overcome. Then, in the very bosom of fascist and fascistized Italy, new ideas, new programs, and new political parties will slowly ripen and come to life at last.

The fascist intellectuals gathered together in Bologna (29–30 March) for the first time ever have formulated the above document in order to address those in Italy and abroad who wish to better understand the National Fascist Party's doctrine and policies.

translated by Maria G. Stampino and Jeffrey T. Schnapp

Notes

1. Mazzini's Giovine Italia movement aimed to liberate Italy from domestic and foreign tyranny and to unify it under a republican government. Mazzini's profound impact on fascism may be felt in his constant appeal to action as the true test of thought and in his constant recourse to a secularized rhetoric of the sacred.

2. The reference is to "Giovinezza," the anthem that the early Fasci di Combattimento borrowed from the Arditi and made their own. The anthem celebrates the daring of youth.

3. The MVSN, or Milizia Volontaria per la Sicurezza Nazionale (Voluntary Militia for National Security), was created in February 1923 to absorb militant squadrists and Black Shirts into a more controllable state security force. The experiment was a mixed success, with many local commanders retaining control of their units and acting independently of orders from Rome.

CHAPTER 22

A Reply to the
Manifesto of Fascist Intellectuals (1925)
Benedetto Croce

✶

The Manifesto of Fascist Intellectuals *was published on 21 April 1925. Less than a week later, Benedetto Croce replied with a sharply worded counter-manifesto published in Giovanni Amendola's* Il Mondo *in which he exposed the contradictions in Gentile's text. Originally entitled "A Reply from Italian Writers, Professors, and Journalists," the document was accompanied by a list of forty-one signatories, including many intellectuals who would later suffer persecution for their antifascist views. Croce's own rapport with the Mussolini regime, despite his openly critical stance and outspoken defense of liberalism, was ambiguous at times. His initial sympathies gave way to opposition after the Matteotti assassination. But, deeply persuaded that culture ought to be kept separate from politics, Croce usually couched his opposition in abstract philosophical terms.*

✶

At a recent gathering in Bologna, fascist intellectuals addressed a manifesto to intellectuals in every nation aimed at explaining and defending the Fascist Party's politics.

While toiling away on so challenging a endeavor, these eager gentlemen must have forgotten that German intellectuals issued a similar, famous manifesto to the whole world at the beginning of the European war. This manifesto was universally condemned at the time and later on deemed an error by the Germans themselves.

If the truth be told, intellectuals—which is to say, the worshipers of science and of art—exercise a right and fulfill their duty as citizens when they enroll as members of a political party and serve the party faithfully. But as intellectuals their sole duty is to raise every man and every political party to a higher spiritual plane by means of their critical research and artistic creations, so that men and parties alike may fight the necessary battles and reap ever growing benefits. To overstep the limits of the office that is theirs, to contaminate politics with literature or politics with science, is a mistake.

When this mistake is made, as in the present circumstance, in the name of deplorable acts of violence and arrogance and in defense of the suppression of the freedom of the press, it cannot even be considered a generous mistake.

Nor is the fascist intellectuals' gesture one that radiates a refined sensitivity as regards the fatherland, whose travails ought not be paraded before the judgment of foreigners, who, as is perfectly natural, have good reason to view them in terms of the varied and specific political ambitions of their own homelands.

As for its content, the manifesto brims over with half-baked notions worthy of a schoolchild. At every turn one encounters philosophical confusions and faulty reasoning. For example, the authors conflate the atomism of certain eighteenth-century political theories with nineteenth-century liberalism. In so doing, they mistake an antihistorical, abstract, and mathematical democratic doctrine with the concept of free competition among political parties whose assigned role it is to take turns at the helm of political institutions, a thoroughly historical concept that claims that progress is gradually achieved, so to speak, thanks to political opposition. Two other examples. Elsewhere the manifesto celebrates the necessary submission of each individual to the whole with facile rhetorical flourishes, as if this were the crux of the matter and not the ability of authoritarian forms of government to insure a more effective moral uplifting of the nation. It also wrongly advocates a dangerous intermingling of economic institutions, such as labor unions, with ethical institutions, such as legislative assemblies, aspiring to unite or, rather, to contaminate the two orders. (The inevitable outcome would be, if not reciprocal corruption, then reciprocal hindrance.) We leave to one side the well-established arbitrary interpretations and manipulations of historical fact.

The document's abuse of doctrine and history pales in comparison with its abuse of the term "religion." According to these esteemed fascist intellectuals, Italy currently has the good fortune of hosting a religious war. Within its borders the deeds of a new gospel are unfolding: a new apostolic mission against an old superstition that resists its demise, though death hovers over it, and it will succumb sooner or later. Cited as evidence of this state of affairs are the ill feelings and hatreds that, now more than ever, pit one Italian against another. The overall effect is that of a lugubrious joke. It is certainly disingenuous to chalk up to "religious strife" the hatred and ill feelings stirred up by a party that insults the members of other parties by dubbing them "non-Italians" or "foreigners" and that, in so doing, transforms itself into a foreign oppressor in the eyes of these very citizens (a tactic that introduces into the life of the fatherland feelings and habits more characteristic of actual wars). The same goes for the attempt to ennoble as "religion" the air of suspicion and animosity that has become so widespread that it has pitted even university youth against one another, youth heretofore bound together by the old, true brotherhood of youthful shared ideals.

This verbose manifesto is of little help when it comes to explaining what this new gospel, this new religion, this new faith actually consist in. The manifesto itself, in its mute eloquence, confronts the unbiased reader with an incoherent, bizarre mish-mash of demagoguery and appeals to authority, vows of reverence for the law, ultramodern concepts and mildewed old rubbish, absolutist stances and Bolshevik tendencies, expressions of unbelief and flattery of the Catholic Church, blasts against culture, and sterile nods in the direction of a culture devoid of the necessary premises, mystical swoons, and cynical utterances. As for the present government, it has enacted or initiated a number of plausible measures. But, like the manifesto's formulations, they contain nothing original, nothing that points in the direction of a brand new political system bearing the label "fascism."

We feel no urge, therefore, to embrace this chaotic, ungraspable "religion" and to abandon our old faith, a faith that, for two and a half centuries, has formed the core of Italy's resurgent spirit and modern nationhood. A faith that encompasses the love of truth, the pursuit of justice, a global commitment to humane and civic values, a zeal for intellectual and moral edification, and a deep concern for freedom (the driving force and guarantor of all progress). When we turn our gaze toward the leaders of the Risorgimento, men who labored, suffered, and died for the Italian cause, we see expressions of displeasure and dismay creeping over their faces in reaction to our enemies' words and actions. We also see them gravely admonishing us to grasp the flag ever more firmly in our hands. Our faith is neither an artificial or abstract device nor the product of a cerebral delirium induced by uncertain and ill-understood theories. Rather, it requires embrace of a tradition that translates into an array of feelings and a common mental and moral structure.

In their manifesto, the fascist intellectuals repeat the commonplace that the Italian Risorgimento was carried out by a minority. But they show no awareness that it is precisely for this reason that our political and social establishment [costituzione] was frail. On the contrary, they seem to take pride in the (perhaps only apparent) indifference that a majority of Italian citizens demonstrates as regards the conflicts between fascism and its opponents. Italian liberals never took delight in such a state of affairs. They strove instead to insure the involvement of an ever greater number of Italians in public life. Hence their most controversial reforms, like the enactment of universal suffrage. Hence also the favor with which many liberals initially greeted the fascist movement, founded upon the hope that new forces would reinvigorate Italian political life, forces of renewal and (why not?) forces of preservation. Never did liberals contemplate a politics promoting inertia and apathy on the part of the majority, a politics that satisfies most material needs but betrays the ideals of the Risorgimento and replicates the arts of (mis)rule developed by absolutist, quietist governments.

Even today, we are overcome neither by despair nor by a feeling of resignation when faced with the majority's supposed inertia and indifference or with the obstacles being interposed to freedom. What matters most is knowing what we are striving for and striving for that which is intrinsically good. The present political strife in Italy, thanks to the very nature of these conflicts, will revive in our people a far deeper and more concrete understanding of the virtues of liberal laws and methods. As a result it will give rise to a more conscious and heartfelt affection for the latter. The day will come, perhaps, when one can calmly look back upon the past and conclude that the difficult and painful ordeal that Italy is at present undergoing was a necessary stage. A necessary stage beyond which lies a renewal of national life, the completion of Italy's political education, and a more intense sense of responsibility as a civilized people.

translated by Maria G. Stampino and Jeffrey T. Schnapp

CHAPTER 23

The Labor Charter (1927)

After years of policies that effectively stripped the Italian labor movement and fascist trade unions of their independence, the Labor Charter was drafted to set forth the underlying principles for the regulation and protection of labor. The charter's first draft, written by Edmondo Rossoni, head of the fascist unions, contained extensive legal protections for labor and detailed recommendations to that effect. After reviewing the document, the Fascist Grand Council asked Bottai to revise the charter; his more abstract, theoretical version provided only loose guidelines and eliminated many of the safeguards Rossoni had inserted. The text that follows represents the final compromise draft by Alfredo Rocco and was the one adopted by Mussolini in April 1927.[1]

✶

The Corporate State and Its Organization

I. The Italian nation is an organism having ends, a life, and a means of action superior in power and duration to the single individuals or groups of individuals that compose it. It is a moral, political, and economic unity that is integrally realized in the fascist state.

II. Work in all its forms, intellectual, technical, and manual, however organized or carried out, is a social duty. On this score and on this score alone, it is safeguarded by the state.

From the standpoint of the nation, the mass of production forms a totality; it has a single aim: the well-being of individual producers and the growth of national power.

III. Professional and labor organizations enjoy complete freedom. But only unions legally recognized and subject to state control have the right to legally represent the whole category of employers and workers for which they are constituted; to defend their interests with respect to the state and other professional associations; to negotiate collective labor contracts that are binding on all members of the category; and to impose dues and to make use of these dues as a function of the public interest.

IV. The collective labor contract embodies the feelings of solidarity that bind together the various factors of production. It harmonizes the opposing interests of employers and workers, subordinating them to the higher interests of production.

v. The labor court is the organ by means of which the state settles labor disputes, whether these arise from the application of contracts and other existing rules or from deliberations regarding new labor conditions.

vi. Legally recognized professional associations insure the equality of employers and workers before the law, promote discipline in production and labor, and favor the betterment of both.

Corporations constitute the unitary organization of all the forces of production and represent the totality of their interests.

In virtue of the integral character of this representation and given that the interests of production and the national interest are one and the same, the corporations are recognized by the law as organs of the state.

Since they represent the overall interests of production, corporations may enforce binding regulations that discipline labor relations and promote economic coordination whenever they are authorized to do so by affiliated associations.

vii. In the economic sphere, the corporate state regards private enterprise as the most effective and useful means to advance the national interest.

Given that private-sector production is integral to the national interest, an enterprise's chief officer is responsible to the state for his company's production results. Collaboration between the forces involved in production gives rise to reciprocal rights and duties. The employee, be he a technician, a clerk, or a common laborer, is an active participant in the economic enterprise; the employer has leadership responsibilities.

viii. Employers' professional associations must promote both increased and improved production and reductions in production costs by all available means.

Organs representing those who practice a liberal profession or art, together with associations representing civil servants, safeguard the interests of art, science, and letters; promote improvements in production; and advance the moral aims of the corporate system.

ix. State intervention in economic production is required only when private initiative is lacking or insufficient or when the political interests of the state are involved. Such intervention may take the form of state control, assistance, or direct management.

x. Judicial actions cannot be initiated in collective labor disputes unless the corporate organ has first made an attempt at conciliation.

In the case of individual disputes concerning the interpretation and application of collective labor contracts, professional associations are authorized to mediate conciliation efforts.

Ordinary courts have jurisdiction over these disputes and may be assisted by assessors appointed by the professional associations directly concerned.

Collective Labor Contracts and Workers' Rights

XI. Professional associations are required to regulate relations between the categories of employers and workers that they represent by means of collective contracts.

Collective labor contracts are to be negotiated between lower level associations [*associazioni di primo grado*] under the guidance and control of central organizations, except for the power of substitution granted to a higher level association [*associazione di grado superiore*] under conditions specified by the laws and statutes.

All collective labor contracts, under penalty of being rendered null and void, must contain precise rules governing matters such as disciplinary measures, probationary periods, the amount and payment of compensation, and work schedules.

XII. The actions of labor unions, the conciliatory efforts of corporate organs, and the decisions of labor courts all have as their aim to ensure that wages correspond to the ordinary needs of life, to the possibilities of production, and to worker productivity.

Wages shall be determined without reference to any general rules, by agreement between the contracting parties.

XIII. Once they have been coordinated with and expanded upon by the Ministry of Corporations, data furnished by public agencies, by the central statistical bureau, and by legally recognized professional associations concerning production and work conditions, money markets, and variations in the standard of living of workers shall serve as the basis for harmonizing the interests of the various categories and social classes vis-à-vis one another and vis-à-vis the higher goal of increasing production.

XIV. Compensation should be paid out in the form best suited to the needs of employers and laborers.

When compensation is paid on a piecework basis and payments are calculated over intervals of more than two weeks, adequate weekly or fortnightly payments are required.

Night work, with the exception of regularly scheduled periodic night shifts, must be paid at a percentage above the rate for day labor.

In cases in which work is paid on a piecework basis, the rate must be such as to allow a diligent workman with average working skills to achieve earnings that at least minimally exceed the base wage.

xv. Workers are entitled to a weekly day off, on Sundays.

Collective labor contracts must respect this principle, taking into account existing laws and the technical needs of each and every enterprise. Furthermore, they must see to it that civil and religious holidays are observed in accordance with local traditions to the degree that the latter technical needs allow for such observances. Work schedules must be scrupulously and zealously followed by workers.

xvi. After a full year of uninterrupted employment, workers employed by enterprises in operation on a year-round basis are entitled to an annual paid vacation.

xvii. In enterprises operating on a year-round basis the worker has the right, in the case of an interruption of labor relations due to dismissal without fault on the worker's part, to a severance payment proportional to his years of service. A similar indemnity is also to be paid in the event of a worker's death.

xviii. In enterprises operating on a year-round basis changes in ownership do not nullify existing labor contracts, and employees retain the same rights vis-à-vis the new owners. Likewise, illness on the part of an employee that does not exceed a given duration does not nullify the labor contract. Calls to military duty or to serve in the National Militia cannot provide grounds for dismissal.

xix. Breaches in discipline and acts that disrupt the enterprise's normal operations on the part of workers are to be punished according to the gravity of the offense. Punishments may include fines, suspension from work, and, in the most serious cases, immediate dismissal without severance pay.

The circumstances under which an employer may impose fines, suspension from work, or immediate dismissal without severance pay must be clearly defined.

xx. New employees are subject to a probationary period during which both parties have the right to nullify the contract with payment being due only for the time actually worked.

XXI. The benefits and disciplinary mechanisms governing collective labor contracts apply also to domestic workers. Special regulations shall be promulgated by the state in order to ensure the oversight of domestic labor and hygienic standards.

Employment Bureaus

XXII. The state monitors and verifies levels of worker employment and unemployment, levels that are indicative of the general conditions of production and labor within the economy.

XXIII. Employment bureaus are founded on a mutually beneficial basis and are subject to the control of the corporate organs of the fascist state. Employers must avail themselves of the good offices of these bureaus for purposes of hiring. They are free to choose, however, among workers whose names figure on bureau lists, with preference being granted to members of the Fascist Party and labor unions as a function of their seniority [within the fascist ranks].

XXIV. Professional associations of laborers must select from among their best workers in order to continually improve their technical skills and moral standing.

Welfare, Aid, Education, and Training

XXV. Corporate organs must see to it that laws governing the prevention of accidents and workplace discipline on the part of individuals belonging to the affiliated associations are respected.

XXVI. Social security, workman's compensation, and unemployment insurance [*la previdenza*] are among the highest expressions of the principle of [class] collaboration. Employers and employees must both contribute to their costs, each on a proportional basis. By means of its corporate organs and professional associations, the state will endeavor to coordinate and consolidate, as much as possible, the systems and institutions that administer benefits.

XXVII. The fascist state aims to:

1. improve accident insurance;
2. improve and expand maternity assistance;

3. develop insurance coverage for all occupational diseases and tuberculosis as a stepping stone toward insurance coverage for all diseases;

4. improve insurance benefits for the involuntarily unemployed; and

5. devise special forms of endowment insurance [*forme speciali assicurative dotalize*] for young workers.

XXVIII. Workers associations are responsible for protecting the interests of those whom they represent in all administrative and judicial dealings involving accident and social security insurance benefits.

In collective labor contracts provision must be made, whenever it is technically feasible, for the creation of mutual health insurance funds contributed to jointly by employers and employees and administered by representatives of both under the supervision of the corporate bodies.

XXIX. It is the right and duty of professional associations to assist the category of workers they represent, irrespective of whether the workers in question are members or nonmembers. Such assistance must be provided directly. It may not be delegated to other bodies or institutions, except in the name of a higher good that transcends the interests of a single [professional] category.

XXX. One of the principal duties of the professional associations is the education and training—especially the professional training—of the category of workers they represent, irrespective of whether the workers in question are members or nonmembers. The associations are required to work side by side with the fascist after-work organization [*Dopolavoro*] and other educational institutions.

translated by Jeffrey T. Schnapp

Note

1. The original title reads "The Labor Charter (Promulgated by the Grand Council of Fascism on 21 April 1927 and Published in the *Gazzetta Ufficiale* on 3 April 1927)." There exist two prior English translations of the Labor Charter of which I am aware: that found among the appendices to Herbert W. Schneider's *Making the Fascist State* (New York: Oxford, 1928; rpt. New York: Howard Fertig, 1968), 332–36, and the anonymous one reprinted in Mussolini's *Fascism: Doctrine and Institutions* (Rome: Ardita, 1935), 133–42. Neither is very readable or reliable, so I have provided an entirely new version.

CHAPTER 24

Excerpts from the School Charter
The Twenty-nine Declarations: Principles, Goals, and Methods of Fascist Schools (1939)

✶

The first major reform undertaken by Mussolini's government in the wake of the March on Rome was the Gentile reform of public education, a measure that limited access to the universities to a humanistically trained elite and relegated vocational training to non-university-type institutions. The elitism and conservatism of this approach to education was ill adapted to the political realities of the late 1920s and early 1930s as the regime strove to develop both a mass base and new leadership cadres through expansion of the party and development of after-work and youth organizations. The 1939 School Charter, authored by Giuseppe Bottai, attempted to rectify the situation by creating a new series of vocationally and technically oriented institutions that would counterweigh Gentile's elitist classically grounded program. In line with the regime's goal of forging a new fascist humanity, the charter insisted upon the importance of manual labor, physical education, military training, and integration between schools and youth organizations. It reflected the regime's gender politics in its insistence upon a distinct sort of "fascistization" for young women, focused on their role as future mothers, and granted special attention to training in agriculture. The charter received the approbation of the Fascist Grand Council in February 1939, but World War II and internal resistance within the regime slowed the implementation of many of its reforms.

✶

Declaration I

Schools are the cornerstone of the solidarity that binds together all social forces, from the family to the corporation to the party. They shape the human and political conscience of new generations in the moral, political, and economic unity of the Italian nation whose full realization is found in the fascist state.

Fascist schooling has as its aim to introduce a popular culture [*una cultura del popolo*], inspired by the eternal values of the Italian race and its civilization, into the realm of practice by means of study (understood as the shaping of mature human subjects). Through the promotion of work, schools bring this culture to bear on the concrete activities carried out by the trades, arts, professions, sciences, and armed forces.

Declaration II

In the fascist system, school age and political age are the same. Schooling and groups such as the GIL and GUF form part of a unified system of fascist education.[1] Participation in these institutions is obligatory and concerns citizens from early childhood to twenty years of age. Such service consists in school attendance and participation in the GIL from the fourth to the fourteenth year, continuing until the age of twenty, even for those who do not pursue further studies. University students must participate in the GUF. A personal booklet will be attached to every individual's employment card certifying his or her completion of scholastic service and may be used for purposes of job assessment.

Declaration III

Studies in school have as their goal the moral and cultural training of youth and are adapted to the actual intellectual and physical capabilities of individuals. The GIL, in keeping with its educational objectives, has as its special goal preparing youth for politics and for war. Access to and continuation of studies depends only upon demonstrated abilities and aptitudes. A network of state boarding schools guarantees that capable but not only well-to-do youths will be able to pursue their studies.

Declaration IV

Physical education is the responsibility of the GIL. Proceeding by degrees, it reinforces and promotes the laws of growth and physical strengthening as part and parcel of an individual's mental progress. The exercises aim to achieve harmonious growth, fitness, moral high-mindedness, self-assurance, and a strong sense of discipline and duty. In the university context, the GUF are responsible for the athletic and military training of youth.

Declaration V

Work in all its manifestations, whether intellectual, technical, or manual, is treated by the state as a societal duty. Along with study and athletic training, it makes a crucial contribution to the shaping of individual character and intelligence.

Work is integrated into the educational programs of all educational institutions, from elementary schools on up. Special work shifts in factories, in offices, in the fields, and on the sea, regulated and supervised by school authorities, promote the development of the sort of social and economic conscience required by the corporative system.

Declaration VI

Study, physical exercise, and work provide the means for schools to evaluate a student's aptitude. The schools' chief task is to offer cultural direction and professional guidance in accordance with criteria of reason and necessity. The overall aim is to train men capable of addressing the concrete challenges posed by scientific research and industrial production.

The constant use of selection mechanisms in schools safeguards their function as well as the specialized character of certain institutes.

Declaration VII

School and family are natural collaborators. They cooperate closely and regularly in the schooling and guidance of students. Parents and relatives participate in school life and learn there about the shared goals and methods that keep children and adolescents on the path of our fathers' religion and Italy's destiny.

Declaration XIX: The University System

The aim of universities is to promote the progress of science and scholarship and to provide all necessary training for the professions within the framework of a highly developed sense of political and moral responsibility.

Programs and schools of research specialization [*scuole di perfezionamento*] have a purely scientific/scholarly character and objective. Programs and schools of vocational specialization [*scuole di specializzazione*] have mostly practical aims related to particular branches of professional activity.

Military-athletic training and work experience also contribute to the spiritual formation of youth.

Declaration XXI: The Education of Girls

Fascist life distinguishes the destiny and social mission of women from that of men. There exist, accordingly, different and special educational institutions.

Coeducational schooling is being transformed as a function of ongoing efforts to define the new role of women's labor in the corporative system.

The female single-sex educational system [*ordine femminile*] comprises three-year high schools [*Istituto femminile*] (which accept young girls after they graduate from middle school) and teaching colleges [*Magistero*] open to graduates of the girls' high schools. These institutions prepare girls for governing the home and for teaching nursery school.

Declaration XXII: Training for Workers

The aim of worker training and specialization programs is to increase the technical and productive capabilities of employees in the agriculture, industry, commerce, credit, and insurance sectors in harmony with the needs of the national economy. Professional associations have as one of their principal duties the training of their members and provide this training directly or through appropriate agencies under the strict supervision of the Ministry of National Education and the Ministry of Corporations.

Courses for workers can also be instituted by the PNF (and organizations dependent on the Commissariat for War Manufacturing), by the Ministry of Agriculture and Forests, and by private businesses.

Declaration XXVII: Textbooks

The state furnishes all elementary schools with suitable textbooks. Textbooks intended for middle and secondary schools that directly and concretely implement programs of study cannot be printed without prior approval of either the manuscript or proofs by the Ministry of National Education.

translated by Olivia E. Sears

Note

1. The GIL, or Gioventù Italiana del Littorio (Italian Youth of the Littorio), was established in 1937 to place all the fascist youth organizations, including the Balilla (fascist Boy Scouts), the Giovani Italiane (fascist Girl Scouts), the Giovani Fascisti, and Avanguardisti, under a single umbrella and under the control of the National Fascist Party. The GUF, or Gruppi Universitari Fascisti (Fascist University Groups), first arose alongside the Fasci di Combattimento in 1920 but became one of the central breeding grounds for the new fascist elite during the 1920s and 1930s. Until the passage of the School Charter, membership in the GUF was voluntary for university students.

Bibliography in English

✶

The English-language bibliography on the topic of fascism in general and Italian fascism in particular is enormous and growing. The following is a small sample of introductions to and overviews of fascism, of established works in the field, of specialized studies of one aspect or another of fascism, and of collections that contain a variety of methodologies and approaches.

Adamson, Walter L. *Avant-Garde Florence: From Fascism to Modernism.* Cambridge MA: Harvard University Press, 1993.

Cannistraro, Philip V., ed. in chief. *Historical Dictionary of Fascist Italy.* Westport CT: Greenwood Press, 1982.

De Felice, Renzo. *Interpretations of Fascism.* Cambridge MA: Harvard University Press, 1977.

De Felice, Renzo, and Michael Ledeen. *Fascism: An Informal Introduction to Its Theory and Practice.* New Brunswick NJ: Transaction Books, 1976.

De Grand, Alexander. *Italian Fascism: Its Origins and Development.* 3rd ed. Lincoln: University of Nebraska Press, 2000.

——. *The Italian Nationalist Association and the Rise of Fascism.* Lincoln: University of Nebraska Press, 1978.

De Grazia, Victoria. *The Culture of Consent: Mass Organization of Leisure in Fascist Italy.* Cambridge: Cambridge University Press, 1981.

——. *How Fascism Ruled Women: Italy 1922–1945.* Berkeley: University of California Press, 1994.

Gentile, Emilio. *The Cult of the Lictor: The Sacralization of Politics in Fascist Italy.* Trans. Keith Botsford. Cambridge MA: Harvard University Press, 1995.

Golsan, Richard, ed. *Fascism, Aesthetics, and Politics.* Hanover NH: University Press of New England, 1992.

Gregor, A. James. *The Fascist Persuasion in Radical Politics.* Princeton NJ: Princeton University Press, 1974.

——. *Interpretations of Fascism.* Morristown NJ: General Learning Press, 1974.

——. *Italian Fascism and Developmental Dictatorship.* Princeton NJ: Princeton University Press, 1979.

——. *The Young Mussolini and the Intellectual Origins of Fascism.* Berkeley: University of California Press, 1979.

Griffin, Roger, ed. *Fascism.* Oxford: Oxford University Press, 1995.

——. *The Nature of Fascism.* London: Routledge, 1993.

Koon, Tracy. *Believe, Obey, Fight: Political Socialization of Youth in Fascist Italy 1922–1943.* Chapel Hill: University of North Carolina Press, 1985.

Laqueur, Walter, ed. *Fascism, a Reader's Guide*. Berkeley: University of California Press, 1976.

———. *Fascism: Past, Present, and Future*. New York: Oxford University Press, 1996.

Ledeen, Michael. *Universal Fascism: The Theory and Practice of the Fascist International 1928–1936*. New York: H. Fertig, 1972.

Lyttelton, Adrian. *Italian Fascisms from Pareto to Gentile*. London: Cape, 1973.

———. *The Seizure of Power: Fascism in Italy 1919–1929*. London: Weidenfeld and Nicolson, 1973.

Mosse, George, ed. *International Fascism: New Thoughts and Approaches*. London: Sage Publications, 1979.

Mosse, George, and Jeffrey T. Schnapp, eds. "The Aesthetics of Fascism." Special issue, *Journal of Contemporary History* 31.2 (April 1996).

Nolte, Ernst. *Three Faces of Fascism*. New York: Holt, Rinehart and Winston, 1963.

Payne, Stanley G. *Fascism: Comparison and Definition*. Madison: University of Wisconsin Press, 1980.

———. *Fascism: History and Interpretation*. Madison: University of Wisconsin Press, 1995.

Schnapp, Jeffrey T., and Barbara Spackman, eds. "Fascism and Culture." Special issue, *Stanford Italian Review* 8.1/2 (1988).

Sternhell, Zeev. *Neither Right nor Left: Fascist Ideology in France*. Trans. David Maisel. Berkeley: University of California Press, 1986.

Sternhell, Zeev, with Mario Sznajder and Maia Asheri. *The Birth of Fascist Ideology: From Cultural Rebellion to Political Revolution*. Trans. David Maisel. Princeton NJ: Princeton University Press, 1994.

Tannenbaum, E. R. *The Fascist Experience: Italian Society and Culture 1922–1945*. New York: Basic Books, 1972.

Weber, Eugen. *Varieties of Fascism*. Princeton NJ: Van Nostrand, 1964.

Index

✶